Informix® Guide to SQL

Tutorial

Second Edition

ISBN 0-13-016165-9

Informix® Press

ADMINISTERING INFORMIX DYNAMIC SERVER ON WINDOWS NT
Carlton Doe

DATA WAREHOUSING WITH INFORMIX: BEST PRACTICES
Angela Sanchez, Editor

DYNAMIC WEB PROGRAMMING: USING JAVA, JAVASCRIPT AND INFORMIX
Graham Harrison

INFORMIX BASICS
Glenn Miller

INFORMIX DBA SURVIVAL GUIDE, 2/E
Joe Lumbley

INFORMIX DYNAMIC SERVER.2000: SERVER-SIDE PROGRAMMING IN C
Jacques Roy

INFORMIX DYNAMIC SERVER WITH UNIVERSAL DATA OPTION:
BEST PRACTICES
Angela Sanchez, Editor

INFORMIX GUIDE TO DESIGNING DATABASES AND DATA WAREHOUSES
Informix Software

INFORMIX GUIDE TO SQL: REFERENCE & SYNTAX, 2/E
Informix Software

INFORMIX GUIDE TO SQL: TUTORIAL, 2/E
Informix Software

THE INFORMIX HANDBOOK
Ron Flannery

INFORMIX-ONLINE DYNAMIC SERVER HANDBOOK
Carlton Doe

INFORMIX: POWER REFERENCE
Art Taylor

INFORMIX SQL REFERENCE LIBRARY
Informix Software

JDBC DEVELOPER'S RESOURCE, 2/E
Art Taylor

PROGRAMMING INFORMIX SQL/4GL: A STEP-BY-STEP APPROACH, 2/E
Cathy Kipp

SAP R/3 FOR THE INFORMIX DBA
Sari Nathans

For a complete list of Informix Press titles, please visit
www.phptr.com or www.informix.com/ipress

Informix® Guide to SQL

Tutorial

Second Edition

Informix® Press

Informix Enterprise Decision Server, Version 8.3
Informix Dynamic Server.2000, Version 9.2

Prentice Hall PTR
Upper Saddle River, NJ 07458
www.phptr.com

Editorial/Production Supervision: *Nicholas Radhuber*
Acquisitions Editor: *Miles Williams*
Marketing Manager: *Kate Hargett*
Manufacturing Manager: *Alexis Heydt*
Cover Design: *Talar Agasyan*
Cover Design Direction: *Jerry Votta*
Series Design: *Gail Cocker-Bogusz*
Manager, Informix Press: *Judy Bowman*

Published by Prentice Hall PTR
Prentice-Hall, Inc.
Upper Saddle River, NJ 07458

The following are trademarks of Informix Corporation or its affiliates, one or more of which may be registered in the United States or other jurisdictions:

Answers OnLine™; C-ISAM®; Client SDK™; DataBlade®; Data Director™; Decision Frontier™; Dynamic Scalable Architecture™; Dynamic Server™; Dynamic Server™, Developer Edition™; Dynamic Server™ with Advanced Decision Support Option™; Dynamic Server™ with Extended Parallel Option™; Dynamic Server™ with MetaCube®; Dynamic Server™ with Universal Data Option™; Dynamic Server™ with Web Integration Option™; Dynamic Server™, Workgroup Edition™; Dynamic Virtual Machine™; Enterprise Decision Server™; Formation™; Formation Architect™; Formation Flow Engine™; Gold Mine Data Access®; IIF.2000™; i.Reach™; i.Sell™; Illustra®; Informix®; Informix® 4GL; Informix® Inquire℠; Informix® Internet Foundation.2000™; InformixLink®; Informix® Red Brick® Decision Server™; Informix Session Proxy™; Informix® Vista™; InfoShelf™; Interforum™; I-Spy™; Mediazation™; MetaCube®; NewEra™; ON-Bar™; OnLine Dynamic Server™; OnLine/Secure Dynamic Server™; OpenCase®; Orca™; PaVER™; Red Brick® and Design; Red Brick® Data Mine™; Red Brick® Mine Builder™; Red Brick® Decisionscape™; Red Brick® Ready™; Red Brick Systems®; Regency Support®; Rely on Red Brick℠; RISQL®; Solution Design℠; STARindex™; STARjoin™; SuperView®; TARGETindex™; TARGETjoin™; The Data Warehouse Company®; The one with the smartest data wins.™; The world is being digitized. We're indexing it.℠; Universal Data Warehouse Blueprint™; Universal Database Components™; Universal Web Connect™; ViewPoint®; Visionary™; Web Integration Suite™. The Informix logo is registered with the United States Patent and Trademark Office. The DataBlade logo is registered with the United States Patent and Trademark Office.

Documentation Team: *Linda Briscoe, Brian Deutscher, Jennifer Leland, Richelle White*

Prentice Hall books are widely used by corporations and government agencies for training, marketing, and resale.

The publisher offers discounts on this book when ordered in bulk quantities. For more information, contact Corporate Sales Department, Phone: 800-382-3419; fax: 201-236-7141; email: corpsales@prenhall.com or write Corporate Sales Department, Prentice Hall PTR, One Lake Street, Upper Saddle River, NJ 07458.

Printed in the United States of America

10 9 8 7 6 5 4 3 2 1

ISBN 0-13-016165-9

Prentice-Hall International (UK) Limited, *London*
Prentice-Hall of Australia Pty. Limited, *Sydney*
Prentice-Hall Canada Inc., *Toronto*
Prentice-Hall Hispanoamericana, S.A., *Mexico*
Prentice-Hall of India Private Limited, *New Delhi*
Prentice-Hall of Japan, Inc., *Tokyo*
Prentice-Hall (Singapore) Pte. Ltd., *Singapore*
Editora Prentice-Hall do Brasil, Ltda., *Rio de Janeiro*

Table of Contents

Introduction

In This Introduction	3
About This Manual	3
Types of Users	3
Software Dependencies	4
Assumptions About Your Locale	4
Demonstration Databases	5
New Features	5
New Features in Version 8.3	5
New Features in Version 9.2	7
Documentation Conventions	8
Typographical Conventions	9
Icon Conventions	10
Sample-Code Conventions	12
Additional Documentation	13
On-Line Manuals	13
Printed Manuals	13
On-Line Help	14
Error Message Documentation	14
Documentation Notes, Release Notes, Machine Notes	14
Related Reading	16
Compliance with Industry Standards	16
Informix Welcomes Your Comments	16

Chapter 1   **Database Concepts**

In This Chapter 1-3
Illustration of a Data Model 1-3
    Storing Data 1-5
    Querying Data 1-6
    Modifying Data 1-8
Concurrent Use and Security 1-8
    Controlling Database Use 1-8
    Centralized Management 1-9
Important Database Terms 1-9
    The Object-Relational Model 1-10
    Tables 1-10
    Columns 1-11
    Rows 1-11
    Operations on Tables 1-12
    The Object-Relational Model 1-13
Structured Query Language 1-14
    Standard SQL 1-15
    Informix SQL and ANSI SQL 1-15
    Interactive SQL 1-16
    General Programming 1-16
    ANSI-Compliant Databases 1-17
    GLS Databases 1-17
Summary 1-17

Chapter 2   **Composing SELECT Statements**

In This Chapter 2-3
Introducing the SELECT Statement 2-4
    Some Basic Concepts 2-5
    The Forms of SELECT 2-9
    Special Data Types 2-10
Single-Table SELECT Statements 2-10
    Selecting All Columns and Rows 2-11
    Selecting Specific Columns 2-17
    Using the WHERE Clause 2-25
    Creating a Comparison Condition 2-26
    Using a FIRST Clause to Select Specific Rows 2-41
    Expressions and Derived Values 2-44
    Using Rowid Values In SELECT Statements 2-52

Multiple-Table SELECT Statements 2-56
    Creating a Cartesian Product 2-56
    Creating a Join 2-58
    Some Query Shortcuts 2-64
Selecting Tables from a Database Other Than
    the Current Database 2-69
Summary 2-70

Chapter 3   Selecting Data From Complex Types

In This Chapter 3-3
Selecting Row-Type Data 3-4
    Selecting Columns of a Typed Table 3-5
    Selecting Columns That Contain Row-Type Data 3-6
Selecting from a Collection 3-11
    Selecting Nested Collections 3-12
    Using the IN Keyword to Search for Elements
       in a Collection 3-13
Selecting Rows Within a Table Hierarchy 3-15
    Selecting Rows of the Supertable Without the
       ONLY Keyword 3-16
    Selecting Rows from a Supertable with the
       ONLY Keyword 3-17
    Using an Alias for a Supertable 3-17
Summary 3-18

Chapter 4   Using Functions in Select Statements

In This Chapter 4-3
Using Functions in SELECT Statements 4-4
    Aggregate Functions 4-4
    Time Functions 4-10
    Date-Conversion Functions 4-15
    Cardinality Function 4-19
    Smart-Large-Object Functions 4-20
    String-Manipulation Functions 4-21
    Other Functions 4-29
Using SPL Routines in SELECT Statements 4-36
Using Rowid Values In SELECT Statements 4-38
    Using Rowid Values with the USER Function 4-39
    Using Rowid Values with the DBSERVERNAME
       Function 4-41
Summary 4-42

Chapter 5	**Composing Advanced SELECT Statements**	
	In This Chapter	5-3
	Using the GROUP BY and HAVING Clauses	5-4
	Using the GROUP BY Clause	5-5
	Using the HAVING Clause	5-8
	Creating Advanced Joins	5-11
	Self-Joins	5-11
	Outer Joins	5-15
	Subqueries in SELECT Statements	5-20
	Subqueries in a Select List	5-22
	Subqueries in WHERE Clauses	5-22
	Handling Collections in SELECT Statements	5-30
	Collection Subqueries	5-30
	Collection-Derived Tables	5-32
	Set Operations	5-34
	Union	5-35
	Difference	5-43
	Summary	5-44
Chapter 6	**Modifying Data**	
	In This Chapter	6-5
	Statements That Modify Data	6-6
	Deleting Rows	6-6
	Deleting All Rows of a Table	6-6
	Deleting a Known Number of Rows	6-7
	Deleting an Unknown Number of Rows	6-7
	Deleting Rows That Contain Row Types	6-8
	Deleting Rows That Contain Collection Types	6-9
	Deleting Rows from a Supertable	6-9
	Complicated Delete Conditions	6-9
	Inserting Rows	6-11
	Single Rows	6-11
	Inserting Rows into Typed Tables	6-14
	Inserting into Row-Type Columns	6-15
	Inserting Rows into Supertables	6-17
	Inserting Collection Values into Columns	6-18
	Inserting Smart Large Objects	6-20
	Multiple Rows and Expressions	6-21
	Restrictions on the Insert Selection	6-22

Updating Rows 6-23
    Selecting Rows to Update 6-24
    Updating with Uniform Values 6-25
    Restrictions on Updates 6-26
    Updating with Selected Values 6-26
    Updating Row Types 6-27
    Updating Collection Types 6-29
    Updating Rows of a Supertable 6-30
    Using a CASE Expression to Update a Column 6-31
    Using SQL Functions to Update Smart Large Objects 6-31
    Using a Join to Update a Column. 6-32
Privileges on a Database 6-32
    Database-Level Privileges 6-33
    Table-Level Privileges 6-33
    Displaying Table Privileges. 6-34
Data Integrity 6-35
    Entity Integrity 6-36
    Semantic Integrity 6-37
    Referential Integrity 6-37
    Object Modes and Violation Detection 6-41
Interrupted Modifications 6-51
    Transactions 6-52
    Transaction Logging 6-53
    Specifying Transactions 6-55
Backups and Logs with Informix Database Servers 6-56
Concurrency and Locks 6-57
Informix Data Replication 6-58
Summary 6-59

Chapter 7   Programming with SQL

In This Chapter 7-3
SQL in Programs 7-4
    SQL in SQL APIs 7-4
    SQL in Application Languages 7-5
    Static Embedding 7-5
    Dynamic Statements 7-5
    Program Variables and Host Variables 7-6

Calling the Database Server 7-8
  SQL Communications Area 7-8
  SQLCODE Field 7-9
  SQLERRD Array 7-10
  SQLWARN Array 7-11
  SQLERRM Character String 7-13
  SQLSTATE Value 7-13
Retrieving Single Rows 7-14
  Data Type Conversion 7-15
  Working with Null Data 7-16
  Dealing with Errors 7-17
Retrieving Multiple Rows 7-19
  Declaring a Cursor 7-20
  Opening a Cursor 7-21
  Fetching Rows 7-21
  Cursor Input Modes 7-23
  Active Set of a Cursor 7-24
  Using a Cursor: A Parts Explosion 7-26
Dynamic SQL 7-29
  Preparing a Statement 7-29
  Executing Prepared SQL 7-31
  Dynamic Host Variables 7-31
  Freeing Prepared Statements 7-32
  Quick Execution 7-33
Embedding Data-Definition Statements 7-33
Embedding Grant and Revoke Privileges 7-33
Summary 7-37

Chapter 8   **Modifying Data Through SQL Programs**
In This Chapter 8-3
Using DELETE 8-3
  Direct Deletions 8-4
  Deleting with a Cursor 8-7
Using INSERT 8-9
  Using an Insert Cursor 8-9
  Rows of Constants 8-12
  An Insert Example 8-12
Using UPDATE 8-15
  Using an Update Cursor 8-15
  Cleaning Up a Table 8-17
Summary 8-18

Chapter 9   **Programming for a Multiuser Environment**

In This Chapter 9-3
Concurrency and Performance 9-3
Locking and Integrity 9-4
Locking and Performance 9-4
Concurrency Issues 9-5
How Locks Work 9-6
    Kinds of Locks 9-7
    Lock Scope 9-7
    Duration of a Lock 9-13
    Locks While Modifying 9-13
Locking with the SELECT Statement 9-14
    Setting the Isolation Level 9-14
    Update Cursors 9-20
Retaining Update Locks 9-21
Locks Placed with INSERT, UPDATE, and DELETE 9-22
Understanding the Behavior of the Lock Types 9-22
Controlling Data Modification with Access Modes 9-24
Setting the Lock Mode 9-24
    Waiting for Locks 9-25
    Not Waiting for Locks 9-25
    Waiting a Limited Time 9-26
    Handling a Deadlock 9-26
    Handling External Deadlock 9-26
Simple Concurrency 9-27
Hold Cursors 9-27
Using the SQL Statement Cache 9-29
Summary 9-30

Chapter 10   **Creating and Using SPL Routines**

In This Chapter 10-5
Introduction to SPL Routines 10-6
    What You Can Do with SPL Routines 10-6
    SPL Routine Behavior for Enterprise Decision Server 10-7
Writing SPL Routines 10-8
    Using the CREATE PROCEDURE or
        CREATE FUNCTION Statement 10-8
    Example of a Complete Routine 10-18
    Creating an SPL Routine in a Program 10-18
    Dropping an SPL Routine 10-19

Defining and Using Variables 10-20
    Declaring Local Variables 10-21
    Declaring Global Variables 10-29
    Assigning Values to Variables 10-30
Expressions in SPL Routines 10-33
Writing the Statement Block 10-34
    Implicit and Explicit Statement Blocks 10-34
    Using Cursors 10-35
    Using the FOREACH Loop to Define Cursors 10-35
    Using an IF - ELIF - ELSE Structure 10-38
    Adding WHILE and FOR Loops 10-40
    Exiting a Loop 10-42
Returning Values from an SPL Function 10-43
    Returning a Single Value 10-44
    Returning Multiple Values 10-44
Handling Row-Type Data 10-46
    Precedence of Dot Notation 10-46
    Updating a Row-Type Expression 10-47
Handling Collections 10-48
    Collection Examples 10-48
    The First Steps 10-49
    Declaring a Collection Variable 10-50
    Declaring an Element Variable 10-50
    Selecting a Collection into a Collection Variable . . 10-50
    Inserting Elements into a Collection Variable 10-51
    Selecting Elements from a Collection 10-54
    Deleting a Collection Element 10-57
    Updating a Collection Element 10-61
    Updating the Entire Collection 10-63
    Inserting into a Collection 10-66
Executing Routines 10-71
    Using the EXECUTE Statements 10-71
    Using the CALL Statement 10-73
    Executing Routines in Expressions 10-74
    Executing an External Function with the RETURN Statement . 10-75
    Executing Cursor Functions from an SPL Routine 10-75
    Dynamic Routine-Name Specification 10-76

Privileges on Routines 10-78
   Privileges for Registering a Routine 10-79
   Privileges for Executing a Routine 10-79
   Privileges on Objects Associated with a Routine 10-81
   DBA Privileges for Executing a Routine 10-82
Finding Errors in an SPL Routine 10-84
   Looking at Compile-Time Warnings 10-85
   Generating the Text of the Routine 10-85
Debugging an SPL Routine 10-86
Exception Handling 10-88
   Trapping an Error and Recovering 10-89
   Scope of Control of an ON EXCEPTION Statement 10-90
   User-Generated Exceptions 10-91
Checking the Number of Rows Processed in an SPL Routine . . . 10-93
Summary 10-93

Chapter 11   **Creating and Using Triggers**

In This Chapter 11-3
When to Use Triggers 11-3
How to Create a Trigger 11-4
   Assigning a Trigger Name 11-5
   Specifying the Trigger Event 11-5
   Defining the Triggered Actions 11-6
   A Complete CREATE TRIGGER Statement 11-7
Using Triggered Actions 11-7
   Using BEFORE and AFTER Triggered Actions 11-7
   Using FOR EACH ROW Triggered Actions 11-9
   Using SPL Routines as Triggered Actions 11-11
Triggers in a Table Hierarchy 11-13
Using Select Triggers 11-13
   SELECT Statements that Execute Triggered Actions 11-13
   Restrictions on Execution of Select Triggers 11-15
   Select Triggers on Tables in a Table Hierarchy 11-16
Re-Entrant Triggers 11-16
Tracing Triggered Actions 11-17
   Example of TRACE Statements in an SPL Routine 11-17
   Example of TRACE Output 11-18

Generating Error Messages 11-18
    Applying a Fixed Error Message 11-19
    Generating a Variable Error Message 11-20
Summary 11-22

Index

Introduction

In This Introduction 3

About This Manual. 3
   Types of Users 3
   Software Dependencies 4
   Assumptions About Your Locale 4
   Demonstration Databases 5

New Features. 5
   New Features in Version 8.3 5
      Performance Enhancements 6
      New SQL Functionality 6
      Version 8.3 Features from Version 7.30 6
   New Features in Version 9.2 7
      Extensibility Enhancements 7
      Performance Improvements 7
      Special Features 8

Documentation Conventions 8
   Typographical Conventions 9
   Icon Conventions 10
      Comment Icons 10
      Feature, Product, and Platform Icons 10
      Compliance Icons 11
   Sample-Code Conventions 12

Additional Documentation   13
   On-Line Manuals   13
   Printed Manuals   13
   On-Line Help   14
   Error Message Documentation   14
   Documentation Notes, Release Notes, Machine Notes   14
   Related Reading   16

Compliance with Industry Standards.   16

Informix Welcomes Your Comments   16

In This Introduction

This introduction provides an overview of the information in this book and describes the conventions it uses.

About This Book

This book shows how to use basic and advanced structured query language (SQL) to access and manipulate the data in your databases. It discusses the data manipulation language (DML) statements as well as triggers and stored procedure language (SPL) routines, which DML statements often use.

This book is one of a series of books that discusses the Informix implementation of SQL. The *Informix Guide to SQL: Reference and Syntax, Second Edition* provides reference information for aspects of SQL other than the language statements and contains all the syntax descriptions for SQL and SPL. The *Informix Guide to Designing Databases and Data Warehouses* shows how to use SQL to implement and manage your databases.

Types of Users

This book is written for the following users:

- Database users
- Database administrators
- Database-application programmers

This book assumes that you have the following background:

- A working knowledge of your computer, your operating system, and the utilities that your operating system provides
- Some experience working with relational databases or exposure to database concepts
- Some experience with computer programming

If you have limited experience with relational databases, SQL, or your operating system, refer to the *Getting Started* manual for your database server for a list of supplementary titles.

Software Dependencies

This book assumes that you are using one of the following database servers:

- Informix Enterprise Decision Server, Version 8.3
- Informix Dynamic Server 2000, Version 9.2

Assumptions About Your Locale

Informix products can support many languages, cultures, and code sets. All culture-specific information is brought together in a single environment, called a Global Language Support (GLS) locale.

This book assumes that you use the U.S. 8859-1 English locale as the default locale. The default is **en_us.8859-1** (ISO 8859-1) on UNIX platforms or **en_us.1252** (Microsoft 1252) for Windows NT environments. This locale supports U.S. English format conventions for dates, times, and currency, and also supports the ISO 8859-1 or Microsoft 1252 code set, which includes the ASCII code set plus many 8-bit characters such as é, è, and ñ.

If you plan to use nondefault characters in your data or your SQL identifiers, or if you want to conform to the nondefault collation rules of character data, you need to specify the appropriate nondefault locale.

For instructions on how to specify a nondefault locale, additional syntax, and other considerations related to GLS locales, see the *Informix Guide to GLS Functionality*.

Demonstration Databases

The DB-Access utility, which is provided with your Informix database server products, includes one or more of the following demonstration databases:

- The **stores_demo** database illustrates a relational schema with information about a fictitious wholesale sporting-goods distributor. Many examples in Informix manuals are based on the **stores_demo** database.

EDS

- The **sales_demo** database illustrates a dimensional schema for data-warehousing applications. For conceptual information about dimensional data modeling, see the *Informix Guide to Database Design and Implementation*. ♦

IDS

- The **superstores_demo** database illustrates an object-relational schema. The **superstores_demo** database includes examples of extended data types, type and table inheritance, and user-defined routines. ♦

For information about how to create and populate the demonstration databases, see the *DB-Access User's Manual*. For descriptions of the databases and their contents, see the *Informix Guide to SQL: Reference*.

The scripts that you use to install the demonstration databases reside in the **$INFORMIXDIR/bin** directory on UNIX and in the **%INFORMIXDIR%\bin** directory in Windows.

New Features

For a comprehensive list of new database server features, see the release notes. This section lists new features relevant to this book.

New Features in Version 8.3

This book describes new features in Version 8.3 of Enterprise Decision Server. The features fall into the following areas:

- Performance enhancements
- New SQL functionality
- Version 8.3 features from Dynamic Server 7.30

Performance Enhancements

This book describes the following performance enhancements to Version 8.3 of Enterprise Decision Server:

- Coarse-grain index locks
- Updates with subquery in SET clause

New SQL Functionality

This book describes the following new SQL functionality in Version 8.3 of Enterprise Decision Server:

- DELETE ... USING statement to delete rows based on a table join
- Load and unload simple large objects to external tables
- TRUNCATE statement

Version 8.3 Features from Version 7.30

This book describes the following features from Version 7.3 of Dynamic Server in Version 8.3 of Enterprise Decision Server:

- Ability to retain update locks
- COUNT function
- Insert from SPL procedures
- NVL and DECODE functions
- REPLACE, SUBSTR, LPAD, and RPAD functions for string manipulation
- Slow ALTER TABLE
- TO_CHAR and TO_DATE functions for date conversion
- Triggers
- UPDATE SET clause subqueries
- UPPER, LOWER, and INITCAP functions for case-insensitive search
- Violations table

New Features in Version 9.2

This book describes new features in Version 9.2 of Dynamic Server. The features fall into the following areas:

- Extensibility enhancements
- Performance improvements
- Special features

Extensibility Enhancements

This book describes the following extensibility enhancements to Version 9.2 of Dynamic Server:

- Enhancements to the database server: dynamic lock allocation
- General enhancements to SQL:
    - Embedded newline characters in quoted strings
    - Nested dot expressions
- Triggers on SELECT statements
- Enhancements to collections:
    - Collection constructors that use arbitrary expression elements
    - Collection-derived tables
    - Collection subqueries

Performance Improvements

This book describes the following performance improvements to Version 9.2 of Dynamic Server:

- SQL statement cache
- For UDRs:
    - Expensive-function optimization
    - Parallel UDRs

Special Features

This book describes the following special features in Version 9.2 of Dynamic Server:

- Long identifiers:
  - ❏ 128-character identifier
  - ❏ 32-character user names
- Ability to retain update locks

Documentation Conventions

This section describes the conventions that this book uses. These conventions make it easier to gather information from this and other volumes in the documentation set.

The following conventions are discussed:

- Typographical conventions
- Icon conventions
- Sample-code conventions

Typographical Conventions

This book uses the following conventions to introduce new terms, illustrate screen displays, describe command syntax, and so forth.

Convention	Meaning
KEYWORD	All primary elements in a programming language statement (keywords) appear in uppercase letters in a serif font.
italics **italics** *italics*	Within text, new terms and emphasized words appear in italics. Within syntax and code examples, variable values that you are to specify appear in italics.
boldface *boldface*	Names of program entities (such as classes, events, and tables), environment variables, file and pathnames, and interface elements (such as icons, menu items, and buttons) appear in boldface.
`monospace` `monospace`	Information that the product displays and information that you enter appear in a monospace typeface.
KEYSTROKE	Keys that you are to press appear in uppercase letters in a sans serif font.
◆	This symbol indicates the end of one or more product- or platform-specific paragraphs.
→	This symbol indicates a menu item. For example, "Choose **Tools→Options**" means choose the **Options** item from the **Tools** menu.

Tip: *When you are instructed to "enter" characters or to "execute" a command, immediately press* RETURN *after the entry. When you are instructed to "type" the text or to "press" other keys, no* RETURN *is required.*

Icon Conventions

Throughout the documentation, you will find text that is identified by several different types of icons. This section describes these icons.

Comment Icons

Comment icons identify three types of information, as the following table describes. This information always appears in italics.

Icon	Label	Description
⚠	**Warning:**	Identifies paragraphs that contain vital instructions, cautions, or critical information
⇒	**Important:**	Identifies paragraphs that contain significant information about the feature or operation that is being described
💡	**Tip:**	Identifies paragraphs that offer additional details or shortcuts for the functionality that is being described

Feature, Product, and Platform Icons

Feature, product, and platform icons identify paragraphs that contain feature-specific, product-specific, or platform-specific information.

Icon	Description
EDS	Identifies information or syntax that is specific to Informix Enterprise Decision Server
E/C	Identifies information that is specific to the INFORMIX-ESQL/C product
GLS	Identifies information that relates to the Informix Global Language Support (GLS) feature

(1 of 2)

Icon	Description
IDS	Identifies information that is specific to Informix Dynamic Server 2000
UNIX	Identifies information that is specific to UNIX
WIN NT	Identifies information that is specific to Windows NT

(2 of 2)

These icons can apply to an entire section or to one or more paragraphs within a section. If an icon appears next to a section heading, the information that applies to the indicated feature, product, or platform ends at the next heading at the same or higher level. A ♦ symbol indicates the end of feature-, product-, or platform-specific information that appears within one or more paragraphs within a section.

Compliance Icons

Compliance icons indicate paragraphs that provide guidelines for complying with a standard.

Icon	Description
ANSI	Identifies information that is specific to an ANSI-compliant database

These icons can apply to an entire section or to one or more paragraphs within a section. If an icon appears next to a section heading, the information that applies to the indicated feature, product, or platform ends at the next heading at the same or higher level. A ♦ symbol indicates the end of feature-, product-, or platform-specific information that appears within one or more paragraphs within a section.

Sample-Code Conventions

Examples of SQL code occur throughout this book. Except where noted, the code is not specific to any single Informix application development tool. If only SQL statements are listed in the example, they are not delimited by semicolons. For instance, you might see the code in the following example:

```
CONNECT TO stores_demo
...

DELETE FROM customer
    WHERE customer_num = 121
...

COMMIT WORK
DISCONNECT CURRENT
```

To use this SQL code for a specific product, you must apply the syntax rules for that product. For example, if you are using DB-Access, you must delimit multiple statements with semicolons. If you are using an SQL API, you must use EXEC SQL at the start of each statement and a semicolon (or other appropriate delimiter) at the end of the statement.

 Tip: *Ellipsis points in a code example indicate that more code would be added in a full application, but it is not necessary to show it to describe the concept being discussed.*

For detailed directions on using SQL statements for a particular application development tool or SQL API, see the manual for your product.

Additional Documentation

For additional information, you might want to refer to the following types of documentation:

- On-line manuals
- Printed manuals
- On-line help
- Error message documentation
- Documentation notes, release notes, and machine notes
- Related reading

On-Line Manuals

An Answers OnLine CD that contains Informix manuals in electronic format is provided with your Informix products. You can install the documentation or access it directly from the CD. For information about how to install, read, and print on-line manuals, see the installation insert that accompanies Answers OnLine.

Informix on-line manuals are also available on the following Web site:

```
www.informix.com/answers
```

Printed Manuals

To order printed manuals, call 1-800-331-1763 or send email to moreinfo@informix.com. Please provide the following information when you place your order:

- The documentation that you need
- The quantity that you need
- Your name, address, and telephone number

WIN NT

On-Line Help

Informix provides on-line help with each graphical user interface (GUI) that displays information about those interfaces and the functions that they perform. Use the help facilities that each GUI provides to display the on-line help.

Error Message Documentation

Informix software products provide ASCII files that contain all of the Informix error messages and their corrective actions.

UNIX

To read error messages and corrective actions on UNIX, use one of the following utilities.

Utility	Description
finderr	Displays error messages on line
rofferr	Formats error messages for printing

♦

WIN NT

To read error messages and corrective actions in Windows environments, use the **Informix Find Error** utility. To display this utility, choose **Start→Programs→Informix** from the Task Bar. ♦

Instructions for using the preceding utilities are available in Answers OnLine. Answers OnLine also provides a listing of error messages and corrective actions in HTML format.

Documentation Notes, Release Notes, Machine Notes

In addition to printed documentation, the following sections describe the on-line files that supplement the information in this book. Please examine these files before you begin using your database server. They contain vital information about application and performance issues.

UNIX

On UNIX platforms, the following on-line files appear in the **$INFORMIXDIR/release/en_us/0333** directory. Replace *x.y* in the filenames with the version number of your database server.

On-Line File	Purpose
SQLTDOC_*x.y*	The documentation notes file for your version of this manual describes topics that are not covered in the manual or that were modified since publication.
SERVERS_*x.y*	The release notes file describes feature differences from earlier versions of Informix products and how these differences might affect current products. This file also contains information about any known problems and their workarounds.
IDS_*x.y* or IDS_EDS_*x.y*	The machine notes file describes any special actions that you must take to configure and use Informix products on your computer. Machine notes are named for the product described.

♦

WIN NT

The following items appear in the **Informix** folder. To display this folder, choose **Start→Programs→Informix** from the Task Bar.

Program Group Item	Description
Documentation Notes	This item includes additions or corrections to manuals and information about features that might not be covered in the manuals or that have been modified since publication.
Release Notes	This item describes feature differences from earlier versions of Informix products and how these differences might affect current products. This file also contains information about any known problems and their workarounds.

Machine notes do not apply to Windows environments. ♦

Related Reading

For a list of publications that provide an introduction to database servers and operating-system platforms, refer to your *Getting Started* manual.

Compliance with Industry Standards

The American National Standards Institute (ANSI) has established a set of industry standards for SQL. Informix SQL-based products are fully compliant with SQL-92 Entry Level (published as ANSI X3.135-1992), which is identical to ISO 9075:1992. In addition, many features of Informix database servers comply with the SQL-92 Intermediate and Full Level and X/Open SQL CAE (common applications environment) standards.

Informix Welcomes Your Comments

Let us know what you like or dislike about our books. To help us with future versions of our books, we want to know about any corrections or clarifications that you would find useful. Include the following information:

- The name and version of the book that you are using
- Any comments that you have about the manual
- Your name, address, and phone number

Send electronic mail to us at the following address:

doc@informix.com

The **doc** alias is reserved exclusively. The **doc** alias is reserved exclusively for reporting errors and omissions in our documentation.

We appreciate your suggestions.

Database Concepts

In This Chapter 1-3

Illustration of a Data Model 1-3
    Storing Data 1-5
    Querying Data 1-6
    Modifying Data 1-8

Concurrent Use and Security 1-8
    Controlling Database Use 1-8
    Centralized Management 1-9

Important Database Terms 1-9
    The Object-Relational Model 1-10
    Tables 1-10
    Columns 1-11
    Rows 1-11
    Operations on Tables 1-12
    The Object-Relational Model 1-13

Structured Query Language 1-14
    Standard SQL 1-15
    Informix SQL and ANSI SQL 1-15
    Interactive SQL 1-16
    General Programming 1-16
    ANSI-Compliant Databases 1-17
    GLS Databases 1-17

Summary 1-17

In This Chapter

This chapter describes fundamental concepts of databases and defines some terms that this book uses. The chapter emphasizes the following topics:

- How does the data model differentiate a database from a file?
- What issues are involved when many users use the database as a common resource?
- What terms are used to describe the main components of a database?
- What language is used to create, query, and modify a database?

Your real use of a database begins with the SELECT statement, which Chapter 2, "Composing SELECT Statements," describes.

Illustration of a Data Model

The principal difference between information collected in a database versus information collected in a file is the way the data is organized. A flat file is organized physically; certain items precede or follow other items. But the contents of a database are organized according to a *data model*. A data model is a plan, or map, that defines the units of data and specifies how each unit relates to the others.

For example, a number can appear in either a file or a database. In a file, it is simply a number that occurs at a certain point in the file. A number in a database, however, has a role that the data model assigns to it. The role might be a *price* that is associated with a *product* that was sold as one *item* of an *order* that a *customer* placed. Each of these components, price, product, item, order, and customer, also has a role that the data model specifies. For an illustration of a data model, see Figure 1-1.

Figure 1-1
The Advantage of Using a Data Model

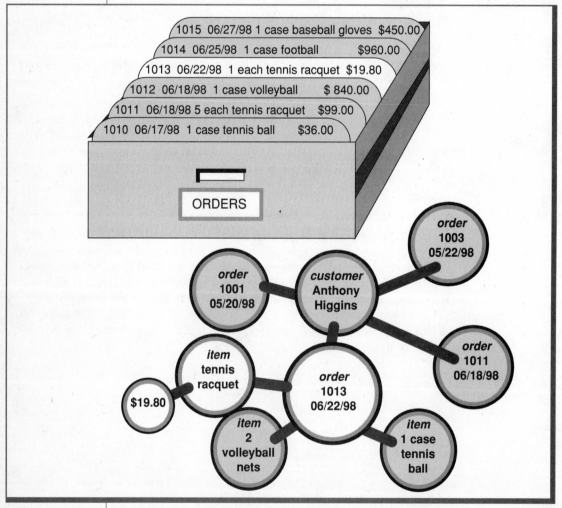

You design the data model when you create the database. You then insert units of data according to the plan that the model lays out. Some books use the term *schema* instead of *data model*.

Storing Data

Another difference between a database and a file is that the organization of the database is stored with the database.

A file can have a complex inner structure, but the definition of that structure is not within the file; it is in the programs that create or use the file. For example, a document file that a word-processing program stores might contain detailed structures that describe the format of the document. However, only the word-processing program can decipher the contents of the file because the structure is defined within the program, not within the file.

A data model, however, is contained in the database it describes. It travels with the database and is available to any program that uses the database. The model defines not only the names of the data items but also their data types, so a program can adapt itself to the database. For example, a program can find out that, in the current database, a *price* item is a decimal number with eight digits, two to the right of the decimal point; then it can allocate storage for a number of that type. How programs work with databases is the subject of Chapter 7, "Programming with SQL," and Chapter 8, "Modifying Data Through SQL Programs."

Querying Data

Another difference between a database and a file is the way you can access them. You can search a file sequentially, looking for particular values at particular physical locations in each line or record. That is, you might ask, "What records have the number 1013 in the first field?" Figure 1-2 shows this type of search.

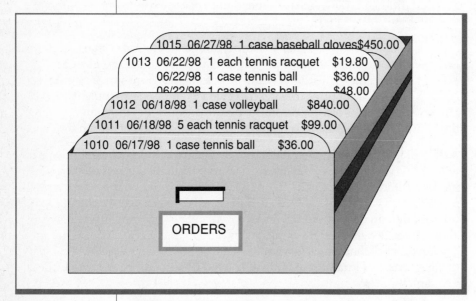

Figure 1-2
Searching a File
Sequentially

In contrast, when you query a database, you use the terms that the model defines. You can query the database with questions such as, "What *orders* have been placed for *products* made by the Shimara Corporation, by *customers* in New Jersey, with *ship dates* in the third quarter?" Figure 1-3 shows this type of query.

Figure 1-3
Querying a Database

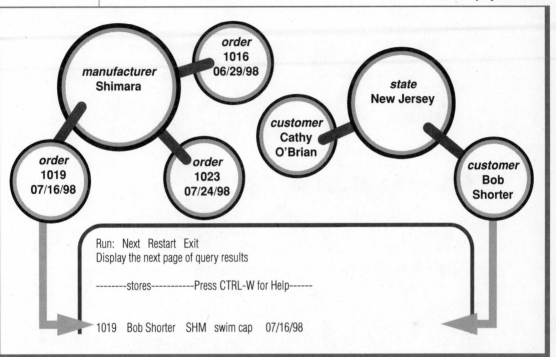

In other words, when you access data that is stored in a file, you must state
your question in terms of the physical layout of the file. When you query a
database, you can ignore the arcane details of computer storage and state
your query in terms that reflect the real world, at least to the extent that the
data model reflects the real world.

Chapter 2, "Composing SELECT Statements," and Chapter 5, "Composing,"
discuss the language you use to make queries.

For information about how to build and implement your data model, see the
Informix Guide to Database Design and Implementation.

Modifying Data

The data model also makes it possible to modify the contents of the database with less chance for error. You can query the database with statements such as, "Find every *stock item* with a *manufacturer* of Presta or Schraeder, and increase its *price* by 13 percent." You state changes in terms that reflect the meaning of the data. You do not have to waste time and effort thinking about details of fields within records in a file, so the chances for error are less.

The statements you use to modify stored data are covered in Chapter 6, "Modifying Data."

Concurrent Use and Security

A database can be a common resource for many users. Multiple users can query and modify a database simultaneously. The database server (the program that manages the contents of all databases) ensures that the queries and modifications are done in sequence and without conflict.

Having concurrent users on a database provides great advantages but also introduces new problems of security and privacy. Some databases are private; individuals set them up for their own use. Other databases contain confidential material that must be shared but among only a select group of persons; still other databases provide public access.

Controlling Database Use

Informix database software provides the means to control database use. When you design a database, you can perform any of the following functions:

- Keep the database completely private
- Open its entire contents to all users or to selected users
- Restrict the selection of data that some users can view. (In fact, you can reveal entirely different selections of data to different groups of users.)
- Allow specified users to view certain items but not modify them

- Allow specified users to add new data but not modify old data
- Allow specified users to modify all, or specified items of, existing data
- Ensure that added or modified data conforms to the data model

For information about how to grant and limit access to your database, see the *Informix Guide to Database Design and Implementation*.

Centralized Management

Databases that many people use are valuable and must be protected as important business assets. You create a significant problem when you compile a store of valuable data and simultaneously allow many employees to access it. You handle this problem by protecting data while maintaining performance. The database server lets you centralize these tasks.

Databases must be guarded against loss or damage. The hazards are many: failures in software and hardware, and the risks of fire, flood, and other natural disasters. Losing an important database creates a huge potential for damage. The damage could include not only the expense and difficulty of re-creating the lost data but also the loss of productive time by the database users as well as the loss of business and goodwill while users cannot work. A plan for regular backups helps avoid or mitigate these potential disasters.

A large database that many people use must be maintained and tuned. Someone must monitor its use of system resources, chart its growth, antic-ipate bottlenecks, and plan for expansion. Users will report problems in the application programs; someone must diagnose these problems and correct them. If rapid response is important, someone must analyze the performance of the system and find the causes of slow responses.

Important Database Terms

You should know a number of terms before you begin the next chapter. Depending on the database server you use, a different set of terms can describe the database and the data model that apply.

IDS

The Object-Relational Model

The databases you create with an Informix database server are *object-relational* databases. In practical terms this means that all data is presented in the form of *tables* with *rows* and *columns* where the following simple corresponding relationships apply.

Relationship	Description
table = entity	A table represents all that the database knows about one subject or kind of thing.
column = attribute	A column represents one feature, characteristic, or fact that is true of the table subject.
row = instance	A row represents one individual instance of the table subject.

Some rules apply about how you choose entities and attributes, but they are important only when you are designing a new database. (For more information about database design, see the *Informix Guide to Database Design and Implementation*.) The data model in an existing database is already set. To use the database, you need to know only the names of the tables and columns and how they correspond to the real world.

Tables

A database is a collection of information that is grouped into one or more tables. A table is an array of data *items* organized into rows and columns. A demonstration database is distributed with every Informix product. A partial table from the demonstration database follows.

stock_num	manu_code	description	unit_price	unit	unit_descr
...	...	...	...	...	...
1	HRO	baseball gloves	250.00	case	10 gloves/case
1	HSK	baseball gloves	800.00	case	10 gloves/case

(1 of 2)

stock_num	manu_code	description	unit_price	unit	unit_descr
1	SMT	baseball gloves	450.00	case	10 gloves/case
2	HRO	baseball	126.00	case	24/case
3	HSK	baseball bat	240.00	case	12/case
4	HSK	football	960.00	case	24/case
4	HRO	football	480.00	case	24/case
5	NRG	tennis racquet	28.00	each	each
...	...	...	...	...	...
313	ANZ	swim cap	60.00	case	12/box

(2 of 2)

A table represents all that the database administrator (DBA) wants to store about one *entity*, one type of thing that the database describes. The example table, **stock**, represents all that the DBA wants to store about the merchandise that a sporting-goods store stocks. Other tables in the demonstration database represent such entities as **customer** and **orders**.

Think of a database as a collection of tables. To create a database is to create a set of tables. The right to query or modify tables can be controlled on a table-by-table basis, so that some users can view or modify some tables but not others.

Columns

Each column of a table contains one *attribute*, which is one characteristic, feature, or fact that describes the subject of the table. The **stock** table has columns for the following facts about items of merchandise: stock numbers, manufacturer codes, descriptions, prices, and units of measure.

Rows

Each row of a table is one *instance* of the subject of the table, which is one particular example of that entity. Each row of the **stock** table stands for one item of merchandise that the sporting-goods store sells.

Operations on Tables

Because a database is really a collection of tables, database operations are operations on tables. The object-relational model supports three fundamental operations: selection, projection, and joining. Figure 1-4 shows the selection and projection operations. (All three operations are defined in detail, with many examples, in the following chapters.)

Figure 1-4
Illustration of Selection and Projection

stock table

stock_num	manu_code	description	unit_price	unit	unit_descr
...	...	...	...	...	...
1	HRO	baseball gloves	250.00	case	10 gloves/case
1	HSK	baseball gloves	800.00	case	10 gloves/case
1	SMT	baseball gloves	450.00	case	10 gloves/case
2	HRO	baseball	126.00	case	24/case
3	HSK	baseball bat	240.00	case	12/case
4	HSK	football	960.00	case	24/case
4	HRO	football	480.00	case	24/case
5	NRG	tennis racquet	28.00	each	each
...	...	...	...	...	...
313	ANZ	swim cap	60.00	case	12/box

SELECTION

P R O J E C T I O N

When you *select* data from a table, you are choosing certain rows and ignoring others. For example, you can query the **stock** table by asking the database management system to, "Select all rows in which the manufacturer code is HSK and the unit price is between 200.00 and 300.00."

When you *project* from a table, you are choosing certain columns and ignoring others. For example, you can query the **stock** table by asking the database management system to "project the **stock_num**, **unit_descr**, and **unit_price** columns."

A table contains information about only one entity; when you want information about multiple entities, you must *join* their tables. You can join tables in many ways. (The join operation is the subject of Chapter 5.)

The Object-Relational Model

Dynamic Server allows you to build *object-relational* databases. In addition to supporting alphanumeric data such as character strings, integers, date, and decimal, an object-relational database extends the features of a relational model with the following object-oriented capabilities:

- **Extensibility.** You can extend the capability of the database server by defining new data types (and the access methods and functions to support them) and user-defined routines (UDRs) that allow you to store and manage images, audio, video, large text documents, and so forth.

  Informix, as well as third-party vendors, package some data types and their access methods into *DataBlade modules,* or shared class libraries, that you can add on to the database server, if they suit your needs. DataBlade modules enable you to store non-traditional data types such as two-dimensional spatial objects (lines, polygons, ellipses, and circles) and to access them through R-tree indexes. A DataBlade module might also provide new types of access to large text documents, including phrase matching, fuzzy searches, and synonym matching.

  You can also extend the database server on your own by using the features of Dynamic Server that enable you to add data types and access methods. For more information, see *Extending Informix Dynamic Server 2000*.

  You can create UDRs in SPL and the C programming language to encapsulate application logic or to enhance the functionality of the Dynamic Server. For more information, see Chapter 10, "Creating and Using SPL Routines."

- **Complex Types**. You can define new data types that combine one or more existing data types. Complex types enable greater flexibility in how you organize data at the level of columns and tables. For example, with complex types you can define columns that contain collections of values of a single type and columns that contain multiple component types.

- **Inheritance**. You can define objects (types and tables) that acquire the properties of other objects and add new properties that are specific to the object that you define.

The Dynamic Server provides object-oriented capabilities beyond those of the relational model but represents all data in the form of *tables* with *rows* and *columns*. Although the object-relational model extends the capabilities of the relational model, you can implement your data model as a traditional relational database if you choose.

Some rules apply about how you choose entities and attributes, but they are important only when you are designing a new database. For more information about object-relational database design, see the *Informix Guide to Database Design and Implementation*.

Structured Query Language

Most computer software has not yet reached a point where you can literally ask a database, "What orders have been placed by customers in New Jersey with ship dates in the third quarter?" You must still phrase questions in a restricted syntax that the software can easily parse. You can pose the same question to the demonstration database in the following terms:

```
SELECT * FROM customer, orders
    WHERE customer.customer_num = orders.customer_num
        AND customer.state = 'NJ'
        AND orders.ship_date
        BETWEEN DATE('7/1/98') AND DATE('9/30/98')
```

This question is a sample of Structured Query Language (SQL). It is the language that you use to direct all operations on the database. SQL is composed of statements, each of which begins with one or two keywords that specify a function. The Informix implementation of SQL includes a large number of SQL statements, from ALLOCATE DESCRIPTOR to WHENEVER.

You will use most of the statements only when you set up or tune your database. You will use three or four statements regularly to query or update your database. For details on SQL statements, see the *Informix Guide to SQL: Syntax*.

One statement, SELECT, is in almost constant use. SELECT is the only statement that you can use to retrieve data from the database. It is also the most complicated statement, and the next two chapters of this book explore its many uses.

Standard SQL

SQL and the relational model were invented and developed at IBM in the early and middle 1970s. Once IBM proved that it was possible to implement practical relational databases and that SQL was a usable language for manipulating them, other vendors began to provide similar products for non-IBM computers.

For reasons of performance or competitive advantage, or to take advantage of local hardware or software features, each SQL implementation differed in small ways from the others and from the IBM version of the language. To ensure that the differences remained small, a standards committee was formed in the early 1980s.

Committee X3H2, sponsored by the American National Standards Institute (ANSI), issued the SQL1 standard in 1986. This standard defines a core set of SQL features and the syntax of statements such as SELECT.

Informix SQL and ANSI SQL

The SQL version that Informix products support is compatible with standard SQL (it is also compatible with the IBM version of the language). However, it does contain *extensions* to the standard; that is, extra options or features for certain statements, and looser rules for others. Most of the differences occur in the statements that are not in everyday use. For example, few differences occur in the SELECT statement, which accounts for 90 percent of the SQL use for a typical person.

However, the extensions do exist and create a conflict. Thousands of Informix customers have embedded Informix-style SQL in programs and stored routines. They rely on Informix to keep its language the same. Other customers require the ability to use databases in a way that conforms exactly to the ANSI standard. They rely on Informix to change its language to conform.

Informix resolves the conflict with the following compromise:

- The Informix version of SQL, with its extensions to the standard, is available by default.
- You can ask any Informix SQL language processor to check your use of SQL and post a warning flag whenever you use an Informix extension.

This resolution is fair but makes the SQL documentation more complicated. Wherever a difference exists between Informix and ANSI SQL, the *Informix Guide to SQL: Syntax* describes both versions. Because you probably intend to use only one version, simply ignore the version you do not need.

Interactive SQL

To carry out the examples in this book and to experiment with SQL and database design, you need a program that lets you execute SQL statements interactively. DB-Access and the Relational Object Manager are examples of such programs. They help you compose SQL statements, and then they pass your SQL statements to the database server for execution and display the results to you.

General Programming

You can write programs that incorporate SQL statements and exchange data with the database server. That is, you can write a program to retrieve data from the database and format it however you choose. You can also write programs that take data from any source in any format, prepare it, and insert it into the database.

You can also write programs called stored routines to work with database data and objects. The stored routines that you write are stored directly in a database in tables. You can then execute a stored routine from DB-Access, the Relational Object Manager, or an SQL application programming interface (SQL API) such as Informix ESQL/C.

Chapter 7 and Chapter 8 present an overview of how SQL is used in programs.

ANSI-Compliant Databases

Use the MODE ANSI keywords when you create a database to designate it as ANSI compliant. Within such a database, certain characteristics of the ANSI standard apply. For example, all actions that modify data take place within a transaction automatically, which means that the changes are made in their entirety or not at all. Differences in the behavior of ANSI-compliant databases are noted where appropriate in the statement descriptions in the *Informix Guide to SQL: Syntax*. For a detailed discussion of ANSI-compliant databases, see the *Informix Guide to Database Design and Implementation*.

GLS

GLS Databases

Informix database server products provide the Global Language Support (GLS) feature. In addition to U.S. ASCII English, GLS allows you to work in other locales and use non-ASCII characters in SQL data and identifiers. You can use the GLS feature to conform to the customs of a specific locale. The locale files contain culture-specific information such as various money and date formats and collation orders. For more GLS information, see the *Informix Guide to GLS Functionality*.

Summary

A database contains a collection of related information but differs in a fundamental way from other methods of storing data. The database contains not only the data but also a data model that defines each data item and specifies its meaning with respect to the other items and to the real world.

More than one user can access and modify a database at the same time. Each user has a different view of the contents of a database, and each user's access to those contents can be restricted in several ways.

A relational database consists of tables, and the tables consist of columns and rows. The relational model supports three fundamental operations on tables: selections, projections, and joins.

An object-relational database extends the features of a relational database. You can define new data types to store and manage audio, video, large text documents, and so forth. You can define complex types that combine one or more existing data types to provide greater flexibility in how you organize your data in columns and tables. You can define types and tables that inherit the properties of other database objects and add new properties that are specific to the object that you define.

To manipulate and query a database, use SQL. IBM pioneered SQL and ANSI standardized it. Informix added extensions to the ANSI-defined language that you can use to your advantage. Informix tools also make it possible to maintain strict compliance with ANSI standards.

Two layers of software mediate all your work with databases. The bottom layer is always a database server that executes SQL statements and manages the data on disk and in computer memory. The top layer is one of many applications, some from Informix and some written by you, by other vendors, or your colleagues. Middleware is the component that links the database server to the application, and is provided by the database vendor to bind the client programs with the data server. Informix Stored Procedure Language is an example of such a tool.

Composing SELECT Statements

In This Chapter 2-3

Introducing the SELECT Statement 2-4
  Some Basic Concepts 2-5
    Privileges 2-5
    Relational Operations 2-5
    Selection and Projection 2-6
    Joining 2-8
  The Forms of SELECT 2-9
  Special Data Types. 2-10

Single-Table SELECT Statements 2-10
  Selecting All Columns and Rows. 2-11
    Using the Asterisk Symbol (*) 2-11
    Reordering the Columns 2-12
    Sorting the Rows 2-12
  Selecting Specific Columns 2-17
    Selecting Substrings 2-22
    ORDER BY and Non-English Data 2-23
  Using the WHERE Clause 2-25
  Creating a Comparison Condition 2-26
    Including Rows 2-27
    Excluding Rows 2-28
    Specifying A Range of Rows 2-29
    Excluding a Range of Rows 2-30
    Using a WHERE Clause to Find a Subset of Values 2-30
    Identifying Null Values. 2-32
    Forming Compound Conditions 2-33
    Using Exact-Text Comparisons 2-34

Using Variable-Text Searches 2-35
Using a Single-Character Wildcard 2-35
MATCHES and Non-English Data 2-39
Protecting Special Characters 2-40
Using Subscripting in a WHERE Clause 2-40
Using a FIRST Clause to Select Specific Rows 2-41
FIRST Clause Without an ORDER BY Clause 2-42
FIRST Clause with an ORDER BY Clause 2-43
FIRST Clause in a Union Query 2-44
Expressions and Derived Values 2-44
Arithmetic Expressions 2-45
CASE Expressions 2-49
Sorting on Derived Columns 2-51
Using Rowid Values In SELECT Statements 2-52
Using Rowid Values with the USER Function 2-54
Using Rowid Values with the DBSERVERNAME Function . . 2-55

Multiple-Table SELECT Statements 2-56
Creating a Cartesian Product 2-56
Creating a Join 2-58
Equi-Join 2-58
Natural Join 2-61
Multiple-Table Join 2-63
Some Query Shortcuts 2-64
Using Aliases 2-64
The INTO TEMP Clause 2-67

Selecting Tables from a Database Other Than the Current Database . . 2-69

Summary 2-70

In This Chapter

SELECT is the most important and the most complex SQL statement. You can use it and the SQL statements INSERT, UPDATE, and DELETE to manipulate data. You can use the SELECT statement in the following ways:

- By itself to retrieve data from a database
- As part of an INSERT statement to produce new rows
- As part of an UPDATE statement to update information

The SELECT statement is the primary way to query information in a database. It is your key to retrieving data in a program, report, screen form, or spreadsheet.

This chapter introduces the basic methods for how you can use the SELECT statement to query and retrieve data from relational databases. It discusses how to tailor your statements to select columns or rows of information from one or more tables, how to include expressions and functions in SELECT statements, and how to create various join conditions between database tables. The syntax and usage for the SELECT statement are described in detail in the *Informix Guide to SQL: Syntax*.

Most examples in this manual come from the tables in the **stores_demo** database, which is included with the software for your Informix SQL API or database utility. In the interest of brevity, the examples show only part of the data that is retrieved for each SELECT statement. For information on the structure and contents of the demonstration database, see the *Informix Guide to SQL: Reference*. For emphasis, keywords are shown in uppercase letters in the examples, although SQL is not case sensitive.

Introducing the SELECT Statement

The SELECT statement is constructed of clauses that let you look at data in a relational database. These clauses let you select columns and rows from one or more database tables or views, specify one or more conditions, order and summarize the data, and put the selected data in a temporary table.

This chapter shows how to use five SELECT statement clauses. You must include these clauses in a SELECT statement in the following order:

1. SELECT clause
2. FROM clause
3. WHERE clause
4. ORDER BY clause
5. INTO TEMP clause

Only the SELECT and FROM clauses are required. These two clauses form the basis for every database query because they specify the tables and columns to be retrieved. Use one or more of the other clauses from the following list:

- Add a WHERE clause to select specific rows or create a *join* condition.
- Add an ORDER BY clause to change the order in which data is produced.
- Add an INTO TEMP clause to save the results as a table for further queries.

Two additional SELECT statement clauses, GROUP BY and HAVING, let you perform more complex data retrieval. They are introduced in Chapter 5. Another clause, INTO, specifies the program or host variable to receive data from a SELECT statement in INFORMIX-NewEra and SQL APIs. Complete syntax and rules for using the SELECT statement are in the *Informix Guide to SQL: Syntax*.

Some Basic Concepts

The SELECT statement, unlike INSERT, UPDATE, and DELETE statements, does not modify the data in a database. It simply queries the data. Whereas only one user at a time can modify data, multiple users can query or *select* the data concurrently. The statements that modify data appear in Chapter 6. The syntax descriptions of the INSERT, UPDATE, and DELETE statements appear in the *Informix Guide to SQL: Syntax.*

In a relational database, a *column* is a data element that contains a particular type of information that occurs in every row in the table. A *row* is a group of related items of information about a single entity across all columns in a database table.

You can select columns and rows from a database table; from a *system-catalog table*, a special table that contains information on the database; or from a *view*, a virtual table created to contain a customized set of data. System catalog tables are described in the *Informix Guide to SQL: Reference*. Views are discussed in the *Informix Guide to Database Design and Implementation*.

Privileges

Before you make a query against data, make sure you have the Connect privilege on the database and the Select privilege on the table. These privileges are normally granted to all users. Database access privileges are discussed in the *Informix Guide to Database Design and Implementation* and in the GRANT and REVOKE statements in the *Informix Guide to SQL: Syntax.*

Relational Operations

A *relational operation* involves manipulating one or more tables, or *relations*, to result in another table. The three kinds of relational operations are selection, projection, and join. This chapter includes examples of selection, projection, and simple joining.

Selection and Projection

In relational terminology, *selection* is defined as taking the *horizontal* subset of rows of a single table that satisfies a particular condition. This kind of SELECT statement returns some of the rows and all the columns in a table. Selection is implemented through the WHERE clause of a SELECT statement, as Query 2-1 shows.

Query 2-1

```
SELECT * FROM customer
    WHERE state = 'NJ'
```

Query Result 2-1 contains the same number of columns as the **customer** table, but only a subset of its rows. Because the data in the selected columns does not fit on one line of the DB-Access or the Relational Object Manager screen, the data is displayed vertically instead of horizontally.

Query Result 2-1

```
customer_num  119
fname     Bob
lname     Shorter
company   The Triathletes Club
address1  2405 Kings Highway
address2
city      Cherry Hill
state     NJ
zipcode   08002
phone     609-663-6079


customer_num  122
fname     Cathy
lname     O'Brian
company   The Sporting Life
address1  543d Nassau
address2
city      Princeton
state     NJ
zipcode   08540
phone     609-342-0054
```

In relational terminology, *projection* is defined as taking a *vertical* subset from the columns of a single table that retains the unique rows. This kind of SELECT statement returns some of the columns and all the rows in a table.

Projection is implemented through the *select list* in the SELECT clause of a SELECT statement, as Query 2-2 shows.

```
SELECT city, state, zipcode
    FROM customer
```

Query Result 2-2 contains the same number of rows as the **customer** table, but it *projects* only a subset of the columns in the table.

```
city              state zipcode

Bartlesville      OK    74006
Blue Island       NY    60406
Brighton          MA    02135
Cherry Hill       NJ    08002
Denver            CO    80219
Jacksonville      FL    32256
Los Altos         CA    94022
Menlo Park        CA    94025
Mountain View     CA    94040
Mountain View     CA    94063
Oakland           CA    94609
Palo Alto         CA    94303
Palo Alto         CA    94304
Phoenix           AZ    85008
Phoenix           AZ    85016
Princeton         NJ    08540
Redwood City      CA    94026
Redwood City      CA    94062
Redwood City      CA    94063
San Francisco     CA    94117
Sunnyvale         CA    94085
Sunnyvale         CA    94086
Wilmington        DE    19898
```

The most common kind of SELECT statement uses both selection and projection. A query of this kind returns some of the rows and some of the columns in a table, as Query 2-3 shows.

```
SELECT UNIQUE city, state, zipcode
    FROM customer
    WHERE state = 'NJ'
```

Query Result 2-3 contains a subset of the rows and a subset of the columns in the **customer** table.

```
city            state zipcode

Cherry Hill     NJ    08002
Princeton       NJ    08540
```

Joining

A join occurs when two or more tables are connected by one or more columns in common, which creates a new table of results. Figure 2-1 shows a query that uses a subset of the **items** and **stock** tables to illustrate the concept of a join.

Figure 2-1
A Join Between Two Tables

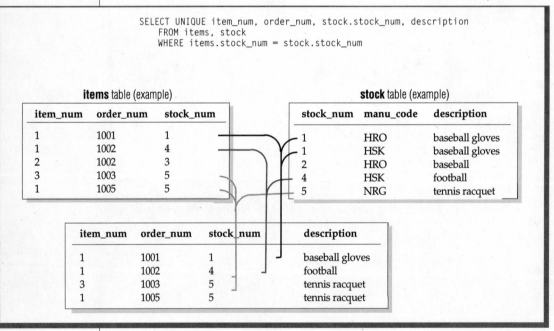

Query 2-4 joins the **customer** and **state** tables.

```
SELECT UNIQUE city, state, zipcode, sname
    FROM customer, state
    WHERE customer.state = state.code
```

Query Result 2-4 consists of specified rows and columns from both the **customer** and **state** tables.

```
city            state zipcode sname

Bartlesville    OK    74006   Oklahoma
Blue Island     NY    60406   New York
Brighton        MA    02135   Massachusetts
Cherry Hill     NJ    08002   New Jersey
Denver          CO    80219   Colorado
Jacksonville    FL    32256   Florida
Los Altos       CA    94022   California
Menlo Park      CA    94025   California
Mountain View   CA    94040   California
Mountain View   CA    94063   California
Oakland         CA    94609   California
Palo Alto       CA    94303   California
Palo Alto       CA    94304   California
Phoenix         AZ    85008   Arizona
Phoenix         AZ    85016   Arizona
Princeton       NJ    08540   New Jersey
Redwood City    CA    94026   California
Redwood City    CA    94062   California
Redwood City    CA    94063   California
San Francisco   CA    94117   California
Sunnyvale       CA    94085   California
Sunnyvale       CA    94086   California
Wilmington      DE    19898   Delaware
```

The Forms of SELECT

Although the syntax remains the same across all Informix products, the form of a SELECT statement and the location and formatting of the resulting output depends on the application. The examples in this chapter and in Chapter 5 display the SELECT statements and their output as they appear when you use the interactive Query-language option in DB-Access or the Relational Object Manager. You can also embed SELECT statements in a language such as Informix ESQL/C (where the statements are treated as executable code).

Special Data Types

With DB-Access or the Relational Object Manager, when you issue a SELECT statement that includes a TEXT or BYTE data type, also called a simple large object, or a BLOB or CLOB data type, also called a smart large object, the results of the query are displayed differently, as follows:

- If you select a TEXT or CLOB column, the contents of the TEXT or CLOB column are displayed, and you can scroll through them.

- If you query a BYTE column, the words `<BYTE value>` are displayed instead of the actual value.

- If you query a BLOB column, the words `<SBlob data>` are displayed instead of the actual value.

Differences specific to TEXT, BYTE, BLOB, and CLOB are noted as appropriate throughout this chapter.

GLS

You can issue a SELECT statement that queries NCHAR columns instead of CHAR columns or NVARCHAR columns instead of VARCHAR columns.

For more global language support (GLS) information, see the *Informix Guide to GLS Functionality*. For additional information on GLS and other data types, see the *Informix Guide to Database Design and Implementation* and the *Informix Guide to SQL: Reference.* ◆

Single-Table SELECT Statements

You can query a single table in a database in many ways. You can tailor a SELECT statement to perform the following actions:

- Retrieve all or specific columns
- Retrieve all or specific rows
- Perform computations or other functions on the retrieved data
- Order the data in various ways

Selecting All Columns and Rows

The most basic SELECT statement contains only the two required clauses, SELECT and FROM.

Using the Asterisk Symbol (*)

Query 2-5a specifies all the columns in the **manufact** table in a *select list*. A select list is a list of the column names or expressions that you want to project from a table.

Query 2-5a

```
SELECT manu_code, manu_name, lead_time
    FROM manufact
```

Query 2-5b uses the *wildcard* asterisk symbol (*) as shorthand in the select list to represent the names of all the columns in the table. You can use the asterisk symbol (*) when you want all the columns in their defined order.

Query 2-5b

```
SELECT * FROM manufact
```

Query 2-5a and Query 2-5b are equivalent and display the same results; that is, a list of every column and row in the **manufact** table. Query Result 2-5 shows the results as they would appear on a DB-Access or a Relational Object Manager screen.

Query Result 2-5

```
manu_code manu_name      lead_time

  SMT      Smith              3
  ANZ      Anza               5
  NRG      Norge              7
  HSK      Husky              5
  HRO      Hero               4
  SHM      Shimara           30
  KAR      Karsten           21
  NKL      Nikolus            8
  PRC      ProCycle           9
```

Reordering the Columns

Query 2-6 shows how you can change the order in which the columns are listed by changing their order in your select list.

Query 2-6

```
SELECT manu_name, manu_code, lead_time
    FROM manufact
```

Query Result 2-6 includes the same columns as the previous query result, but because the columns are specified in a different order, the display is also different.

Query Result 2-6

```
manu_name       manu_code lead_time

  Smith         SMT          3
  Anza          ANZ          5
  Norge         NRG          7
  Husky         HSK          5
  Hero          HRO          4
  Shimara       SHM         30
  Karsten       KAR         21
  Nikolus       NKL          8
  ProCycle      PRC          9
```

Sorting the Rows

You can add an ORDER BY clause to your SELECT statement to direct the system to sort the data in a specific order. You must include the columns that you want to use in the ORDER BY clause in the select list either explicitly or implicitly.

Query 2-7a shows an *explicit* select list, which includes all the column names that you want to retrieve.

Query 2-7a

```
SELECT manu_code, manu_name, lead_time
    FROM manufact
    ORDER BY lead_time
```

An *implicit* select list uses the asterisk symbol (*), as Query 2-7b shows.

Query 2-7b

```
SELECT * FROM manufact
   ORDER BY lead_time
```

Query 2-7a and Query 2-7b produce the same display. Query Result 2-7 shows a list of every column and row in the **manufact** table, in order of **lead_time**.

Query Result 2-7

```
manu_code manu_name      lead_time

  SMT       Smith            3
  HRO       Hero             4
  HSK       Husky            5
  ANZ       Anza             5
  NRG       Norge            7
  NKL       Nikolus          8
  PRC       ProCycle         9
  KAR       Karsten         21
  SHM       Shimara         30
```

Ascending Order

The retrieved data is sorted and displayed, by default, in *ascending* order. Ascending order is uppercase A to lowercase z for character data types, and lowest to highest value for numeric data types. DATE and DATETIME data is sorted from earliest to latest, and INTERVAL data is ordered from shortest to longest span of time.

Descending Order

Descending order is the opposite of ascending order, from lowercase z to uppercase A for character types and highest to lowest for numeric data types. DATE and DATETIME data is sorted from latest to earliest, and INTERVAL data is ordered from longest to shortest span of time. Query 2-8 shows an example of descending order.

Query 2-8

```
SELECT * FROM manufact
   ORDER BY lead_time DESC
```

The keyword DESC following a column name causes the retrieved data to be sorted in *descending* order, as Query Result 2-8 shows.

```
manu_code manu_name      lead_time

  SHM     Shimara           30
  KAR     Karsten           21
  PRC     ProCycle           9
  NKL     Nikolus            8
  NRG     Norge              7
  HSK     Husky              5
  ANZ     Anza               5
  HRO     Hero               4
  SMT     Smith              3
```

You can specify any column (except TEXT, BYTE, BLOB, or CLOB) in the ORDER BY clause, and the database server sorts the data based on the values in that column.

Sorting on Multiple Columns

You can also ORDER BY two or more columns, which creates a *nested sort*. The default is still ascending, and the column that is listed first in the ORDER BY clause takes precedence.

Query 2-9 and Query 2-10 and corresponding query results show nested sorts. To modify the order in which selected data is displayed, change the order of the two columns that are named in the ORDER BY clause.

```
SELECT * FROM stock
    ORDER BY manu_code, unit_price
```

In Query Result 2-9, the **manu_code** column data appears in alphabetical order and, within each set of rows with the same **manu_code** (for example, ANZ, HRO), the **unit_price** is listed in ascending order.

```
stock_num manu_code description     unit_price unit unit_descr

        5 ANZ       tennis racquet     $19.80 each each
        9 ANZ       volleyball net     $20.00 each each
        6 ANZ       tennis ball        $48.00 case 24 cans/case
      313 ANZ       swim cap           $60.00 box  12/box
      201 ANZ       golf shoes         $75.00 each each
      310 ANZ       kick board         $84.00 case 12/case
...
      113 SHM       18-spd, assmbld   $685.90 each each
        5 SMT       tennis racquet     $25.00 each each
        6 SMT       tennis ball        $36.00 case 24 cans/case
        1 SMT       baseball gloves   $450.00 case 10 gloves/case
```

Query 2-10 shows the reverse order of the columns in the ORDER BY clause.

```
SELECT * FROM stock
    ORDER BY unit_price, manu_code
```

In Query Result 2-10, the data appears in ascending order of **unit_price** and, where two or more rows have the same **unit_price** (for example, $20.00, $48.00, $312.00), the **manu_code** is in alphabetical order.

```
stock_num manu_code description     unit_price unit unit_descr

      302 HRO       ice pack           $4.50 each each
      302 KAR       ice pack           $5.00 each each
        5 ANZ       tennis racquet    $19.80 each each
        9 ANZ       volleyball net    $20.00 each each
      103 PRC       frnt derailleur   $20.00 each each
      106 PRC       bicycle stem      $23.00 each each
        5 SMT       tennis racquet    $25.00 each each
 ...
      301 HRO       running shoes     $42.50 each each
      204 KAR       putter            $45.00 each each
      108 SHM       crankset          $45.00 each each
        6 ANZ       tennis ball       $48.00 case 24 cans/case
      305 HRO       first-aid kit     $48.00 case 4/case
      303 PRC       socks             $48.00 box  24 pairs/box
      311 SHM       water gloves      $48.00 box  4 pairs/box
 ...
      102 PRC       bicycle brakes   $480.00 case 4 sets/case
      111 SHM       10-spd, assmbld  $499.99 each each
      112 SHM       12-spd, assmbld  $549.00 each each
        7 HRO       basketball       $600.00 case 24/case
      203 NKL       irons/wedge      $670.00 case 2 sets/case
      113 SHM       18-spd, assmbld  $685.90 each each
        1 HSK       baseball gloves  $800.00 case 10 gloves/case
        8 ANZ       volleyball       $840.00 case 24/case
        4 HSK       football         $960.00 case 24/case
```

The order of the columns in the ORDER BY clause is important, and so is the
position of the DESC keyword. Although the statements in Query 2-11 contain
the same components in the ORDER BY clause, each produces a different
result (not shown).

```
SELECT * FROM stock
    ORDER BY manu_code, unit_price DESC

SELECT * FROM stock
    ORDER BY unit_price, manu_code DESC

SELECT * FROM stock
    ORDER BY manu_code DESC, unit_price

SELECT * FROM stock
    ORDER BY unit_price DESC, manu_code
```

Selecting Specific Columns

The previous section shows how to select and order all data from a table. However, often all you want to see is the data in one or more specific columns. Again, the formula is to use the SELECT and FROM clauses, specify the columns and table, and perhaps order the data in ascending or descending order with an ORDER BY clause.

If you want to find all the customer numbers in the **orders** table, use a statement such as the one in Query 2-12.

Query 2-12

```
SELECT customer_num FROM orders
```

Query Result 2-12 shows how the statement simply selects all data in the **customer_num** column in the **orders** table and lists the customer numbers on all the orders, including duplicates.

Query Result 2-12

```
customer_num

        104
        101
        104
...
        122
        123
        124
        126
        127
```

The output includes several duplicates because some customers have placed more than one order. Sometimes you want to see duplicate rows in a projection. At other times, you want to see only the distinct values, not how often each value appears.

To suppress duplicate rows, you can include the keyword DISTINCT or its synonym UNIQUE at the start of the select list, once in each level of a query, as Query 2-13 shows.

Query 2-13

```
SELECT DISTINCT customer_num FROM orders

SELECT UNIQUE customer_num FROM orders
```

To produce a more readable list, Query 2-13 limits the display to show each customer number in the **orders** table only once, as Query Result 2-13 shows.

```
customer_num

        101
        104
        106
        110
        111
        112
        115
        116
        117
        119
        120
        121
        122
        123
        124
        126
        127
```

Suppose you are handling a customer call, and you want to locate purchase order number DM354331. To list all the purchase order numbers in the **orders** table, use a statement such as the one that Query 2-14 shows.

```
SELECT po_num FROM orders
```

Query Result 2-14 shows how the statement retrieves data in the **po_num** column in the **orders** table.

```
po_num

B77836
9270
B77890
8006
2865
Q13557
278693
LZ230
4745
429Q
B77897
278701
...
```

However, the list is not in a useful order. You can add an ORDER BY clause to
sort the column data in ascending order and make it easier to find that
particular **po_num**, as Query Result 2-15 shows.

Query 2-15

```
SELECT po_num FROM orders
    ORDER BY po_num
```

Query Result 2-15

```
po_num

 278693
 278701
 2865
 429Q
 4745
 8006
 8052
 9270
 B77836
 B77890
 ...
```

To select multiple columns from a table, list them in the select list in the
SELECT clause. Query 2-16 shows that the order in which the columns are
selected is the order in which they are produced, from left to right.

Query 2-16

```
SELECT paid_date, ship_date, order_date,
     customer_num, order_num, po_num
    FROM orders
    ORDER BY paid_date, order_date
```

As "Sorting on Multiple Columns" on page 2-14 shows, you can use the ORDER BY clause to sort the data in ascending or descending order and perform nested sorts. Query Result 2-16 shows ascending order.

```
paid_date   ship_date  order_date customer_num   order_num po_num

            05/30/1998 05/22/1998        106        1004 8006
                       05/30/1998        112        1006 Q13557
            06/05/1998 05/31/1998        117        1007 278693
            06/29/1998 06/18/1998        117        1012 278701
            07/12/1998 06/29/1998        119        1016 PC6782
            07/13/1998 07/09/1998        120        1017 DM354331
06/03/1998  05/26/1998 05/21/1998        101        1002 9270
06/14/1998  05/23/1998 05/22/1998        104        1003 B77890
06/21/1998  06/09/1998 05/24/1998        116        1005 2865
07/10/1998  07/03/1998 06/25/1998        106        1014 8052
07/21/1998  07/06/1998 06/07/1998        110        1008 LZ230
07/22/1998  06/01/1998 05/20/1998        104        1001 B77836
07/31/1998  07/10/1998 06/22/1998        104        1013 B77930
08/06/1998  07/13/1998 07/10/1998        121        1018 S22942
08/06/1998  07/16/1998 07/11/1998        122        1019 Z55709
08/21/1998  06/21/1998 06/14/1998        111        1009 4745
08/22/1998  06/29/1998 06/17/1998        115        1010 429Q
08/22/1998  07/25/1998 07/23/1998        124        1021 C3288
08/22/1998  07/30/1998 07/24/1998        127        1023 KF2961
08/29/1998  07/03/1998 06/18/1998        104        1011 B77897
08/31/1998  07/16/1998 06/27/1998        110        1015 MA003
09/02/1998  07/30/1998 07/24/1998        126        1022 W9925
09/20/1998  07/16/1998 07/11/1998        123        1020 W2286
```

When you use SELECT and ORDER BY on several columns in a table, you might find it helpful to use integers to refer to the position of the columns in the ORDER BY clause. The statements in Query 2-17 retrieve and display the same data, as Query Result 2-17 shows.

```
SELECT customer_num, order_num, po_num, order_date
    FROM orders
    ORDER BY 4, 1

SELECT customer_num, order_num, po_num, order_date
    FROM orders
    ORDER BY order_date, customer_num
```

```
customer_num   order_num po_num    order_date

         104        1001 B77836    05/20/1998
         101        1002 9270      05/21/1998
         104        1003 B77890    05/22/1998
         106        1004 8006      05/22/1998
         116        1005 2865      05/24/1998
         112        1006 Q13557    05/30/1998
         117        1007 278693    05/31/1998
         110        1008 LZ230     06/07/1998
         111        1009 4745      06/14/1998
         115        1010 429Q      06/17/1998
         104        1011 B77897    06/18/1998
         117        1012 278701    06/18/1998
         104        1013 B77930    06/22/1998
         106        1014 8052      06/25/1998
         110        1015 MA003     06/27/1998
         119        1016 PC6782    06/29/1998
         120        1017 DM354331  07/09/1998
         121        1018 S22942    07/10/1998
         122        1019 Z55709    07/11/1998
         123        1020 W2286     07/11/1998
         124        1021 C3288     07/23/1998
         126        1022 W9925     07/24/1998
         127        1023 KF2961    07/24/1998
```

You can include the DESC keyword in the ORDER BY clause when you assign integers to column names, as Query 2-18 shows.

```
SELECT customer_num, order_num, po_num, order_date
    FROM orders
    ORDER BY 4 DESC, 1
```

In this case, data is first sorted in descending order by **order_date** and in ascending order by **customer_num**.

Selecting Substrings

To select part of the value of a character column, include a *substring* in the select list. Suppose your marketing department is planning a mailing to your customers and wants their geographical distribution based on zip codes. You could write a query similar to the one that Query 2-19 shows.

```
SELECT zipcode[1,3], customer_num
    FROM customer
    ORDER BY zipcode
```

Query 2-19 uses a substring to select the first three characters of the **zipcode** column (which identify the state) and the full **customer_num**, and lists them in ascending order by zip code, as Query Result 2-19 shows.

Query Result 2-19

```
zipcode customer_num

021        125
080        119
085        122
198        121
322        123
...
943        103
943        107
946        118
```

GLS

ORDER BY and Non-English Data

By default, Informix database servers use the U.S. English language environment, called a locale, for database data. The U.S. English locale specifies data sorted in code-set order. This default locale uses the ISO 8859-1 code set.

If your database contains non-English data, you should store non-English data in NCHAR (or NVARCHAR) columns to obtain results sorted by the language. The ORDER BY clause should return data in the order appropriate to that language. Query 2-20 uses a SELECT statement with an ORDER BY clause to search the table, **abonnés**, and to order the selected information by the data in the **nom** column.

Query 2-20

```
SELECT numéro,nom,prénom
    FROM abonnés
    ORDER BY nom
```

The collation order for the results of this query can vary, depending on the following system variations:

- Whether the **nom** column is CHAR or NCHAR data type. The database server sorts data in CHAR columns by the order the characters appear in the code set. The database server sorts data in NCHAR columns by the order the characters are listed in the collation portion of the locale.

- Whether the database server is using the correct non-English locale when it accesses the database. To use a non-English locale, you must set the CLIENT_LOCALE and DB_LOCALE environment variables to the appropriate locale name.

For Query 2-20 to return expected results, the **nom** column should be NCHAR data type in a database that uses a French locale. Other operations, such as less than, greater than, or equal to, are also affected by the user-specified locale. For more information on non-English data and locales, see the *Informix Guide to GLS Functionality*.

Query Result 2-20a and Query Result 2-20b show two sample sets of output.

Query Result 2-20a

```
numéro  nom           prénom

13612   Azevedo       Edouardo Freire
13606   Dupré         Michèle Françoise
13607   Hammer        Gerhard
13602   Hämmer        le Greta
13604   LaForêt       Jean-Noël
13610   LeMaître      Héloïse
13613   Llanero       Gloria Dolores
13603   Montaña       José Antonio
13611   Oatfield      Emily
13609   Tiramisù      Paolo Alfredo
13600   da Sousa      João Lourenço Antunes
13615   di Girolamo   Giuseppe
13601   Ålesund       Sverre
13608   Étaix         Émile
13605   Ötker         Hans-Jürgen
13614   Øverst        Per-Anders
```

Query Result 2-20a follows the ISO 8859-1 code-set order, which ranks uppercase letters before lowercase letters and moves names that contain an accented character (Ålesund, Étaix, Ötker, and Øverst) to the end of the list.

```
numéro    nom           prénom

13601    Ålesund       Sverre
13612    Azevedo       Edouardo Freire
13600    da Sousa      João Lourenço Antunes
13615    di Girolamo   Giuseppe
13606    Dupré         Michèle Françoise
13608    Étaix         Émile
13607    Hammer        Gerhard
13602    Hämmer        le Greta
13604    LaForêt       Jean-Noël
13610    LeMaître      Héloïse
13613    Llanero       Gloria Dolores
13603    Montaña       José Antonio
13611    Oatfield      Emily
13605    Ötker         Hans-Jürgen
13614    Øverst        Per-Anders
13609    Tiramisù      Paolo Alfredo
```

Query Result 2-20b shows that when the appropriate locale file is referenced by the database server, names including non-English characters (Ålesund, Étaix, Ötker, and Øverst) are collated differently than they are in the ISO 8859-1 code set. They are sorted correctly for the locale. It does not distinguish between uppercase and lowercase letters.

Using the WHERE Clause

The set of rows that a SELECT statement returns is its *active set*. A *singleton* SELECT statement returns a single row. You can add a WHERE clause to a SELECT statement if you want to see only specific rows. For example, you use a WHERE clause to restrict the rows that the database server returns to only the orders that a particular customer placed or the calls that a particular customer service representative entered.

You can use the WHERE clause to set up a *comparison condition* or a *join condition*. This section demonstrates only the first use. Join conditions are described in a later section and in the next chapter.

Creating a Comparison Condition

The WHERE clause of a SELECT statement specifies the rows that you want to see. A comparison condition employs specific *keywords* and *operators* to define the search criteria.

For example, you might use one of the keywords BETWEEN, IN, LIKE, or MATCHES to test for equality, or the keywords IS NULL to test for null values. You can combine the keyword NOT with any of these keywords to specify the opposite condition.

The following table lists the *relational operators* that you can use in a WHERE clause in place of a keyword to test for equality.

Operator	Operation
=	equals
!= or <>	does not equal
>	greater than
>=	greater than or equal to
<	less than
<=	less than or equal to

For CHAR expressions, *greater than* means *after* in ASCII collating order, where lowercase letters are after uppercase letters, and both are after numerals. See the ASCII Character Set chart in the *Informix Guide to SQL: Syntax*. For DATE and DATETIME expressions, *greater than* means *later in time*, and for INTERVAL expressions, it means *of longer duration*.

Important: *You cannot use TEXT or BYTE columns to create a comparison condition, except when you use the IS NULL or IS NOT NULL keywords to test for null values.*

You cannot specify BLOB or CLOB columns to create a comparison condition on Dynamic Server, except when you use the IS NULL or IS NOT NULL keywords to test for null values. ♦

You can use the preceding keywords and operators in a WHERE clause to create comparison-condition queries that perform the following actions:

- Include values
- Exclude values
- Find a range of values
- Find a subset of values
- Identify null values

To perform variable text searches using the following criteria, use the preceding keywords and operators in a WHERE clause to create comparison-condition queries:

- Exact-text comparison
- Single-character wildcards
- Restricted single-character wildcards
- Variable-length wildcards
- Subscripting

The following section contains examples that illustrate these types of queries.

Including Rows

Use the equal sign (=) relational operator to include rows in a WHERE clause, as Query 2-21 shows.

Query 2-21

```
SELECT customer_num, call_code, call_dtime, res_dtime
    FROM cust_calls
    WHERE user_id = 'maryj'
```

Query 2-21 returns the set of rows that Query Result 2-21 shows.

Query Result 2-21

```
customer_num call_code call_dtime      res_dtime

         106 D         1998-06-12 08:20 1998-06-12 08:25
         121 0         1998-07-10 14:05 1998-07-10 14:06
         127 I         1998-07-31 14:30
```

Excluding Rows

Use the relational operators != or <> to exclude rows in a WHERE clause.

Query 2-22 assumes that you are selecting from an ANSI-compliant database; the statements specify the *owner* or login name of the creator of the **customer** table. This qualifier is not required when the creator of the table is the current user, or when the database is not ANSI compliant. However, you can include the qualifier in either case. For a detailed discussion of owner naming, see the *Informix Guide to SQL: Syntax*.

Query 2-22

```
SELECT customer_num, company, city, state
    FROM odin.customer
    WHERE state != 'CA'

SELECT customer_num, company, city, state
    FROM odin.customer
    WHERE state <> 'CA'
```

Both statements in Query 2-22 exclude values by specifying that, in the **customer** table that the user **odin** owns, the value in the **state** column should not be equal to CA, as Query Result 2-22 shows.

Query Result 2-22

```
customer_num  company              city          state

         119  The Triathletes Club Cherry Hill   NJ
         120  Century Pro Shop     Phoenix       AZ
         121  City Sports          Wilmington    DE
         122  The Sporting Life    Princeton     NJ
         123  Bay Sports           Jacksonville  FL
         124  Putnum's Putters     Bartlesville  OK
         125  Total Fitness Sports Brighton      MA
         126  Neelie's Discount Sp Denver        CO
         127  Big Blue Bike Shop   Blue Island   NY
         128  Phoenix College      Phoenix       AZ
```

Specifying A Range of Rows

Query 2-23 shows two ways to specify a range of rows in a WHERE clause.

```
SELECT catalog_num, stock_num, manu_code, cat_advert
    FROM catalog
    WHERE catalog_num BETWEEN 10005 AND 10008

SELECT catalog_num, stock_num, manu_code, cat_advert
    FROM catalog
    WHERE catalog_num >= 10005 AND catalog_num <= 10008
```

Each statement in Query 2-23 specifies a range for **catalog_num** from 10005 through 10008, inclusive. The first statement uses keywords, and the second statement uses relational operators to retrieve the rows as Query Result 2-23 shows.

```
catalog_num   10005
stock_num     3
manu_code     HSK
cat_advert    High-Technology Design Expands the Sweet Spot

catalog_num   10006
stock_num     3
manu_code     SHM
cat_advert    Durable Aluminum for High School and Collegiate Athletes

catalog_num   10007
stock_num     4
manu_code     HSK
cat_advert    Quality Pigskin with Joe Namath Signature

catalog_num   10008
stock_num     4
manu_code     HRO
cat_advert    Highest Quality Football for High School
              and Collegiate Competitions
```

Although the **catalog** table includes a column with the BYTE data type, that column is not included in this SELECT statement because the output would show only the words <BYTE value> by the column name. You can write an SQL API application to display TEXT and BYTE values.

Excluding a Range of Rows

Query 2-24 uses the keywords NOT BETWEEN to exclude rows that have the character range 94000 through 94999 in the **zipcode** column, as Query Result 2-24 shows.

Query 2-24

```
SELECT fname, lname, company, city, state
    FROM customer
    WHERE zipcode NOT BETWEEN '94000' AND '94999'
    ORDER BY state
```

Query Result 2-24

fname	lname	company	city	state
Frank	Lessor	Phoenix University	Phoenix	AZ
Fred	Jewell	Century* Pro Shop	Phoenix	AZ
Eileen	Neelie	Neelie's Discount Sp	Denver	CO
Jason	Wallack	City Sports	Wilmington	DE
Marvin	Hanlon	Bay Sports	Jacksonville	FL
James	Henry	Total Fitness Sports	Brighton	MA
Bob	Shorter	The Triathletes Club	Cherry Hill	NJ
Cathy	O'Brian	The Sporting Life	Princeton	NJ
Kim	Satifer	Big Blue Bike Shop	Blue Island	NY
Chris	Putnum	Putnum's Putters	Bartlesville	OK

Using a WHERE Clause to Find a Subset of Values

As "Excluding Rows" on page 2-28 shows, Query 2-25 also assumes the use of an ANSI-compliant database. The owner qualifier is in quotation marks to preserve the case sensitivity of the literal string.

Query 2-25

```
SELECT lname, city, state, phone
    FROM 'Aleta'.customer
    WHERE state = 'AZ' OR state = 'NJ'
    ORDER BY lname

SELECT lname, city, state, phone
    FROM 'Aleta'.customer
    WHERE state IN ('AZ', 'NJ')
    ORDER BY lname
```

Each statement in Query 2-25 retrieves rows that include the subset of AZ or NJ in the **state** column of the **Aleta.customer** table, as Query Result 2-25 shows.

```
lname           city          state phone

Jewell          Phoenix       AZ    602-265-8754
Lessor          Phoenix       AZ    602-533-1817
O'Brian         Princeton     NJ    609-342-0054
Shorter         Cherry Hill   NJ    609-663-6079
```

IDS

Important: *You cannot test TEXT or BYTE columns with the IN keyword.*

Also, when you use Dynamic Server, you cannot test BLOB or CLOB columns with the IN keyword. ♦

In Query 2-26, an example of a query on an ANSI-compliant database, no quotation marks exist around the table owner name. Whereas the two statements in Query 2-25 searched the **Aleta.customer** table, Query 2-26 searches the table **ALETA.customer**, which is a different table, because of the way ANSI-compliant databases look at owner names.

```
SELECT lname, city, state, phone
    FROM Aleta.customer
    WHERE state NOT IN ('AZ', 'NJ')
    ORDER BY state
```

Query 2-26 adds the keywords NOT IN, so the subset changes to exclude the subsets AZ and NJ in the **state** column. Query Result 2-26 shows the results in order of the **state** column.

```
lname            city            state phone

Pauli            Sunnyvale        CA    408-789-8075
Sadler           San Francisco    CA    415-822-1289
Currie           Palo Alto        CA    415-328-4543
Higgins          Redwood City     CA    415-368-1100
Vector           Los Altos        CA    415-776-3249
Watson           Mountain View    CA    415-389-8789
Ream             Palo Alto        CA    415-356-9876
Quinn            Redwood City     CA    415-544-8729
Miller           Sunnyvale        CA    408-723-8789
Jaeger           Redwood City     CA    415-743-3611
Keyes            Sunnyvale        CA    408-277-7245
Lawson           Los Altos        CA    415-887-7235
Beatty           Menlo Park       CA    415-356-9982
Albertson        Redwood City     CA    415-886-6677
Grant            Menlo Park       CA    415-356-1123
Parmelee         Mountain View    CA    415-534-8822
Sipes            Redwood City     CA    415-245-4578
Baxter           Oakland          CA    415-655-0011
Neelie           Denver           CO    303-936-7731
Wallack          Wilmington       DE    302-366-7511
Hanlon           Jacksonville     FL    904-823-4239
Henry            Brighton         MA    617-232-4159
Satifer          Blue Island      NY    312-944-5691
Putnum           Bartlesville     OK    918-355-2074
```

Identifying Null Values

Use the IS NULL or IS NOT NULL option to check for null values. A null value represents either the absence of data or an unknown value. A null value is not the same as a zero or a blank.

Query 2-27 returns all rows that have a null **paid_date**, as Query Result 2-27 shows.

```
SELECT order_num, customer_num, po_num, ship_date
   FROM orders
   WHERE paid_date IS NULL
   ORDER BY customer_num
```

```
order_num  customer_num  po_num   ship_date

    1004           106   8006     05/30/1998
    1006           112   Q13557
    1007           117   278693   06/05/1998
    1012           117   278701   06/29/1998
    1016           119   PC6782   07/12/1998
    1017           120   DM354331 07/13/1998
```

Forming Compound Conditions

To connect two or more comparison conditions, or *Boolean* expressions, use the *logical operators* AND, OR, and NOT. A Boolean expression evaluates as `true` or `false` or, if null values are involved, as `unknown`.

In Query 2-28, the operator AND combines two comparison expressions in the WHERE clause.

Query 2-28

```
SELECT order_num, customer_num, po_num, ship_date
    FROM orders
    WHERE paid_date IS NULL
        AND ship_date IS NOT NULL
    ORDER BY customer_num
```

The query returns all rows that have null **paid_date** or a not null **ship_date**, as Query Result 2-28 shows.

Query Result 2-28

```
order_num customer_num po_num    ship_date

    1004          106 8006       05/30/1998
    1007          117 278693     06/05/1998
    1012          117 278701     06/29/1998
    1016          119 PC6782     07/12/1998
    1017          120 DM354331   07/13/1998
```

Using Exact-Text Comparisons

The following examples include a WHERE clause that searches for exact-text comparisons by using the keyword LIKE or MATCHES or the equal sign (=) relational operator. Unlike earlier examples, these examples illustrate how to query a table that is not in the current database. You can access a table that is not in the current database only if the database that contains the table has the same ANSI status as the current database. If the current database is an ANSI-compliant database, the table you want to access must also reside in an ANSI-compliant database. If the current database is not an ANSI-compliant database, the table you want to access must also reside in a database that is not an ANSI-compliant database.

Although the database used previously in this chapter is the demonstration database, the FROM clause in the following examples specifies the **manatee** table, created by the owner **bubba**, which resides in an ANSI-compliant database named **syzygy**. For more information on how to access tables that are not in the current database, see the *Informix Guide to SQL: Syntax*

Each statement in Query 2-29 retrieves all the rows that have the single word helmet in the **description** column, as Query Result 2-29 shows.

Query 2-29

```
SELECT * FROM syzygy:bubba.manatee
    WHERE description = 'helmet'
    ORDER BY mfg_code

SELECT * FROM syzygy:bubba.manatee
    WHERE description LIKE 'helmet'
    ORDER BY mfg_code

SELECT * FROM syzygy:bubba.manatee
    WHERE description MATCHES 'helmet'
    ORDER BY mfg_code
```

Query Result 2-29

stock_no	mfg_code	description	unit_price	unit	unit_type
991	ANT	helmet	$222.00	case	4/case
991	BKE	helmet	$269.00	case	4/case
991	JSK	helmet	$311.00	each	4/case
991	PRM	helmet	$234.00	case	4/case
991	SHR	helmet	$245.00	case	4/case

Using Variable-Text Searches

You can use the keywords LIKE and MATCHES for *variable-text* queries that are based on substring searches of fields. Include the keyword NOT to indicate the opposite condition. The keyword LIKE is the ANSI standard, whereas MATCHES is an Informix extension.

Variable-text search strings can include the wildcards listed with LIKE or MATCHES in the following table.

Keyword	Symbol	Meaning
LIKE	%	Evaluates to zero or more characters
LIKE	_	Evaluates to a single character
LIKE	\	Escapes special significance of next character
MATCHES	*	Evaluates to zero or more characters
MATCHES	?	Evaluates to a single character (except null)
MATCHES	[ ]	Evaluates to a single character or range of values
MATCHES	\	Escapes special significance of next character

Important: *You cannot test TEXT or BYTE columns with the LIKE or MATCHES keywords.*

Also, when you use Dynamic Server, you cannot test BLOB or CLOB columns with the LIKE or MATCHES keywords. ♦

Using a Single-Character Wildcard

The statements in Query 2-30 illustrate the use of a single-character wildcard in a WHERE clause. Further, they demonstrate a query on a table that is not in the current database. The **stock** table is in the database **sloth**. Besides being outside the current demonstration database, **sloth** is on a separate database server called **meerkat**.

For more information, see "Selecting Tables from a Database Other Than the Current Database" on page 2-69 and the *Informix Guide to SQL: Syntax*.

Query 2-30

```
SELECT * FROM sloth@meerkat:stock
    WHERE manu_code LIKE '_R_'
        AND unit_price >= 100
    ORDER BY description, unit_price

SELECT * FROM sloth@meerkat:stock
    WHERE manu_code MATCHES '?R?'
        AND unit_price >= 100
    ORDER BY description, unit_price
```

Each statement in Query 2-30 retrieves only those rows for which the middle letter of the **manu_code** is R, as Query Result 2-30 shows.

Query Result 2-30

stock_num	manu_code	description	unit_price	unit	unit_descr
205	HRO	3 golf balls	$312.00	case	24/case
2	HRO	baseball	$126.00	case	24/case
1	HRO	baseball gloves	$250.00	case	10 gloves/case
7	HRO	basketball	$600.00	case	24/case
102	PRC	bicycle brakes	$480.00	case	4 sets/case
114	PRC	bicycle gloves	$120.00	case	10 pairs/case
4	HRO	football	$480.00	case	24/case
110	PRC	helmet	$236.00	case	4/case
110	HRO	helmet	$260.00	case	4/case
307	PRC	infant jogger	$250.00	each	each
306	PRC	tandem adapter	$160.00	each	each
308	PRC	twin jogger	$280.00	each	each
304	HRO	watch	$280.00	box	10/box

The comparison '_R_' (for LIKE) or '?R?' (for MATCHES) specifies, from left to right, the following items:

- Any single character
- The letter R
- Any single character

WHERE Clause with Restricted Single-Character Wildcard

Query 2-31 selects only those rows where the **manu_code** begins with A
through H and returns the rows that Query Result 2-31 shows. The test '[A-H]'
specifies any single letter from A through H, inclusive. No equivalent
wildcard symbol exists for the LIKE keyword.

Query 2-31

```
SELECT * FROM stock
     WHERE manu_code MATCHES '[A-H]*'
     ORDER BY description, manu_code, unit_price
```

Query Result 2-31

```
stock_num manu_code description     unit_price unit unit_descr

      205 ANZ       3 golf balls      $312.00 case 24/case
      205 HRO       3 golf balls      $312.00 case 24/case
        2 HRO       baseball          $126.00 case 24/case
        3 HSK       baseball bat      $240.00 case 12/case
        1 HRO       baseball gloves   $250.00 case 10 gloves/case
        1 HSK       baseball gloves   $800.00 case 10 gloves/case
        7 HRO       basketball        $600.00 case 24/case
...
      301 ANZ       running shoes      $95.00 each each
      301 HRO       running shoes      $42.50 each each
      313 ANZ       swim cap           $60.00 box  12/box
        6 ANZ       tennis ball        $48.00 case 24 cans/case
        5 ANZ       tennis racquet     $19.80 each each
        8 ANZ       volleyball        $840.00 case 24/case
        9 ANZ       volleyball net     $20.00 each each
      304 ANZ       watch             $170.00 box  10/box
      304 HRO       watch             $280.00 box  10/box
```

WHERE Clause with Variable-Length Wildcard

The statements in Query 2-32 use a wildcard at the end of a string to retrieve
all the rows where the **description** begins with the characters bicycle.

Query 2-32

```
SELECT * FROM stock
    WHERE description LIKE 'bicycle%'
    ORDER BY description, manu_code

SELECT * FROM stock
    WHERE description MATCHES 'bicycle*'
    ORDER BY description, manu_code
```

Either statement returns the rows that Query Result 2-32 shows.

```
stock_num manu_code description    unit_price unit unit_descr

      102 PRC        bicycle brakes    $480.00 case 4 sets/case
      102 SHM        bicycle brakes    $220.00 case 4 sets/case
      114 PRC        bicycle gloves    $120.00 case 10 pairs/case
      107 PRC        bicycle saddle     $70.00 pair pair
      106 PRC        bicycle stem       $23.00 each each
      101 PRC        bicycle tires      $88.00 box  4/box
      101 SHM        bicycle tires      $68.00 box  4/box
      105 PRC        bicycle wheels     $53.00 pair pair
      105 SHM        bicycle wheels     $80.00 pair pair
```

The comparison 'bicycle%' or 'bicycle*' specifies the characters bicycle followed by any sequence of zero or more characters. It matches bicycle stem with stem matched by the wildcard. It matches to the characters bicycle alone, if a row exists with that description.

Query 2-33 narrows the search by adding another comparison condition that excludes a **manu_code** of PRC.

```
SELECT * FROM stock
    WHERE description LIKE 'bicycle%'
        AND manu_code NOT LIKE 'PRC'
    ORDER BY description, manu_code
```

The statement retrieves only the rows that Query Result 2-33 shows.

```
stock_num manu_code description    unit_price unit unit_descr

      102 SHM        bicycle brakes    $220.00 case 4 sets/case
      101 SHM        bicycle tires      $68.00 box  4/box
      105 SHM        bicycle wheels     $80.00 pair pair
```

When you select from a large table and use an initial wildcard in the comparison string (such as '%cycle'), the query often takes longer to execute. Because indexes cannot be used, every row is searched.

MATCHES and Non-English Data

By default, Informix database servers use the U.S. English language environment, called a locale, for database data. This default locale uses the ISO 8859-1 code set. The U.S. English locale specifies that MATCHES will use code-set order.

If your database contains non-English data, the MATCHES clause uses the correct non-English code set for that language. Query 2-34 uses a SELECT statement with a MATCHES clause in the WHERE clause to search the table, **abonnés**, and to compare the selected information with the data in the **nom** column.

Query 2-34

```
SELECT numéro,nom,prénom
    FROM abonnés
    WHERE nom MATCHES '[E-P]*'
    ORDER BY nom
```

In Query Result 2-34, the rows for Étaix, Ötker, and Øverst are not selected and listed because, with ISO 8859-1 code-set order, the accented first letter of each name is not in the E through P MATCHES range for the **nom** column.

Query Result 2-34

numéro	nom	prénom
13607	Hammer	Gerhard
13602	Hämmer	Greta
13604	LaForêt	Jean-Noël
13610	LeMaître	Héloïse
13613	Llanero	Gloria Dolores
13603	Montaña	José Antonio
13611	Oatfield	Emily

For more information on non-English data and locales, see the *Informix Guide to GLS Functionality*.

Protecting Special Characters

Query 2-35 uses the keyword ESCAPE with LIKE or MATCHES so you can protect a special character from misinterpretation as a wildcard symbol.

Query 2-35

```
SELECT * FROM cust_calls
    WHERE res_descr LIKE '%!%%' ESCAPE '!'
```

The ESCAPE keyword designates an *escape character* (it is ! in this example) that protects the next character so that it is interpreted as data and not as a wildcard. In the example, the escape character causes the middle percent sign (%) to be treated as data. By using the ESCAPE keyword, you can search for occurrences of a percent sign (%) in the **res_descr** column by using the LIKE wildcard percent sign (%). The query retrieves the row that Query Result 2-35 shows.

Query Result 2-35

```
customer_num   116
call_dtime     1997-12-21 11:24
user_id        mannyn
call_code      I
call_descr     Second complaint from this customer! Received
               two cases right-handed outfielder gloves
               (1 HRO) instead of one case lefties.
res_dtime      1997-12-27 08:19
res_descr      Memo to shipping (Ava Brown) to send case of
               left-handed gloves, pick up wrong case; memo
               to billing requesting 5% discount to placate
               customer due to second offense and lateness
               of resolution because of holiday
```

Using Subscripting in a WHERE Clause

You can use *subscripting* in the WHERE clause of a SELECT statement to specify a range of characters or numbers in a column, as Query 2-36 shows.

Query 2-36

```
SELECT catalog_num, stock_num, manu_code, cat_advert,
       cat_descr
    FROM catalog
    WHERE cat_advert[1,4] = 'High'
```

The subscript [1,4] causes Query 2-36 to retrieve all rows in which the first four letters of the **cat_advert** column are High, as Query Result 2-36 shows.

```
  catalog_num  10004
  stock_num    2
  manu_code    HRO
  cat_advert   Highest Quality Ball Available, from
               Hand-Stitching to the Robinson Signature
  cat_descr
Jackie Robinson signature ball. Highest professional quality, used by National
League.

  catalog_num  10005
  stock_num    3
  manu_code    HSK
  cat_advert   High-Technology Design Expands the Sweet Spot
  cat_descr
Pro-style wood. Available in sizes: 31, 32, 33, 34, 35.
...
  catalog_num  10045
  stock_num    204
  manu_code    KAR
  cat_advert   High-Quality Beginning Set of Irons
               Appropriate for High School Competitions
  cat_descr
Ideally balanced for optimum control. Nylon covered shaft.

  catalog_num  10068
  stock_num    310
  manu_code    ANZ
  cat_advert   High-Quality Kickboard
  cat_descr
White. Standard size.
```

Using a FIRST Clause to Select Specific Rows

You can include a FIRST clause in a SELECT statement to specify that the query returns only a specified number of the first rows that match the conditions of the SELECT statement. You include a number immediately following the FIRST keyword to specify the maximum number of rows that the query can return. The rows that the database server returns when you execute a SELECT statement with a FIRST clause might differ, depending on whether the statement also includes an ORDER BY clause.

You cannot use a FIRST clause when the SELECT statement is a subquery or part of a view definition.

For information about restrictions on use of the FIRST clause, see the description of the SELECT statement in the *Informix Guide to SQL: Syntax*.

FIRST Clause Without an ORDER BY Clause

If you do not include an ORDER BY clause in a SELECT statement with a FIRST clause, any rows that match the conditions of the SELECT statement might be returned. In other words, the database server determines which of the qualifying rows to return, and the query result can vary depending on the query plan that the optimizer chooses.

Query 2-37 uses the FIRST clause to return the first five rows from the **state** table.

Query 2-37

```
SELECT FIRST 5 *
    FROM state
```

Query Result 2-37

```
code sname

AK   Alaska
HI   Hawaii
CA   California
OR   Oregon
WA   Washington
```

You can use a FIRST clause when you simply want to know the names of all the columns, and the type of data that a table contains, or to test a query that otherwise would return many rows. Query 2-38 shows how to use the FIRST clause to return column values for the first row of a table.

Query 2-38

```
SELECT FIRST 1 *
    FROM orders
```

Query Result 2-38

```
order_num      1001
order_date     05/20/1998
customer_num   104
ship_instruct  express
backlog        n
po_num         B77836
ship_date      06/01/1998
ship_weight    20.40
ship_charge    $10.00
paid_date      07/22/1998
```

FIRST Clause with an ORDER BY Clause

You can include an ORDER BY clause in a SELECT statement with a FIRST clause to return rows that contain the highest or lowest values for a specified column. Query 2-38 shows a query that includes an ORDER BY clause to return (by alphabetical order) the first five states contained in the **state** table. Query 2-39, which is the same as Query 2-37 except for the ORDER BY clause, returns a different set of rows than Query 2-37.

Query 2-39

```
SELECT FIRST 5 *
    FROM state ORDER BY sname
```

Query Result 2-39

```
code sname

AL   Alabama
AK   Alaska
AZ   Arizona
AR   Arkansas
CA   California
```

Query 2-40 shows how to use a FIRST clause in a query with an ORDER BY clause to find the 10 most expensive items listed in the **stock** table.

Query 2-40

```
SELECT FIRST 10 description, unit_price
    FROM stock ORDER BY unit_price DESC
```

Query Result 2-40

```
description      unit_price

football         $960.00
volleyball       $840.00
baseball gloves  $800.00
18-spd, assmbld  $685.90
irons/wedge      $670.00
basketball       $600.00
12-spd, assmbld  $549.00
10-spd, assmbld  $499.99
football         $480.00
bicycle brakes   $480.00
```

EDS

FIRST Clause in a Union Query

Enterprise Decision Server allows you to use the FIRST clause to select the first rows that result from a union query. Query 2-41 uses a FIRST clause to return the first five rows of a union between the **stock** and **items** tables.

Query 2-41

```
SELECT FIRST 5 DISTINCT stock_num, manu_code
    FROM stock
    WHERE unit_price < 55.00

UNION

SELECT stock_num, manu_code
    FROM items
    WHERE quantity > 3
```

Query Result 2-41

```
stock_num manu_code

311       SHM
9         ANZ
301       HRO
6         ANZ
204       KAR
```

Expressions and Derived Values

You are not limited to selecting columns by name. You can list an *expression* in the SELECT clause of a SELECT statement to perform computations on column data and to display information *derived* from the contents of one or more columns.

An expression consists of a column name, a constant, a quoted string, a keyword, or any combination of these items connected by operators. It can also include host variables (program data) when the SELECT statement is embedded in a program.

Arithmetic Expressions

An arithmetic expression contains at least one of the *arithmetic operators* listed in the following table and produces a number.

Operator	Operation
+	addition
-	subtraction
*	multiplication
/	division

Important: *You cannot use TEXT or BYTE columns in arithmetic expressions.*

With Dynamic Server, you cannot specify BLOB or CLOB in arithmetic expressions. ♦

Arithmetic operations enable you to see the results of proposed computations without actually altering the data in the database. You can add an INTO TEMP clause to save the altered data in a temporary table for further reference, computations, or impromptu reports. Query 2-42 calculates a 7 percent sales tax on the **unit_price** column when the **unit_price** is $400 or more (but does not update it in the database).

Query 2-42

```
SELECT stock_num, description, unit, unit_descr,
       unit_price, unit_price * 1.07
    FROM stock
    WHERE unit_price >= 400
```

If you are using DB-Access or the Relational Object Manager, the result appears in the **expression** column, as Query Result 2-42 shows.

```
stock_num description    unit unit_descr     unit_price  (expression)

        1 baseball gloves case 10 gloves/case    $800.00    $856.0000
        1 baseball gloves case 10 gloves/case    $450.00    $481.5000
        4 football        case 24/case           $960.00   $1027.2000
        4 football        case 24/case           $480.00    $513.6000
        7 basketball      case 24/case           $600.00    $642.0000
        8 volleyball      case 24/case           $840.00    $898.8000
      102 bicycle brakes  case 4 sets/case       $480.00    $513.6000
      111 10-spd, assmbld each each              $499.99    $534.9893
      112 12-spd, assmbld each each              $549.00    $587.4300
      113 18-spd, assmbld each each              $685.90    $733.9130
      203 irons/wedge     case 2 sets/case       $670.00    $716.9000
```

Query 2-43 calculates a surcharge of $6.50 on orders when the quantity ordered is less than 5.

```
SELECT item_num, order_num, quantity,
     total_price, total_price + 6.50
   FROM items
   WHERE quantity < 5
```

If you are using DB-Access or the Relational Object Manager, the result appears in the **expression** column, as Query Result 2-43 shows.

```
item_num   order_num quantity total_price (expression)

       1      1001       1     $250.00    $256.50
       1      1002       1     $960.00    $966.50
       2      1002       1     $240.00    $246.50
       1      1003       1      $20.00     $26.50
       2      1003       1     $840.00    $846.50
       1      1004       1     $250.00    $256.50
       2      1004       1     $126.00    $132.50
       3      1004       1     $240.00    $246.50
       4      1004       1     $800.00    $806.50
...
       1      1023       2      $40.00     $46.50
       2      1023       2     $116.00    $122.50
       3      1023       1      $80.00     $86.50
       4      1023       1     $228.00    $234.50
       5      1023       1     $170.00    $176.50
       6      1023       1     $190.00    $196.50
```

Query 2-44 calculates and displays in the **expression** column (if you are using DB-Access or the Relational Object Manager) the interval between when the customer call was received (**call_dtime**) and when the call was resolved (**res_dtime**), in days, hours, and minutes.

Query 2-44

```
SELECT customer_num, user_id, call_code,
       call_dtime, res_dtime - call_dtime
    FROM cust_calls
    ORDER BY user_id
```

Query Result 2-44

customer_num	user_id	call_code	call_dtime	(expression)
116	mannyn	I	1997-12-21 11:24	5 20:55
116	mannyn	I	1997-11-28 13:34	0 03:13
106	maryj	D	1998-06-12 08:20	0 00:05
121	maryj	O	1998-07-10 14:05	0 00:01
127	maryj	I	1998-07-31 14:30	
110	richc	L	1998-07-07 10:24	0 00:06
119	richc	B	1998-07-01 15:00	0 17:21

Using Display Labels

You can assign a *display label* to a computed or derived data column to replace the default column header **expression**. In Query 2-42, Query 2-43, and Query 2-44, the derived data appears in the **expression** column. Query 2-45 also presents derived values, but the column that displays the derived values has the descriptive header **taxed**.

Query 2-45

```
SELECT stock_num, description, unit, unit_descr,
       unit_price, unit_price * 1.07 taxed
    FROM stock
    WHERE unit_price >= 400
```

Query Result 2-45 shows that the label **taxed** is assigned to the expression in the select list that displays the results of the operation unit_price * 1.07.

```
stock_num description      unit unit_descr     unit_price      taxed

        1 baseball gloves case 10 gloves/case    $800.00    $856.0000
        1 baseball gloves case 10 gloves/case    $450.00    $481.5000
        4 football        case 24/case           $960.00   $1027.2000
        4 football        case 24/case           $480.00    $513.6000
        7 basketball      case 24/case           $600.00    $642.0000
        8 volleyball      case 24/case           $840.00    $898.8000
      102 bicycle brakes  case 4 sets/case       $480.00    $513.6000
      111 10-spd, assmbld each each              $499.99    $534.9893
      112 12-spd, assmbld each each              $549.00    $587.4300
      113 18-spd, assmbld each each              $685.90    $733.9130
      203 irons/wedge     case 2 sets/case       $670.00    $716.9000
```

In Query 2-46, the label **surcharge** is defined for the column that displays the results of the operation total_price + 6.50.

```
SELECT item_num, order_num, quantity,
       total_price, total_price + 6.50 surcharge
   FROM items
   WHERE quantity < 5
```

The **surcharge** column is labeled in the output, as Query Result 2-46 shows.

```
item_num   order_num quantity total_price    surcharge

       1      1001      1      $250.00       $256.50
       1      1002      1      $960.00       $966.50
       2      1002      1      $240.00       $246.50
       1      1003      1       $20.00        $26.50
       2      1003      1      $840.00       $846.50
...
       1      1023      2       $40.00        $46.50
       2      1023      2      $116.00       $122.50
       3      1023      1       $80.00        $86.50
       4      1023      1      $228.00       $234.50
       5      1023      1      $170.00       $176.50
       6      1023      1      $190.00       $196.50
```

Query 2-47 assigns the label **span** to the column that displays the results of subtracting the DATETIME column **call_dtime** from the DATETIME column **res_dtime**.

Query 2-47

```
SELECT customer_num, user_id, call_code,
       call_dtime, res_dtime - call_dtime span
    FROM cust_calls
    ORDER BY user_id
```

The **span** column is labeled in the output, as Query Result 2-47 shows.

Query Result 2-47

customer_num	user_id	call_code	call_dtime	span
116	mannyn	I	1997-12-21 11:24	5 20:55
116	mannyn	I	1997-11-28 13:34	0 03:13
106	maryj	D	1998-06-12 08:20	0 00:05
121	maryj	0	1998-07-10 14:05	0 00:01
127	maryj	I	1998-07-31 14:30	
110	richc	L	1998-07-07 10:24	0 00:06
119	richc	B	1998-07-01 15:00	0 17:21

CASE Expressions

A CASE expression is a conditional expression, which is similar to the concept of the CASE statement in programming languages. You can use a CASE expression when you want to change the way data is represented. The CASE expression allows a statement to return one of several possible results, depending on which of several condition tests evaluates to TRUE.

TEXT or BYTE values are not allowed in a CASE expression.

Consider a column that represents marital status numerically as 1, 2, 3, 4 with the corresponding values meaning single, married, divorced, widowed. In some cases, you might prefer to store the short values (1, 2, 3, 4) for database efficiency, but employees in human resources might prefer the more descriptive values (single, married, divorced, widowed). The CASE expression makes such conversions between different sets of values easy.

IDS

The CASE expression also supports extended data types and cast expressions. ◆

The following example shows a CASE expression with multiple WHEN clauses that returns more descriptive values for the **manu_code** column of the **stock** table. If none of the WHEN conditions is true, NULL is the default result. (You can omit the ELSE NULL clause.)

```
SELECT
    CASE
         WHEN manu_code = "HRO" THEN "Hero"
         WHEN manu_code = "SHM" THEN "Shimara"
         WHEN manu_code = "PRC" THEN "ProCycle"
         WHEN manu_code = "ANZ" THEN "Anza"
         ELSE NULL
    END
FROM stock
```

You must include at least one WHEN clause within the CASE expression; subsequent WHEN clauses and the ELSE clause are optional. If no WHEN condition evaluates to true, the resulting value is null. You can use the IS NULL expression to handle null results. For information on handling null values, see the *Informix Guide to SQL: Syntax*.

The following example shows a simple CASE expression that returns a character string value to flag any orders from the **orders** table that have not been shipped to the customer.

Query 2-48

```
SELECT order_num, order_date,
CASE
     WHEN ship_date IS NULL
     THEN "order not shipped"
     END
FROM orders
```

Query Result 2-48

```
order_num order_date (expression)

1001      05/20/1998
1002      05/21/1998
1003      05/22/1998
1004      05/22/1998
1005      05/24/1998
1006      05/30/1998 order not shipped
....
1021      07/23/1998
1022      07/24/1998
1023      07/24/1998
```

For information about how to use the CASE expression to update a column, see "Using a CASE Expression to Update a Column" on page 6-31.

Sorting on Derived Columns

When you want to use ORDER BY as an expression, you can use either the display label assigned to the expression or an integer, as Query 2-49 and Query 2-50 show.

Query 2-49

```
SELECT customer_num, user_id, call_code,
       call_dtime, res_dtime - call_dtime span
    FROM cust_calls
    ORDER BY span
```

Query 2-49 retrieves the same data from the **cust_calls** table as Query 2-47. In Query 2-49, the ORDER BY clause causes the data to be displayed in ascending order of the derived values in the **span** column, as Query Result 2-49 shows.

Query Result 2-49

```
customer_num user_id        call_code call_dtime        span
         127 maryj          I         1998-07-31 14:30
         121 maryj          0         1998-07-10 14:05  0 00:01
         106 maryj          D         1998-06-12 08:20  0 00:05
         110 richc          L         1998-07-07 10:24  0 00:06
         116 mannyn         I         1997-11-28 13:34  0 03:13
         119 richc          B         1998-07-01 15:00  0 17:21
         116 mannyn         I         1997-12-21 11:24  5 20:55
```

Query 2-50 uses an integer to represent the result of the operation `res_dtime - call_dtime` and retrieves the same rows that appear in Query Result 2-49.

Query 2-50

```
SELECT customer_num, user_id, call_code,
       call_dtime, res_dtime - call_dtime span
    FROM cust_calls
    ORDER BY 5
```

Using Rowid Values In SELECT Statements

The database server assigns a unique rowid to rows in nonfragmented tables. However, rows in fragmented tables do not automatically contain the rowid column.

Informix recommends that you use primary keys as a method of access in your applications rather than rowids. Because primary keys are defined in the ANSI specification of SQL, using them to access data makes your applications more portable. In addition, the database server requires less time to access data in a fragmented table when it uses a primary key than it requires to access the same data when it uses rowid.

You can use a rowid to locate the internal record number that is associated with a row in a table. The rowid is, in effect, a hidden column in every table. The sequential values of rowid have no special significance and can vary depending on the location of the physical data in the chunk. Your rowid might vary from the following examples.

For more information about rowids, see the *Informix Guide to Database Design and Implementation* and your *Administrator's Guide*.

Query 2-51 uses the rowid and the wildcard asterisk symbol (*) in the SELECT clause to retrieve every row in the **manufact** table and their corresponding rowids.

Query 2-51

```
SELECT rowid, * FROM manufact
```

Query Result 2-51

```
   rowid manu_code manu_name      lead_time

     257 SMT       Smith              3
     258 ANZ       Anza               5
     259 NRG       Norge              7
     260 HSK       Husky              5
     261 HRO       Hero               4
     262 SHM       Shimara           30
     263 KAR       Karsten           21
     264 NKL       Nikolus            8
     265 PRC       ProCycle           9
```

You can also use the rowid when you select a specific column, as Query 2-52 shows.

```
SELECT rowid, manu_code FROM manufact
```

```
    rowid manu_code

      258 ANZ
      261 HRO
      260 HSK
      263 KAR
      264 NKL
      259 NRG
      265 PRC
      262 SHM
      257 SMT
```

You can use the rowid in the WHERE clause to retrieve rows based on their internal record number. This method is handy when no other unique column exists in a table. Query 2-53 uses a rowid from Query 2-52.

```
SELECT * FROM manufact WHERE rowid = 263
```

Query 2-53 returns the row that Query Result 2-53 shows.

```
manu_code manu_name       lead_time

KAR       Karsten            21
```

Using Rowid Values with the USER Function

To obtain additional information about a table, you can combine the rowid with the USER function.

Query 2-54 assigns the label **username** to the USER expression column and returns this information about the **cust_calls** table.

Query 2-54

```
SELECT USER username, rowid FROM cust_calls
```

Query Result 2-54

```
username          rowid

zenda              257
zenda              258
zenda              259
zenda              513
zenda              514
zenda              515
zenda              769
```

You can also use the USER function in a WHERE clause when you select the rowid.

Query 2-55 returns the rowid for only those rows that are inserted or updated by the user who performs the query.

Query 2-55

```
SELECT rowid FROM cust_calls WHERE user_id = USER
```

For example, if the user **richc** uses Query 2-55, the output is as Query Result 2-55 shows.

Query Result 2-55

```
    rowid
      258
      259
```

Using Rowid Values with the DBSERVERNAME Function

You can add the DBSERVERNAME function (or its synonym, SITENAME) to a
query to find out where the current database resides.

Query 2-56 finds the database server name and the user name as well as the
rowid and the *tabid*, which is the serial-interval table identifier for system
catalog tables.

Query 2-56

```
SELECT DBSERVERNAME server, tabid, rowid, USER username
     FROM systables
     WHERE tabid >= 105 OR rowid <= 260
     ORDER BY rowid
```

Query 2-56 assigns display labels to the DBSERVERNAME and USER
expressions and returns the 10 rows from the **systables** system catalog table,
as Query Result 2-56 shows.

Query Result 2-56

server	tabid	rowid	username
manatee	1	257	zenda
manatee	2	258	zenda
manatee	3	259	zenda
manatee	4	260	zenda
manatee	105	274	zenda
manatee	106	1025	zenda
manatee	107	1026	zenda
manatee	108	1027	zenda
manatee	109	1028	zenda
manatee	110	1029	zenda

Never store a rowid in a *permanent* table or attempt to use it as a foreign key
because the rowid can change. For example, if a table is dropped and then
reloaded from external data, all the rowids are different.

Multiple-Table SELECT Statements

To select data from two or more tables, name these tables in the FROM clause. Add a WHERE clause to create a *join* condition between at least one related column in each table. This WHERE clause creates a temporary composite table in which each pair of rows that satisfies the join condition is linked to form a single row.

A *simple join* combines information from two or more tables based on the relationship between one column in each table. A *composite join* is a join between two or more tables based on the relationship between two or more columns in each table.

To create a join, you must specify a relationship, called a *join condition*, between at least one column from each table. Because the columns are being compared, they must have compatible data types. When you join large tables, performance improves when you index the columns in the join condition.

Data types are described in the *Informix Guide to SQL: Reference* and the *Informix Guide to Database Design and Implementation*. Indexing is discussed in detail in the *Administrator's Guide*.

Creating a Cartesian Product

When you perform a multiple-table query that does not explicitly state a join condition among the tables, you create a *Cartesian product*. A Cartesian product consists of every possible combination of rows from the tables. This result is usually large and unwieldy, and the data is inaccurate.

Query 2-57 selects from two tables and produces a Cartesian product.

Query 2-57

```
SELECT * FROM customer, state
```

Although only 52 rows exist in the **state** table and 28 rows in the **customer** table, the effect of Query 2-57 is to multiply the rows of one table by the rows of the other and retrieve an impractical 1,456 rows, as Query Result 2-57 shows.

```
customer_num  101
fname         Ludwig
lname         Pauli
company       All Sports Supplies
address1      213 Erstwild Court
address2
city          Sunnyvale
state         CA
zipcode       94086
phone         408-789-8075
code          AK
sname         Alaska

customer_num  101
fname         Ludwig
lname         Pauli
company       All Sports Supplies
address1      213 Erstwild Court
address2
city          Sunnyvale
state         CA
zipcode       94086
phone         408-789-8075
code          HI
sname         Hawaii

customer_num  101
fname         Ludwig
lname         Pauli
company       All Sports Supplies
address1      213 Erstwild Court
address2
city          Sunnyvale
state         CA
zipcode       94086
phone         408-789-8075
code          CA
sname         California
...
```

Some of the data that is displayed in the concatenated rows is inaccurate. For example, although the **city** and **state** from the **customer** table indicate an address in California, the **code** and **sname** from the **state** table might be for a different state.

Creating a Join

Conceptually, the first stage of any join is the creation of a Cartesian product. To refine or constrain this Cartesian product and eliminate meaningless rows of data, include a WHERE clause with a valid join condition in your SELECT statement.

This section illustrates *equi-joins*, *natural joins*, and *multiple-table joins*. Additional complex forms, such as *self-joins* and *outer joins,* are discussed in Chapter 5.

Equi-Join

An equi-join is a join based on equality or matching values. This equality is indicated with an equal sign (=) in the comparison operation in the WHERE clause, as Query 2-58 shows.

Query 2-58

```
SELECT * FROM manufact, stock
    WHERE manufact.manu_code = stock.manu_code
```

Query 2-58 joins the **manufact** and **stock** tables on the **manu_code** column. It retrieves only those rows for which the values for the two columns are equal, as Query Result 2-58 shows.

```
manu_code     SMT
manu_name     Smith
lead_time        3
stock_num     1
manu_code     SMT
description   baseball gloves
unit_price    $450.00
unit          case
unit_descr    10 gloves/case

manu_code     SMT
manu_name     Smith
lead_time        3
stock_num     5
manu_code     SMT
description   tennis racquet
unit_price    $25.00
unit          each
unit_descr    each

manu_code     SMT
manu_name     Smith
lead_time        3
stock_num     6
manu_code     SMT
description   tennis ball
unit_price    $36.00
unit          case
unit_descr    24 cans/case

manu_code     ANZ
manu_name     Anza
lead_time        5
stock_num     5
manu_code     ANZ
description   tennis racquet
unit_price    $19.80
unit          each
unit_descr    each
....
```

In this equi-join, Query Result 2-58 includes the **manu_code** column from both the **manufact** and **stock** tables because the select list requested every column.

You can also create an equi-join with additional constraints, one where the comparison condition is based on the inequality of values in the joined columns. These joins use a relational operator in addition to the equal sign (=) in the comparison condition that is specified in the WHERE clause.

To join tables that contain columns with the same name, precede each column name with a period and its table name, as Query 2-59 shows.

Query 2-59

```
SELECT order_num, order_date, ship_date, cust_calls.*
    FROM orders, cust_calls
    WHERE call_dtime >= ship_date
        AND cust_calls.customer_num = orders.customer_num
    ORDER BY customer_num
```

Query 2-59 joins the **customer_num** column and then selects only those rows where the **call_dtime** in the **cust_calls** table is greater than or equal to the **ship_date** in the **orders** table. Query Result 2-59 shows the rows that it returns.

Query Result 2-59

```
order_num      1004
order_date     05/22/1998
ship_date      05/30/1998
customer_num   106
call_dtime     1998-06-12 08:20
user_id        maryj
call_code      D
call_descr     Order received okay, but two of the cans of
               ANZ tennis balls within the case were empty
res_dtime      1998-06-12 08:25
res_descr      Authorized credit for two cans to customer,
               issued apology. Called ANZ buyer to report
               the qa problem.

order_num      1008
order_date     06/07/1998
ship_date      07/06/1998
customer_num   110
call_dtime     1998-07-07 10:24
user_id        richc
call_code      L
call_descr     Order placed one month ago (6/7) not received.
res_dtime      1998-07-07 10:30
res_descr      Checked with shipping (Ed Smith). Order out
               yesterday-was waiting for goods from ANZ.
               Next time will call with delay if necessary.

order_num      1023
order_date     07/24/1998
ship_date      07/30/1998
customer_num   127
call_dtime     1998-07-31 14:30
user_id        maryj
call_code      I
call_descr     Received Hero watches (item # 304) instead
               of ANZ watches
res_dtime
res_descr      Sent memo to shipping to send ANZ item 304
               to customer and pickup HRO watches. Should
               be done tomorrow, 8/1
```

Natural Join

A natural join is structured so that the join column does not display data
redundantly, as Query 2-60 shows.

Query 2-60

```
SELECT manu_name, lead_time, stock.*
    FROM manufact, stock
    WHERE manufact.manu_code = stock.manu_code
```

Like the example for equi-join, Query 2-60 joins the **manufact** and **stock**
tables on the **manu_code** column. Because the select list is more closely
defined, the **manu_code** is listed only once for each row retrieved, as Query
Result 2-60 shows.

Query Result 2-60

```
manu_name     Smith
lead_time        3
stock_num     1
manu_code     SMT
description   baseball gloves
unit_price    $450.00
unit          case
unit_descr    10 gloves/case

manu_name     Smith
lead_time        3
stock_num     5
manu_code     SMT
description   tennis racquet
unit_price    $25.00
unit          each
unit_descr    each

manu_name     Smith
lead_time        3
stock_num     6
manu_code     SMT
description   tennis ball
unit_price    $36.00
unit          case
unit_descr    24 cans/case

manu_name     Anza
lead_time        5
stock_num     5
manu_code     ANZ
description   tennis racquet
unit_price    $19.80
unit          each
unit_descr    each
...
```

All joins are *associative*; that is, the order of the joining terms in the WHERE clause does not affect the meaning of the join.

Both statements in Query 2-61 create the same natural join.

Query 2-61

```
SELECT catalog.*, description, unit_price, unit, unit_descr
    FROM catalog, stock
    WHERE catalog.stock_num = stock.stock_num
        AND catalog.manu_code = stock.manu_code
        AND catalog_num = 10017

SELECT catalog.*, description, unit_price, unit, unit_descr
    FROM catalog, stock
    WHERE catalog_num = 10017
        AND catalog.manu_code = stock.manu_code
        AND catalog.stock_num = stock.stock_num
```

Each statement retrieves the row that Query Result 2-61 shows.

Query Result 2-61

```
catalog_num   10017
stock_num     101
manu_code     PRC
cat_descr
Reinforced, hand-finished tubular. Polyurethane belted.
Effective against punctures. Mixed tread for super wear
and road grip.
cat_picture   <BYTE value>

cat_advert    Ultimate in Puncture Protection. Tires
              Designed for In-City Riding
description    bicycle tires
unit_price    $88.00
unit          box
unit_descr    4/box
```

Query 2-61 includes a TEXT column, **cat_descr**; a BYTE column, **cat_picture**; and a VARCHAR column, **cat_advert**.

Multiple-Table Join

A multiple-table join connects more than two tables on one or more associated columns; it can be an equi-join or a natural join.

Query 2-62 creates an equi-join on the **catalog**, **stock**, and **manufact** tables.

```
SELECT * FROM catalog, stock, manufact
    WHERE catalog.stock_num = stock.stock_num
        AND stock.manu_code = manufact.manu_code
        AND catalog_num = 10025
```

Query 2-62 retrieves the rows that Query Result 2-62 shows.

```
catalog_num  10025
stock_num    106
manu_code    PRC
cat_descr
Hard anodized alloy with pearl finish; 6mm hex bolt hardware.
Available in lengths of 90-140mm in 10mm increments.
cat_picture  <BYTE value>

cat_advert   ProCycle Stem with Pearl Finish
stock_num    106
manu_code    PRC
description  bicycle stem
unit_price   $23.00
unit         each
unit_descr   each
manu_code    PRC
manu_name    ProCycle
lead_time        9
```

The **manu_code** is repeated three times, once for each table, and **stock_num** is repeated twice.

To avoid the considerable duplication of a multiple-table query such as Query 2-62, include specific columns in the select list to define the SELECT statement more closely, as Query 2-63 shows.

```
SELECT catalog.*, description, unit_price, unit,
    unit_descr, manu_name, lead_time
    FROM catalog, stock, manufact
    WHERE catalog.stock_num = stock.stock_num
        AND stock.manu_code = manufact.manu_code
        AND catalog_num = 10025
```

Query 2-63 uses a wildcard to select all columns from the table with the most columns and then specifies columns from the other two tables. Query Result 2-63 shows the natural join that Query 2-63 produces. It displays the same information as the previous example, but without duplication.

Query Result 2-63

```
catalog_num   10025
stock_num     106
manu_code     PRC
cat_descr
Hard anodized alloy with pearl finish. 6mm hex bolt hardware.
Available in lengths of 90-140mm in 10mm increments.
cat_picture   <BYTE value>

cat_advert    ProCycle Stem with Pearl Finish
description   bicycle stem
unit_price    $23.00
unit          each
unit_descr    each
manu_name     ProCycle
lead_time      9
```

Some Query Shortcuts

You can use aliases, the INTO TEMP clause, and display labels to speed your way through joins and multiple-table queries and to produce output for other uses.

Using Aliases

You can assign *aliases* to the tables in a SELECT statement to make multiple-table queries shorter and more readable. You can use an alias wherever the table name would be used, for instance, as a prefix to the column names in the other clauses.

Query 2-64a

```
SELECT s.stock_num, s.manu_code, s.description,
       s.unit_price, s.unit, c.catalog_num,
       c.cat_descr, c.cat_advert, m.lead_time
    FROM stock s, catalog c, manufact m
    WHERE s.stock_num = c.stock_num
        AND s.manu_code = c.manu_code
        AND s.manu_code = m.manu_code
        AND s.manu_code IN ('HRO', 'HSK')
        AND s.stock_num BETWEEN 100 AND 301
    ORDER BY catalog_num
```

The associative nature of the SELECT statement allows you to use an alias before you define it. In Query 2-64a, the aliases **s** for the **stock** table, **c** for the **catalog** table, and **m** for the **manufact** table are specified in the FROM clause and used throughout the SELECT and WHERE clauses as column prefixes.

Compare the length of Query 2-64a with Query 2-64b, which does not use aliases.

Query 2-64b

```
SELECT stock.stock_num, stock.manu_code, stock.description,
       stock.unit_price, stock.unit, catalog.catalog_num,
       catalog.cat_descr, catalog.cat_advert,
       manufact.lead_time
    FROM stock, catalog, manufact
    WHERE stock.stock_num = catalog.stock_num
        AND stock.manu_code = catalog.manu_code
        AND stock.manu_code = manufact.manu_code
        AND stock.manu_code IN ('HRO', 'HSK')
        AND stock.stock_num BETWEEN 100 AND 301
    ORDER BY catalog_num
```

Query 2-64a and Query 2-64b are equivalent and retrieve the data that Query Result 2-64 shows.

```
stock_num    110
manu_code    HRO
description   helmet
unit_price   $260.00
unit         case
catalog_num  10033
cat_descr
Newest ultralight helmet uses plastic shell. Largest ventilation
channels of any helmet on the market. 8.5 oz.
cat_advert   Lightweight Plastic Slatted with Vents Assures Cool
             Comfort Without Sacrificing Protection
lead_time    4

stock_num    110
manu_code    HSK
description   helmet
unit_price   $308.00
unit         each
catalog_num  10034
cat_descr
Aerodynamic (teardrop) helmet covered with anti-drag fabric.
Credited with shaving 2 seconds/mile from winner's time in
Tour de France time-trial. 7.5 oz.
cat_advert   Teardrop Design Endorsed by Yellow Jerseys,
             You Can Time the Difference
lead_time    5

stock_num    205
manu_code    HRO
description   3 golf balls
unit_price   $312.00
unit         each
catalog_num  10048
cat_descr
Combination fluorescent yellow and standard white.
cat_advert   HiFlier Golf Balls: Case Includes Fluorescent
             Yellow and Standard White
lead_time    4

...
```

You cannot use the ORDER BY clause for the TEXT column **cat_descr** or the BYTE column **cat_picture**.

You can use aliases to shorten your queries on tables that are not in the current database.

Query 2-65 joins columns from two tables that reside in different databases and systems, neither of which is the current database or system.

```
SELECT order_num, lname, fname, phone
FROM masterdb@central:customer c, sales@western:orders o
    WHERE c.customer_num = o.customer_num
        AND order_num <= 1010
```

By assigning the aliases **c** and **o** to the long *database@system:table* names, **masterdb@central:customer** and **sales@western:orders**, respectively, you can use the aliases to shorten the expression in the WHERE clause and retrieve the data, as Query Result 2-65 shows.

Query Result 2-65

```
order_num lname           fname           phone

    1001 Higgins         Anthony         415-368-1100
    1002 Pauli           Ludwig          408-789-8075
    1003 Higgins         Anthony         415-368-1100
    1004 Watson          George          415-389-8789
    1005 Parmelee        Jean            415-534-8822
    1006 Lawson          Margaret        415-887-7235
    1007 Sipes           Arnold          415-245-4578
    1008 Jaeger          Roy             415-743-3611
    1009 Keyes           Frances         408-277-7245
    1010 Grant           Alfred          415-356-1123
```

For more information on how to access tables that are not in the current database, see "Selecting Tables from a Database Other Than the Current Database" on page 2-69 and the *Informix Guide to SQL: Syntax*.

You can also use *synonyms* as shorthand references to the long names of tables that are not in the current database as well as current tables and views. For details on how to create and use synonyms, see the *Informix Guide to Database Design and Implementation*.

The INTO TEMP Clause

By adding an INTO TEMP clause to your SELECT statement, you can temporarily save the results of a multiple-table query in a separate table that you can query or manipulate without modifying the database. Temporary tables are dropped when you end your SQL session or when your program or report terminates.

Query 2-66 creates a temporary table called **stockman** and stores the results of the query in it. Because all columns in a temporary table must have names, the alias **adj_price** is required.

```
SELECT DISTINCT stock_num, manu_name, description,
                unit_price, unit_price * 1.05  adj_price
    FROM stock, manufact
    WHERE manufact.manu_code = stock.manu_code
    INTO TEMP stockman
```

stock_num	manu_name	description	unit_price	adj_price
1	Hero	baseball gloves	$250.00	$262.5000
1	Husky	baseball gloves	$800.00	$840.0000
1	Smith	baseball gloves	$450.00	$472.5000
2	Hero	baseball	$126.00	$132.3000
3	Husky	baseball bat	$240.00	$252.0000
4	Hero	football	$480.00	$504.0000
4	Husky	football	$960.00	$1008.0000
...				
306	Shimara	tandem adapter	$190.00	$199.5000
307	ProCycle	infant jogger	$250.00	$262.5000
308	ProCycle	twin jogger	$280.00	$294.0000
309	Hero	ear drops	$40.00	$42.0000
309	Shimara	ear drops	$40.00	$42.0000
310	Anza	kick board	$84.00	$88.2000
310	Shimara	kick board	$80.00	$84.0000
311	Shimara	water gloves	$48.00	$50.4000
312	Hero	racer goggles	$72.00	$75.6000
312	Shimara	racer goggles	$96.00	$100.8000
313	Anza	swim cap	$60.00	$63.0000
313	Shimara	swim cap	$72.00	$75.6000

You can query this table and join it with other tables, which avoids a multiple sort and lets you move more quickly through the database. For more information on temporary tables, see the *Informix Guide to SQL: Syntax* and the *Administrator's Guide*.

Selecting Tables from a Database Other Than the Current Database

The database that a CONNECT DATABASE or CREATE DATABASE statement opens is the *current* database. To refer to a table in a database other than the current database, include the database name as part of the table name, as the following SELECT statement illustrates:

```
SELECT name, number FROM salesdb:contacts
```

The database is **salesdb**. The table in **salesdb** is named **contacts**. You can use the same notation in a join. When you must specify the database name explicitly, the long table names can become cumbersome unless you use aliases to shorten them, as the following example shows:

```
SELECT C.custname, S.phone
    FROM salesdb:contacts C, stores:customer S
    WHERE C.custname = S.company
```

You must qualify the database name with a *database server name* to specify a table in a database that a different database server manages. For example, the following SELECT statement refers to table **customer** from database **masterdb**, which resides on the database server **central**:

```
SELECT O.order_num, C.fname, C.lname
    FROM masterdb@central:customer C, sales@boston:orders O
    WHERE C.customer_num = O.Customer_num
    INTO TEMP mycopy
```

In the example, two tables are being joined. The joined rows are stored in a temporary table called **mycopy** in the current database. The tables are located in two database servers, **central** and **boston**.

Informix allows you to *over qualify* table names (to give more information than is required). Because both table names are fully qualified, you cannot tell whether the current database is **masterdb** or **sales**.

Summary

This chapter introduced sample syntax and results for basic kinds of SELECT statements that are used to query a relational database. The section "Single-Table SELECT Statements" on page 2-10 shows how to perform the following actions:

- Select columns and rows from a table with the SELECT and FROM clauses

- Select rows from a table with the SELECT, FROM, and WHERE clauses

- Use the DISTINCT or UNIQUE keyword in the SELECT clause to eliminate duplicate rows from query results

- Sort retrieved data with the ORDER BY clause and the DESC keyword

- Select and order data that contains non-English characters

- Use the BETWEEN, IN, MATCHES, and LIKE keywords and various relational operators in the WHERE clause to create a comparison condition

- Create comparison conditions that include values, exclude values, find a range of values (with keywords, relational operators, and subscripting), and find a subset of values

- Use exact-text comparisons, variable-length wildcards, and restricted and unrestricted wildcards to perform variable text searches

- Use the logical operators AND, OR, and NOT to connect search conditions or Boolean expressions in a WHERE clause

- Use the ESCAPE keyword to protect special characters in a query

- Search for null values with the IS NULL and IS NOT NULL keywords in the WHERE clause

- Use the FIRST clause to specify that a query returns only a specified number of the rows that match the conditions of the SELECT statement

- Use arithmetic operators in the SELECT clause to perform computations on number fields and display derived data

- Use substrings and subscripting to tailor your queries

- Assign display labels to computed columns as a formatting tool for reports

This chapter also introduced simple join conditions that enable you to select and display data from two or more tables. The section "Multiple-Table SELECT Statements" on page 2-56 describes how to perform the following actions:

- Create a Cartesian product
- Include a WHERE clause with a valid join condition in your query to constrain a Cartesian product
- Define and create a natural join and an equi-join
- Join two or more tables on one or more columns
- Select rows from tables within a table hierarchy
- Use aliases as a shortcut in multiple-table queries
- Retrieve selected data into a separate, temporary table with the INTO TEMP clause to perform computations outside the database
- Select tables from a database other than the current database

Selecting Data From Complex Types

In This Chapter 3-3

Selecting Row-Type Data 3-4
   Selecting Columns of a Typed Table 3-5
   Selecting Columns That Contain Row-Type Data 3-6
      Field Projections 3-8
      Using Field Projections to Select Nested Fields 3-9
      Using Asterisk Notation to Access All Fields of a Row Type . . 3-10

Selecting from a Collection 3-11
   Selecting Nested Collections 3-12
   Using the IN Keyword to Search for Elements in a Collection . . . 3-13

Selecting Rows Within a Table Hierarchy 3-15
   Selecting Rows of the Supertable Without the ONLY Keyword . . 3-16
   Selecting Rows from a Supertable with the ONLY Keyword . . . 3-17
   Using an Alias for a Supertable 3-17

Summary 3-18

In This Chapter

This chapter describes how to query *complex data types*. A complex data type is built from a combination of other data types with an SQL type constructor. An SQL statement can access individual components within the complex type. The two kinds of complex data types are as follows:

- *Row types* have instances that combine one or more related data fields. The two kinds of row types are named and unnamed.

- *Collection types* have instances where each collection value contains a group of elements of the same data type, which can be any fundamental or complex data type. A collection can consist of a LIST, SET, or MULTISET.

For a more complete description of the data types that the database server supports, see the chapter on data types in the *Informix Guide to SQL: Reference*.

For information about how to create and use complex types, see the *Informix Guide to Database Design and Implementation*, the *Informix Guide to SQL: Reference*, and the *Informix Guide to SQL: Syntax*.

Selecting Row-Type Data

This section describes how to query data that is defined as row-type data. A row type is a complex type that combines one or more related data fields.

The two kinds of row types are as follows:

- **Named row types**. A named row type can define tables, columns, fields of another row-type column, program variables, statement local variables, and routine return values.

- **Unnamed row types**. An unnamed row type can define columns, fields of another row-type column, program variables, statement local variables, routine return values, and constants.

The examples used throughout this section use the named row types **zip_t,** **address_t,** and **employee_t,** which define the **employee** table. Figure 3-1 shows the SQL syntax that creates the row types and table.

Figure 3-1

```
CREATE ROW TYPE zip_t
(
    z_code      CHAR(5),
    z_suffix    CHAR(4)
)

CREATE ROW TYPE address_t
(
    street   VARCHAR(20),
    city     VARCHAR(20),
    state    CHAR(2),
    zip      zip_t
)

CREATE ROW TYPE employee_t
(
name     VARCHAR(30),
address  address_t,
salary   INTEGER
)

CREATE TABLE employee OF TYPE employee_t
```

The named row types **zip_t, address_t** and **employee_t** serve as templates for the fields and columns of the typed table, **employee**. A *typed table* is a table that is defined on a named row type. The **employee_t** type that serves as the template for the **employee** table uses the **address_t** type as the data type of the **address** field. The **address_t** type uses the **zip_t** type as the data type of the **zip** field.

Figure 3-2 shows the SQL syntax that creates the **student** table. The **s_address** column of the **student** table is defined on an unnamed row type. (The **s_address** column could also have been defined as a named row type.)

Figure 3-2

```
CREATE TABLE student
(
s_name        VARCHAR(30),
s_address     ROW(street VARCHAR (20), city VARCHAR(20),
                  state CHAR(2), zip VARCHAR(9)),
                  grade_point_avg DECIMAL(3,2)
)
```

Selecting Columns of a Typed Table

A query on a typed table is no different than a query on any other table. For example, Query 3-1 uses the asterisk symbol (*) to construct an implicit SELECT statement that returns all columns of the **employee** table.

Query 3-1

```
SELECT *
     FROM employee
```

The implicit SELECT statement on the **employee** table returns all rows for all columns, as Query Result 3-1 shows.

Query Result 3-1

```
name       Paul, J.
address    ROW(102 Ruby, Belmont, CA, 49932, 1000)
salary     78000

name       Davis, J.
address    ROW(133 First, San Jose, CA, 85744, 4900)
salary     75000
...
```

Query 3-2 shows how to construct a query that returns rows for the **name** and **address** columns of the **employee** table.

Query 3-2

```
SELECT name, address
    FROM employee
```

Query Result 3-2

```
name        Paul, J.
address     ROW(102 Ruby, Belmont, CA, 49932, 1000)

name        Davis, J.
address     ROW(133 First, San Jose, CA, 85744, 4900)
....
```

Selecting Columns That Contain Row-Type Data

A *row-type column* is a column that is defined on a named row type or unnamed row type. You use the same SQL syntax to query a named row-type or an unnamed row-type column.

A query on a row-type column returns data from all the fields of the row type. A *field* is a component data type within a row type. For example, the **address** column of the **employee** table contains the **street**, **city**, **state**, and **zip** fields. Query 3-3 shows how to construct a query that returns all fields of the **address** column.

Query 3-3

```
SELECT address
    FROM employee
```

Query Result 3-3

```
address     ROW(102 Ruby, Belmont, CA, 49932, 1000)

address     ROW(133 First, San Jose, CA, 85744, 4900)

address     ROW(152 Topaz, Willits, CA, 69445, 1000))
...
```

To access individual fields that a column contains, use single-dot notation to project the individual fields of the column. For example, suppose you want to access specific fields from the **address** column of the **employee** table. The following SELECT statement projects the **city** and **state** fields from the **address** column.

Query 3-4

```
SELECT address.city, address.state
    FROM employee
```

Query Result 3-4

```
city          state

Belmont       CA
San Jose      CA
Willits       CA
...
```

You construct a query on an unnamed row-type column in the same way you construct a query on a named row-type column. For example, suppose you want to access data from the **s_address** column of the **student** table in Figure 3-2. You can use *dot notation* to query the individual fields of a column that are defined on an unnamed row type. Query 3-5 shows how to construct a SELECT statement on the **student** table that returns rows for the **city** and **state** fields of the **s_address** column.

Query 3-5

```
SELECT s_address.city, s_address.state
    FROM student
```

Query Result 3-5

```
city            state

Belmont         CA
Mount Prospect  IL
Greeley         CO
...
```

Field Projections

Do not confuse fields with columns. Columns are only associated with tables, and column projections use conventional dot notation of the form *name_1.name_2* for a table and column, respectively. A *field* is a component data type within a row type. With row types (and the capability to assign a row type to a single column), you can project individual fields of a column with single dot notation of the form: *name_a.name_b.name_c.name_d*. Informix uses the following precedence rules to interpret dot notation:

1.   schema *name_a* . table *name_b* . column *name_c* . field *name_d*
2.   table name_a . column *name_b* . field *name_c* . field *name_d*
3.   column name_a . field *name_b* . field *name_c* . field *name_d*

When the meaning of a particular identifier is ambiguous, the database server uses precedence rules to determine which database object the identifier specifies. Consider the following two statements:

```
CREATE TABLE b (c ROW(d INTEGER, e CHAR(2)))
CREATE TABLE c (d INTEGER)
```

In the following SELECT statement, the expression c.d references column **d** of table **c** (rather than field **d** of column **c** in table **b**) because a table identifier has a higher precedence than a column identifier:

```
SELECT *
    FROM b,c
    WHERE c.d = 10
```

To avoid referencing the wrong database object, you can specify the full notation for a field projection. Suppose, for example, you want to reference field **d** of column **c** in table **b** (not column **d** of table **c**). The following statement specifies the table, column, and field identifiers of the object you want to reference:

```
SELECT *
    FROM b,c
    WHERE b.c.d = 10
```

Important: Although precedence rules reduce the chance of the database server misinterpreting field projections, Informix recommends that you use unique names for all table, column, and field identifiers.

Using Field Projections to Select Nested Fields

Typically the row type is a column, but you can use any row-type expression for field projection. When the row-type expression itself contains other row types, the expression contains *nested fields*. To access nested fields within an expression or individual fields, use dot notation. To access all the fields of the row type, use an asterisk (*). This section describes both methods of row-type access.

For a discussion of how to use dot notation and asterisk notation with row-type expressions, see the Expression segment in the *Informix Guide to SQL: Syntax*.

Selecting Individual Fields of a Row Type

Consider the **address** column of the **employee** table, which contains the fields **street**, **city**, **state**, and **zip**. In addition, the **zip** field contains the nested fields: **z_code** and **z_suffix**. (You might want to review the row type and table definitions of Figure 3-1 on page 3-4.) A query on the **zip** field returns rows for the **z_code** and **z_suffix** fields. However, you can specify that a query returns only specific nested fields. Query 3-6 shows how to use dot notation to construct a SELECT statement that returns rows for the **z_code** field of the **address** column only.

Query 3-6

```
SELECT address.zip.z_code
    FROM employee
```

Query Result 3-6

```
z_code

39444
6500
76055
19004
...
```

Using Asterisk Notation to Access All Fields of a Row Type

Asterisk notation is supported only within the select list of a SELECT statement. When you specify the column name for a row-type column in a select list, the database server returns values for all fields of the column. You can also use asterisk notation when you want to project all the fields within a row type.

Query 3-7 uses asterisk notation to return all fields of the **address** column in the **employee** table.

Query 3-7

```
SELECT address.*
    FROM employee
```

Query Result 3-7

```
address     ROW(102 Ruby, Belmont, CA, 49932, 1000)

address     ROW(133 First, San Jose, CA, 85744, 4900)

address     ROW(152 Topaz, Willits, CA, 69445, 1000))
...
```

The asterisk notation makes it easier to perform some SQL tasks. Suppose you create a function **new_row()** that returns a row-type value and you want to call this function and insert the row that is returned into a table. The database server provides no easy way to handle such operations. However, Query 3-8 shows how to use asterisk notation to return all fields of **new_row()** and insert the returned fields into the **tab_2** table.

Query 3-8

```
INSERT INTO tab_2 SELECT new_row(exp).* FROM tab_1
```

For information about how to use the INSERT statement, see Chapter 6, "Modifying Data."

Important: *An expression that uses the .* notation is evaluated only once.*

Selecting from a Collection

This section describes how to query columns that are defined on collection types. A *collection type* is a complex data type in which each collection value contains a group of elements of the same data type. For a detailed description of collection data types, see the *Informix Guide to Database Design and Implementation*. For information about how to access the individual elements that a collection contains, see "Handling Collections in SELECT Statements" on page 5-30.

Figure 3-3 shows the **manager** table, which is used in examples throughout this section. The **manager** table contains both simple and nested collection types. A *simple collection* is a collection type that does not contain any fields that are themselves collection types. The **direct_reports** column of the **manager** table is a simple collection. A *nested collection* is a collection type that contains another collection type. The **projects** column of the **manager** table is a nested collection.

Figure 3-3

```
CREATE TABLE manager
(
     mgr_name          VARCHAR(30),
     department        VARCHAR(12),
     direct_reports    SET(VARCHAR(30) NOT NULL),
     projects          LIST(ROW(pro_name VARCHAR(15),
                        pro_members SET(VARCHAR(20)
                        NOT NULL) ) NOT NULL)
)
```

A query on a column that is a collection type returns, for each row in the table, all the elements that the particular collection contains. For example, Query 3-9 shows a query that returns data in the **department** column and all elements in the **direct_reports** column for each row of the **manager** table.

```
SELECT department, direct_reports
    FROM manager
```

```
department       marketing
direct_reports   SET {Smith, Waters, Adams, Davis, Kurasawa}

department       engineering
direct_reports   SET {Joshi, Davis, Smith, Waters, Fosmire, Evans, Jones}

department       publications
direct_reports   SET {Walker, Fremont, Porat, Johnson}

department       accounting
direct_reports   SET {Baker, Freeman, Jacobs}
....
```

The output of a query on a collection type always includes the type
constructor that specifies whether the collection is a SET, MULTISET, or LIST.
For example, in Query Result 3-9, the SET constructor precedes the elements
of each collection. Braces ({}) demarcate the elements of a collection; commas
separate individual elements of a collection.

Selecting Nested Collections

The **projects** column of the **manager** table (see Figure 3-3 on page 3-11) is a
nested collection. A query on a nested collection type returns all the elements
that the particular collection contains. Query 3-10 shows a query that returns
all elements from the **projects** column for a specified row. The WHERE clause
limits the query to a single row in which the value in the **mgr_name** column
is Sayles.

```
SELECT projects
    FROM manager
    WHERE mgr_name = 'Sayles'
```

Query Result 3-10 shows a **project** column collection for a single row of the **manager** table. The query returns the names of those projects that the manager Sayles oversees. The collection contains, for each element in the LIST, the project name (**pro_name**) and the SET of individuals (**pro_members**) who are assigned to each project.

Query Result 3-10

```
projects    LIST {ROW(voyager_project, SET(Simonian, Waters, Adams, Davis))}

projects    LIST {ROW(horizon_project, SET(Freeman, Jacobs, Walker, Cannan))}

projects    LIST {ROW(saphire_project, SET(Villers, Reeves, Doyle, Strongin))}
....
```

Using the IN Keyword to Search for Elements in a Collection

You can use the IN keyword in the WHERE clause of an SQL statement to determine whether a collection contains a certain element. For example, Query 3-11 shows how to construct a query that returns values for **mgr_name** and **department** where Adams is an element of a collection in the **direct_reports** column.

Query 3-11

```
SELECT mgr_name, department
    FROM manager
    WHERE 'Adams' IN direct_reports
```

Query Result 3-11

```
mgr_name        Sayles
department      marketing
```

Although you can use a WHERE clause with the IN keyword to search for a particular element in a simple collection, the query always returns the complete collection. For example, Query 3-12 returns all the elements of the collection where Adams is an element of a collection in the **direct_reports** column.

Query 3-12

```
SELECT mgr_name, direct_reports
    FROM manager
    WHERE 'Adams' IN direct_reports
```

Query Result 3-12

```
mgr_name          Sayles
direct_reports    SET {Smith, Waters, Adams, Davis, Kurasawa}
```

As Query Result 3-12 shows, a query on a collection column returns the entire collection, not a particular element within the collection.

You can use the IN keyword in a WHERE clause to reference a simple collection only. You cannot use the IN keyword to reference a collection that contains fields that are themselves collections. For example, you cannot use the IN keyword to reference the **projects** column in the **manager** table because **projects** is a nested collection.

You can combine the NOT and IN keywords in the WHERE clause of a SELECT statement to search for collections that do not contain a certain element. For example, Query 3-13 shows a query that returns values for **mgr_name** and **department** where Adams is not an element of a collection in the **direct_reports** column.

Query 3-13

```
SELECT mgr_name, department
    FROM manager
    WHERE 'Adams' NOT IN direct_reports
```

Query Result 3-13

```
mgr_name          Williams
department        engineering

mgr_name          Lyman
department        publications

mgr_name          Cole
department        accounting
```

For information about how to count the elements in a collection column, see "Cardinality Function" on page 4-19.

Selecting Rows Within a Table Hierarchy

This section describes how to query rows from tables within a table hierarchy. For more information about how to create and use a table hierarchy, see the *Informix Guide to Database Design and Implementation*.

Figure 3-4 shows the statements that create the type and table hierarchies that the examples in this section use.

Figure 3-4

```
CREATE ROW TYPE address_t
(
    street  VARCHAR (20),
    city    VARCHAR(20),
    state   CHAR(2),
    zip     VARCHAR(9)
)

CREATE ROW TYPE person_t
(
    name    VARCHAR(30),
    address address_t,
    soc_sec CHAR(9)
)

CREATE ROW TYPE employee_t
(
salary   INTEGER
)
UNDER person_t

CREATE ROW TYPE sales_rep_t
(
    rep_num SERIAL8,
    region_num INTEGER
)
UNDER employee_t

CREATE TABLE person OF TYPE person_t

CREATE TABLE employee OF TYPE employee_t
UNDER person

CREATE TABLE sales_rep OF TYPE sales_rep_t
UNDER employee
```

Figure 3-5 shows the hierarchical relationships of the row types and tables in Figure 3-4.

Figure 3-5
Type and Table Hierarchies

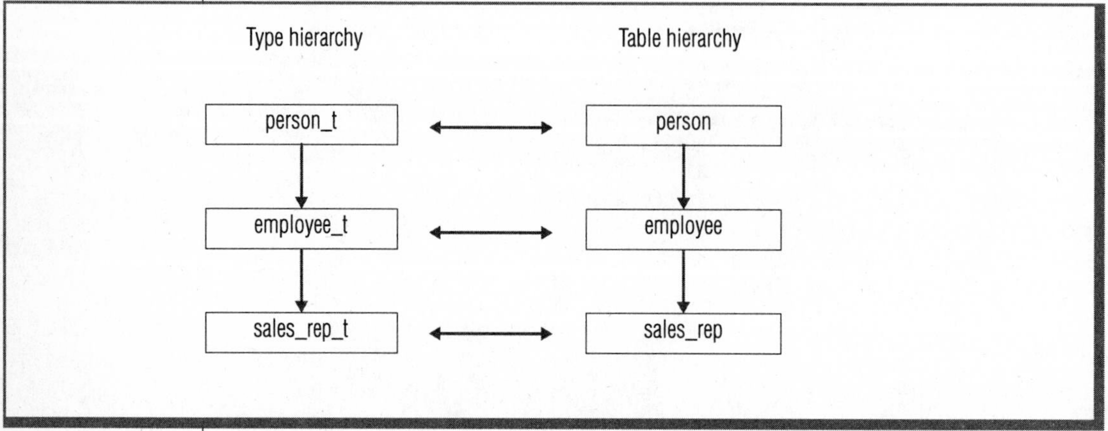

Selecting Rows of the Supertable Without the ONLY Keyword

A table hierarchy allows you to construct a query whose scope is a supertable and its subtables in a single SQL statement. A query on a supertable returns rows from both the supertable and its subtables. Query 3-14 shows a query on the **person** table, which is the root supertable in the table hierarchy.

Query 3-14

```
SELECT * FROM person
```

Query Result 2-15 returns all columns in the supertable and those columns in subtables (**employee** and **sales_rep**) that are inherited from the supertable. A query on a supertable does not return columns from subtables that are not in the supertable. Query Result 3-14 shows the **name, address,** and **soc_sec** columns in the **person, employee,** and **sales_rep** tables.

```
name        Rogers, J.
address     ROW(102 Ruby Ave, Belmont, CA, 69055)
soc_sec     454849344

name        Sallie, A.
address     ROW(134 Rose St, San Carlos, CA, 69025)
soc_sec     348441214
...
```

Selecting Rows from a Supertable with the ONLY Keyword

Although a SELECT statement on a supertable returns rows from both the
supertable and its subtables, you cannot tell which rows come from the
supertable and which rows come from the subtables. To limit the results of a
query to the supertable only, you must include the ONLY keyword in the
SELECT statement. For example, Query 3-15 returns rows in the **person** table
only.

```
SELECT * FROM ONLY(person)
```

```
name        Rogers, J.
address     ROW(102 Ruby Ave, Belmont, CA, 69055)
soc_sec     454849344
...
```

Using an Alias for a Supertable

An *alias* is a word that immediately follows the name of a table in the FROM
clause. You can specify an alias for a typed table in a SELECT or UPDATE
statement and then use the alias as an expression by itself. If you create an
alias for a supertable, the alias can represent values from the supertable or the
subtables that inherit from the supertable. In DB-Access, Query 3-16 returns
row values for all instances of the **person, employee**, and **sales_rep** tables.

```
SELECT p FROM person p
```

In an ESQL/C program, Query 3-16 returns an error.

Summary

This chapter introduced sample syntax and results for selecting data from complex types using SELECT statements to query a relational database. The section "Selecting Row-Type Data" on page 3-4 shows how to perform the following actions:

- Select row-type data from typed tables and columns
- Use row-type expressions for field projections

The section "Selecting from a Collection" on page 3-11 shows how to perform the following actions:

- Query columns that are defined on collection types
- Search for elements in a collection
- Query columns that are defined on collection types

The section "Selecting Rows Within a Table Hierarchy" on page 3-15 shows how to perform the following actions:

- Query a supertable with or without the ONLY keyword
- Specify an alias for a supertable

Using Functions in Select Statements

In This Chapter   4-3

Using Functions in SELECT Statements   4-4
  Aggregate Functions   4-4
    Using the COUNT Function   4-5
    Using the AVG Function   4-6
    Using the MAX and MIN Functions   4-7
    Using the SUM Function   4-7
    Using the RANGE Function   4-7
    Using the STDEV Function   4-8
    Using the VARIANCE Function   4-9
    Applying Functions to Expressions   4-10
  Time Functions   4-10
    Using DAY and CURRENT Functions   4-11
    Using the MONTH Function   4-12
    Using the WEEKDAY Function   4-13
    Using the YEAR Function   4-14
    Formatting DATETIME Values   4-14
  Date-Conversion Functions   4-15
    Using the DATE Function   4-15
    Using the TO_CHAR Function   4-16
    Using the TO_DATE Function   4-17
  Cardinality Function   4-19
  Smart-Large-Object Functions   4-20
  String-Manipulation Functions   4-21
    Using the LOWER Function   4-22
    Using the UPPER Function   4-22
    Using the INITCAP Function   4-23
    Using the REPLACE Function   4-24
    Using the SUBSTRING and SUBSTR Functions   4-24
    Using the SUBSTRING Function   4-25

Using the SUBSTR Function 4-26
Using the LPAD Function 4-27
Using the RPAD Function 4-28
Other Functions. 4-29
Using the LENGTH Function. 4-29
Using the USER Function 4-30
Using the TODAY Function 4-31
Using the DBSERVERNAME and SITENAME Functions . . . 4-31
Using the HEX Function 4-32
Using the DBINFO Function 4-32
Using the DECODE Function. 4-33
Using the NVL Function 4-35

Using SPL Routines in SELECT Statements 4-36

Using Rowid Values In SELECT Statements 4-38
Using Rowid Values with the USER Function 4-39
Using Rowid Values with the DBSERVERNAME Function 4-41

Summary 4-42

In This Chapter

In addition to column names and operators, an expression can also include one or more functions. This chapter shows how to use functions in SELECT statements to perform more complex database queries and data manipulation. The following functions are described in this chapter:

- Aggregate functions
- Time functions
- Date-conversion functions
- Cardinality function
- Smart-large-object functions
- String-manipulation functions
- Other functions

For information about the syntax of the following SQL functions and other SQL functions, see the Expressions segment in the *Informix Guide to SQL: Syntax*.

Tip: *You can also use functions that you create yourself. For information about user-defined functions, see Chapter 10 and "Extending Informix Dynamic Server 2000."*

Using Functions in SELECT Statements

You can use any basic type of expression (column, constant, function, aggregate function, and procedure), or combination thereof, in the select list.

A function expression uses a function that is evaluated for each row in the query. All function expressions require arguments. This set of expressions contains the time function and the length function when they are used with a column name as an argument.

Aggregate Functions

All Informix database servers support the following *aggregate* functions:

- AVG
- COUNT
- MAX
- MIN
- RANGE
- STDEV
- SUM
- VARIANCE

An aggregate function returns one value for a set of queried rows. The aggregate functions take on values that depend on the set of rows that the WHERE clause of the SELECT statement returns. In the absence of a WHERE clause, the aggregate functions take on values that depend on all the rows that the FROM clause forms.

You cannot use aggregate functions for expressions that contain the following data types:

- TEXT
- BYTE
- CLOB

IDS

- BLOB
- opaque data types (unless user creates aggregate functions)
- collection data types
- row types ♦

Aggregates are often used to summarize information about groups of rows in a table. This use is discussed in Chapter 5. When you apply an aggregate function to an entire table, the result contains a single row that summarizes all the selected rows.

Using the COUNT Function

Query 4-1 counts and displays the total number of rows in the **stock** table.

Query 4-1

```
SELECT COUNT(*)
    FROM stock
```

Query Result 4-1

```
(count(*))

    73
```

Query 4-2 includes a WHERE clause to count specific rows in the **stock** table; in this case, only those rows that have a **manu_code** of SHM.

Query 4-2

```
SELECT COUNT (*)
    FROM stock
    WHERE manu_code = 'SHM'
```

Query Result 4-2

```
(count(*))

    17
```

By including the keyword DISTINCT (or its synonym UNIQUE) and a column name in Query 4-3, you can tally the number of different manufacturer codes in the **stock** table.

Query 4-3

```
SELECT COUNT (DISTINCT manu_code)
    FROM stock
```

Query Result 4-3

```
    (count)
      9
```

Using the AVG Function

Query 4-4 computes the average **unit_price** of all rows in the **stock** table.

Query 4-4

```
SELECT AVG (unit_price)
    FROM stock
```

Query Result 4-4

```
    (avg)
  $197.14
```

Query 4-5 computes the average **unit_price** of just those rows in the **stock** table that have a **manu_code** of SHM.

Query 4-5

```
SELECT AVG (unit_price)
    FROM stock
    WHERE manu_code = 'SHM'
```

Query Result 4-5

```
    (avg)
  $204.93
```

Using the MAX and MIN Functions

You can combine aggregate functions in the same SELECT statement. For example, you can include both the **MAX** and the **MIN** functions in the select list, as Query 4-6 shows.

Query 4-6

```
SELECT MAX (ship_charge), MIN (ship_charge)
    FROM orders
```

Query 4-6 finds and displays both the highest and lowest **ship_charge** in the **orders** table, as Query Result 4-6 shows.

Query Result 4-6

```
  (max)     (min)

 $25.20    $5.00
```

Using the SUM Function

Query 4-7 calculates the total **ship_weight** of orders that were shipped on July 13, 1998.

Query 4-7

```
SELECT SUM (ship_weight)
    FROM orders
    WHERE ship_date = '07/13/1998'
```

Query Result 4-7

```
  (sum)

  130.5
```

Using the RANGE Function

The **RANGE** function computes the difference between the maximum and the minimum values for the selected rows.

You can apply the **RANGE** function only to numeric columns. Query 4-8 finds the range of prices for items in the **stock** table.

Query 4-8

```
SELECT RANGE(unit_price) FROM stock
```

Query Result 4-8

```
(range)

955.50
```

As with other aggregates, the **RANGE** function applies to the rows of a group when the query includes a GROUP BY clause, which Query 4-9 shows.

Query 4-9

```
SELECT RANGE(unit_price) FROM stock
    GROUP BY manu_code
```

Query Result 4-9

```
(range)

820.20
595.50
720.00
225.00
632.50
0.00
460.00
645.90
425.00
```

Using the STDEV Function

The **STDEV** function computes the standard deviation for the selected rows. It is the square root of the **VARIANCE** function.

You can apply the **STDEV** function only to numeric columns. The following query finds the standard deviation on a population:

```
SELECT STDEV(age) FROM u_pop WHERE age > 21
```

As with the other aggregates, the **STDEV** function applies to the rows of a group when the query includes a GROUP BY clause, as the following example shows:

```
SELECT STDEV(age) FROM u_pop
    GROUP BY state
    WHERE STDEV(age) > 21
```

Nulls are ignored unless every value in the specified column is null. If every column value is null, the **STDEV** function returns a null for that column. For more information about the **STDEV** function, see the Expression segment in the *Informix Guide to SQL: Syntax*.

Using the VARIANCE Function

The **VARIANCE** function returns the variance for a sample of values as an unbiased estimate of the variance for all rows selected. It computes the following value:

```
(SUM(Xi**2) - (SUM(Xi)**2)/N)/(N-1)
```

In this example, Xi is each value in the column and N is the total number of values in the column. You can apply the **VARIANCE** function only to numeric columns. The following query finds the variance on a population:

```
SELECT VARIANCE(age) FROM u_pop WHERE age > 21
```

As with the other aggregates, the **VARIANCE** function applies to the rows of a group when the query includes a GROUP BY clause, which the following example shows:

```
SELECT VARIANCE(age) FROM u_pop
    GROUP BY birth
    WHERE VARIANCE(age) > 21
```

Nulls are ignored unless every value in the specified column is null. If every column value is null, the **VARIANCE** function returns a null for that column. For more information about the **VARIANCE** function, see the Expression segment in the *Informix Guide to SQL: Syntax*.

Applying Functions to Expressions

Query 4-10 shows how you can apply functions to expressions, and you can supply display labels for their results.

Query 4-10

```
SELECT MAX (res_dtime - call_dtime) maximum,
    MIN (res_dtime - call_dtime) minimum,
    AVG (res_dtime - call_dtime) average
    FROM cust_calls
```

Query 4-10 finds and displays the maximum, minimum, and average amount of time (in days, hours, and minutes) between the reception and resolution of a customer call and labels the derived values appropriately. Query Result 4-10 shows these amounts of time.

Query Result 4-10

```
maximum         minimum         average

5 20:55         0 00:01         1 02:56
```

Time Functions

You can use the *time* functions **DAY, MDY, MONTH, WEEKDAY,** and **YEAR** in either the SELECT clause or the WHERE clause of a query. These functions return a value that corresponds to the expressions or arguments that you use to call the function. You can also use the **CURRENT** function to return a value with the current date and time, or use the **EXTEND** function to adjust the precision of a DATE or DATETIME value.

Using DAY and CURRENT Functions

Query 4-11 returns the day of the month for the **call_dtime** and **res_dtime** columns in two *expression* columns.

```
SELECT customer_num, DAY (call_dtime), DAY (res_dtime)
    FROM cust_calls
```

```
customer_num (expression) (expression)

       106          12          12
       110           7           7
       119           1           2
       121          10          10
       127          31
       116          28          28
       116          21          27
```

Query 4-12 uses the **DAY** and **CURRENT** functions to compare column values to the current day of the month. It selects only those rows where the value is earlier than the current day. In this example, the CURRENT day is 15.

```
SELECT customer_num, DAY (call_dtime), DAY (res_dtime)
    FROM cust_calls
    WHERE DAY (call_dtime) < DAY (CURRENT)
```

```
customer_num (expression) (expression)

       106          12          12
       110           7           7
       119           1           2
       121          10          10
```

Query 4-13 uses the **CURRENT** function to select all calls except those that came in today.

Query 4-13

```
SELECT customer_num, call_code, call_descr
    FROM cust_calls
    WHERE call_dtime < CURRENT YEAR TO DAY
```

Query Result 4-13

```
customer_num  106
call_code     D
call_descr    Order was received, but two of the cans of ANZ tennis balls
              within the case were empty

customer_num  110
call_code     L
call_descr    Order placed one month ago (6/7) not received.
....
customer_num  116
call_code     I
call_descr    Second complaint from this customer! Received two cases
              right-handed outfielder gloves (1 HRO) instead of one case
              lefties.
```

Using the MONTH Function

Query 4-14 uses the **MONTH** function to extract and show what month the customer call was received and resolved, and it uses display labels for the resulting columns. However, it does not make a distinction between years.

Query 4-14

```
SELECT customer_num,
    MONTH (call_dtime) call_month,
    MONTH (res_dtime) res_month
    FROM cust_calls
```

Query Result 4-14

```
customer_num   call_month   res_month

        106           6           6
        110           7           7
        119           7           7
        121           7           7
        127           7
        116          11          11
        116          12          12
```

Query 4-15 uses the **MONTH** function plus **DAY** and **CURRENT** to show what month the customer call was received and resolved if **DAY** is earlier than the current day.

Query 4-15

```
SELECT customer_num,
    MONTH (call_dtime) called,
    MONTH (res_dtime) resolved
    FROM cust_calls
    WHERE DAY (res_dtime) < DAY (CURRENT)
```

Query Result 4-15

customer_num	called	resolved
106	6	6
119	7	7
121	7	7

Using the WEEKDAY Function

Query 4-16 uses the **WEEKDAY** function to indicate which day of the week calls are received and resolved (0 represents Sunday, 1 is Monday, and so on), and the expression columns are labeled.

Query 4-16

```
SELECT customer_num,
    WEEKDAY (call_dtime) called,
    WEEKDAY (res_dtime) resolved
    FROM cust_calls
    ORDER BY resolved
```

Query Result 4-16

customer_num	called	resolved
127	3	
110	0	0
119	1	2
121	3	3
116	3	3
106	3	3
116	5	4

Query 4-17 uses the **COUNT** and **WEEKDAY** functions to count how many calls were received on a weekend. This kind of statement can give you an idea of customer-call patterns or indicate whether overtime pay might be required.

Query 4-17

```
SELECT COUNT(*)
    FROM cust_calls
    WHERE WEEKDAY (call_dtime) IN (0,6)
```

Query Result 4-17

```
(count(*))

        4
```

Using the YEAR Function

Query 4-18 retrieves rows where the **call_dtime** is earlier than the beginning of the current year.

Query 4-18

```
SELECT customer_num, call_code,
    YEAR (call_dtime) call_year,
    YEAR (res_dtime) res_year
    FROM cust_calls
    WHERE YEAR (call_dtime) < YEAR (TODAY)
```

Query Result 4-18

```
customer_num call_code call_year res_year

        116 I         1997      1997
        116 I         1997      1997
```

Formatting DATETIME Values

In Query 4-19, the **EXTEND** function displays only the specified subfields to restrict the two DATETIME values.

Query 4-19

```
SELECT customer_num,
    EXTEND (call_dtime, month to minute) call_time,
    EXTEND (res_dtime, month to minute) res_time
    FROM cust_calls
    ORDER BY res_time
```

Query Result 4-19 returns the month-to-minute range for the columns labeled **call_time** and **res_time** and gives an indication of the work load.

```
customer_num call_time   res_time

        127 07-31 14:30
        106 06-12 08:20 06-12 08:25
        119 07-01 15:00 07-02 08:21
        110 07-07 10:24 07-07 10:30
        121 07-10 14:05 07-10 14:06
        116 11-28 13:34 11-28 16:47
        116 12-21 11:24 12-27 08:19
```

IDS

Date-Conversion Functions

The following conversion functions convert between date and character values:

- **DATE**
- **TO_CHAR**
- **TO_DATE**

You can use a date-conversion function anywhere you use an expression.

Using the DATE Function

The **DATE** function converts a character string to a DATE value. In Query 4-20, the **DATE** function converts a character string to a DATE value to allow for comparisons with DATETIME values. The query retrieves DATETIME values only when **call_dtime** is later than the specified DATE.

```
SELECT customer_num, call_dtime, res_dtime
    FROM cust_calls
    WHERE call_dtime > DATE ('12/31/97')
```

```
customer_num call_dtime        res_dtime

        106 1998-06-12 08:20 1998-06-12 08:25
        110 1998-07-07 10:24 1998-07-07 10:30
        119 1998-07-01 15:00 1998-07-02 08:21
        121 1998-07-10 14:05 1998-07-10 14:06
        127 1998-07-31 14:30
```

Query 4-21 converts DATETIME values to DATE format and displays the
values, with labels, only when **call_dtime** is greater than or equal to the
specified date.

Query 4-21

```
SELECT customer_num,
    DATE (call_dtime) called,
    DATE (res_dtime) resolved
    FROM cust_calls
    WHERE call_dtime >= DATE ('1/1/98')
```

Query Result 4-21

```
customer_num called     resolved

         106 06/12/1998  06/12/1998
         110 07/07/1998  07/07/1998
         119 07/01/1998  07/02/1998
         121 07/10/1998  07/10/1998
         127 07/31/1998
```

Using the TO_CHAR Function

The **TO_CHAR** function converts DATETIME or DATE values to character
string values. The **TO_CHAR** function evaluates a DATETIME value according
to the date-formatting directive that you specify and returns an NVARCHAR
value. For a complete list of the supported date-formatting directives, see the
description of the **GL_DATETIME** environment variable in the *Informix Guide
to GLS Functionality*.

You can also use the **TO_CHAR** function to convert a DATETIME or DATE
value to an LVARCHAR value.

Query 4-22 uses the **TO_CHAR** function to convert a DATETIME value to a
more readable character string.

Query 4-22

```
SELECT customer_num,
    TO_CHAR(call_dtime, "%A %B %d %Y") call_date
    FROM cust_calls
    WHERE call_code = "B"
```

Query Result 4-22

```
customer_num  119
call_date     Friday July 01 1998
```

Query 4-23 uses the **TO_CHAR** function to convert DATE values to more readable character strings.

Query 4-23

```
SELECT order_num,
       TO_CHAR(ship_date,"%A %B %d %Y") date_shipped
       FROM orders
       WHERE paid_date IS NULL
```

Query Result 4-23

```
order_num      1004
date_shipped   Monday May 30 1998

order_num      1006
date_shipped

order_num      1007
date_shipped   Sunday June 05 1998

order_num      1012
date_shipped   Wednesday June 29 1998

order_num      1016
date_shipped   Tuesday July 12 1998

order_num      1017
date_shipped   Wednesday July 13 1998
```

Using the TO_DATE Function

The **TO_DATE** function accepts an argument of a character data type and converts this value to a DATETIME value. The **TO_DATE** function evaluates a character string according to the date-formatting directive that you specify and returns a DATETIME value. For a complete list of the supported date-formatting directives, see the description of the **GL_DATETIME** environment variable in the *Informix Guide to GLS Functionality*.

You can also use the **TO_DATE** function to convert an LVARCHAR value to a DATETIME value.

Date-Conversion Functions

Query 4-24 uses the **TO_DATE** function to convert character string values to DATETIME values whose format you specify.

Query 4-24

```
SELECT customer_num, call_descr
    FROM cust_calls
    WHERE call_dtime = TO_DATE("1998-07-07 10:24",
    "%Y-%m-%d %H:%M").
```

Query Result 4-24

```
customer_num   110

call_descr     Order placed one month ago (6/7) not received.
```

You can use the **DATE** or **TO_DATE** function to convert a character string to a DATE value. One advantage of the **TO_DATE** function is that it allows you to specify a format for the value returned. (You can use the **TO_DATE** function, which always returns a DATETIME value, to convert a character string to a DATE value because the database server implicitly handles conversions between DATE and DATETIME values.)

Query 4-25 uses the **TO_DATE** function to convert character string values to DATE values whose format you specify.

Query 4-25

```
SELECT order_num, paid_date
    FROM orders
    WHERE order_date = TO_DATE("6/7/98", "%m/%d/%iY")
```

Query Result 4-25

```
order_num   paid_date

1008        07/21/1998
```

Cardinality Function

The **CARDINALITY()** function counts the number of elements that a collection contains. You can use the **CARDINALITY()** function with simple or nested collections. Any duplicates in a collection are counted as individual elements. Query 4-26 shows a query that returns, for every row in the **manager** table, **department** values and the number of elements in each **direct_reports** collection.

Query 4-26

```
SELECT department, CARDINALITY(direct_reports)
    FROM manager
```

Query Result 4-26

```
department    marketing 5

department    engineering 7

department    publications 4

department    accounting 3
```

You can also evaluate the number of elements in a collection from within a predicate expression, as Query 4-27 shows.

Query 4-27

```
SELECT department, CARDINALITY(direct_reports)
    FROM manager
    WHERE CARDINALITY(direct_reports) < 6
    GROUP BY department
```

Query Result 4-27

```
department    accounting 3

department    marketing 5

department    publications 4
```

IDS

Smart-Large-Object Functions

The database server provides four SQL functions that you can call from within an SQL statement to import and export smart large objects. Figure 4-1 shows the smart-large-object functions.

Figure 4-1
SQL Functions for Smart Large Objects

Function Name	Purpose
FILETOBLOB()	Copies a file into a BLOB column.
FILETOCLOB()	Copies a file into a CLOB column.
LOCOPY()	Copies BLOB or CLOB data into another BLOB or CLOB column.
LOTOFILE()	Copies a BLOB or CLOB into a file.

For detailed information and the syntax of smart-large-object functions, see the Expression segment in the *Informix Guide to SQL: Syntax*.

You can use any of the functions that Figure 4-1 shows in SELECT, UPDATE, and INSERT statements. For examples of how to use the preceding functions in INSERT and UPDATE statements, see Chapter 6.

Suppose you create the **inmate** and **fbi_list** tables, as Figure 4-2 shows.

Figure 4-2

```
CREATE TABLE inmate
(
    id_num  INT,
    picture BLOB,
    felony  CLOB
)

CREATE TABLE fbi_list
(
    id      INTEGER,
    mugshot  BLOB
) PUT mugshot IN (sbspace1)
```

The following SELECT statement uses the **LOTOFILE()** function to copy data from the **felony** column into the **felon_322.txt** file that is located on the client computer:

```
SELECT id_num, LOTOFILE(felony, 'felon_322.txt', 'client')
    FROM inmate
    WHERE id = 322
```

The first argument for **LOTOFILE()** specifies the name of the column from which data is to be exported. The second argument specifies the name of the file into which data is to be copied. The third argument specifies whether the target file is located on the client computer ('client') or server computer ('server').

The following rules apply for specifying the path of a filename in a function argument, depending on whether the file resides on the client or server computer:

- If the source file resides on the server computer, you must specify the full pathname to the file (not the pathname relative to the current working directory).

- If the source file resides on the client computer, you can specify either the full or relative pathname to the file.

String-Manipulation Functions

IDS

String-manipulation functions accept arguments of type CHAR, NCHAR, VARCHAR, NVARCHAR, or LVARCHAR. You can use a string-manipulation function anywhere you use an expression.

The following functions convert between upper and lowercase letters in a character string:

- **LOWER**
- **UPPER**
- **INITCAP**

The following functions manipulate character strings in various ways:

- **REPLACE**
- **SUBSTR**
- **SUBSTRING**
- **LPAD**
- **RPAD**

You cannot overload any of the string-manipulation functions to handle extended data types.

Using the LOWER Function

Use the **LOWER** function to replace every uppercase letter in a character string with a lowercase letter. The **LOWER** function accepts an argument of a character data type and returns a value of the same data type as the argument you specify.

Query 4-28 uses the **LOWER** function to convert any uppercase letters in a character string to lowercase letters.

Query 4-28

```
SELECT manu_code, LOWER(manu_code)
    FROM items
    WHERE order_num = 1018
```

Query Result 4-28

```
manu_code  (expression)

PRC        prc
KAR        kar
PRC        prc
SMT        smt
HRO        hro
```

Using the UPPER Function

Use the **UPPER** function to replace every lowercase letter in a character string with an uppercase letter. The **UPPER** function accepts an argument of a character data type and returns a value of the same data type as the argument you specify.

Query 4-29 uses the **UPPER** function to convert any uppercase letters in a character string to lowercase letters.

Query 4-29

```
SELECT call_code, UPPER(code_descr)
    FROM call_type
```

Query Result 4-29

```
call_code  (expression)

B          BILLING ERROR
D          DAMAGED GOODS
I          INCORRECT MERCHANDISE SENT
L          LATE SHIPMENT
O          OTHER
```

Using the INITCAP Function

Use the **INITCAP** function to replace the first letter of every word in a character string with an uppercase letter. The **INITCAP** function assumes a new word whenever the function encounters a letter that is preceded by any character other than a letter. The **INITCAP** function accepts an argument of a character data type and returns a value of the same data type as the argument you specify.

Query 4-30 uses the **INITCAP** function to convert the first letter of every word in a character string to an uppercase letter.

Query 4-30

```
SELECT INITCAP(description)
    FROM stock
    WHERE manu_code = "ANZ"
```

Query Result 4-30

```
(expression)

3 Golf Balls
Golf Shoes
Helmet
Kick Board
Running Shoes
Swim Cap
Tennis Ball
Tennis Racquet
Volleyball
Volleyball Net
Watch
```

Using the REPLACE Function

Use the **REPLACE** function to replace a certain set of characters in a character string with other characters.

In Query 4-31, the **REPLACE** function replaces the **unit** column value each with item for every row that the query returns. The first argument of the **REPLACE** function is the expression to be evaluated. The second argument specifies the characters that you want to replace. The third argument specifies a new character string to replace the characters removed.

Query 4-31

```
SELECT stock_num, REPLACE(unit,"each", "item") cost_per,
unit_price
      FROM stock
      WHERE manu_code = "HRO"
```

Query Result 4-31

stock_num	cost_per	unit_price
1	case$	$250.00
2	case	$126.00
4	case	$480.00
7	case	$600.00
110	case	$260.00
205	case	$312.00
301	item	$ 42.50
302	item	$ 4.50
304	box	$280.00
305	case	$ 48.00
309	case	$ 40.00
312	box	$ 72.00

Using the SUBSTRING and SUBSTR Functions

You can use the **SUBSTRING** and **SUBSTR** functions to return a portion of a character string. You specify the *start position* and *length* (optional) to determine which portion of the character string the function returns.

Using the SUBSTRING Function

You can use the **SUBSTRING** function to return some portion of a character string. You specify the *start position* and *length* (optional) to determine which portion of the character string the function returns. You can specify a positive or negative number for the start position. A start position of 1 specifies that the **SUBSTRING** function begins from the first position in the string. When the start position is zero (0) or a negative number, the **SUBSTRING** function counts backward from the beginning of the string.

Query 4-32 shows an example of the **SUBSTRING** function, which returns the first four characters for any **sname** column values that the query returns. In this example, the **SUBSTRING** function starts at the beginning of the string and returns four characters counting forward from the start position.

Query 4-32

```
SELECT sname, SUBSTRING(sname FROM 1 FOR 4)
    FROM state
    WHERE code = "AZ"
```

Query Result 4-32

sname	(expression)
Arizona	Ariz

In Query 4-33, the **SUBSTRING** function specifies a start position of 6 but does not specify the length. The function returns a character string that extends from the sixth position to the end of the string.

Query 4-33

```
SELECT sname, SUBSTRING(sname FROM 6)
    FROM state
    WHERE code = "WV"
```

Query Result 4-33

sname	(expression)
West Virginia	Virginia

In Query 4-34, the **SUBSTRING** function returns only the first character for any **sname** column value that the query returns. For the **SUBSTRING** function, a start position of -2 counts backward three positions (0, -1, -2) from the start position of the string (for a start position of 0, the function counts backward one position from the beginning of the string).

Query 4-34

```
SELECT sname, SUBSTRING(sname FROM -2 FOR 4)
    FROM state
    WHERE code = "AZ"
```

Query Result 4-34

```
sname           (expression)

Arizona         A
```

Using the SUBSTR Function

The **SUBSTR** function serves the same purpose as the **SUBSTRING** function, but the syntax of the two functions differs.

To return a portion of a character string, specify the *start position* and *length* (optional) to determine which portion of the character string the **SUBSTR** function returns. The start position that you specify for the **SUBSTR** function can be a positive or a negative number. However, the **SUBSTR** function treats a negative number in the start position differently than does the **SUBSTRING** function. When the start position is a negative number, the **SUBSTR** function counts backward from the end of the character string, which depends on the length of the string, not the character length of a word or visible characters that the string contains. The **SUBSTR** function recognizes zero (0) or 1 in the start position as the first position in the string.

Query 4-35 shows an example of the **SUBSTR** function that includes a negative number for the start position. Given a start position of -15, the **SUBSTR** function counts backward 15 positions from the end of the string to find the start position and then returns the next five characters.

Query 4-35

```
SELECT sname, SUBSTR(sname, -15, 5)
    FROM state
    WHERE code = "CA"
```

Query Result 4-35

sname	(expression)
California	Calif
Arizona	

To use a negative number for the start position, you need to know the length of the value that is evaluated. The **sname** column is defined as CHAR(15), so a **SUBSTR** function that accepts an argument of type **sname** can use a start position of 0, 1, or -15 for the function to return a character string that begins from the first position in the string.

Query 4-36 returns the same result as Query 4-35.

Query 4-36

```
SELECT sname, SUBSTR(sname, 1, 5)
    FROM state
    WHERE code = "CA
```

Using the LPAD Function

Use the **LPAD** function to return a copy of a string that has been left padded with a sequence of characters that are repeated as many times as necessary or truncated, depending on the specified length of the padded portion of the string. Specify the source string, the length of the string to be returned, and the character string to serve as padding.

The data type of the source string and the character string that serves as padding can be any data type that converts to VARCHAR or NVARCHAR.

Query 4-37 shows an example of the **LPAD** function with a specified length of 21 bytes. Because the source string has a length of 15 bytes (**sname** is defined as CHAR(15)), the **LPAD** function pads the first six positions to the left of the source string.

Query 4-37

```
SELECT sname, LPAD(sname, 21, "-")
    FROM state
    WHERE code = "CA" OR code = "AZ"
```

Query Result 4-37

```
sname           (expression)

California      ------California
Arizona         ------Arizona
```

Using the RPAD Function

Use the **RPAD** function to return a copy of a string that has been right padded with a sequence of characters that are repeated as many times as necessary or truncated, depending on the specified length of the padded portion of the string. Specify the source string, the length of the string to be returned, and the character string to serve as padding.

The data type of the source string and the character string that serves as padding can be any data type that converts to VARCHAR or NVARCHAR.

Query 4-38 shows an example of the **RPAD** function with a specified length of 21 bytes. Because the source string has a length of 15 bytes (**sname** is defined as CHAR(15)), the **RPAD** function pads the first six positions to the right of the source string.

Query 4-38

```
SELECT sname, RPAD(sname, 21, "-")
    FROM state
    WHERE code = "WV" OR code = "AZ"
```

Query Result 4-38

```
sname           (expression)

West Virginia   West Virginia ------
Arizona         Arizona       ------
```

Other Functions

You can also use the **LENGTH, USER, CURRENT,** and **TODAY** functions anywhere in an SQL expression that you would use a constant. In addition, you can include the **DBSERVERNAME** function in a SELECT statement to display the name of the database server where the current database resides.

You can use these functions to select an expression that consists entirely of constant values or an expression that includes column data. In the first instance, the result is the same for all rows of output.

In addition, you can use the **HEX** function to return the hexadecimal encoding of an expression, the **ROUND** function to return the rounded value of an expression, and the **TRUNC** function to return the truncated value of an expression. For more information on the preceding functions, see the *Informix Guide to SQL: Syntax.*

Using the LENGTH Function

In Query 4-39, the **LENGTH** function calculates the number of bytes in the combined **fname** and **lname** columns for each row where the length of **company** is greater than 15.

Query 4-39

```
SELECT customer_num,
    LENGTH (fname) + LENGTH (lname) namelength
    FROM customer
    WHERE LENGTH (company) > 15
```

Query Result 4-39

customer_num	namelength
101	11
105	13
107	11
112	14
115	11
118	10
119	10
120	10
122	12
124	11
125	10
126	12
127	10
128	11

Although the **LENGTH** function might not be useful when you work with DB-Access or the Relational Object Manager, it can be important to determine the string length for programs and reports. The **LENGTH** function returns the clipped length of a CHARACTER or VARCHAR string and the full number of bytes in a TEXT or BYTE string.

Using the USER Function

Use the **USER** function when you want to define a restricted view of a table that contains only rows that include your user id. For information about how to create views, see the *Informix Guide to Database Design and Implementation* and the GRANT and CREATE VIEW statements in the *Informix Guide to SQL: Syntax*.

Query 4-40 returns the user name (login account name) of the user who executes the query. It is repeated once for each row in the table.

Query 4-40

```
SELECT * FROM cust_calls
    WHERE user_id = USER
```

If the user name of the current user is **richc**, Query 4-40 retrieves only those rows in the **cust_calls** table where user_id = richc, as Query Result 4-40 shows.

Query Result 4-40

```
customer_num  110
call_dtime    1998-07-07 10:24
user_id       richc
call_code     L
call_descr    Order placed one month ago (6/7) not received.
res_dtime     1998-07-07 10:30
res_descr     Checked with shipping (Ed Smith). Order sent yesterday- we
              were waiting for goods from ANZ. Next time will call with
              delay if necessary

customer_num  119
call_dtime    1998-07-01 15:00
user_id       richc
call_code     B
call_descr    Bill does not reflect credit from previous order
res_dtime     1998-07-02 08:21
res_descr     Spoke with Jane Akant in Finance. She found the error and is
              sending new bill to customer
```

Using the TODAY Function

The **TODAY** function returns the current system date. If Query 4-41 is issued when the current system date is July 10, 1998, it returns this one row.

```
SELECT * FROM orders
    WHERE order_date = TODAY
```

```
order_num      1018
order_date     07/10/1998
customer_num   121
ship_instruct  SW corner of Biltmore Mall
backlog        n
po_num         S22942
ship_date      07/13/1998
ship_weight    70.50
ship_charge    $20.00
paid_date      08/06/1998
```

Using the DBSERVERNAME and SITENAME Functions

You can include the function **DBSERVERNAME** (or its synonym, **SITENAME**) in a SELECT statement to find the name of the database server. You can query the **DBSERVERNAME** for any table that has rows, including system catalog tables.

In Query 4-42, you assign the label **server** to the **DBSERVERNAME** expression and also select the **tabid** column from the **systables** system catalog table. This table describes database tables, and **tabid** is the table identifier.

```
SELECT DBSERVERNAME server, tabid
    FROM systables
    WHERE tabid <= 4
```

```
server         tabid

montague       1
montague       2
montague       3
montague       4
```

The WHERE clause restricts the numbers of rows displayed. Otherwise, the database server name would be displayed once for each row of the **systables** table.

Using the HEX Function

In Query 4-43, the **HEX** function returns the hexadecimal format of three specified columns in the **customer** table, as Query Result 4-43 shows.

Query 4-43

```
SELECT HEX (customer_num) hexnum, HEX (zipcode) hexzip,
       HEX (rowid) hexrow
       FROM customer
```

Query Result 4-43

```
hexnum       hexzip      hexrow

0x00000065  0x00016F86  0x00000001
0x00000066  0x00016FA5  0x00000002
0x00000067  0x0001705F  0x00000003
0x00000068  0x00016F4A  0x00000004
0x00000069  0x00016F46  0x00000005
...
0x0000007D  0x00000857  0x00000019
0x0000007E  0x0001395B  0x0000001A
0x0000007F  0x0000EBF6  0x0000001B
0x00000080  0x00014C10  0x0000001C
```

For information about rowids, see "Using Rowid Values In SELECT Statements" on page 4-38.

Using the DBINFO Function

You can use the **DBINFO** function in a SELECT statement to find any of the following information:

- The name of a dbspace corresponding to a tablespace number or expression

- The last serial value inserted in a table

- The number of rows processed by selects, inserts, deletes, updates, and execute routine statements

IDS

- The session ID of the current session
- The name of the host computer on which the database server runs
- The exact version of the database server to which a client application is connected ◆

You can use the **DBINFO** function anywhere within SQL statements and within SPL routines.

Query 4-44 shows how you might use the **DBINFO** function to find out the name of the host computer on which the database server runs.

Query 4-44

```
SELECT DBINFO('dbhostname')
    FROM systables
    WHERE tabid = 1
```

Query Result 4-44

```
(constant)

lyceum
```

Without the WHERE clause to restrict the values in the **tabid**, the host name of the computer on which the database server runs would be repeated for each row of the **systables** table. Query 4-45 shows how you might use the **DBINFO** function to find out the complete version number and the type of the current database server.

Query 4-45

```
SELECT DBINFO('version','full')
    FROM systables
    WHERE tabid = 1
```

For more information about how to use the **DBINFO** function to find information about your current database server, database session, or database, see the *Informix Guide to SQL: Syntax*.

IDS

Using the DECODE Function

You can use the **DECODE** function to convert an expression of one value to another value. The **DECODE** function has the following form:

```
DECODE(test, a, a_value, b, b_value, ..., n, n_value, exp_m )
```

DECODE returns *a_value* when *a* equals *test*, and returns *b_value* when *b* equals *test*, and, in general, returns *n_value* when *n* equals *test*.

If several expressions match *test*, DECODE returns *n_value* for the first expression found. If no expression matches *test*, DECODE returns *exp_m*; if no expression matches *test* and there is no *exp_m*, DECODE returns NULL.

The DECODE function does not support arguments of type TEXT or BYTE.

Suppose an **employee** table exists that includes **emp_id** and **evaluation** columns. Suppose also that execution of Query 4-46 on the **employee** table returns the rows that Query Result 4-46 shows.

Query 4-46

```
SELECT emp_id, evaluation
    FROM employee
```

Query Result 4-46

emp_id	evaluation
012233	great
012344	poor
012677	NULL
012288	good
012555	very good

In some cases, you might want to convert a set of values. For example, suppose you want to convert the descriptive values of the **evaluation** column in the preceding example to corresponding numeric values. Query 4-47 shows how you might use the DECODE function to convert values from the **evaluation** column to numeric values for each row in the **employee** table.

Query 4-47

```
SELECT emp_id, DECODE(evaluation, "poor", 0, "fair", 25,
    "good", 50, "very good", 75, "great", 100, -1) AS evaluation
    FROM employee
```

Query Result 4-47

emp_id	evaluation
012233	100
012344	0
012677	-1
012288	50
012555	75

You can specify any data type for the arguments of the **DECODE** function provided that the arguments meet the following requirements:

- The arguments *test, a,b, ..., n* all have the same data type or evaluate to a common compatible data type.

- The arguments *a_value, b_value, ..., n_value* all have the same data type or evaluate to a common compatible data type.

Using the NVL Function

You can use the **NVL** function to convert an expression that evaluates to null to a value that you specify. The **NVL** function accepts two arguments: the first argument takes the name of the expression to be evaluated; the second argument specifies the value that the function returns when the first argument evaluates to null. If the first argument does not evaluate to null, the function returns the value of the first argument. Suppose a **student** table exists that includes **name** and **address** columns. Suppose also that execution of Query 4-48 on the **student** table returns the rows that Query Result 4-48 shows.

Query 4-48

```
SELECT name, address
     FROM student
```

Query Result 4-48

```
name            address

John Smith      333 Vista Drive
Lauren Collier  1129 Greenridge Street
Fred Frith      NULL
Susan Jordan    NULL
```

Query 4-49 includes the **NVL** function, which returns a new value for each row in the table where the **address** column contains a null value.

Query 4-49

```
SELECT name, NVL(address, "address is unknown") AS address
     FROM student
```

Query Result 4-49

```
name                address

John Smith          333 Vista Drive
Lauren Collier      1129 Greenridge Street
Fred Frith          address is unknown
Susan Jordan        address is unknown
```

You can specify any data type for the arguments of the **NVL** function provided that the two arguments evaluate to a common compatible data type.

If both arguments of the **NVL** function evaluate to null, the function returns null.

Using SPL Routines in SELECT Statements

Previous examples in this chapter show SELECT statement expressions that consist of column names, operators, and SQL functions. This section shows expressions that contain an SPL routine call.

SPL routines contain special Stored Procedure Language (SPL) statements as well as SQL statements. For more information on SPL routines, see Chapter 10.

IDS

Dynamic Server allows you to write external routines in C language. For more information, see *Extending Informix Dynamic Server 2000*. ◆

When you include an SPL routine expression in a select list, the SPL routine must be one that returns a single value (one column of one row). For example, the following statement is valid only if **test_func()** returns a single value:

```
SELECT col_a, test_func(col_b) FROM tab1
    WHERE col_c = "Davis"
```

SPL routines that return more than a single value are not supported in the select list of SELECT statements. In the preceding example, if **test_func()** returns more than one value, the database server returns an error message.

SPL routines provide a way to extend the range of functions available by allowing you to perform a subquery on each row you select.

For example, suppose you want a listing of the customer number, the customer's last name, and the number of orders the customer has made. Query 4-50 shows one way to retrieve this information. The **customer** table has **customer_num** and **lname** columns but no record of the number of orders each customer has made. You could write a **get_orders** routine, which queries the **orders** table for each **customer_num** and returns the number of corresponding orders (labeled **n_orders**).

Query 4-50

```
SELECT customer_num, lname, get_orders(customer_num) n_orders
      FROM customer
```

Query Result 4-50 shows the output from this SPL routine.

Query Result 4-50

```
customer_num lname n_orders

        101 Pauli      1
        102 Sadler     0
        103 Currie     0
        104 Higgins    4
...
        123 Hanlon     1
        124 Putnum     1
        125 Henry      0
        126 Neelie     1
        127 Satifer    1
        128 Lessor     0
```

Use SPL routines to encapsulate operations that you frequently perform in your queries. For example, the condition in Query 4-51 contains a routine, **conv_price**, that converts the unit price of a stock item to a different currency and adds any import tariffs.

Query 4-51

```
SELECT stock_num, manu_code, description
    FROM stock
    WHERE conv_price(unit_price, ex_rate = 1.50,
    tariff = 50.00) < 1000
```

Using Rowid Values In SELECT Statements

The database server assigns a unique rowid to rows in nonfragmented tables. However, rows in fragmented tables do not automatically contain the rowid column.

Informix recommends that you use primary keys as a method of access in your applications rather than rowids. Because primary keys are defined in the ANSI specification of SQL, using them to access data makes your applications more portable. In addition, the database server requires less time to access data in a fragmented table when it uses a primary key than it requires to access the same data when it uses rowid.

You can use a rowid to locate the internal record number that is associated with a row in a table. The rowid is, in effect, a hidden column in every table. The sequential values of rowid have no special significance and can vary depending on the location of the physical data in the chunk. Your rowid might vary from the following examples.

For more information about rowids, see the *Informix Guide to Database Design and Implementation* and your *Administrator's Guide*.

Query 4-52 uses the rowid and the wildcard asterisk symbol (*) in the SELECT clause to retrieve every row in the **manufact** table and their corresponding rowids.

Query 4-52

```
SELECT rowid, * FROM manufact
```

Query Result 4-52

```
rowid manu_code manu_name    lead_time

  257 SMT       Smith             3
  258 ANZ       Anza              5
  259 NRG       Norge             7
  260 HSK       Husky             5
  261 HRO       Hero              4
  262 SHM       Shimara          30
  263 KAR       Karsten          21
  264 NKL       Nikolus           8
  265 PRC       ProCycle          9
```

You can also use the rowid when you select a specific column, as Query 4-53 shows.

Query 4-53

```
SELECT rowid, manu_code FROM manufact
```

Query Result 4-53

```
    rowid manu_code

      258 ANZ
      261 HRO
      260 HSK
      263 KAR
      264 NKL
      259 NRG
      265 PRC
      262 SHM
      257 SMT
```

You can use the rowid in the WHERE clause to retrieve rows based on their internal record number. This method is handy when no other unique column exists in a table. Query 4-54 uses a rowid from Query 4-53.

Query 4-54

```
SELECT * FROM manufact WHERE rowid = 263
```

Query 4-54 returns the row that Query Result 4-54 shows.

Query Result 4-54

```
manu_code manu_name      lead_time

KAR       Karsten            21
```

Using Rowid Values with the USER Function

To obtain additional information about a table, you can combine the rowid with the **USER** function.

Query 4-55 assigns the label **username** to the USER expression column and returns this information about the **cust_calls** table.

Query 4-55

```
SELECT USER username, rowid FROM cust_calls
```

Query Result 4-55

```
username        rowid

zenda             257
zenda             258
zenda             259
zenda             513
zenda             514
zenda             515
zenda             769
```

You can also use the **USER** function in a WHERE clause when you select the rowid.

Query 4-56 returns the rowid for only those rows that are inserted or updated by the user who performs the query.

Query 4-56

```
SELECT rowid FROM cust_calls WHERE user_id = USER
```

For example, if the user **richc** uses Query 4-56, the output is as Query Result 4-56 shows.

Query Result 4-56

```
     rowid

       258
       259
```

Using Rowid Values with the DBSERVERNAME Function

You can add the **DBSERVERNAME** function (or its synonym, **SITENAME**) to a query to find out where the current database resides.

Query 4-57 finds the database server name and the user name as well as the rowid and the *tabid*, which is the serial-interval table identifier for system catalog tables.

Query 4-57

```
SELECT DBSERVERNAME server, tabid, rowid, USER username
    FROM systables
    WHERE tabid >= 105 OR rowid <= 260
    ORDER BY rowid
```

Query 4-57 assigns display labels to the **DBSERVERNAME** and **USER** expressions and returns the 10 rows from the **systables** system catalog table, as Query Result 4-57 shows.

Query Result 4-57

```
server         tabid       rowid username

manatee            1         257 zenda
manatee            2         258 zenda
manatee            3         259 zenda
manatee            4         260 zenda
manatee          105         274 zenda
manatee          106        1025 zenda
manatee          107        1026 zenda
manatee          108        1027 zenda
manatee          109        1028 zenda
manatee          110        1029 zenda
```

Never store a rowid in a *permanent* table or attempt to use it as a foreign key because the rowid can change. For example, if a table is dropped and then reloaded from external data, all the rowids are different.

Summary

This chapter introduced sample syntax and results for functions in basic SELECT statements to query a relational database and to manipulate the returned data. "Using Functions in SELECT Statements" on page 4-4 shows how to perform the following actions:

- Use the aggregate functions in the SELECT clause to calculate and retrieve specific data

- Include the time functions **DATE, DAY, MDY, MONTH, WEEKDAY, YEAR, CURRENT,** and **EXTEND** plus the **TODAY, LENGTH,** and **USER** functions in your SELECT statements

- Use functions to copy BLOB and CLOB data to and from columns and files

- Use conversion functions in the SELECT clause to convert between date and character values

- Use string-manipulation functions in the SELECT clause to convert between upper and lower case letters or to manipulate character strings in various ways

"Using SPL Routines in SELECT Statements" on page 4-36 shows how to include SPL routines in your SELECT statements.

"Using Rowid Values In SELECT Statements" on page 4-38 shows how to use the rowid to retrieve internal record numbers from tables and system catalog tables and discusses the internal table identifier or tabid.

Composing Advanced SELECT Statements

In This Chapter 5-3

Using the GROUP BY and HAVING Clauses 5-4
   Using the GROUP BY Clause 5-5
   Using the HAVING Clause 5-8

Creating Advanced Joins 5-11
   Self-Joins 5-11
   Outer Joins 5-15
      Simple Join 5-16
      Simple Outer Join on Two Tables 5-17
      Outer Join for a Simple Join to a Third Table 5-18
      Outer Join of Two Tables to a Third Table 5-18
      Joins That Combine Outer Joins 5-19

Subqueries in SELECT Statements 5-20
   Subqueries in a Select List 5-22
   Subqueries in WHERE Clauses 5-22
      Using ALL 5-23
      Using ANY 5-24
      Single-Valued Subqueries 5-24
      Correlated Subqueries 5-26
      Using EXISTS 5-27

Handling Collections in SELECT Statements 5-30
   Collection Subqueries 5-30
      Omitting the Item Keyword in a Collection Subquery 5-31
      Specifying the ITEM Keyword in a Collection Subquery . . . 5-32
   Collection-Derived Tables 5-32

Set Operations 5-34
    Union 5-35
    Difference 5-43

Summary 5-44

In This Chapter

This chapter increases the scope of what you can do with the SELECT statement and enables you to perform more complex database queries and data manipulation.

Whereas Chapter 2 focused on five of the clauses in the SELECT statement syntax, this chapter adds two more: the GROUP BY clause and the HAVING clause. You can use the GROUP BY clause with aggregate functions to organize rows returned by the FROM clause. You can include a HAVING clause to place conditions on the values that the GROUP BY clause returns.

This chapter also extends the earlier discussion of joins. It illustrates *self-joins*, which enable you to join a table to itself, and four kinds of *outer joins*, in which you apply the keyword OUTER to treat two or more joined tables unequally. It also introduces correlated and uncorrelated subqueries and their operational keywords, shows how to combine queries with the UNION operator, and defines the set operations known as union, intersection, and difference.

Examples in this chapter show how to use some or all of the SELECT statement clauses in your queries. The clauses must appear in the following order:

1. SELECT
2. FROM
3. WHERE
4. GROUP BY
5. HAVING
6. ORDER BY
7. INTO TEMP

For an example of a SELECT statement that uses all these clauses in the correct order, see Query 5-8 on page 5-10.

An additional SELECT statement clause, INTO, which you can use to specify program and host variables in SQL APIs, is described in Chapter 7 as well as in the manuals that come with the product.

Using the GROUP BY and HAVING Clauses

The optional GROUP BY and HAVING clauses add functionality to your SELECT statement. You can include one or both in a basic SELECT statement to increase your ability to manipulate aggregates.

The GROUP BY clause combines similar rows, producing a single result row for each *group* of rows that have the same values for each column listed in the select list. The HAVING clause sets conditions on those groups after you form them. You can use a GROUP BY clause without a HAVING clause, or a HAVING clause without a GROUP BY clause.

IDS

The GROUP BY and HAVING clauses support only *hashable* data types. With a hashable data type, the built-in hashing function that the database server provides is sufficient to hash the data. For a hashable data type, the database server takes the data, byte by byte, and processes it to derive a hash value. In contrast, an opaque data type that is defined with the CANNOTHASH modifier is not hashable.

Any complex data type that contains only hashable types is hashable. However, if an opaque type **my_udt** is defined as not hashable, then any row type or collection data type that contains **my_udt** is not hashable. For example, values of type ROW(a INT, b my_udt) or SET(my_udt NOT NULL) would not be allowed in a GROUP BY or HAVING clause because the data types are not hashable. In addition, BLOB and CLOB data types are not hashable types and are not allowed in a GROUP BY or HAVING clause. ♦

Using the GROUP BY Clause

The GROUP BY clause divides a table into sets. This clause is most often combined with aggregate functions that produce summary values for each of those sets. Some examples in Chapter 2 show the use of aggregate functions applied to a whole table. This chapter illustrates aggregate functions applied to groups of rows.

Using the GROUP BY clause without aggregates is much like using the DISTINCT (or UNIQUE) keyword in the SELECT clause. Query 5-1 is described in "Selecting Specific Columns" on page 2-17.

Query 5-1

```
SELECT DISTINCT customer_num FROM orders
```

You could also write the statement as Query 5-1a shows.

Query 5-1a

```
SELECT customer_num
    FROM orders
    GROUP BY customer_num
```

Query 5-1 and Query 5-1a return the rows that Query Result 5-1 shows.

Query Result 5-1

```
customer_num

         101
         104
         106
         110
          .
          .
          .
         124
         126
         127
```

The GROUP BY clause collects the rows into sets so that each row in each set has equal customer numbers. With no other columns selected, the result is a list of the unique **customer_num** values.

The power of the GROUP BY clause is more apparent when you use it with aggregate functions.

Query 5-2 retrieves the number of items and the total price of all items for each order.

```
SELECT order_num, COUNT (*) number, SUM (total_price) price
    FROM items
    GROUP BY order_num
```

The GROUP BY clause causes the rows of the **items** table to be collected into groups, each group composed of rows that have identical **order_num** values (that is, the items of each order are grouped together). After you form the groups, the aggregate functions COUNT and SUM are applied within each group.

Query 5-2 returns one row for each group. It uses labels to give names to the results of the COUNT and SUM expressions, as Query Result 5-2 shows.

order_num	number	price
1001	1	$250.00
1002	2	$1200.00
1003	3	$959.00
1004	4	$1416.00
⋮		
1021	4	$1614.00
1022	3	$232.00
1023	6	$824.00

Query Result 5-2 collects the rows of the **items** table into groups that have identical order numbers and computes the COUNT of rows in each group and the sum of the prices.

You cannot include a TEXT or BYTE column in a GROUP BY clause. To *group*, you must be able to *sort*, and no natural sort order exists for TEXT or BYTE data.

Unlike the ORDER BY clause, the GROUP BY clause does not order data. Include an ORDER BY clause *after* your GROUP BY clause if you want to sort data in a particular order or sort on an aggregate in the select list.

Query 5-3 is the same as Query 5-2 but includes an ORDER BY clause to sort the retrieved rows in ascending order of **price**, as Query Result 5-3 shows.

Query 5-3

```
SELECT order_num, COUNT(*) number, SUM (total_price) price
    FROM items
    GROUP BY order_num
    ORDER BY price
```

Query Result 5-3

order_num	number	price
1010	2	$84.00
1011	1	$99.00
1013	4	$143.80
1022	3	$232.00
1001	1	$250.00
1020	2	$438.00
1006	5	$448.00
⋮		
1002	2	$1200.00
1004	4	$1416.00
1014	2	$1440.00
1019	1	$1499.97
1021	4	$1614.00
1007	5	$1696.00

The section "Selecting Specific Columns" on page 2-17 describes how to use an integer in an ORDER BY clause to indicate the position of a column in the select list. You can also use an integer in a GROUP BY clause to indicate the position of column names or display labels in the group list.

Query 5-4 returns the same rows as Query 5-3, as Query Result 5-3 shows.

Query 5-4

```
SELECT order_num, COUNT(*) number, SUM (total_price) price
    FROM items
    GROUP BY 1
    ORDER BY 3
```

When you build a query, remember that all nonaggregate columns that are in the select list in the SELECT clause must also be included in the group list in the GROUP BY clause. The reason is that a SELECT statement with a GROUP BY clause must return only one row per group. Columns that are listed after GROUP BY are certain to reflect only one distinct value within a group, and that value can be returned. However, a column not listed after GROUP BY might contain different values in the rows that are contained in a group.

Query 5-5 shows how to use the GROUP BY clause in a SELECT statement that joins tables.

```
SELECT o.order_num, SUM (i.total_price)
    FROM orders o, items i
    WHERE o.order_date > '01/01/98'
        AND o.customer_num = 110
        AND o.order_num = i.order_num
    GROUP BY o.order_num
```

Query 5-5 joins the **orders** and **items** tables, assigns table aliases to them, and returns the rows that Query Result 5-5 shows.

```
    order_num              (sum)

         1008          $940.00
         1015          $450.00
```

Using the HAVING Clause

To complement a GROUP BY clause, use a HAVING clause to apply one or more qualifying conditions to groups after they are formed. The effect of the HAVING clause on groups is similar to the way the WHERE clause qualifies individual rows. One advantage of using a HAVING clause is that you can include aggregates in the search condition, whereas you cannot include aggregates in the search condition of a WHERE clause.

Each HAVING condition compares one column or aggregate expression of the group with another aggregate expression of the group or with a constant. You can use HAVING to place conditions on both column values and aggregate values in the group list.

Query 5-6 returns the average total price per item on all orders that have more than two items. The HAVING clause tests each group as it is formed and selects those that are composed of more than two rows.

```
SELECT order_num, COUNT(*) number, AVG (total_price) average
    FROM items
    GROUP BY order_num
    HAVING COUNT(*) > 2
```

Query Result 5-6

```
order_num        number          average

       1003          3          $319.67
       1004          4          $354.00
       1005          4          $140.50
       1006          5           $89.60
       1007          5          $339.20
       1013          4           $35.95
       1016          4          $163.50
       1017          3          $194.67
       1018          5          $226.20
       1021          4          $403.50
       1022          3           $77.33
       1023          6          $137.33
```

If you use a HAVING clause without a GROUP BY clause, the HAVING condition applies to all rows that satisfy the search condition. In other words, all rows that satisfy the search condition make up a single group.

Query 5-7, a modified version of Query 5-6, returns just one row, the average of all **total_price** values in the table, as Query Result 5-7 shows.

Query 5-7

```
SELECT AVG (total_price) average
    FROM items
    HAVING count(*) > 2
```

Query Result 5-7

```
        average

      $270.97
```

If Query 5-7, like Query 5-6, had included the nonaggregate column **order_ num** in the select list, you would have to include a GROUP BY clause with that column in the group list. In addition, if the condition in the HAVING clause was not satisfied, the output would show the column heading and a message would indicate that no rows were found.

Query 5-8 contains all the SELECT statement clauses that you can use in the Informix version of interactive SQL (the INTO clause that names host variables is available only in an SQL API).

Query 5-8

```
SELECT o.order_num, SUM (i.total_price) price,
     paid_date - order_date span
   FROM orders o, items i
   WHERE o.order_date > '01/01/98'
     AND o.customer_num > 110
     AND o.order_num = i.order_num
   GROUP BY 1, 3
   HAVING COUNT (*) < 5
   ORDER BY 3
   INTO TEMP temptab1
```

Query 5-8 joins the **orders** and **items** tables; employs display labels, table aliases, and integers that are used as column indicators; groups and orders the data; and puts the results in a temporary table, as Query Result 5-8 shows.

Query Result 5-8

order_num	price	span
1017	$584.00	
1016	$654.00	
1012	$1040.00	
1019	$1499.97	26
1005	$562.00	28
1021	$1614.00	30
1022	$232.00	40
1010	$84.00	66
1009	$450.00	68
1020	$438.00	71

Creating Advanced Joins

The section "Creating a Join" on page 2-58 shows how to include a WHERE clause in a SELECT statement to join two or more tables on one or more columns. It illustrates natural joins and equi-joins.

This chapter discusses how to use two more complex kinds of joins, self-joins and outer joins. As described for simple joins, you can define aliases for tables and assign display labels to expressions to shorten your multiple-table queries. You can also issue a SELECT statement with an ORDER BY clause that sorts data into a temporary table.

Self-Joins

A join does not always have to involve two different tables. You can join a table to itself, creating a *self-join*. Joining a table to itself can be useful when you want to compare values in a column to other values in the same column.

To create a self-join, list a table twice in the FROM clause, and assign it a different alias each time. Use the aliases to refer to the table in the SELECT and WHERE clauses as if it were two separate tables. (Aliases in SELECT statements are discussed in "Using Aliases" on page 2-64 and in the *Informix Guide to SQL: Syntax*.)

Just as in joins between tables, you can use arithmetic expressions in self-joins. You can test for null values, and you can use an ORDER BY clause to sort the values in a specified column in ascending or descending order.

Query 5-9 finds pairs of orders where the **ship_weight** differs by a factor of five or more and the **ship_date** is not null. The query then orders the data by **ship_date**.

Query 5-9

```
SELECT x.order_num, x.ship_weight, x.ship_date,
       y.order_num, y.ship_weight, y.ship_date
    FROM orders x, orders y
    WHERE x.ship_weight >= 5 * y.ship_weight
        AND x.ship_date IS NOT NULL
        AND y.ship_date IS NOT NULL
    ORDER BY x.ship_date
```

```
order_num ship_weight ship_date    order_num ship_weight ship_date

     1004      95.80 05/30/1998          1011      10.40 07/03/1998
     1004      95.80 05/30/1998          1020      14.00 07/16/1998
     1004      95.80 05/30/1998          1022      15.00 07/30/1998
     1007     125.90 06/05/1998          1015      20.60 07/16/1998
     1007     125.90 06/05/1998          1020      14.00 07/16/1998
...
```

If you want to store the results of a self-join into a temporary table, append an INTO TEMP clause to the SELECT statement and assign display labels to at least one set of columns to rename them. Otherwise, the duplicate column names cause an error and the temporary table is not created.

Query 5-10, which is similar to Query 5-9, labels all columns selected from the **orders** table and puts them in a temporary table called **shipping**.

```
SELECT x.order_num orders1, x.po_num purch1,
       x.ship_date ship1, y.order_num orders2,
       y.po_num purch2, y.ship_date ship2
    FROM orders x, orders y
    WHERE x.ship_weight >= 5 * y.ship_weight
        AND x.ship_date IS NOT NULL
        AND y.ship_date IS NOT NULL
    ORDER BY orders1, orders2
    INTO TEMP shipping
```

If you query with SELECT * from table **shipping**, you see the rows that Query Result 5-10 shows.

```
orders1 purch1     ship1      orders2 purch2     ship2

   1004 8006       05/30/1998    1011 B77897     07/03/1998
   1004 8006       05/30/1998    1020 W2286      07/16/1998
   1004 8006       05/30/1998    1022 W9925      07/30/1998
   1005 2865       06/09/1998    1011 B77897     07/03/1998
...
   1019 Z55709     07/16/1998    1020 W2286      07/16/1998
   1019 Z55709     07/16/1998    1022 W9925      07/30/1998
   1023 KF2961     07/30/1998    1011 B77897     07/03/1998
```

You can join a table to itself more than once. The maximum number of self-joins depends on the resources available to you.

The self-join in Query 5-11 creates a list of those items in the **stock** table that are supplied by three manufacturers. The self-join includes the last two conditions in the WHERE clause to eliminate duplicate manufacturer codes in rows that are retrieved.

Query 5-11

```
SELECT s1.manu_code, s2.manu_code, s3.manu_code,
       s1.stock_num, s1.description
    FROM stock s1, stock s2, stock s3
    WHERE s1.stock_num = s2.stock_num
        AND s2.stock_num = s3.stock_num
        AND s1.manu_code < s2.manu_code
        AND s2.manu_code < s3.manu_code
    ORDER BY stock_num
```

Query Result 5-11

```
manu_code  manu_code  manu_code  stock_num  description

HRO        HSK        SMT                1  baseball gloves
ANZ        NRG        SMT                5  tennis racquet
ANZ        HRO        HSK              110  helmet
ANZ        HRO        PRC              110  helmet
ANZ        HRO        SHM              110  helmet
ANZ        HSK        PRC              110  helmet
ANZ        HSK        SHM              110  helmet
ANZ        PRC        SHM              110  helmet
HRO        HSK        PRC              110  helmet
HRO        HSK        SHM              110  helmet
HRO        PRC        SHM              110  helmet
...
KAR        NKL        PRC              301  running shoes
KAR        NKL        SHM              301  running shoes
KAR        PRC        SHM              301  running shoes
NKL        PRC        SHM              301  running shoes
```

If you want to select rows from a payroll table to determine which employees earn more than their manager, you can construct the self-join that Query 5-12a shows.

Query 5-12a

```
SELECT emp.employee_num, emp.gross_pay, emp.level,
       emp.dept_num, mgr.employee_num, mgr.gross_pay,
       mgr.dept_num, mgr.level
    FROM payroll emp, payroll mgr
    WHERE emp.gross_pay > mgr.gross_pay
        AND emp.level < mgr.level
        AND emp.dept_num = mgr.dept_num
    ORDER BY 4
```

Query 5-12b uses a *correlated subquery* to retrieve and list the 10 highest-priced items ordered.

Query 5-12b

```
SELECT order_num, total_price
    FROM items a
    WHERE 10 >
        (SELECT COUNT (*)
            FROM items b
            WHERE b.total_price < a.total_price)
    ORDER BY total_price
```

Query 5-12b returns the 10 rows that Query Result 5-12 shows.

Query Result 5-12

```
order_num    total_price

    1018     $15.00
    1013     $19.80
    1003     $20.00
    1005     $36.00
    1006     $36.00
    1013     $36.00
    1010     $36.00
    1013     $40.00
    1022     $40.00
    1023     $40.00
```

You can create a similar query to find and list the 10 employees in the company who have the most seniority.

Correlated and uncorrelated subqueries are described in "Subqueries in SELECT Statements" on page 5-20.

You can use the hidden *rowid* column in a self-join to locate duplicate values in a table. In the following example, the condition x.rowid != y.rowid is equivalent to saying "row *x* is not the same row as row *y*."

Query 5-13 selects data twice from the **cust_calls** table, assigning it the table aliases **x** and **y**.

Query 5-13

```
SELECT x.rowid, x.customer_num
    FROM cust_calls x, cust_calls y
    WHERE x.customer_num = y.customer_num
        AND x.rowid != y.rowid
```

Query 5-13 searches for duplicate values in the **customer_num** column and for their rowids, finding the pair that Query Result 5-13 shows.

```
rowid customer_num

  515        116
  769        116
```

For information about rowids, see "Using Rowid Values In SELECT Statements" on page 2-52.

Outer Joins

The section "Creating a Join" on page 2-58 shows how to create and use some simple joins. Whereas a simple join treats two or more joined tables equally, an *outer join* treats two or more joined tables *asymmetrically.* An outer join makes one of the tables *dominant* (also called *preserved*) over the other *subservient* tables.

The database server supports the following three basic types of outer joins:

- A simple outer join on two tables
- An outer join for a simple join to a third table
- An outer join of two tables to a third table

This section discusses these types of outer joins. For more information on the syntax, use, and logic of outer joins, see the *Informix Guide to SQL: Syntax.*

In a *simple join,* the result contains only the combinations of rows from the tables that satisfy the join conditions. *Rows that do not satisfy the join conditions are discarded.*

In an *outer join,* the result contains the combinations of rows from the tables that satisfy the join conditions. In addition, the result preserves rows from the dominant table that would otherwise be discarded because no matching row was found in the subservient table. The dominant-table rows that do not have a matching subservient-table row receive nulls for the columns of the subservient table.

An outer join applies conditions to the subservient table while it sequentially applies the join conditions to the rows of the dominant table. The conditions are expressed in a WHERE clause.

An outer join must have a SELECT clause, a FROM clause, and a WHERE clause. To transform a simple join into an outer join, insert the keyword OUTER directly before the name of the subservient tables in the FROM clause. As shown later in this section, you can include the OUTER keyword more than once in your query.

Before you use outer joins heavily, determine whether one or more simple joins can work. You can often use a simple join when you do not need supplemental information from other tables.

The examples in this section use table aliases for brevity. The section "Using Aliases" on page 2-64 discusses table aliases.

Simple Join

Query 5-14 is an example of a simple join on the **customer** and **cust_calls** tables.

Query 5-14

```
SELECT c.customer_num, c.lname, c.company,
       c.phone, u.call_dtime, u.call_descr
   FROM customer c, cust_calls u
   WHERE c.customer_num = u.customer_num
```

Query 5-14 returns only those rows in which the customer has made a call to customer service, as Query Result 5-14 shows.

Query Result 5-14

```
customer_num  106
lname         Watson
company       Watson & Son
phone         415-389-8789
call_dtime    1998-06-12 08:20
call_descr    Order was received, but two of the cans of
              ANZ tennis balls within the case were empty

...

customer_num  116
lname         Parmelee
company       Olympic City
phone         415-534-8822
call_dtime    1997-12-21 11:24
call_descr    Second complaint from this customer! Received
              two cases right-handed outfielder gloves (1 HRO)
              instead of one case lefties.
```

Simple Outer Join on Two Tables

Query 5-15 uses the same select list, tables, and comparison condition as the preceding example, but this time it creates a simple outer join.

```
SELECT c.customer_num, c.lname, c.company,
       c.phone, u.call_dtime, u.call_descr
   FROM customer c, OUTER cust_calls u
   WHERE c.customer_num = u.customer_num
```

The addition of the keyword OUTER before the **cust_calls** table makes it the subservient table. An outer join causes the query to return information on *all* customers, whether or not they have made calls to customer service. All rows from the dominant **customer** table are retrieved, and null values are assigned to columns of the subservient **cust_calls** table, as Query Result 5-15 shows.

```
customer_num   101
lname          Pauli
company        All Sports Supplies
phone          408-789-8075
call_dtime
call_descr

customer_num   102
lname          Sadler
company        Sports Spot
phone          415-822-1289
call_dtime
call_descr
...
customer_num   107
lname          Ream
company        Athletic Supplies
phone          415-356-9876
call_dtime
call_descr

customer_num   108
lname          Quinn
company        Quinn's Sports
phone          415-544-8729
call_dtime
call_descr
```

Outer Join for a Simple Join to a Third Table

Query 5-16 shows an outer join that is the result of a simple join to a third table. This second type of outer join is known as a *nested simple join*.

Query 5-16

```
SELECT c.customer_num, c.lname, o.order_num,
    i.stock_num, i.manu_code, i.quantity
    FROM customer c, OUTER (orders o, items i)
    WHERE c.customer_num = o.customer_num
        AND o.order_num = i.order_num
        AND manu_code IN ('KAR', 'SHM')
    ORDER BY lname
```

Query 5-16 first performs a simple join on the **orders** and **items** tables, retrieving information on all orders for items with a **manu_code** of KAR or SHM. It then performs an outer join to combine this information with data from the dominant **customer** table. An optional ORDER BY clause reorganizes the data into the form that Query Result 5-16 shows.

Query Result 5-16

```
customer_num lname              order_num stock_num manu_code quantity

         114 Albertson
         118 Baxter
         113 Beatty
...
         105 Vector
         121 Wallack            1018      302       KAR              3
         106 Watson
```

Outer Join of Two Tables to a Third Table

Query 5-17 shows an outer join that is the result of an outer join of each of two tables to a third table. In this third type of outer join, join relationships are possible *only* between the dominant table and the subservient tables.

Query 5-17

```
SELECT c.customer_num, lname, o.order_num,
    order_date, call_dtime
    FROM customer c, OUTER orders o, OUTER cust_calls x
    WHERE c.customer_num = o.customer_num
        AND c.customer_num = x.customer_num
    ORDER BY lname
    INTO TEMP service
```

Query 5-17 individually joins the subservient tables **orders** and **cust_calls** to the dominant **customer** table; it does not join the two subservient tables. An INTO TEMP clause selects the results into a temporary table for further manipulation or queries, as Query Result 5-17 shows.

Query Result 5-17

```
customer_num lname              order_num order_date call_dtime

         114 Albertson
         118 Baxter
         113 Beatty
         103 Currie
         115 Grant                   1010 06/17/1998
  ...
         117 Sipes                   1012 06/18/1998
         105 Vector
         121 Wallack                 1018 07/10/1998 1998-07-10 14:05
         106 Watson                  1004 05/22/1998 1998-06-12 08:20
         106 Watson                  1014 06/25/1998 1998-06-12 08:20
```

If Query 5-17 had tried to create a join condition between the two subservient tables **o** and **x**, as Query 5-18 shows, an error message would indicate the creation of a two-sided outer join.

Query 5-18

```
WHERE o.customer_num = x.customer_num
```

Joins That Combine Outer Joins

To achieve multiple levels of nesting, you can create a join that employs any combination of the three types of outer joins. Query 5-19 creates a join that is the result of a combination of a simple outer join on two tables and a second outer join.

Query 5-19

```
SELECT c.customer_num, lname, o.order_num,
       stock_num, manu_code, quantity
    FROM customer c, OUTER (orders o, OUTER items i)
    WHERE c.customer_num = o.customer_num
        AND o.order_num = i.order_num
        AND manu_code IN ('KAR', 'SHM')
    ORDER BY lname
```

Query 5-19 first performs an outer join on the **orders** and **items** tables, retrieving information on all orders for items with a **manu_code** of KAR or SHM. It then performs a second outer join that combines this information with data from the dominant **customer** table.

Query Result 5-19

```
customer_num lname                order_num stock_num manu_code quantity

         114 Albertson
         118 Baxter
         113 Beatty
         103 Currie
         115 Grant                  1010
...
         117 Sipes                  1012
         117 Sipes                  1007
         105 Vector
         121 Wallack                1018      302 KAR             3
         106 Watson                 1014
         106 Watson                 1004
```

You can state the join conditions in two ways when you apply an outer join to the result of an outer join to a third table. The two subservient tables are joined, but you can join the dominant table to either subservient table without affecting the results if the dominant table and the subservient table share a common column.

Subqueries in SELECT Statements

The following situations define the types of subqueries the database server supports:

- A SELECT statement nested in the SELECT list of another SELECT statement

- A SELECT statement nested in the WHERE clause of another SELECT statement (or in an INSERT, DELETE, or UPDATE statement)

Each subquery must contain a SELECT clause and a FROM clause. Subqueries can be *correlated* or *uncorrelated*. A subquery (or *inner* SELECT statement) is correlated when the value it produces depends on a value produced by the *outer* SELECT statement that contains it. Any other kind of subquery is considered uncorrelated.

The important feature of a correlated subquery is that, because it depends on a value from the outer SELECT, it must be executed repeatedly, once for every value that the outer SELECT produces. An uncorrelated subquery is executed only once.

You can construct a SELECT statement with a subquery to replace two separate SELECT statements.

Subqueries in SELECT statements allow you to perform the following actions:

- Compare an expression to the result of another SELECT statement
- Determine whether the results of another SELECT statement include an expression
- Determine whether another SELECT statement selects any rows

An optional WHERE clause in a subquery is often used to narrow the search condition.

A subquery selects and returns values to the first or outer SELECT statement. A subquery can return no value, a single value, or a set of values, as follows:

- If a subquery returns *no* value, the query does not return any rows. Such a subquery is equivalent to a null value.
- If a subquery returns *one* value, the value is in the form of either one aggregate expression or exactly one row and one column. Such a subquery is equivalent to a single number or character value.
- If a subquery returns a list or *set* of values, the values represent either one row or one column.

Subqueries in a Select List

A subquery can occur in the select list of another SELECT statement. Query 5-20 shows how you might use a subquery in a select list to return the total shipping charges (from the **orders** table) for each customer in the **customer** table. You could also write this query as a join between two tables.

Query 5-20

```
SELECT customer.customer_num,
    (SELECT SUM(ship_charge)
       FROM orders
          WHERE customer.customer_num = orders.customer_num)
             AS total_ship_chg
    FROM customer
```

Query Result 5-20

```
customer_num total_ship_chg

101            $15.30
102
103
104            $38.00
105
...
123             $8.50
124            $12.00
125
126            $13.00
127            $18.00
128
```

Subqueries in WHERE Clauses

This section describes subqueries that occur as a SELECT statement *nested* in the WHERE clause of another SELECT statement.

The following keywords introduce a subquery in the WHERE clause of a SELECT statement:

- ALL
- ANY
- IN
- EXISTS

You can use any relational operator with ALL and ANY to compare something to every one of (ALL) or to any one of (ANY) the values that the subquery produces. You can use the keyword SOME in place of ANY. The operator IN is equivalent to = ANY. To create the opposite search condition, use the keyword NOT or a different relational operator.

The EXISTS operator tests a subquery to see if it found any values; that is, it asks if the result of the subquery is not null. You cannot use the EXISTS keyword in a subquery that contains a column with a TEXT or BYTE data type.

For the syntax that you use to create a condition with a subquery, see the *Informix Guide to SQL: Syntax.*

Using ALL

Use the keyword ALL preceding a subquery to determine whether a comparison is true for every value returned. If the subquery returns no values, the search condition is *true*. (If it returns no values, the condition is true of all the zero values.)

Query 5-21 lists the following information for all orders that contain an item for which the total price is less than the total price on *every* item in order number 1023.

Query 5-21

```
SELECT order_num, stock_num, manu_code, total_price
    FROM items
    WHERE total_price < ALL
        (SELECT total_price FROM items
            WHERE order_num = 1023)
```

Query Result 5-21

order_num	stock_num	manu_code	total_price
1003	9	ANZ	$20.00
1005	6	SMT	$36.00
1006	6	SMT	$36.00
1010	6	SMT	$36.00
1013	5	ANZ	$19.80
1013	6	SMT	$36.00
1018	302	KAR	$15.00

Using ANY

Use the keyword ANY (or its synonym SOME) before a subquery to determine whether a comparison is true for at least one of the values returned. If the subquery returns no values, the search condition is *false*. (Because no values exist, the condition cannot be true for one of them.)

Query 5-22 finds the order number of all orders that contain an item for which the total price is greater than the total price of *any one* of the items in order number 1005.

Query 5-22

```
SELECT DISTINCT order_num
    FROM items
    WHERE total_price > ANY
        (SELECT total_price
            FROM items
            WHERE order_num = 1005)
```

Query Result 5-22

```
order_num

     1001
     1002
     1003
     1004
...
     1020
     1021
     1022
     1023
```

Single-Valued Subqueries

You do not need to include the keyword ALL or ANY if you know the subquery can return *exactly one value* to the outer-level query. A subquery that returns exactly one value can be treated like a function. This kind of subquery often uses an aggregate function because aggregate functions always return single values.

Subqueries in WHERE Clauses

Query 5-23 uses the aggregate function **MAX** in a subquery to find the
order_num for orders that include the maximum number of volleyball nets.

Query 5-23

```
SELECT order_num FROM items
    WHERE stock_num = 9
        AND quantity =
            (SELECT MAX (quantity)
                FROM items
                WHERE stock_num = 9)
```

Query Result 5-23

```
order_num

    1012
```

Query 5-24 uses the aggregate function **MIN** in the subquery to select items
for which the total price is higher than 10 times the minimum price.

Query 5-24

```
SELECT order_num, stock_num, manu_code, total_price
    FROM items x
    WHERE total_price >
        (SELECT 10 * MIN (total_price)
            FROM items
            WHERE order_num = x.order_num)
```

Query Result 5-24

```
order_num stock_num manu_code   total_price

    1003        8 ANZ           $840.00
    1018      307 PRC           $500.00
    1018      110 PRC           $236.00
    1018      304 HRO           $280.00
```

Composing Advanced SELECT Statements   **5-25**

Correlated Subqueries

Query 5-25 is an example of a correlated subquery that returns a list of the 10 latest shipping dates in the **orders** table. It includes an ORDER BY clause after the subquery to order the results because you cannot include ORDER BY within a subquery.

Query 5-25

```
SELECT po_num, ship_date FROM orders main
    WHERE 10 >
        (SELECT COUNT (DISTINCT ship_date)
            FROM orders sub
            WHERE sub.ship_date < main.ship_date)
    AND ship_date IS NOT NULL
    ORDER BY ship_date, po_num
```

The subquery is correlated because the number that it produces depends on **main.ship_date**, a value that the outer SELECT produces. Thus, the subquery must be re-executed for every row that the outer query considers.

Query 5-25 uses the **COUNT** function to return a value to the main query. The ORDER BY clause then orders the data. The query locates and returns the 16 rows that have the 10 latest shipping dates, as Query Result 5-25 shows.

Query Result 5-25

```
po_num     ship_date

4745       06/21/1998
278701     06/29/1998
4290       06/29/1998
8052       07/03/1998
B77897     07/03/1998
LZ230      07/06/1998
B77930     07/10/1998
PC6782     07/12/1998
DM354331   07/13/1998
S22942     07/13/1998
MA003      07/16/1998
W2286      07/16/1998
Z55709     07/16/1998
C3288      07/25/1998
KF2961     07/30/1998
W9925      07/30/1998
```

If you use a correlated subquery, such as Query 5-25, on a large table, you should index the **ship_date** column to improve performance. Otherwise, this SELECT statement is inefficient because it executes the subquery once for every row of the table. For information about indexing and performance issues, see the *Administrator's Guide* and your *Performance Guide*.

Using EXISTS

The keyword EXISTS is known as an *existential qualifier* because the subquery is true only if the outer SELECT, as Query 5-26a shows, finds at least one row.

Query 5-26a

```
SELECT UNIQUE manu_name, lead_time
    FROM manufact
    WHERE EXISTS
        (SELECT * FROM stock
            WHERE description MATCHES '*shoe*'
                AND manufact.manu_code = stock.manu_code)
```

You can often construct a query with EXISTS that is equivalent to one that uses IN. Query 5-26b uses an IN predicate to construct a query that returns the same result as Query 5-26a.

Query 5-26b

```
SELECT UNIQUE manu_name, lead_time
    FROM stock, manufact
    WHERE manufact.manu_code IN
        (SELECT manu_code FROM stock
            WHERE description MATCHES '*shoe*')
                AND stock.manu_code = manufact.manu_code
```

Query 5-26a and Query 5-26b return rows for the manufacturers that produce a kind of shoe as well as the lead time for ordering the product. Query Result 5-26 shows the return values.

Query Result 5-26

```
manu_name       lead_time

Anza             5
Hero             4
Karsten         21
Nikolus          8
ProCycle         9
Shimara         30
```

Add the keyword NOT to IN or to EXISTS to create a search condition that is the opposite of the condition in the preceding queries. You can also substitute !=ALL for NOT IN.

Query 5-27 shows two ways to do the same thing. One way might allow the database server to do less work than the other, depending on the design of the database and the size of the tables. To find out which query might be better, use the SET EXPLAIN command to get a listing of the query plan. SET EXPLAIN is discussed in your *Performance Guide* and the *Informix Guide to SQL: Syntax*.

Query 5-27

```
SELECT customer_num, company FROM customer
    WHERE customer_num NOT IN
        (SELECT customer_num FROM orders
            WHERE customer.customer_num = orders.customer_num)

SELECT customer_num, company FROM customer
    WHERE NOT EXISTS
        (SELECT * FROM orders
            WHERE customer.customer_num = orders.customer_num)
```

Each statement in Query 5-27 returns the rows that Query Result 5-27 shows, which identify customers who have not placed orders.

Query Result 5-27

```
customer_num company

         102 Sports Spot
         103 Phil's Sports
         105 Los Altos Sports
         107 Athletic Supplies
         108 Quinn's Sports
         109 Sport Stuff
         113 Sportstown
         114 Sporting Place
         118 Blue Ribbon Sports
         125 Total Fitness Sports
         128 Phoenix University
```

The keywords EXISTS and IN are used for the set operation known as *intersection*, and the keywords NOT EXISTS and NOT IN are used for the set operation known as *difference*. These concepts are discussed in "Set Operations" on page 5-34.

Query 5-28 performs a subquery on the **items** table to identify all the items in the **stock** table that have not yet been ordered.

Query 5-28

```
SELECT * FROM stock
    WHERE NOT EXISTS
        (SELECT * FROM items
            WHERE stock.stock_num = items.stock_num
                AND stock.manu_code = items.manu_code)
```

Query 5-28 returns the rows that Query Result 5-28 shows.

```
stock_num manu_code description unit_price unit unit_descr


   101  PRC       bicycle tires    $88.00  box   4/box
   102  SHM       bicycle brakes  $220.00  case  4 sets/case
   102  PRC       bicycle brakes  $480.00  case  4 sets/case
   105  PRC       bicycle wheels   $53.00  pair  pair
 .


 .
 .
   312  HRO       racer goggles    $72.00  box   12/box
   313  SHM       swim cap         $72.00  box   12/box
   313  ANZ       swim cap         $60.00  box   12/box
```

No logical limit exists to the number of subqueries a SELECT statement can have, but the size of any statement is physically limited when it is considered as a character string. However, this limit is probably larger than any practical statement that you are likely to compose.

Perhaps you want to check whether information has been entered correctly in the database. One way to find errors in a database is to write a query that returns output only when errors exist. A subquery of this type serves as a kind of *audit query*, as Query 5-29 shows.

```
SELECT * FROM items
    WHERE total_price != quantity *
        (SELECT unit_price FROM stock
            WHERE stock.stock_num = items.stock_num
                AND stock.manu_code = items.manu_code)
```

Query 5-29 returns only those rows for which the total price of an item on an order is not equal to the stock unit price times the order quantity. If no discount has been applied, such rows were probably entered incorrectly in the database. The query returns rows only when errors occur. If information is correctly inserted into the database, no rows are returned.

```
item_num order_num stock_num manu_code quantity total_price

    1      1004        1 HRO            1        $960.00
    2      1006        5 NRG            5        $190.00
```

Handling Collections in SELECT Statements

The database server provides the following SQL features to handle collection expressions:

- A *collection subquery* takes a virtual table (the result of a subquery) and converts it into a collection.

  A collection subquery always returns a collection of type MULTISET. You can use a collection subquery to convert a query result of relational data into a MULTISET collection. For information about the collection data types, see the *Informix Guide to Database Design and Implementation*.

- A *collection-derived table* takes a collection and converts it into a virtual table.

  Each element of the collection is constructed as a row in the collection-derived table. You can use a collection-derived table to access the individual elements of a collection.

The collection subquery and collection-derived table features represent inverse operations: the collection subquery converts row values from a relational table into a collection whereas the collection-derived table converts the elements of a collection into rows of a relational table.

Collection Subqueries

A collection subquery enables users to construct a collection expression from a subquery expression. A collection subquery uses the MULTISET keyword immediately before the subquery to convert the values returned into a MULTISET collection. However, when you use the MULTISET keyword before a subquery expression, the database server does not change the rows of the underlying table but only modifies a copy of the table rows. For example, if a collection subquery is passed to a user-defined routine that modifies the collection, then a copy of the collection is modified but not the underlying table.

A collection subquery is an expression that can take either of the following forms:

```
MULTISET(SELECT expression1, expression2... FROM tab_name...)
```

or

```
MULTISET(SELECT ITEM expression FROM tab_name...)
```

Omitting the Item Keyword in a Collection Subquery

If you omit the ITEM keyword in the collection subquery expression, the collection subquery is a MULTISET whose element type is always an unnamed row type. The fields of the unnamed row type match the expressions specified in the projection list of the subquery.

Suppose you create the following table that contains a column of type MULTISET:

```
CREATE TABLE tab2
(
id_num INT,
ms_col MULTISET(ROW(a INT) NOT NULL)
)
```

Query 5-30 shows how you might use a collection subquery in a WHERE clause to convert the rows of INT values that the subquery returns to a collection of type MULTISET. In this example, the database server returns rows when the **ms_col** column of **tab2** is equal to the result of the collection subquery expression.

Query 5-30

```
SELECT id_num FROM tab2
WHERE ms_col = (MULTISET(SELECT int_col FROM tab1))
```

Query 5-30 omits the ITEM keyword in the collection subquery, so the INT values the subquery returns are of type MULTISET (ROW(a INT) NOT NULL) that matches the data type of the **ms_col** column of **tab2**.

Specifying the ITEM Keyword in a Collection Subquery

When the projection list of the subquery contains a single expression, you can preface the projection list of the subquery with the ITEM keyword to specify that the element type of the MULTISET matches the data type of the subquery result. In other words, when you include the ITEM keyword, the database server does not put a row wrapper around the projection list. For example, if the subquery (that immediately follows the MULTISET keyword) returns INT values, the collection subquery is of type MULTISET(INT NOT NULL).

Suppose you create a function **int_func()** that accepts an argument of type MULTISET(INT NOT NULL). Query 5-31 shows a collection subquery that converts rows of INT values to a MULTISET and uses the collection subquery as an argument in the function **int_func()**.

Query 5-31

```
EXECUTE FUNCTION int_func(MULTISET(SELECT ITEM int_col
    FROM tab1
    WHERE int_col BETWEEN 1 AND 10))
```

Query 5-31 includes the ITEM keyword in the subquery, so the **int_col** values that the query returns are converted to a collection of type MULTISET (INT NOT NULL). Without the ITEM keyword, the collection subquery would return a collection of type MULTISET (ROW(a INT) NOT NULL).

For more information about syntax and restrictions for collection subqueries, see the *Informix Guide to SQL: Syntax*.

Collection-Derived Tables

A *collection-derived table* enables you to handle the elements of a collection expression as rows in a virtual table. Use the TABLE keyword in the FROM clause of a SELECT statement to create a collection-derived table. The database server supports collection-derived tables in SELECT, INSERT, UPDATE, and DELETE statements.

Query 5-32 uses a collection-derived table named **c_table** to access elements from the **sales** column of the **sales_rep** table in the **superstores_demo** database. The **sales** column is a collection of an unnamed row type whose two fields, **month** and **amount**, store sales data. Query 5-32 returns an element for **sales.amount** when **sales.month** equals 98-03. Because the inner select is itself an expression, it cannot return more than one column value per iteration of the outer query. The outer query specifies how many rows of the **sales_rep** table are evaluated.

Query 5-32

```
SELECT (SELECT c_table.amount FROM TABLE (sales_rep.sales)
c_table WHERE c_table.month = '98-03')
FROM sales_rep
```

Query Result 5-32

```
(expression)

$47.22
$53.22
```

Query 5-33 uses a collection-derived table to access elements from the **sales** collection column where the **rep_num** column equals 102. With a collection-derived table, you can specify aliases for the table and columns. If no table name is specified for a collection-derived table, the database server creates one automatically. This example specifies the derived column list **s_month** and **s_amount** for the collection-derived table **c_table**.

Query 5-33

```
SELECT * FROM TABLE((SELECT sales FROM sales_rep
WHERE sales_rep.rep_num = 102)) c_table(s_month, s_amount)
```

Query Result 5-33

```
s_month        s_amount

1998-03          $53.22
1998-04          $18.22
```

Query 5-34 creates a collection-derived table but does not specify a derived table or derived column names. Query 5-34 returns the same result as Query 5-33 except the derived columns assume the default field names of the **sales** column in the **sales_rep** table.

Query 5-34

```
SELECT * FROM TABLE((SELECT sales FROM sales_rep
WHERE sales_rep.rep_num = 102))
```

Query Result 5-34

```
month          amount

1998-03        $53.22
1998-04        $18.22
```

Important: *A collection-derived table is read only, so it cannot be the target table of INSERT, UPDATE, or DELETE statements or the underlying table of an updateable cursor or view.*

For a complete description of the syntax and restrictions on collection-derived tables, see the *Informix Guide to SQL: Syntax.*

Set Operations

The standard set operations *union, intersection,* and *difference* let you manipulate database information. These three operations let you use SELECT statements to check the integrity of your database after you perform an update, insert, or delete. They can be useful when you transfer data to a history table, for example, and want to verify that the correct data is in the history table before you delete the data from the original table.

Union

The union operation uses the UNION keyword, or *operator*, to combine two queries into a single *compound query*. You can use the UNION operator between two or more SELECT statements to *unite* them and produce a temporary table that contains rows that exist in any or all of the original tables. You can also use the UNION operator in the definition of a view.

You cannot use a UNION operator inside a subquery.

IDS

Dynamic Server does not support ordering on row types. Because a union operation requires a sort to remove duplicate values, you cannot use a UNION operator when either query in the union operation includes row type data. However, the database server does support UNION ALL with row type data since this type of operation does not require sort. ♦

Figure 5-1 illustrates the union set operation.

Figure 5-1
The Union Set Operation

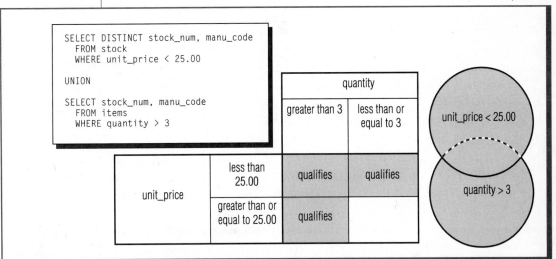

The UNION keyword selects all rows from the two queries, removes duplicates, and returns what is left. Because the results of the queries are combined into a single result, the select list in each query must have the same number of columns. Also, the corresponding columns that are selected from each table must contain compatible data types (CHARACTER data type columns must be the same length), and these corresponding columns must all allow or all disallow nulls.

Query 5-35 performs a union on the **stock_num** and **manu_code** columns in the **stock** and **items** tables.

Query 5-35

```
SELECT DISTINCT stock_num, manu_code
    FROM stock
    WHERE unit_price < 25.00

UNION

SELECT stock_num, manu_code
    FROM items
    WHERE quantity > 3
```

Query 5-35 selects those items that have a unit price of less than $25.00 or that have been ordered in quantities greater than three and lists their **stock_num** and **manu_code**, as Query Result 5-35 shows.

Query Result 5-35

```
stock_num manu_code

        5 ANZ
        5 NRG
        5 SMT
        9 ANZ
      103 PRC
      106 PRC
      201 NKL
      301 KAR
      302 HRO
      302 KAR
```

As Query 5-36 shows, when you include an ORDER BY clause, it must follow the final SELECT statement and use an integer, not an identifier, to refer to the ordering column. Ordering takes place after the set operation is complete.

Query 5-36

```
SELECT DISTINCT stock_num, manu_code
    FROM stock
    WHERE unit_price < 25.00

UNION

SELECT stock_num, manu_code
    FROM items
    WHERE quantity > 3
    ORDER BY 2
```

The compound query in Query 5-36 selects the same rows as Query 5-35 but displays them in order of the manufacturer code, as Query Result 5-36 shows.

Query Result 5-36

```
stock_num manu_code

      5 ANZ
      9 ANZ
    302 HRO
    301 KAR
    302 KAR
    201 NKL
      5 NRG
    103 PRC
    106 PRC
      5 SMT
```

By default, the UNION keyword excludes duplicate rows. To retain the duplicate values, add the optional keyword ALL, as Query 5-37 shows.

Query 5-37

```
SELECT stock_num, manu_code
    FROM stock
    WHERE unit_price < 25.00

UNION ALL

SELECT stock_num, manu_code
    FROM items
    WHERE quantity > 3
    ORDER BY 2
    INTO TEMP stockitem
```

Query 5-37 uses the UNION ALL keywords to unite two SELECT statements and adds an INTO TEMP clause after the final SELECT to put the results into a temporary table. It returns the same rows as Query 5-36 but also includes duplicate values.

```
stock_num manu_code

        9 ANZ
        5 ANZ
        9 ANZ
        5 ANZ
        9 ANZ
        5 ANZ
        5 ANZ
        5 ANZ
      302 HRO
      302 KAR
      301 KAR
      201 NKL
        5 NRG
        5 NRG
      103 PRC
      106 PRC
        5 SMT
        5 SMT
```

Corresponding columns in the select lists for the combined queries must have compatible data types, but the columns do not need to use the same column names.

Query 5-38 selects the **state** column from the **customer** table and the corresponding **code** column from the **state** table.

Query 5-38

```
SELECT DISTINCT state
    FROM customer
    WHERE customer_num BETWEEN 120 AND 125

UNION

SELECT DISTINCT code
    FROM state
    WHERE sname MATCHES '*a'
```

Query Result 5-38 returns state code abbreviations for customer numbers 120 through 125 and for states whose **sname** ends in a.

```
state

AK
AL
AZ
CA
...
SD
VA
WV
```

In compound queries, the column names or display labels in the first SELECT statement are the ones that appear in the results. Thus, in Query 5-38, the column name **state** from the first SELECT statement is used instead of the column name **code** from the second.

Query 5-39 performs a union on three tables. The maximum number of unions depends on the practicality of the application and any memory limitations.

```
SELECT stock_num, manu_code
    FROM stock
    WHERE unit_price > 600.00

UNION ALL

SELECT stock_num, manu_code
    FROM catalog
    WHERE catalog_num = 10025

UNION ALL

SELECT stock_num, manu_code
    FROM items
    WHERE quantity = 10
    ORDER BY 2
```

Query 5-39 selects items where the **unit_price** in the **stock** table is greater than $600, the **catalog_num** in the **catalog** table is 10025, or the **quantity** in the **items** table is 10; and the query orders the data by **manu_code**. Query Result 5-39 shows the return values.

Query Result 5-39

```
stock_num manu_code

        5 ANZ
        9 ANZ
        8 ANZ
        4 HSK
        1 HSK
      203 NKL
        5 NRG
      106 PRC
      113 SHM
```

For the complete syntax of the SELECT statement and the UNION operator, see the *Informix Guide to SQL: Syntax*. For information specific to the Informix ESQL/C product and any limitations that involve the INTO clause and compound queries, see the *Informix ESQL/C Programmer's Manual*.

Query 5-40 uses a combined query to select data into a temporary table and then adds a simple query to order and display it. You must separate the combined and simple queries with a semicolon.

The combined query uses a literal in the select list to tag the output of part of a union so it can be distinguished later. The tag is given the label **sortkey**. The simple query uses that tag as a sort key to order the retrieved rows.

Query 5-40

```
SELECT '1' sortkey, lname, fname, company,
    city, state, phone
    FROM customer x
    WHERE state = 'CA'

UNION

SELECT '2' sortkey, lname, fname, company,
    city, state, phone
    FROM customer y
    WHERE state <> 'CA'
    INTO TEMP calcust;

SELECT * FROM calcust
    ORDER BY 1
```

Query 5-40 creates a list in which the most frequently called customers, those from California, appear first, as Query Result 5-40 shows.

```
sortkey   1
lname     Baxter
fname     Dick
company   Blue Ribbon Sports
city      Oakland
state     CA
phone     415-655-0011

sortkey   1
lname     Beatty
fname     Lana
company   Sportstown
city      Menlo Park    .
state     CA
phone     415-356-9982
...
sortkey   2
lname     Wallack
fname     Jason
company   City Sports
city      Wilmington
state     DE
phone     302-366-7511
```

The *intersection* of two sets of rows produces a table that contains rows that exist in both the original tables. Use the keyword EXISTS or IN to introduce subqueries that show the intersection of two sets. Figure 5-2 illustrates the intersection set operation.

Figure 5-2
The Intersection Set Operation

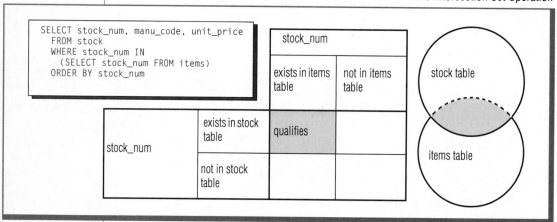

Query 5-41 is an example of a nested SELECT statement that shows the intersection of the **stock** and **items** tables.

Query 5-41

```
SELECT stock_num, manu_code, unit_price
    FROM stock
    WHERE stock_num IN
        (SELECT stock_num FROM items)
    ORDER BY stock_num
```

Query Result 5-41 contains all the elements from both sets and returns the following 57 rows.

Query Result 5-41

```
stock_num manu_code unit_price

        1 HRO         $250.00
        1 HSK         $800.00
        1 SMT         $450.00
        2 HRO         $126.00
        3 HSK         $240.00
        3 SHM         $280.00
...
      304 ANZ         $170.00
      304 HRO         $280.00
      306 PRC         $160.00
      306 SHM         $190.00
      307 PRC         $250.00
      309 HRO          $40.00
      309 SHM          $40.00
```

Difference

The *difference* between two sets of rows produces a table that contains rows in the first set that are not also in the second set. Use the keywords NOT EXISTS or NOT IN to introduce subqueries that show the difference between two sets. Figure 5-3 illustrates the difference set operation.

Figure 5-3
The Difference Set Operation

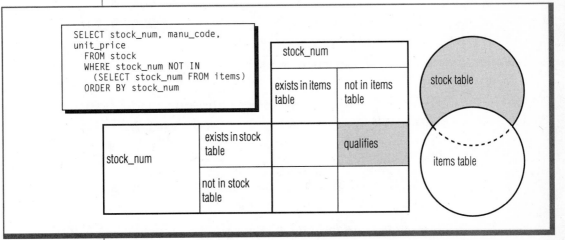

Query 5-42 is an example of a nested SELECT statement that shows the difference between the **stock** and **items** tables.

Query 5-42

```
SELECT stock_num, manu_code, unit_price
    FROM stock
    WHERE stock_num NOT IN
        (SELECT stock_num FROM items)
    ORDER BY stock_num
```

Query Result 5-42 contains all the elements from only the first set, which returns 17 rows.

```
stock_num manu_code unit_price

      102 PRC        $480.00
      102 SHM        $220.00
      106 PRC         $23.00
 .
 .
 .
      312 HRO         $72.00
      312 SHM         $96.00
      313 ANZ         $60.00
      313 SHM         $72.00
```

Summary

This chapter builds on concepts introduced in Chapter 2. It provides sample syntax and results for more advanced kinds of SELECT statements, which are used to query a relational database. This chapter presents the following material:

- Introduces the GROUP BY and HAVING clauses, which you can use with aggregates to return groups of rows and apply conditions to those groups

- Shows how to join a table to itself with a self-join to compare values in a column with other values in the same column and to identify duplicates

- Introduces the keyword OUTER, explains how an outer join treats two or more tables asymmetrically, and provides examples of the four kinds of outer join

- Describes how to nest a SELECT statement in the WHERE clause of another SELECT statement to create correlated and uncorrelated subqueries and shows how to use aggregate functions in subqueries

- Demonstrates how to use the keywords ALL, ANY, EXISTS, IN, and SOME to create subqueries, and the effect of adding the keyword NOT or a relational operator

- Describes how to use collection subqueries to convert relational data to a collection of type MULTISET and how to use collection-derived tables to access elements within a collection
- Discusses the union, intersection, and difference set operations
- Shows how to use the UNION and UNION ALL keywords to create compound queries that consist of two or more SELECT statements

Modifying Data

In This Chapter 6-5

Statements That Modify Data 6-6

Deleting Rows 6-6
    Deleting All Rows of a Table 6-6
    Deleting a Known Number of Rows 6-7
    Deleting an Unknown Number of Rows 6-7
    Deleting Rows That Contain Row Types 6-8
    Deleting Rows That Contain Collection Types 6-9
    Deleting Rows from a Supertable 6-9
    Complicated Delete Conditions 6-9
        Using a Join to Delete Rows 6-10

Inserting Rows 6-11
    Single Rows 6-11
        Possible Column Values 6-12
        Listing Specific Column Names 6-13
    Inserting Rows into Typed Tables 6-14
    Inserting into Row-Type Columns 6-15
        Rows That Contain Named Row Types 6-15
        Rows That Contain Unnamed Row Types 6-16
        Specifying Null Values for Row Types 6-16
    Inserting Rows into Supertables 6-17
    Inserting Collection Values into Columns 6-18
        Inserting into Simple Collections and Nested Collections . . . 6-19
        Inserting Null Values into a Collection That Contains
            a Row Type 6-19
    Inserting Smart Large Objects 6-20
    Multiple Rows and Expressions 6-21
    Restrictions on the Insert Selection 6-22

Updating Rows 6-23
  Selecting Rows to Update 6-24
  Updating with Uniform Values 6-25
  Restrictions on Updates 6-26
  Updating with Selected Values 6-26
  Updating Row Types 6-27
    Updating Rows That Contain Named Row Types. 6-27
    Updating Rows That Contain Unnamed Row Types 6-28
    Specifying Null Values for the Fields of a Row Type 6-28
  Updating Collection Types 6-29
  Updating Rows of a Supertable 6-30
  Using a CASE Expression to Update a Column 6-31
  Using SQL Functions to Update Smart Large Objects 6-31
  Using a Join to Update a Column. 6-32

Privileges on a Database 6-32
  Database-Level Privileges 6-33
  Table-Level Privileges 6-33
  Displaying Table Privileges. 6-34

Data Integrity. 6-35
  Entity Integrity 6-36
  Semantic Integrity 6-37
  Referential Integrity 6-37
    Using the ON DELETE CASCADE Option 6-39
    Example of Cascading Deletes 6-40
    Restrictions on Cascading Deletes 6-41
  Object Modes and Violation Detection 6-41
    Definitions of Object Modes 6-41
    Example of Modes with Data Manipulation Statements . . . 6-43
    Violations and Diagnostics Tables 6-46

Interrupted Modifications 6-51
  Transactions 6-52
  Transaction Logging 6-53
    Transaction Logging for Enterprise Decision Server 6-53
    Logging and Cascading Deletes 6-54
  Specifying Transactions 6-55

Backups and Logs with Informix Database Servers 6-56

Concurrency and Locks 6-57

Informix Data Replication 6-58

Summary 6-59

In This Chapter

This chapter describes how to modify the data in your databases. Modifying data is fundamentally different than querying data. To query data involves examining the contents of tables. To modify data involves *changing* the contents of tables.

Think about what happens if the system hardware or software fails during a query. In this case, the effect on the application can be severe, but the database itself is unharmed. However, if the system fails while a modification is under way, the state of the database is in doubt. Obviously, a database in an uncertain state has far-reaching implications. Before you delete, insert, or update rows in a database, ask yourself the following questions:

- Is user access to the database and its tables secure; that is, are specific users given limited database and table-level privileges?
- Does the modified data preserve the existing integrity of the database?
- Are systems in place that make the database relatively immune to external events that might cause system or hardware failures?

If you cannot answer yes to each of these questions, do not panic. Solutions to all these problems are built into the Informix database servers. After a description of the statements that modify data, this chapter discusses these solutions. The *Informix Guide to Database Design and Implementation* covers these topics in greater detail.

Statements That Modify Data

The following statements modify data:

- DELETE
- INSERT
- UPDATE

Although these SQL statements are relatively simple when compared with the more advanced SELECT statements, use them carefully because they change the contents of the database.

Deleting Rows

The DELETE statement removes any row or combination of rows from a table. You cannot recover a deleted row after the transaction is committed. (Transactions are discussed under "Interrupted Modifications" on page 6-51. For now, think of a transaction and a statement as the same thing.)

When you delete a row, you must also be careful to delete any rows of other tables whose values depend on the deleted row. If your database enforces referential constraints, you can use the ON DELETE CASCADE option of the CREATE TABLE or ALTER TABLE statements to allow deletes to cascade from one table in a relationship to another. For more information on referential constraints and the ON DELETE CASCADE option, refer to "Referential Integrity" on page 6-37.

Deleting All Rows of a Table

The DELETE statement specifies a table and usually contains a WHERE clause that designates the row or rows that are to be removed from the table. If the WHERE clause is left out, all rows are deleted. *Do not execute the following statement*:

```
DELETE FROM customer
```

Because this DELETE statement does not contain a WHERE clause, all rows from the **customer** table are deleted. If you attempt an unconditional delete using the DB-Access or the Relational Object Manager menu options, the program warns you and asks for confirmation. However, an unconditional delete from within a program can occur without warning.

Deleting a Known Number of Rows

The WHERE clause in a DELETE statement has the same form as the WHERE clause in a SELECT statement. You can use it to designate exactly which row or rows should be deleted. You can delete a customer with a specific customer number, as the following example shows:

```
DELETE FROM customer WHERE customer_num = 175
```

In this example, because the **customer_num** column has a unique constraint, you can ensure that no more than one row is deleted.

Deleting an Unknown Number of Rows

You can also choose rows that are based on nonindexed columns, as the following example shows:

```
DELETE FROM customer WHERE company = 'Druid Cyclery'
```

Because the column that is tested does not have a unique constraint, this statement might delete more than one row. (Druid Cyclery might have two stores, both with the same name but different customer numbers.)

To find out how many rows a DELETE statement affects, select the count of qualifying rows from the **customer** table for Druid Cyclery.

```
SELECT COUNT(*) FROM customer WHERE company = 'Druid Cyclery'
```

You can also select the rows and display them to ensure that they are the ones you want to delete.

Using a SELECT statement as a test is only an approximation, however, when the database is available to multiple users concurrently. Between the time you execute the SELECT statement and the subsequent DELETE statement, other users could have modified the table and changed the result. In this example, another user might perform the following actions:

- Insert a new row for another customer named Druid Cyclery
- Delete one or more of the Druid Cyclery rows before you insert the new row
- Update a Druid Cyclery row to have a new company name, or update some other customer to have the name Druid Cyclery

Although it is not likely that other users would do these things in that brief interval, the possibility does exist. This same problem affects the UPDATE statement. Ways of addressing this problem are discussed under "Concurrency and Locks" on page 6-57, and in greater detail in Chapter 9, "Programming for a Multiuser Environment."

Another problem you might encounter is a hardware or software failure before the statement finishes. In this case, the database might have deleted no rows, some rows, or all specified rows. The *state* of the database is unknown, which is undesirable. To prevent this situation, use transaction logging, as "Interrupted Modifications" on page 6-51 discusses.

Deleting Rows That Contain Row Types

IDS

When a row contains a column that is defined on a row type, you can use dot notation to specify that the only rows deleted are those that contain a specific field value. For example, the following statement deletes only those rows from the **employee** table in which the value of the **city** field in the **address** column is San Jose:

```
DELETE FROM employee
    WHERE address.city = 'San Jose'
```

In the preceding statement, the **address** column might be a named row type or an unnamed row type. The syntax you use to specify field values of a row type is the same.

IDS

Deleting Rows That Contain Collection Types

When a row contains a column that is defined on a collection type, you can search for a particular element in a collection and delete the row or rows in which that element is found. For example, the following statement deletes rows in which the **direct_reports** column contains a collection with the element `Baker`:

```
DELETE FROM manager
    WHERE 'Baker' IN direct_reports
```

IDS

Deleting Rows from a Supertable

When you delete the rows of a supertable, the scope of the delete is a supertable and its subtables. Suppose you create a supertable **person** that has two subtables **employee** and **sales_rep** defined under it. The following DELETE statement on the **person** table can delete rows from all the tables **person**, **employee**, and **sales_rep**:

```
DELETE FROM person
    WHERE name ='Walker'
```

To limit a delete to rows of the supertable only, you must use the ONLY keyword in the DELETE statement. For example, the following statement deletes rows of the **person** table only:

```
DELETE FROM ONLY(person)
    WHERE name ='Walker'
```

Warning: *Use caution when you delete rows from a supertable because the scope of a delete on a supertable includes the supertable and all its subtables.*

Complicated Delete Conditions

The WHERE clause in a DELETE statement can be almost as complicated as the one in a SELECT statement. It can contain multiple conditions that are connected by AND and OR, and it might contain subqueries.

Suppose you discover that some rows of the **stock** table contain incorrect manufacturer codes. Rather than update them, you want to delete them so that they can be re-entered. You know that these rows, unlike the correct ones, have no matching rows in the **manufact** table. The fact that these incorrect rows have no matching rows in the **manufact** table allows you to write a DELETE statement such as the one in the following example:

```
DELETE FROM stock
    WHERE 0 = (SELECT COUNT(*) FROM manufact
        WHERE manufact.manu_code = stock.manu_code)
```

The subquery counts the number of rows of **manufact** that match; the count is 1 for a correct row of **stock** and 0 for an incorrect one. The latter rows are chosen for deletion.

One way to develop a DELETE statement with a complicated condition is to first develop a SELECT statement that returns precisely the rows to be deleted. Write it as SELECT *; when it returns the desired set of rows, change SELECT * to read DELETE and execute it once more.

The WHERE clause of a DELETE statement cannot use a subquery that tests the same table. That is, when you delete from **stock**, you cannot use a subquery in the WHERE clause that also selects from **stock**.

The key to this rule is in the FROM clause. If a table is named in the FROM clause of a DELETE statement, it cannot also appear in the FROM clause of a subquery of the DELETE statement.

EDS

Using a Join to Delete Rows

Instead of writing a subquery in the WHERE clause, in Enterprise Decision Server, you can use a delete join to join rows from various tables and delete these rows from a target table based on the join results.

As in the above example, suppose you discover that some rows of the **stock** table contain incorrect manufacturer codes. Rather than update them, you want to delete them so that they can be re-entered. You can use a delete join query such as the one in the following example:

```
DELETE FROM stock USING stock, manufact
    WHERE stock.maun_code != manufact.manu_code
```

All tables being joined should be listed in the USING clause. Even if the target table is not being used for the join, it should be listed in the USING clause. For more information on delete joins, see the DELETE statement in the *Informix Guide to SQL: Syntax*.

Inserting Rows

The INSERT statement adds a new row, or rows, to a table. The statement has two basic functions. It can create a single new row using column values you supply, or it can create a group of new rows using data selected from other tables.

Single Rows

In its simplest form, the INSERT statement creates one new row from a list of column values and puts that row in the table. The following statement shows how to add a row to the **stock** table:

```
INSERT INTO stock
    VALUES(115, 'PRC', 'tire pump', 108, 'box', '6/box')
```

The **stock** table has the following columns:

- **stock_num** (a number that identifies the type of merchandise)
- **manu_code** (a foreign key to the **manufact** table)
- **description** (a description of the merchandise)
- **unit_price** (the unit price of the merchandise)
- **unit** (of measure)
- **unit_descr** (characterizes the unit of measure)

The values that are listed in the VALUES clause in the preceding example have a one-to-one correspondence with the columns of the **stock** table. To write a VALUES clause, you must know the columns of the tables as well as their sequence from first to last.

Possible Column Values

The VALUES clause accepts *only* constant values, *not* expressions. You can supply the following values:

- Literal numbers
- Literal datetime values
- Literal interval values
- Quoted strings of characters
- The word NULL for a null value
- The word TODAY for the current date
- The word CURRENT for the current date and time
- The word USER for your user name
- The word DBSERVERNAME (or SITENAME) for the name of the computer where the database server is running

Some columns of a table might not allow null values. If you attempt to insert NULL in such a column, the statement is rejected, or a column in the table might not permit duplicate values. If you specify a value that is a duplicate of one that is already in such a column, the statement is rejected. Some columns might even *restrict* the possible column values allowed. Use data integrity constraints to restrict columns. For more information, see "Data Integrity" on page 6-35.

Only one column in a table can have the SERIAL data type. The database server generates values for a serial column. To make this happen when you insert values, specify the value zero for the serial column. The database server generates the next actual value in sequence. Serial columns do not allow null values.

You can specify a nonzero value for a serial column (as long as it does not duplicate any existing value in that column), and the database server uses the value. However, that nonzero value might set a new starting point for values that the database server generates. The next value the database server generates for you is one greater than the maximum value in the column.

Do not specify the currency symbols for columns that contain money values. Just specify the numeric value of the amount.

The database server can convert between numeric and character data types. You can give a string of numeric characters (for example, '-0075.6') as the value of a numeric column. The database server converts the numeric string to a number. An error occurs only if the string does not represent a number.

You can specify a number or a date as the value for a character column. The database server converts that value to a character string. For example, if you specify TODAY as the value for a character column, a character string that represents the current date is used. (The **DBDATE** environment variable specifies the format that is used.)

Listing Specific Column Names

You do not have to specify values for every column. Instead, you can list the column names after the table name and then supply values for only those columns that you named. The following example shows a statement that inserts a new row into the **stock** table:

```
INSERT INTO stock (stock_num,description,unit_price,manu_code)
   VALUES (115,'tyre pump',114,'SHM')
```

Only the data for the stock number, description, unit price, and manufacturer code is provided. The database server supplies the following values for the remaining columns:

- It generates a serial number for an unlisted serial column.

- It generates a default value for a column with a specific default associated with it.

- It generates a null value for any column that allows nulls but it does not specify a default value for any column that specifies null as the default value.

  You must list and supply values for all columns that do not specify a default value or do not permit nulls.

You can list the columns in any order, as long as the values for those columns are listed in the same order. For information about how to designate null or default values for a column, see the *Informix Guide to Database Design and Implementation*.

After the INSERT statement in the preceding example is executed, the following new row is inserted into the **stock** table:

```
stock_num  manu_code description  unit_price  unit  unit_descr

115        SHM        tyre pump    114
```

Both **unit** and **unit_descr** are blank, which indicates that null values exist in those two columns. Because the **unit** column permits nulls, the number of tire pumps that were purchased for $114 is not known. Of course, if a default value of box were specified for this column, then box would be the unit of measure. In any case, when you insert values into specific columns of a table, pay attention to what data is needed for that row.

IDS

Inserting Rows into Typed Tables

You can insert rows into a typed table in the same way you insert rows into a table not based on a row type.

When a typed table contains a row-type column (the named row type that defines the typed table contains a nested row type), you insert into the row-type column in the same way you insert into a row-type column for a table not based on a row type. The following section, "Inserting into Row-Type Columns," describes how to perform inserts on row-type columns.

This section uses row types **zip_t**, **address_t**, and **employee_t** and typed table **employee** for examples. Figure 6-1 shows the SQL syntax that creates the row types and table.

Figure 6-1

```
CREATE ROW TYPE zip_t
(
    z_code      CHAR(5),
    z_suffix    CHAR(4)
);

CREATE ROW TYPE address_t
(
    street  VARCHAR(20),
    city    VARCHAR(20),
    state   CHAR(2),
    zip     zip_t
);

CREATE ROW TYPE employee_t
(
name    VARCHAR(30),
address address_t,
salary  INTEGER
);

CREATE TABLE employee OF TYPE employee_t;
```

IDS

Inserting into Row-Type Columns

The following syntax rules apply for inserts on columns that are defined on named row types or unnamed row types:

- Specify the ROW constructor before the field values to be inserted.
- Enclose the field values of the row type in parentheses.
- Cast the row expression to the appropriate named row type (for named row types).

Rows That Contain Named Row Types

The following statement shows you how to insert a row into the **employee** table in Figure 6-1 on page 6-15:

```
INSERT INTO employee
    VALUES ('Poole, John',
    ROW('402 High St', 'Willits', 'CA',
    ROW('69055','1450'))::address_t, 35000 )
```

Because the **address** column of the **employee** table is a named row type, you must use a cast operator and the name of the row type (**address_t**) to insert a value of type **address_t**.

Rows That Contain Unnamed Row Types

Suppose you create the table that Figure 6-2 shows. The **student** table defines the **s_address** column as an unnamed row type.

Figure 6-2

```
CREATE TABLE student
(
s_name        VARCHAR(30),
s_address     ROW(street VARCHAR (20), city VARCHAR(20),
                  state CHAR(2), zip VARCHAR(9)),
              grade_point_avg DECIMAL(3,2)
);
```

The following statement shows you how to add a row to the **student** table. To insert into the unnamed row-type column **s_address**, use the ROW constructor but do not cast the row-type value.

```
INSERT INTO student
    VALUES (
        'Keene, Terry',
        ROW('53 Terra Villa', 'Wheeling', 'IL', '45052'),
        3.75
        )
```

Specifying Null Values for Row Types

The fields of a row-type column can contain null values. You can specify null values either at the level of the column or the field.

The following statement specifies a null value at the column level to insert null values for all fields of the **s_address** column. When you insert a null value at the column level, do not include the ROW constructor.

```
INSERT INTO student
    VALUES ('Brauer, Howie', NULL, 3.75)
```

When you insert a null value for particular fields of a row type, you must include the ROW constructor. The following INSERT statement shows how you might insert null values into particular fields of the **address** column of the **employee** table. (The **address** column is defined as a named row type.)

```
INSERT INTO employee
    VALUES (
        'Singer, John',
        ROW(NULL, 'Davis', 'CA', ROW(97000,
            2000))::address_t,
        67000
        )
```

When you specify a null value for the field of a row type, you do not need to explicitly cast the null value when the row type occurs in an INSERT statement, an UPDATE statement, or a program variable assignment.

The following INSERT statement shows how you insert null values for the **street** and **zip** fields of the **s_address** column for the **student** table:

```
INSERT INTO student
    VALUES(
        Henry, John',
        ROW(NULL, s_address.city, s_address.state, NULL)
        )
```

Inserting Rows into Supertables

No special considerations exist when you insert a row into a supertable. An INSERT statement applies only to the table that is specified in the statement. For example, the following statement inserts values into the supertable but does not insert values into any subtables:

```
INSERT INTO person
    VALUES (
        'Poole, John',
        ROW('402 Saphire St.', 'Elmondo', 'CA', 69055'),
        345605900
        )
```

IDS

Inserting Collection Values into Columns

This section describes how to insert a collection value into a column with DB-Access or the Relational Object Manager. It does not discuss how to insert individual elements into a collection column. To access or modify the individual elements of a collection, use an ESQL/C program or SPL routine. For information about how to create an ESQL/C program to insert into a collection, see the *Informix ESQL/C Programmer's Manual*. For information about how to create an SPL routine to insert into a collection, see Chapter 10.

The examples that this section provides are based on the **manager** table in Figure 6-3. The **manager** table contains both simple and nested collection types.

Figure 6-3

```
CREATE TABLE manager
(
    mgr_name         VARCHAR(30),
    department       VARCHAR(12),
    direct_reports   SET(VARCHAR(30) NOT NULL),
    projects         LIST(ROW(pro_name VARCHAR(15),
                     pro_members SET(VARCHAR(20)
                     NOT NULL) ) NOT NULL)
);
```

Inserting into Simple Collections and Nested Collections

When you insert values into a row that contains a collection column, you insert the values of all the elements that the collection contains as well as values for the other columns. For example, the following statement inserts a single row into the **manager** table, which includes columns for both simple collections and nested collections:

```
INSERT INTO manager(mgr_name, department, direct_reports,
projects)
VALUES
(
'Sayles', 'marketing',
"SET{'Simonian', 'Waters', 'Adams', 'Davis', 'Jones'}",
"LIST{
    ROW('voyager_project', SET{'Simonian', 'Waters',
    'Adams', 'Davis'}),
    ROW ('horizon_project', SET{'Freeman', 'Jacobs',
    'Walker', 'Smith', 'Cannan'}),
    ROW ('saphire_project', SET{'Villers', 'Reeves',
    'Doyle', 'Strongin'})
    }"
)
```

Inserting Null Values into a Collection That Contains a Row Type

To insert values into a collection that is a row type, you must specify a value for each field in the row type.

In general, null values are not allowed in a collection. However, if the element type of the collection is a row type, you can insert null values into individual fields of the row type.

You can also specify an empty collection. An *empty collection* is a collection that contains no elements. To specify an empty collection, use the braces ({}). For example, the following statement inserts data into a row in the **manager** table but specifies that the **direct_reports** and **projects** columns are empty collections:

```
INSERT INTO manager
    VALUES ('Sayles', 'marketing', "SET{}",
    "LIST{ROW(SET{})}")
```

A collection column cannot contain null elements. The following statement returns an error because null values are specified as elements of collections:

```
INSERT INTO manager
    VALUES ('Cole', 'accounting', "SET{NULL}",
    "LIST{ROW(NULL, ""SET{NULL}"")}"
```

The following syntax rules apply for performing inserts and updates on collection types:

- Use braces ({}) to demarcate the elements that each collection contains
- If the collection is a nested collection, use braces ({}) to demarcate the elements of both the inner and outer collections

IDS

Inserting Smart Large Objects

When you use the INSERT statement to insert an object into a **BLOB** or **CLOB** column, the database server stores the object in an sbspace rather than the table. The database server provides SQL functions that you can call from within an INSERT statement to import and export BLOB or CLOB data, otherwise known as smart large objects. For a description of these functions, see page 4-20.

The following INSERT statement uses the **FILETOBLOB()** and **FILETOCLOB()** functions to insert a row of the **inmate** table. (Figure 4-2 on page 4-20 defines the **inmate** table.)

```
INSERT INTO inmate
    VALUES (437, FILETOBLOB('datafile', 'client'),
        FILETOCLOB('tmp/text', 'server'))
```

In the preceding example, the first argument for the **FILETOBLOB()** and **FILETOCLOB()** functions specifies the path of the source file to be copied into the **BLOB** and **CLOB** columns of the **inmate** table, respectively. The second argument for each function specifies whether the source file is located on the client computer ('client') or server computer ('server'). To specify the path of a filename in the function argument, apply the following rules:

- If the source file resides on the server computer, you must specify the full pathname to the file (not the pathname relative to the current working directory).

- If the source file resides on the client computer, you can specify either the full or relative pathname to the file.

Multiple Rows and Expressions

The other major form of the INSERT statement replaces the VALUES clause with a SELECT statement. This feature allows you to insert the following data:

- Multiple rows with only one statement (each time the SELECT statement returns a row, a row is inserted)

- Calculated values (the VALUES clause permits only constants) because the select list can contain expressions

For example, suppose a follow-up call is required for every order that has been paid for but not shipped. The INSERT statement in the following example finds those orders and inserts a row in **cust_calls** for each order:

```
INSERT INTO cust_calls (customer_num, call_descr)
    SELECT customer_num, order_num FROM orders
        WHERE paid_date IS NOT NULL
        AND ship_date IS NULL
```

This SELECT statement returns two columns. The data from these columns (in each selected row) is inserted into the named columns of the **cust_calls** table. Then an order number (from **order_num**, a serial column) is inserted into the call description, which is a character column. Remember that the database server allows you to insert integer values into a character column. It automatically converts the serial number to a character string of decimal digits.

Restrictions on the Insert Selection

The following list contains the restrictions on the SELECT statement for inserting rows:

- It cannot contain an INTO clause.
- It cannot contain an INTO TEMP clause.
- It cannot contain an ORDER BY clause.
- It cannot refer to the table into which you are inserting rows.

EDS

Enterprise Decision Server allows you to use a SELECT statement that contains an ORDER BY clause in an INSERT SELECT statement. ♦

The INTO, INTO TEMP, and ORDER BY clause restrictions are minor. The INTO clause is not useful in this context. (For more information, see Chapter 7.) To work around the INTO TEMP clause restriction, first select the data you want to insert into a temporary table and then insert the data from the temporary table with the INSERT statement. Likewise, the lack of an ORDER BY clause is not important. If you need to ensure that the new rows are physically ordered in the table, you can first select them into a temporary table and order it, and then insert from the temporary table. You can also apply a physical order to the table using a clustered index after all insertions are done.

Important: *The last restriction is more serious because it prevents you from naming the same table in both the INTO clause of the INSERT statement and the FROM clause of the SELECT statement. Naming the same table in both the INTO clause of the INSERT statement and the FROM clause of the SELECT statement causes the database server to enter an endless loop in which each inserted row is reselected and reinserted.*

In some cases, however, you might want to select from the same table into which you must insert data. For example, suppose that you have learned that the Nikolus company supplies the same products as the Anza company, but at half the price. You want to add rows to the **stock** table to reflect the difference between the two companies. Optimally, you want to select data from all the Anza stock rows and reinsert it with the Nikolus manufacturer code. However, you cannot select from the same table into which you are inserting.

To get around this restriction, select the data you want to insert into a temporary table. Then select from that temporary table in the INSERT statement, as the following example shows:

```
SELECT stock_num, 'NIK' temp_manu, description, unit_price/2
       half_price, unit, unit_descr FROM stock
    WHERE manu_code = 'ANZ'
       AND stock_num < 110
    INTO TEMP anzrows;

INSERT INTO stock SELECT * FROM anzrows;

DROP TABLE anzrows;
```

This SELECT statement takes existing rows from **stock** and substitutes a literal value for the manufacturer code and a computed value for the unit price. These rows are then saved in a temporary table, **anzrows**, which is immediately inserted into the **stock** table.

When you insert multiple rows, a risk exists that one of the rows contains invalid data that might cause the database server to report an error. When such an error occurs, the statement terminates early. Even if no error occurs, a small risk exists that a hardware or software failure might occur while the statement is executing (for example, the disk might fill up).

In either event, you cannot easily tell how many new rows were inserted. If you repeat the statement in its entirety, you might create duplicate rows, or you might not. Because the database is in an unknown state, you cannot know what to do. The solution lies in using transactions, as "Interrupted Modifications" on page 6-51 discusses.

Updating Rows

Use the UPDATE statement to change the contents of one or more columns in one or more existing rows of a table. This statement takes two fundamentally different forms. One lets you assign specific values to columns by name; the other lets you assign a list of values (that might be returned by a SELECT statement) to a list of columns. In either case, if you are updating rows, and some of the columns have data integrity constraints, the data you change must be within the constraints placed on those columns. For more information, refer to "Data Integrity" on page 6-35.

Selecting Rows to Update

Either form of the UPDATE statement can end with a WHERE clause that determines which rows are modified. If you omit the WHERE clause, all rows are modified. The WHERE clause can be quite complicated to select the precise set of rows that need changing. The only restriction on the WHERE clause is that the table that you update cannot be named in the FROM clause of a subquery.

The first form of an UPDATE statement uses a series of assignment clauses to specify new column values, as the following example shows:

```
UPDATE customer
    SET fname = 'Barnaby', lname = 'Dorfler'
    WHERE customer_num = 103
```

The WHERE clause selects the row you want to update. In the demonstration database, the **customer.customer_num** column is the primary key for that table, so this statement can update no more than one row.

You can also use subqueries in the WHERE clause. Suppose that the Anza Corporation issues a safety recall of their tennis balls. As a result, any unshipped orders that include stock number 6 from manufacturer ANZ must be put on back order, as the following example shows:

```
UPDATE orders
    SET backlog = 'y'
    WHERE ship_date IS NULL
    AND order_num IN
        (SELECT DISTINCT items.order_num FROM items
            WHERE items.stock_num = 6
            AND items.manu_code = 'ANZ')
```

This subquery returns a column of order numbers (zero or more). The UPDATE operation then tests each row of **orders** against the list and performs the update if that row matches.

Updating with Uniform Values

Each assignment after the keyword SET specifies a new value for a column. That value is applied uniformly to every row that you update. In the examples in the previous section, the new values were constants, but you can assign any expression, including one based on the column value itself. Suppose the manufacturer code HRO has raised all prices by 5 percent, and you must update the **stock** table to reflect this increase. Use the following statement:

```
UPDATE stock
    SET unit_price = unit_price * 1.05
    WHERE manu_code = 'HRO'
```

You can also use a subquery as part of the assigned value. When a subquery is used as an element of an expression, it must return exactly one value (one column and one row). Perhaps you decide that for any stock number, you must charge a higher price than any manufacturer of that product. You need to update the prices of all unshipped orders. The SELECT statements in the following example specify the criteria:

```
UPDATE items
    SET total_price = quantity *
        (SELECT MAX (unit_price) FROM stock
            WHERE stock.stock_num = items.stock_num)
    WHERE items.order_num IN
        (SELECT order_num FROM orders
            WHERE ship_date IS NULL)
```

The first SELECT statement returns a single value: the highest price in the **stock** table for a particular product. The first SELECT statement is a correlated subquery because, when a value from **items** appears in the WHERE clause for the first SELECT statement, you must execute it for every row that you update.

The second SELECT statement produces a list of the order numbers of unshipped orders. It is an uncorrelated subquery that is executed once.

Restrictions on Updates

Restrictions exist on the use of subqueries when you modify data. In particular, you cannot query the table that is being modified. You *can* refer to the present value of a column in an expression, as in the example that increments the **unit_price** column by 5 percent. You can also refer to a value of a column in a WHERE clause in a subquery, as in the example that updated the **stock** table, in which the **items** table is updated and **items.stock_num** is used in a join expression.

EDS

Enterprise Decision Server does not allow you to use a subquery in the SET clause of an UPDATE statement. ♦

The need to update and query a table at the same time does not occur often in a well-designed database. (For more information about database design, see the *Informix Guide to Database Design and Implementation.*) However, you might want to update and query at the same time when a database is first being developed, before its design has been carefully thought through. A typical problem arises when a table inadvertently and incorrectly contains a few rows with duplicate values in a column that should be unique. You might want to delete the duplicate rows or update only the duplicate rows. Either way, a test for duplicate rows inevitably requires a subquery on the same table that you want to modify, which is not allowed in an UPDATE statement or DELETE statement. Chapter 8 discusses how to use an *update cursor* to perform this kind of modification.

Updating with Selected Values

The second form of UPDATE statement replaces the list of assignments with a single bulk assignment, in which a list of columns is set equal to a list of values. When the values are simple constants, this form is nothing more than the form of the previous example with its parts rearranged, as the following example shows:

```
UPDATE customer
    SET (fname, lname) = ('Barnaby', 'Dorfler')
    WHERE customer_num = 103
```

No advantage exists to writing the statement this way. In fact, it is harder to read because it is not obvious which values are assigned to which columns.

However, when the values to be assigned come from a single SELECT statement, this form makes sense. Suppose that changes of address are to be applied to several customers. Instead of updating the **customer** table each time a change is reported, the new addresses are collected in a single temporary table named **newaddr**. It contains columns for the customer number and the address-related fields of the **customer** table. Now the time comes to apply all the new addresses at once.

```
UPDATE customer
    SET (address1, address2, city, state, zipcode) =
        ((SELECT address1, address2, city, state, zipcode
            FROM newaddr
            WHERE newaddr.customer_num=customer.customer_num))
    WHERE customer_num IN
        (SELECT customer_num FROM newaddr)
```

A single SELECT statement produces the values for multiple columns. If you rewrite this example in the other form, with an assignment for each updated column, you must write five SELECT statements, one for each column to be updated. Not only is such a statement harder to write but it also takes much longer to execute.

Tip: *In SQL API programs, you can use record or host variables to update values. For more information, refer to Chapter 7.*

Updating Row Types

The syntax you use to update a row-type value differs somewhat depending on whether the column is a named row type or unnamed row type. This section describes those differences and also describes how to specify null values for the fields of a row type.

Updating Rows That Contain Named Row Types

To update a column that is defined on a named row type, you must specify all fields of the row type. For example, the following statement updates only the **street** and **city** fields of the **address** column in the **employee** table, but each field of the row type must contain a value (null values are allowed):

```
UPDATE employee
    SET address = ROW('103 California St',
    'San Francisco', address.state, address.zip)::address_t
    WHERE name = 'zawinul, joe'
```

In this example, the values of the **state** and **zip** fields are read from and then immediately reinserted into the row. Only the **street** and **city** fields of the **address** column are updated.

When you update the fields of a column that are defined on a named row type, you must use a ROW constructor and cast the row value to the appropriate named row type.

Updating Rows That Contain Unnamed Row Types

To update a column that is defined on an unnamed row type, you must specify all fields of the row type. For example, the following statement updates only the **street** and **city** fields of the **address** column in the **student** table, but each field of the row type must contain a value (null values are allowed):

```
UPDATE student
    SET s_address = ROW('13 Sunset', 'Fresno',
    s_address.state, s_address.zip)
    WHERE s_name = 'henry, john'
```

To update the fields of a column that are defined on an unnamed row type, always specify the ROW constructor before the field values to be inserted.

Specifying Null Values for the Fields of a Row Type

The fields of a row-type column can contain null values. When you insert into or update a row-type field with a null value, you must cast the value to the data type of that field.

The following UPDATE statement shows how you might specify null values for particular fields of a named row-type column:

```
UPDATE employee
    SET address = ROW(NULL::VARCHAR(20), 'Davis', 'CA',
    ROW(NULL::CHAR(5), NULL::CHAR(4)))::address_t)
    WHERE name = 'henry, john'
```

The following UPDATE statement shows how you specify null values for the
street and **zip** fields of the **address** column for the **student** table.

```
UPDATE student
    SET address = ROW(NULL::VARCHAR(20), address.city,
    address.state, NULL::VARCHAR(9))
    WHERE s_name = 'henry, john'
```

Important: *You cannot specify null values for a row-type column. You can only specify null values for the individual fields of the row type.*

Updating Collection Types

When you use DB-Access or the Relational Object Manager to update a
collection type, you must update the entire collection. The following
statement shows how to update the **projects** column. To locate the row that
needs to be updated, use the IN keyword to perform a search on the
direct_reports column.

```
UPDATE manager
SET projects = "LIST
{
    ROW('brazil_project', SET{'Pryor', 'Murphy', 'Kinsley',
        'Bryant'}),
    ROW ('cuba_project', SET{'Forester', 'Barth', 'Lewis',
        'Leonard'})
}"
WHERE 'Williams' IN direct_reports
```

The first occurrence of the SET keyword in the preceding statement is part of
the UPDATE statement syntax.

Tip: *Do not confuse the SET keyword of an UPDATE statement with the SET
constructor that indicates that a collection is a SET.*

Although you can use the IN keyword to locate specific elements of a simple
collection, you cannot update individual elements of a collection column
from DB-Access or the Relational Object Manager. However, you can create
ESQL/C programs and SPL routines to update elements within a collection.
For information about how to create an ESQL/C program to update a
collection, see the *Informix ESQL/C Programmer's Manual*. For information
about how to create SPL routines to update a collection, see the section
"Handling Collections" on page 10-48.

IDS

Updating Rows of a Supertable

When you update the rows of a supertable, the scope of the update is a supertable and its subtables.

When you construct an UPDATE statement on a supertable, you can update all columns in the supertable and columns of subtables that are inherited from the supertable. For example, the following statement updates rows from the **employee** and **sales_rep** tables, which are subtables of the supertable **person**:

```
UPDATE person
    SET salary=65000
    WHERE address.state = 'CA'
```

However, an update on a supertable does not allow you to update columns from subtables that are not in the supertable. For example, in the previous update statement, you cannot update the **region_num** column of the **sales_rep** table because the **region_num** column does not occur in the **employee** table.

When you perform updates on supertables, be aware of the scope of the update. For example, an UPDATE statement on the **person** table that does not include a WHERE clause to restrict which rows to update, modifies all rows of the **person, employee**, and **sales_rep** table.

To limit an update to rows of the supertable only, you must use the ONLY keyword in the UPDATE statement. For example, the following statement updates rows of the **person** table only:

```
UPDATE ONLY(person)
    SET address = ROW('14 Jackson St', 'Berkeley',
    address.state, address.zip)
    WHERE name = 'Sallie, A.'
```

Warning: *Use caution when you update rows of a supertable because the scope of an update on a supertable includes the supertable and all its subtables.*

Using a CASE Expression to Update a Column

The CASE expression allows a statement to return one of several possible results, depending on which of several condition tests evaluates to TRUE.

The following example shows how to use a CASE statement in an UPDATE statement to increase the unit price of certain items in the **stock** table:

```
UPDATE stock
    SET unit_price = CASE
        WHEN stock_num = 1
        AND manu_code = "HRO"
        THEN unit_price = unit_price * 1.2
        WHEN stock_num = 1
        AND manu_code = "SMT"
        THEN unit_price = unit_price * 1.1
        ELSE 0
        END
```

You must include at least one WHEN clause within the CASE expression; subsequent WHEN clauses and the ELSE clause are optional. If no WHEN condition evaluates to true, the resulting value is null.

IDS

Using SQL Functions to Update Smart Large Objects

You can use an SQL function that you can call from within an UPDATE statement to import and export smart large objects. For a description of these functions, see page 4-20.

The following UPDATE statement uses the **LOCOPY()** function to copy BLOB data from the **mugshot** column of the **fbi_list** table into the **picture** column of the **inmate** table. (Figure 4-2 on page 4-20 defines the **inmate** and **fbi_list** tables.)

```
UPDATE inmate (picture)
    SET picture = (SELECT LOCOPY(mugshot, 'inmate', 'picture')
                      FROM fbi_list WHERE fbi_list.id = 669)
    WHERE inmate.id_num = 437
```

The first argument for **LOCOPY()** specifies the column (**mugshot**) from which the object is exported. The second and third arguments specify the name of the table (**inmate**) and column (**picture**) whose storage characteristics the newly created object will use. After execution of the UPDATE statement, the **picture** column contains data from the **mugshot** column.

When you specify the path of a filename in the function argument, apply the following rules:

- If the source file resides on the server computer, you must specify the full pathname to the file (not the pathname relative to the current working directory).
- If the source file resides on the client computer, you can specify either the full or relative pathname to the file.

EDS

Using a Join to Update a Column

Enterprise Decision Server allows you to use a join on tables to determine which columns to update. You can use columns from any table that you list in the FROM clause in the SET clause to specify values for the columns and rows to update.

When you use the FROM clause, you must include the name of the table in which the update is to be performed. Otherwise, an error results. The following example illustrates how you can use the UPDATE statement with a FROM clause:

```
UPDATE t SET a = t2.a FROM t, t2 WHERE t.b = t2.b
```

In the preceding example, the statement performs the same action as it does when you omit the FROM clause altogether. You are allowed to specify more than one table in the FROM clause of the UPDATE statement. However, if you specify only one table, it must be the target table.

Privileges on a Database

You can use the following database privileges to control who accesses a database:

- Database-level privileges
- Table-level privileges
- Column-level privileges
- Routine-level privileges

This section briefly describes database- and table-level privileges. For more information about database privileges, see the *Informix Guide to Database Design and Implementation*. For a list of privileges and a description of the GRANT and REVOKE statements, see the *Informix Guide to SQL: Syntax*.

Database-Level Privileges

When you create a database, you are the only one who can access it until you, as the owner or database administrator (DBA) of the database, grant database-level privileges to others. The following table shows the database-level privileges.

Privilege	Purpose
Connect	Allows you to open a database, issue queries, and create and place indexes on temporary tables.
Resource	Allows you to create permanent tables.
DBA	Allows you to perform several additional functions as the DBA.

Table-Level Privileges

When you create a table in a database that is not ANSI compliant, all users have access privileges to the table until you, as the owner of the table, revoke table-level privileges from specific users. The following table introduces the four privileges that govern how users can access a table.

Privilege	Purpose
Select	Granted on a table-by-table basis and allows you to select rows from a table. (This privilege can be limited to specific columns in a table.)
Delete	Allows you to delete rows.

(1 of 2)

Privilege	Purpose
Insert	Allows you to insert rows.
Update	Allows you to update existing rows (that is, to change their content).

(2 of 2)

The people who create databases and tables often grant the Connect and Select privileges to **public** so that all users have them. If you can query a table, you have at least the Connect and Select privileges for that database and table.

You need the other table-level privileges to modify data. The owners of tables often withhold these privileges or grant them only to specific users. As a result, you might not be able to modify some tables that you can query freely.

Because these privileges are granted on a table-by-table basis, you can have only Insert privileges on one table and only Update privileges on another, for example. The Update privileges can be restricted even further to specific columns in a table.

For more information on these and other table-level privileges, see the *Informix Guide to Database Design and Implementation*.

Displaying Table Privileges

If you are the owner of a table (that is, if you created it), you have all privileges on that table. Otherwise, you can determine the privileges you have for a certain table by querying the system catalog. The system catalog consists of system tables that describe the database structure. The privileges granted on each table are recorded in the **systabauth** system table. To display these privileges, you must also know the unique identifier number of the table. This number is specified in the **systables** system table. To display privileges granted on the **orders** table, you might enter the following SELECT statement:

```
SELECT * FROM systabauth
    WHERE tabid = (SELECT tabid FROM systables
                        WHERE tabname = 'orders')
```

The output of the query resembles the following example.

```
grantorgranteetabid       tabauth

tfecitmutator101    su-i-x--
tfecitprocrustes101 s--idx--
tfecitpublic101     s--i-x--
```

The grantor is the user who *grants* the privilege. The grantor is usually the owner of the table but the owner can be another user that the grantor empowered. The grantee is the user to whom the privilege is granted, and the grantee **public** means "any user with Connect privilege." If your user name does not appear, you have only those privileges granted to **public**.

The **tabauth** column specifies the privileges granted. The letters in each row of this column are the initial letters of the privilege names except that i means Insert and x means Index. In this example, **public** has Select, Insert, and Index privileges. Only the user **mutator** has Update privileges, and only the user **procrustes** has Delete privileges.

Before the database server performs any action for you (for example, execution of a DELETE statement), it performs a query similar to the preceding one. If you are not the owner of the table, and if the database server cannot find the necessary privilege on the table for your user name or for **public**, it refuses to perform the operation.

Data Integrity

The INSERT, UPDATE, and DELETE statements modify data in an existing database. Whenever you modify existing data, the *integrity* of the data can be affected. For example, an order for a nonexistent product could be entered into the **orders** table, a customer with outstanding orders could be deleted from the **customer** table, or the order number could be updated in the **orders** table and *not* in the **items** table. In each of these cases, the integrity of the stored data is lost.

Data integrity is actually made up of the following parts:

- Entity integrity

  Each row of a table has a unique identifier.

- Semantic integrity

  The data in the columns properly reflects the types of information the column was designed to hold.

- Referential integrity

  The relationships between tables are enforced.

Well-designed databases incorporate these principles so that when you modify data, the database itself prevents you from doing anything that might harm the integrity of the data.

Entity Integrity

An entity is any person, place, or thing to be recorded in a database. Each table represents an entity, and each row of a table represents an instance of that entity. For example, if *order* is an entity, the **orders** table represents the idea of an order and *each row* in the table represents a specific order.

To identify each row in a table, the table must have a primary key. The primary key is a unique value that identifies each row. This requirement is called the *entity integrity constraint.*

For example, the **orders** table primary key is **order_num**. The **order_num** column holds a unique system-generated order number for each row in the table. To access a row of data in the **orders** table, use the following SELECT statement:

```
SELECT * FROM orders WHERE order_num = 1001
```

Using the order number in the WHERE clause of this statement enables you to access a row easily because the order number uniquely identifies that row. If the table allowed duplicate order numbers, it would be almost impossible to access one single row because all other columns of this table allow duplicate values.

For more information on primary keys and entity integrity, see the *Informix Guide to Database Design and Implementation.*

Semantic Integrity

Semantic integrity ensures that data entered into a row reflects an allowable value for that row. The value must be within the *domain*, or allowable set of values, for that column. For example, the **quantity** column of the **items** table permits only numbers. If a value outside the domain can be entered into a column, the semantic integrity of the data is violated.

The following constraints enforce semantic integrity:

- Data type

  The data type defines the types of values that you can store in a column. For example, the data type SMALLINT allows you to enter values from -32,767 to 32,767 into a column.

- Default value

  The default value is the value inserted into the column when an explicit value is not specified. For example, the **user_id** column of the **cust_calls** table defaults to the login name of the user if no name is entered.

- Check constraint

  The check constraint specifies conditions on data inserted into a column. Each row inserted into a table must meet these conditions. For example, the **quantity** column of the **items** table might check for quantities greater than or equal to one.

  For more information on how to use semantic integrity constraints in database design, see the *Informix Guide to Database Design and Implementation*.

Referential Integrity

Referential integrity refers to the relationship *between* tables. Because each table in a database must have a primary key, this primary key can appear in other tables because of its relationship to data within those tables. When a primary key from one table appears in another table, it is called a foreign key.

Foreign keys *join* tables and establish dependencies between tables. Tables can form a hierarchy of dependencies in such a way that if you change or delete a row in one table, you destroy the meaning of rows in other tables. For example, Figure 6-4 shows that the **customer_num** column of the **customer** table is a primary key for that table and a foreign key in the **orders** and **cust_call** tables. Customer number 106, George Watson, is *referenced* in both the **orders** and **cust_calls** tables. If customer 106 is deleted from the **customer** table, the link between the three tables and this particular customer is destroyed.

Figure 6-4
Referential Integrity in the Demonstration Database

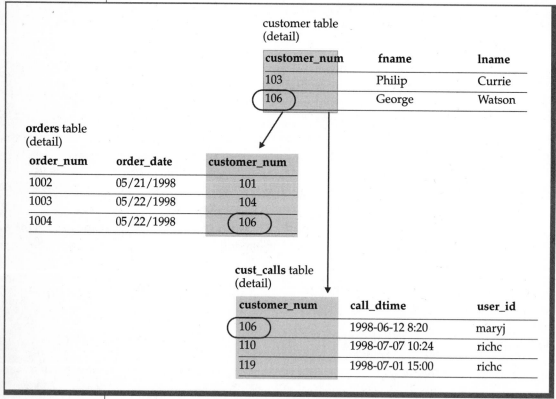

When you delete a row that contains a primary key or update it with a different primary key, you destroy the meaning of any rows that contain that value as a foreign key. Referential integrity is the logical dependency of a foreign key on a primary key. The *integrity* of a row that contains a foreign key depends on the integrity of the row that it *references*—the row that contains the matching primary key.

By default, the database server does not allow you to violate referential integrity and gives you an error message if you attempt to delete rows from the parent table before you delete rows from the child table. You can, however, use the ON DELETE CASCADE option to cause deletes from a parent table to trip deletes on child tables. See "Using the ON DELETE CASCADE Option" on page 6-39.

To define primary and foreign keys, and the relationship between them, use the CREATE TABLE and ALTER TABLE statements. For more information on these statements, see the *Informix Guide to SQL: Syntax*. For information about how to build a data model with primary and foreign keys, see the *Informix Guide to Database Design and Implementation*.

Using the ON DELETE CASCADE Option

To maintain referential integrity when you delete rows from a primary key for a table, use the ON DELETE CASCADE option in the REFERENCES clause of the CREATE TABLE and ALTER TABLE statements. This option allows you to delete a row from a parent table and its corresponding rows in matching child tables with a single delete command.

Locking During Cascading Deletes

During deletes, locks are held on all qualifying rows of the parent and child tables. When you specify a delete, the delete that is requested from the parent table occurs before any referential actions are performed.

What Happens to Multiple Children Tables

If you have a parent table with two child constraints, one child with cascading deletes specified and one child without cascading deletes, and you attempt to delete a row from the parent table that applies to both child tables, the DELETE statement fails, and no rows are deleted from either the parent or child tables.

Logging Must Be Turned On

You must turn on logging in your current database for cascading deletes to work. Logging and cascading deletes are discussed in "Transaction Logging" on page 6-53.

Example of Cascading Deletes

Suppose you have two tables with referential integrity rules applied, a parent table, **accounts**, and a child table, **sub_accounts**. The following CREATE TABLE statements define the referential constraints:

```
CREATE TABLE accounts (
  acc_num SERIAL primary key,
  acc_type INT,
  acc_descr CHAR(20));

CREATE TABLE sub_accounts (
  sub_acc INTEGER primary key,
  ref_num INTEGER REFERENCES accounts (acc_num) ON DELETE CASCADE,
  sub_descr CHAR(20));
```

The primary key of the **accounts** table, the **acc_num** column, uses a SERIAL data type, and the foreign key of the **sub_accounts** table, the **ref_num** column, uses an INTEGER data type. Combining the SERIAL data type on the primary key and the INTEGER data type on the foreign key is allowed. Only in this condition can you mix and match data types. The SERIAL data type is an INTEGER, and the database automatically generates the values for the column. All other primary and foreign key combinations must match explicitly. For example, a primary key that is defined as CHAR must match a foreign key that is defined as CHAR.

The definition of the foreign key of the **sub_accounts** table, the **ref_num** column, includes the ON DELETE CASCADE option. This option specifies that a delete of any row in the parent table **accounts** will automatically cause the corresponding rows of the child table **sub_accounts** to be deleted.

To delete a row from the **accounts** table that will cascade a delete to the **sub_accounts** table, you must turn on logging. After logging is turned on, you can delete the account number 2 from both tables, as the following example shows:

```
DELETE FROM accounts WHERE acc_num = 2
```

Restrictions on Cascading Deletes

You can use cascading deletes for most deletes, including deletes on self-referencing and cyclic queries. The only exception is correlated subqueries. In correlated subqueries, the subquery (or inner SELECT) is correlated when the value it produces depends on a value produced by the outer SELECT statement that contains it. If you have implemented cascading deletes, you cannot write deletes that use a child table in the correlated subquery. You receive an error when you attempt to delete from a correlated subquery.

Important: *You cannot define a DELETE trigger event on a table if the table defines a referential constraint with ON DELETE CASCADE.*

Object Modes and Violation Detection

The object modes and violation detection features of the database can help you monitor data integrity. These features are particularly powerful when they are combined during schema changes or when insert, delete, and update operations are performed on large volumes of data over short periods.

Database objects, within the context of a discussion of the object modes feature, are constraints, indexes, and triggers, and each of them have different modes. Do not confuse database objects that are relevant to the object modes feature with generic database objects. Generic database objects are things like tables and synonyms.

Definitions of Object Modes

You can set disabled, enabled, or filtering modes for a constraint or a unique index. You can set disabled or enabled modes for a trigger or a duplicate index. You can use database object modes to control the effects of INSERT, DELETE, and UPDATE statements.

Enabled Mode

Constraints, indexes, and triggers are enabled by default.

IDS

When a database object is enabled, the database server recognizes the existence of the database object and takes the database object into consideration while it executes an INSERT, DELETE, OR UPDATE statement. Thus, an enabled constraint is enforced, an enabled index updated, and an enabled trigger is executed when the trigger event takes place.

When you enable constraints and unique indexes, if a violating row exists, the data manipulation statement fails (that is no rows change) and the database server returns an error message.

You can identify the reason for the failure when you analyze the information in the violations and diagnostic tables. You can then take corrective action or roll back the operation. ♦

IDS

Disabled Mode

When a database object is disabled, the database server does not take it into consideration during the execution of an INSERT, DELETE, OR UPDATE statement. A disabled constraint is not enforced, a disabled index is not updated, and a disabled trigger is not executed when the trigger event takes place. When you disable constraints and unique indexes, any data manipulation statement that violates the restriction of the constraint or unique index succeeds, (that is the target row is changed) and the database server does not return an error message. ♦

Filtering Mode

When a constraint or unique index is in filtering mode, the statement succeeds and the database server enforces the constraint or the unique index requirement during an INSERT, DELETE, OR UPDATE statement by writing the failed rows to the violations table associated with the target table. Diagnostic information about the constraint violation is written to the diagnostics table associated with the target table.

Example of Modes with Data Manipulation Statements

An example with the INSERT statement can illustrate the differences between the enabled, disabled, and filtering modes. Consider an INSERT statement in which a user tries to add a row that does not satisfy an integrity constraint on a table. For example, assume that user **joe** created a table named **cust_subset**, and this table consists of the following columns: **ssn** (customer's social security number), **fname** (customer's first name), **lname** (customer's last name), and **city** (city in which the customer lives). The **ssn** column has the INT data type. The other three columns have the CHAR data type.

Assume that user **joe** defined the **lname** column as not null but has not assigned a name to the not null constraint, so the database server has implicitly assigned the name **n104_7** to this constraint. Finally, assume that user **joe** created a unique index named **unq_ssn** on the **ssn** column.

Now user **linda** who has the Insert privilege on the **cust_subset** table enters the following INSERT statement on this table:

```
INSERT INTO cust_subset (ssn, fname, city)
    VALUES (973824499, "jane", "los altos")
```

To better understand the distinctions among enabled, disabled, and filtering modes, you can view the results of the preceding INSERT statement in the following three sections.

Results of the Insert Operation When the Constraint Is Enabled

If the not null constraint on the **cust_subset** table is enabled, the INSERT statement fails to insert the new row in this table. Instead user **linda** receives the following error message when she enters the INSERT statement:

```
-292 An implied insert column lname does not accept NULLs.
```

Results of the Insert Operation When the Constraint Is Disabled

If the not null constraint on the **cust_subset** table is disabled, the INSERT statement that user **linda** issues successfully inserts the new row in this table. The new row of the **cust_subset** table has the following column values.

ssn	fname	lname	city
973824499	jane	NULL	los altos

Results of the Insert When Constraint Is in Filtering Mode

If the not null constraint on the **cust_subset** table is set to the filtering mode, the INSERT statement that user **linda** issues fails to insert the new row in this table. Instead the new row is inserted into the violations table, and a diagnostic row that describes the integrity violation is added to the diagnostics table.

Assume that user **joe** has started a violations and diagnostics table for the **cust_subset** table. The violations table is named **cust_subset_vio**, and the diagnostics table is named **cust_subset_dia**. The new row added to the **cust_subset_vio** violations table when user **linda** issues the INSERT statement on the **cust_subset** target table has the following column values.

ssn	fname	lname	city	informix_tupleid	informix_optype	informix_recowner
973824499	jane	NULL	los altos	1	I	linda

This new row in the **cust_subset_vio** violations table has the following characteristics:

- The first four columns of the violations table exactly match the columns of the target table. These four columns have the same names and the same data types as the corresponding columns of the target table, and they have the column values that were supplied by the INSERT statement that user **linda** entered.

- The value 1 in the **informix_tupleid** column is a unique serial identifier that is assigned to the nonconforming row.

- The value I in the **informix_optype** column is a code that identifies the type of operation that has caused this nonconforming row to be created. Specifically, I stands for an insert operation.

- The value linda in the **informix_recowner** column identifies the user who issued the statement that caused this nonconforming row to be created.

The INSERT statement that user **linda** issued on the **cust_subset** target table also causes a diagnostic row to be added to the **cust_subset_dia** diagnostics table. The new diagnostic row added to the diagnostics table has the following column values.

informix_tupleid	objtype	objowner	objname
1	C	joe	n104_7

This new diagnostic row in the **cust_subset_dia** diagnostics table has the following characteristics:

- This row of the diagnostics table is linked to the corresponding row of the violations table by means of the **informix_tupleid** column that appears in both tables. The value 1 appears in this column in both tables.

- The value C in the **objtype** column identifies the type of integrity violation that the corresponding row in the violations table caused. Specifically, the value C stands for a constraint violation.

- The value joe in the **objowner** column identifies the owner of the constraint for which an integrity violation was detected.

- The value n104_7 in the **objname** column gives the name of the constraint for which an integrity violation was detected.

By joining the violations and diagnostics tables, user **joe** (who owns the **cust_subset** target table and its associated special tables) or the DBA can find out that the row in the violations table whose **informix_tupleid** value is 1 was created after an INSERT statement and that this row is violating a constraint. The table owner or DBA can query the **sysconstraints** system catalog table to determine that this constraint is a not null constraint. Now that the reason for the failure of the INSERT statement is known, user **joe** or the DBA can take corrective action.

Multiple Diagnostic Rows for One Violations Row

In the preceding example, only one row in the diagnostics table corresponds to the new row in the violations table. However, more than one diagnostic row can be added to the diagnostics table when a single new row is added to the violations table. For example, if the **ssn** value (973824499) that user **linda** entered in the INSERT statement had been the same as an existing value in the **ssn** column of the **cust_subset** target table, only one new row would appear in the violations table, but the following two diagnostic rows would be present in the **cust_subset_dia** diagnostics table.

informix_tupleid	objtype	objowner	objname
1	C	joe	n104_7
1	I	joe	unq_ssn

Both rows in the diagnostics table correspond to the same row of the violations table because both of these rows have the value 1 in the **informix_tupleid** column. However, the first diagnostic row identifies the constraint violation caused by the INSERT statement that user **linda** issued, while the second diagnostic row identifies the unique-index violation caused by the same INSERT statement. In this second diagnostic row, the value I in the **objtype** column stands for a unique-index violation, and the value unq_ssn in the **objname** column gives the name of the index for which the integrity violation was detected.

For more information about how to set database object modes, see the SET DATABASE OBJECT MODE statement in the *Informix Guide to SQL: Syntax*.

Violations and Diagnostics Tables

When you start a violations table for a target table, any rows that violate constraints and unique indexes during insert, update, and delete operations on the target table do not cause the entire operation to fail, but are filtered out to the violations table. The diagnostics table contains information about the integrity violations caused by each row in the violations table. By examining these tables, you can identify the cause of failure and take corrective action by either fixing the violation or rolling back the operation.

After you create a violations table for a target table, you cannot alter the columns or the fragmentation of the base table or the violations table. If you alter the constraints on a target table after you have started the violations table, nonconforming rows will be filtered to the violations table.

EDS

When you create a violations table for a target table on Enterprise Decision Server, all constraints are in filtering mode. The violations table contains fields that record the diagnostic information, thus no separate diagnostics table exists. ♦

For information about how to start and stop the violations tables, see the START VIOLATIONS TABLE and STOP VIOLATIONS TABLE statements in the *Informix Guide to SQL: Syntax*.

Relationship of Violations Tables and Database Object Modes

If you set the constraints or unique indexes defined on a table to the filtering mode, but you do not create the violations and diagnostics tables for this target table, any rows that violate a constraint or unique-index requirement during an insert, update, or delete operation are not filtered to a violations table. Instead, you receive an error message that indicates that you must start a violations table for the target table.

Similarly, if you set a disabled constraint or disabled unique index to the enabled or filtering mode and you want the ability to identify existing rows that do not satisfy the constraint or unique-index requirement, you must create the violations tables before you issue the SET DATABASE OBJECT MODE statement.

Examples of START VIOLATIONS TABLE Statements

The following examples show different ways to execute the START VIOLATIONS TABLE statement.

Starting Violations and Diagnostics Tables Without Specifying Their Names

To start a violations and diagnostics table for the target table named **customer** in the demonstration database, enter the following statement:

```
START VIOLATIONS TABLE FOR customer
```

Because your START VIOLATIONS TABLE statement does not include a USING clause, the violations table is named **customer_vio** by default, and the diagnostics table is named **customer_dia** by default. The **customer_vio** table includes the following columns:

```
customer_num
fname
lname
company
address1
address2
city
state
zipcode
phone
informix_tupleid
informix_optype
informix_recowner
```

The **customer_vio** table has the same table definition as the **customer** table except that the **customer_vio** table has three additional columns that contain information about the operation that caused the bad row.

The **customer_dia** table includes the following columns:

```
informix_tupleid
objtype
objowner
objname
```

This list of columns shows an important difference between the diagnostics table and violations table for a target table. Whereas the violations table has a matching column for every column in the target table, the columns of the diagnostics table do not match any columns in the target table. The diagnostics table created by any START VIOLATIONS TABLE statement always has the same columns with the same column names and data types.

Starting Violations and Diagnostics Tables and Specifying Their Names

The following statement starts a violations and diagnostics table for the target table named **items**. The USING clause assigns explicit names to the violations and diagnostics tables. The violations table is to be named **exceptions**, and the diagnostics table is to be named **reasons**.

```
START VIOLATIONS TABLE FOR items
    USING exceptions, reasons
```

Specifying the Maximum Number of Rows in the Diagnostics Table

The following statement starts violations and diagnostics tables for the target table named **orders**. The MAX ROWS clause specifies the maximum number of rows that can be inserted into the diagnostics table when a single statement, such as an INSERT or SET DATABASE OBJECT MODE statement, is executed on the target table.

```
START VIOLATIONS TABLE FOR orders MAX ROWS 50000
```

If you do not specify a value for MAX ROWS when you create a violations table, no maximum (other than disk space) will be imposed.

Example of Privileges on the Violations Table

The following example illustrates how the initial set of privileges on a violations table is derived from the current set of privileges on the target table.

For example, assume that we created a table named **cust_subset** and that this table consists of the following columns: **ssn** (customer's social security number), **fname** (customer's first name), **lname** (customer's last name), and **city** (city in which the customer lives).

The following set of privileges exists on the **cust_subset** table:

- User **alvin** is the owner of the table.
- User **barbara** has the Insert and Index privileges on the table. She also has the Select privilege on the **ssn** and **lname** columns.
- User **carrie** has the Update privilege on the **city** column. She also has the Select privilege on the **ssn** column.
- User **danny** has the Alter privilege on the table.

Now user **alvin** starts a violations table named **cust_subset_viols** and a diagnostics table named **cust_subset_diags** for the **cust_subset** table, as follows:

```
START VIOLATIONS TABLE FOR cust_subset
    USING cust_subset_viols, cust_subset_diags
```

The database server grants the following set of initial privileges on the **cust_subset_viols** violations table:

- User **alvin** is the owner of the violations table, so he has all table-level privileges on the table.

- User **barbara** has the Insert, Delete, and Index privileges on the violations table. She also has the Select privilege on the following columns of the violations table: the **ssn** column, the **lname** column, the **informix_tupleid** column, the **informix_optype** column, and the **informix_recowner** column.

- User **carrie** has the Insert and Delete privileges on the violations table. She has the Update privilege on the following columns of the violations table: the **city** column, the **informix_tupleid** column, the **informix_optype** column, and the **informix_recowner** column. She has the Select privilege on the following columns of the violations table: the **ssn** column, the **informix_tupleid** column, the **informix_optype** column, and the **informix_recowner** column.

- User **danny** has no privileges on the violations table.

Example of Privileges on the Diagnostics Table

The following example illustrates how the initial set of privileges on a diagnostics table is derived from the current set of privileges on the target table.

For example, assume that a table called **cust_subset** consists of the following columns: **ssn** (customer's social security number), **fname** (customer's first name), **lname** (customer's last name), and **city** (city in which the customer lives).

The following set of privileges exists on the **cust_subset** table:

- User **alvin** is the owner of the table.

- User **barbara** has the Insert and Index privileges on the table. She also has the Select privilege on the **ssn** and **lname** columns.

- User **carrie** has the Update privilege on the **city** column. She also has the Select privilege on the **ssn** column.

- User **danny** has the Alter privilege on the table.

Now user **alvin** starts a violations table named **cust_subset_viols** and a diagnostics table named **cust_subset_diags** for the **cust_subset** table, as follows:

```
START VIOLATIONS TABLE FOR cust_subset
    USING cust_subset_viols, cust_subset_diags
```

The database server grants the following set of initial privileges on the **cust_subset_diags** diagnostics table:

- User **alvin** is the owner of the diagnostics table, so he has all table-level privileges on the table.
- User **barbara** has the Insert, Delete, Select, and Index privileges on the diagnostics table.
- User **carrie** has the Insert, Delete, Select, and Update privileges on the diagnostics table.
- User **danny** has no privileges on the diagnostics table.

Interrupted Modifications

Even if all the software is error-free and all the hardware is utterly reliable, the world outside the computer can interfere. Lightning might strike the building, interrupting the electrical supply and stopping the computer in the middle of your UPDATE statement. A more likely scenario occurs when a disk fills up or a user supplies incorrect data, causing your multirow insert to stop early with an error. In any case, as you are modifying data, you must assume that some unforeseen event can interrupt the modification.

When an external cause interrupts a modification, you cannot be sure how much of the operation was completed. Even in a single-row operation, you cannot know whether the data reached the disk or the indexes were properly updated.

If multirow modifications are a problem, multistatement modifications are worse. They are usually embedded in programs so you do not see the individual SQL statements being executed. For example, to enter a new order in the demonstration database, perform the following steps:

1. Insert a row in the **orders** table. (This insert generates an order number.)

2. For each item ordered, insert a row in the **items** table.

Two ways to program an order-entry application exist. One way is to make it completely interactive so that the program inserts the first row immediately and then inserts each item as the user enters data. But this approach exposes the operation to the possibility of many more unforeseen events: the customer's telephone disconnecting, the user pressing the wrong key, the user's terminal or computer losing power, and so on.

The following list describes the correct way to build an order-entry application:

- Accept all the data interactively.
- Validate the data, and expand it (look up codes in **stock** and **manufact**, for example).
- Display the information on the screen for inspection.
- Wait for the operator to make a final commitment.
- Perform the insertions quickly.

Even with these steps, an unforeseen circumstance can halt the program after it inserts the order but before it finishes inserting the items. If that happens, the database is in an unpredictable condition: its *data integrity* is compromised.

Transactions

The solution to all these potential problems is called the *transaction*. A transaction is a sequence of modifications that must be accomplished either completely or not at all. The database server guarantees that operations performed within the bounds of a transaction are either completely and perfectly committed to disk, or the database is restored to the same state as before the transaction started.

The transaction is not merely protection against unforeseen failures; it also offers a program a way to escape when the program detects a logical error.

Transaction Logging

The database server can keep a record of each change that it makes to the database during a transaction. If something happens to cancel the transaction, the database server automatically uses the records to reverse the changes. Many things can make a transaction fail. For example, the program that issues the SQL statements can fail or be terminated. As soon as the database server discovers that the transaction failed, which might be only after the computer and the database server are restarted, it uses the records from the transaction to return the database to the same state as before.

The process of keeping records of transactions is called *transaction logging* or simply *logging*. The records of the transactions, called *log records*, are stored in a portion of disk space separate from the database. This space is called the *logical log* because the log records represent logical units of the transactions.

EDS

Only databases on Enterprise Decision Server generate transaction records automatically. ♦

Most Informix databases do not generate transaction records automatically. The DBA decides whether to make a database use transaction logging. Without transaction logging, you cannot roll back transactions.

EDS

Transaction Logging for Enterprise Decision Server

In addition to logical-log files, Enterprise Decision Server allows you to create *logslices* and alter them to add logical logs at any time. A logslice is a set of log files that occupy a dbslice. These log files are owned by multiple coservers, one log file per dbspace. Logslices simplify the process of adding and deleting log files because a logslice treats a set of log files as a single entity. You create, alter, and delete dbslices using the **onutil** utility. For more information about logslices, see the *Administrator's Guide*.

Databases on Enterprise Decision Server must be logged databases and logging cannot be turned off. However, you can specify that individual tables are logging or nonlogging tables. To meet the need for both logging and nonlogging tables, Enterprise Decision Server supports the following types of permanent tables and temporary tables:

- Raw permanent tables (nonlogging)
- Static permanent tables (nonlogging)
- Operational permanent tables (logging)
- Standard permanent tables (logging)
- Scratch temporary tables (nonlogging)
- Temp temporary tables (logging)

For more information about the table types that Enterprise Decision Server supports, see the *Informix Guide to Database Design and Implementation*.

Logging and Cascading Deletes

Logging must be turned on in your database for cascading deletes to work because, when you specify a cascading delete, the delete is first performed on the primary key of the parent table. If the system fails after the rows of the primary key of the parent table are performed but before the rows of the foreign key of the child table are deleted, referential integrity is violated. If logging is turned off, even temporarily, deletes do not cascade. After logging is turned back on, however, deletes can cascade again.

EDS

Databases that you create with Enterprise Decision Server are always logging databases. ♦

IDS

Dynamic Server allows you to turn on logging with the WITH LOG clause in the CREATE DATABASE statement. ♦

Specifying Transactions

You can use two methods to specify the boundaries of transactions with SQL statements. In the most common method, you specify the start of a multi-statement transaction by executing the BEGIN WORK statement. In databases that are created with the MODE ANSI option, no need exists to mark the beginning of a transaction. One is always in effect; you indicate only the end of each transaction.

In both methods, to specify the end of a successful transaction, execute the COMMIT WORK statement. This statement tells the database server that you reached the end of a series of statements that must succeed together. The database server does whatever is necessary to make sure that all modifications are properly completed and committed to disk.

A program can also cancel a transaction deliberately by executing the ROLLBACK WORK statement. This statement asks the database server to cancel the current transaction and undo any changes.

An order-entry application can use a transaction in the following ways when it creates a new order:

- Accept all data interactively
- ·Validate and expand it
- Wait for the operator to make a final commitment
- Execute BEGIN WORK
- Insert rows in the **orders** and **items** tables, checking the error code that the database server returns
- If no errors occurred, execute COMMIT WORK; otherwise execute ROLLBACK WORK

If any external failure prevents the transaction from being completed, the partial transaction rolls back when the system restarts. In all cases, the database is in a predictable state. Either the new order is completely entered, or it is not entered at all.

Backups and Logs with Informix Database Servers

By using transactions, you can ensure that the database is always in a consistent state and that your modifications are properly recorded on disk. But the disk itself is not perfectly safe. It is vulnerable to mechanical failures and to flood, fire, and earthquake. The only safeguard is to keep multiple copies of the data. These redundant copies are called *backup* copies.

The transaction log (also called the logical log) complements the backup copy of a database. Its contents are a history of all modifications that occurred since the last time the database was backed up. If you ever need to restore the database from the backup copy, you can use the transaction log to roll the database forward to its most recent state.

The database server contains elaborate features to support backups and logging. Your database server archive and backup guide describes these features.

The database server has stringent requirements for performance and reliability (for example, it supports making backup copies while databases are in use).

The database server manages its own disk space, which is devoted to logging.

The database server performs logging concurrently for all databases using a limited set of log files. The log files can be copied to another medium (backed up) while transactions are active.

Database users never have to be concerned with these facilities because the DBA usually manages them from a central location.

IDS

Dynamic Server supports the **onload** and **onunload** utilities. Use the **onunload** utility to make a personal backup copy of a single database or table. This program copies a table or a database to tape. Its output consists of binary images of the disk pages as they were stored in the database server. As a result, the copy can be made quickly, and the corresponding **onload** program can restore the file quickly. However, the data format is not meaningful to any other programs. For information about how to use the **onload** and **onunload** utilities, see the *Informix Migration Guide.* ♦

EDS

Enterprise Decision Server uses *external tables* to load or unload data. For information about how to use external tables to load data, see the *Administrator's Guide.* ♦

If your DBA uses ON-Bar to create backups and back up logical logs, you might also be able to create your own backup copies using ON-Bar. For more information, see your *Informix Backup and Restore Guide*.

Concurrency and Locks

If your database is contained in a single-user workstation, without a network connecting it to other computers, concurrency is unimportant. In all other cases, you must allow for the possibility that, while your program is modifying data, another program is also reading or modifying the same data. *Concurrency* involves two or more independent uses of the same data at the same time.

A high level of concurrency is crucial to good performance in a multiuser database system. Unless controls exist on the use of data, however, concurrency can lead to a variety of negative effects. Programs could read obsolete data; modifications could be lost even though it seems they were entered successfully.

To prevent errors of this kind, the database server imposes a system of *locks*. A lock is a claim, or reservation, that a program can place on a piece of data. The database server guarantees that, as long as the data is locked, no other program can modify it. When another program requests the data, the database server either makes the program wait or turns it back with an error.

To control the effect that locks have on your data access, use a combination of SQL statements: SET LOCK MODE and either SET ISOLATION or SET TRANSACTION. You can understand the details of these statements after reading a discussion on the use of *cursors* from within programs. Cursors are covered in Chapter 7 and Chapter 8. For more information about locking and concurrency, see Chapter 9.

IDS

Informix Data Replication

Data replication, in the broadest sense of the term, means that database objects have more than one representation at more than one distinct site. For example, one way to replicate data, so that reports can be run against the data without disturbing client applications that are using the original database, is to copy the database to a database server on a different computer.

The following list describes the advantages of data replication:

- Clients who access replicated data locally, as opposed to remote data that is not replicated, experience improved performance because they do not have to use network services.

- Clients at all sites experience improved availability with replicated data, because if local replicated data is unavailable, a copy of the data is still available, albeit remotely.

These advantages do not come without a cost. Data replication obviously requires more storage for replicated data than for unreplicated data, and updating replicated data can take more processing time than updating a single object.

Data replication can actually be implemented in the logic of client applications, by explicitly specifying where data should be found or updated. However, this method of achieving data replication is costly, error-prone, and difficult to maintain. Instead, the concept of data replication is often coupled with *replication transparency*. Replication transparency is functionality built into a database server (instead of client applications) to handle the details of locating and maintaining data replicas automatically.

Within the broad framework of data replication, an Informix database server implements nearly transparent data replication of entire database servers. All the data that one Informix database server manages is replicated and dynamically updated on another Informix database server, usually at a remote site. Data replication of an Informix database server is sometimes called *hot-site backup*, because it provides a means of maintaining a backup copy of the entire database server that can be used quickly in the event of a catastrophic failure.

Because the database server provides replication transparency, you generally do not need to be concerned with or aware of data replication; the DBA takes care of it. However, if your organization decides to use data replication, you should be aware that special connectivity considerations exist for client applications in a data replication environment. These considerations are described in the *Administrator's Guide*.

The Informix Enterprise Replication feature provides a different method of data replication. For information on this feature, see the *Guide to Informix Enterprise Replication*.

Summary

Database access is regulated by the privileges that the database owner grants to you. The privileges that let you query data are often granted automatically, but the ability to modify data is regulated by specific Insert, Delete, and Update privileges that are granted on a table-by-table basis.

If data integrity constraints are imposed on the database, your ability to modify data is restricted by those constraints. Your database- and table-level privileges and any data constraints control how and when you can modify data. In addition, the object modes and violation detection features of the database affect how you can modify data and help to preserve the integrity of your data.

You can delete one or more rows from a table with the DELETE statement. Its WHERE clause selects the rows; use a SELECT statement with the same clause to preview the deletes.

Rows are added to a table with the INSERT statement. You can insert a single row that contains specified column values, or you can insert a block of rows that a SELECT statement generates.

Use the UPDATE statement to modify the contents of existing rows. You specify the new contents with expressions that can include subqueries, so that you can use data that is based on other tables or the updated table itself. The statement has two forms. In the first form, you specify new values column by column. In the second form, a SELECT statement or a record variable generates a set of new values.

Summary

Use the REFERENCES clause of the CREATE TABLE and ALTER TABLE statements to create relationships between tables. The ON DELETE CASCADE option of the REFERENCES clause allows you to delete rows from parent and associated child tables with one DELETE statement.

Use transactions to prevent unforeseen interruptions in a modification from leaving the database in an indeterminate state. When modifications are performed within a transaction, they are rolled back after an error occurs. The transaction log also extends the periodically made backup copy of the database. If the database must be restored, it can be brought back to its most recent state.

Data replication, which is transparent to users, offers another type of protection from catastrophic failures.

Programming with SQL

In This Chapter 7-3

SQL in Programs 7-4
   SQL in SQL APIs 7-4
   SQL in Application Languages 7-5
   Static Embedding 7-5
   Dynamic Statements 7-5
   Program Variables and Host Variables 7-6

Calling the Database Server 7-8
   SQL Communications Area 7-8
   SQLCODE Field 7-9
      End of Data 7-9
      Negative Codes 7-10
   SQLERRD Array 7-10
   SQLWARN Array 7-11
   SQLERRM Character String 7-13
   SQLSTATE Value 7-13

Retrieving Single Rows 7-14
   Data Type Conversion 7-15
   Working with Null Data 7-16
   Dealing with Errors 7-17
      End of Data 7-17
      End of Data with Databases That Are Not ANSI Compliant . . 7-17
      Serious Errors 7-18
      Interpreting End of Data with Aggregate Functions 7-18
      Using Default Values 7-19

Retrieving Multiple Rows 7-19
　　Declaring a Cursor. 7-20
　　Opening a Cursor 7-21
　　Fetching Rows 7-21
　　　　Detecting End of Data 7-22
　　　　Locating the INTO Clause 7-22
　　Cursor Input Modes 7-23
　　Active Set of a Cursor. 7-24
　　　　Creating the Active Set 7-24
　　　　Active Set for a Sequential Cursor 7-25
　　　　Active Set for a Scroll Cursor 7-25
　　　　Active Set and Concurrency 7-25
　　Using a Cursor: A Parts Explosion 7-26

Dynamic SQL 7-29
　　Preparing a Statement 7-29
　　Executing Prepared SQL. 7-31
　　Dynamic Host Variables 7-31
　　Freeing Prepared Statements 7-32
　　Quick Execution 7-33

Embedding Data-Definition Statements 7-33

Embedding Grant and Revoke Privileges 7-33

Summary 7-37

In This Chapter

The examples in the previous chapters treat SQL as if it were an interactive computer language; that is, as if you could type a SELECT statement directly into the database server and see rows of data rolling back to you.

Of course, that is not the case. Many layers of software stand between you and the database server. The database server retains data in a binary form that must be formatted before it can be displayed. It does not return a mass of data at once; it returns one row at a time, as a program requests it.

You can access information in your database in several ways:

- Through interactive access with DB-Access or the Relational Object Manager
- Through application programs written with an SQL API such as ESQL/C
- Through an application language such as SPL

Almost any program can contain SQL statements, execute them, and retrieve data from a database server. This chapter explains how these activities are performed and indicates how you can write programs that perform them.

This chapter is only an introduction to the concepts that are common to SQL programming in any language. Before you can write a successful program in a particular programming language, you must first become fluent in that language. Then, because the details of the process are different in every language, you must become familiar with the manual for the Informix SQL API specific to that language.

SQL in Programs

You can write a program in any of several languages and mix SQL statements among the other statements of the program, just as if they were ordinary statements of that programming language. These SQL statements are *embedded* in the program, and the program contains *embedded SQL*, which Informix often abbreviates as ESQL.

SQL in SQL APIs

ESQL products are Informix SQL APIs (application programming interfaces). Informix produces an SQL API for the C programming language.

Figure 7-1 shows how an SQL API product works. You write a source program in which you treat SQL statements as executable code. Your source program is processed by an embedded SQL *preprocessor,* a program that locates the embedded SQL statements and converts them into a series of procedure calls and special data structures.

Figure 7-1
Overview of Processing a Program with Embedded SQL Statements

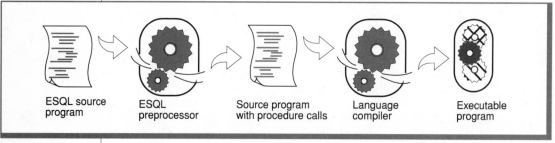

ESQL source program   ESQL preprocessor   Source program with procedure calls   Language compiler   Executable program

The converted source program then passes through the programming language compiler. The compiler output becomes an executable program after it is linked with a static or *dynamic* library of SQL API procedures. When the program runs, the SQL API library procedures are called; they set up communication with the database server to carry out the SQL operations.

If you link your executable program to a threading library package, you can develop ESQL/C *multithreaded applications*. A multithreaded application can have many threads of control. It separates a process into multiple execution threads, each of which runs independently. The major advantage of a multi-threaded ESQL/C application is that each thread can have many active connections to a database server simultaneously. While a nonthreaded ESQL/C application can establish many connections to one or more databases, it can have only one connection active at a time. A multithreaded ESQL/C application can have one active connection per thread and many threads per application.

For more information on multithreaded applications, see the *Informix ESQL/C Programmer's Manual*.

SQL in Application Languages

Whereas an SQL API product allows you to embed SQL in the host language, some languages include SQL as a natural part of their statement set. Informix Stored Procedure Language (SPL) uses SQL as a natural part of its statement set. You use an SQL API product to write application programs. You use SPL to write routines that are stored with a database and called from an application program.

Static Embedding

You can introduce SQL statements into a program through static embedding or dynamic statements. The simpler and more common way is by *static embedding*, which means that the SQL statements are written as part of the code. The statements are *static* because they are a fixed part of the source text. For more information on static embedding, see "Retrieving Single Rows" on page 7-14 and "Retrieving Multiple Rows" on page 7-19.

Dynamic Statements

Some applications require the ability to compose SQL statements *dynamically*, in response to user input. For example, a program might have to select different columns or apply different criteria to rows, depending on what the user wants.

With *dynamic* SQL, the program composes an SQL statement as a string of characters in memory and passes it to the database server to be executed. Dynamic statements are not part of the code; they are constructed in memory during execution. For more information, see "Dynamic SQL" on page 7-29.

Program Variables and Host Variables

Application programs can use program variables within SQL statements. In SPL, you put the program variable in the SQL statement as syntax allows. For example, a DELETE statement can use a program variable in its WHERE clause.

The following code example shows a program variable in SPL:

```
CREATE PROCEDURE delete_item (drop_number INT)
 .
 .
 .
DELETE FROM items WHERE order_num = drop_number
 .
 .
 .
```

In applications that use embedded SQL statements, the SQL statements can refer to the contents of program variables. A program variable that is named in an embedded SQL statement is called a *host variable* because the SQL statement is thought of as a *guest* in the program.

The following example shows a DELETE statement as it might appear when it is embedded in an Informix ESQL/C source program:

```
EXEC SQL delete FROM items
    WHERE order_num = :onum;
```

In this program, you see an ordinary DELETE statement, as Chapter 6 describes. When the ESQL/C program is executed, a row of the **items** table is deleted; multiple rows can also be deleted.

The statement contains one new feature. It compares the **order_num** column to an item written as **:onum**, which is the name of a host variable.

An SQL API product provides a way to delimit the names of host variables when they appear in the context of an SQL statement. In ESQL/C, a host variable can be introduced with either a dollar sign ($) or a colon (:). The colon is the ANSI-compatible format. The example statement asks the database server to delete rows in which the order number equals the current contents of the host variable named **:onum**. This numeric variable was declared and assigned a value earlier in the program.

In Informix ESQL/C, an SQL statement can be introduced with either a leading dollar sign ($) or the words EXEC SQL.

The differences of syntax as illustrated in the preceding examples are trivial; the essential point is that the SQL API and SPL languages let you perform the following tasks:

- Embed SQL statements in a source program as if they were executable statements of the host language.

- Use program variables in SQL expressions the way literal values are used.

If you have programming experience, you can immediately see the possibilities. In the example, the order number to be deleted is passed in the variable **onum**. That value comes from any source that a program can use. It can be read from a file, the program can prompt a user to enter it, or it can be read from the database. The DELETE statement itself can be part of a subroutine (in which case **onum** can be a parameter of the subroutine); the subroutine can be called once or repetitively.

In short, when you embed SQL statements in a program, you can apply all the power of the host language to them. You can hide the SQL statements under many interfaces, and you can embellish the SQL functions in many ways.

Calling the Database Server

Executing an SQL statement is essentially calling the database server as a subroutine. Information must pass from the program to the database server, and information must be returned from the database server to the program.

Some of this communication is done through host variables. You can think of the host variables named in an SQL statement as the parameters of the procedure call to the database server. In the preceding example, a host variable acts as a parameter of the WHERE clause. Host variables receive data that the database server returns, as "Retrieving Multiple Rows" on page 7-19 describes.

SQL Communications Area

The database server always returns a result code, and possibly other information about the effect of an operation, in a data structure known as the SQL Communications Area (SQLCA). If the database server executes an SQL statement in a user-defined routine, the SQLCA of the calling application contains the values that the SQL statement triggers in the routine.

The principal fields of the SQLCA are listed in Figures 7-2 through Figure 7-4. The syntax that you use to describe a data structure such as the SQLCA, as well as the syntax that you use to refer to a field in it, differs among programming languages. For details, see your SQL API manual.

In particular, the subscript by which you name one element of the SQLERRD and SQLWARN arrays differs. Array elements are numbered starting with zero in Informix ESQL/C, but starting with one in other languages. In this discussion, the fields are named with specific words such as *third*, and you must translate these words into the syntax of your programming language.

You can also use the SQLSTATE variable of the GET DIAGNOSTICS statement to detect, handle, and diagnose errors. See "SQLSTATE Value" on page 7-13.

SQLCODE Field

The SQLCODE field is the primary return code of the database server. After every SQL statement, SQLCODE is set to an integer value as Figure 7-2 shows. When that value is zero, the statement is performed without error. In particular, when a statement is supposed to return data into a host variable, a code of zero means that the data has been returned and can be used. Any nonzero code means the opposite. No useful data was returned to host variables.

Figure 7-2
Values of SQLCODE

Return value	Interpretation
value < 0	Specifies an error code.
value = 0	Indicates success.
0 < *value* < 100	After a DESCRIBE statement, an integer value that represents the type of SQL statement that is described.
100	After a successful query that returns no rows, indicates the NOT FOUND condition. NOT FOUND can also occur in an ANSI-compliant database after an INSERT INTO/SELECT, UPDATE, DELETE, or SELECT... INTO TEMP statement fails to access any rows.

End of Data

The database server sets SQLCODE to 100 when the statement is performed correctly but no rows are found. This condition can occur in two situations.

The first situation involves a query that uses a cursor. ("Retrieving Multiple Rows" on page 7-19 describes queries that use cursors.) In these queries, the FETCH statement retrieves each value from the active set into memory. After the last row is retrieved, a subsequent FETCH statement cannot return any data. When this condition occurs, the database server sets SQLCODE to 100, which indicates *end of data, no rows found.*

The second situation involves a query that does not use a cursor. In this case, the database server sets SQLCODE to 100 when no rows satisfy the query condition. In databases that are not ANSI compliant, only a SELECT statement that returns no rows causes SQLCODE to be set to 100.

ANSI

In ANSI-compliant databases, SELECT, DELETE, UPDATE, and INSERT statements all set SQLCODE to 100 if no rows are returned. ♦

Negative Codes

When something unexpected goes wrong during a statement, the database server returns a negative number in SQLCODE to explain the problem. The meanings of these codes are documented in the on-line error message file.

SQLERRD Array

Some error codes that can be reported in SQLCODE reflect general problems. The database server can set a more detailed code in the second field of SQLERRD that reveals the error that the database server I/O routines or the operating system encountered.

The integers in the SQLERRD array are set to different values following different statements. The first and fourth elements of the array are used only in Informix ESQL/C. Figure 7-3 on page 7-11 shows how the fields are used.

These additional details can be useful. For example, you can use the value in the third field to report how many rows were deleted or updated. When your program prepares an SQL statement that the user enters, and an error is found, the value in the fifth field enables you to display the exact point of error to the user. (DB-Access and the Relational Object Manager use this feature to position the cursor when you ask to modify a statement after an error.)

Figure 7-3
Fields of SQLERRD

Field	Interpretation
First	After a successful PREPARE statement for a SELECT, UPDATE, INSERT, or DELETE statement, or after a select cursor is opened, this field contains the estimated number of rows affected.
Second	When **SQLCODE** contains an error code, this field contains either zero or an additional error code, called the ISAM error code, that explains the cause of the main error.
	After a successful insert operation of a single row, this field contains the value of any SERIAL value generated for that row.
Third	After a successful multirow insert, update, or delete operation, this field contains the number of rows that were processed.
	After a multirow insert, update, or delete operation that ends with an error, this field contains the number of rows that were successfully processed before the error was detected.
Fourth	After a successful PREPARE statement for a SELECT, UPDATE, INSERT, or DELETE statement or after a select cursor has been opened, this field contains the estimated weighted sum of disk accesses and total rows processed.
Fifth	After a syntax error in a PREPARE, EXECUTE IMMEDIATE, DECLARE, or static SQL statement, this field contains the offset in the statement text where the error was detected.
Sixth	After a successful fetch of a selected row, or a successful insert, update, or delete operation, this field contains the rowid (physical address) of the last row that was processed. Whether this rowid value corresponds to a row that the database server returns to the user depends on how the database server processes a query, particularly for SELECT statements.

SQLWARN Array

The eight character fields in the SQLWARN array are set to either a blank or to W to indicate a variety of special conditions. Their meanings depend on the statement just executed.

A set of warning flags appears when a database opens, that is, following a CONNECT, DATABASE, or CREATE DATABASE statement. These flags tell you some characteristics of the database as a whole.

A second set of flags appears following any other statement. These flags reflect unusual events that occur during the statement, which are usually not serious enough to be reflected by SQLCODE.

Both sets of SQLWARN values are summarized in Figure 7-4.

Figure 7-4
Fields of SQLWARN

Field	When Opening or Connecting to a Database	All Other Operations
First	Set to W when any other warning field is set to W. If blank, others need not be checked.	Set to W when any other warning field is set to W.
Second	Set to W when the database now open uses a transaction log.	Set to W if a column value is truncated when it is fetched into a host variable using a FETCH or a SELECT...INTO statement. On a REVOKE ALL statement, set to W when not all seven table-level privileges are revoked.
Third	Set to W when the database now open is ANSI compliant.	Set to W when a FETCH or SELECT statement returns an aggregate function (SUM, AVG, MIN, MAX) value that is null.
Fourth	Set to W when the database server is Dynamic Server.	On a SELECT...INTO, FETCH...INTO, or EXECUTE...INTO statement, set to W when the number of items in the select list is not the same as the number of host variables given in the INTO clause to receive them. On a GRANT ALL statement, set to W when not all seven table-level privileges are granted.
Fifth	Set to W when the database server stores the FLOAT data type in DECIMAL form (done when the host system lacks support for FLOAT types).	Set to W after a DESCRIBE statement if the prepared statement contains a DELETE statement or an UPDATE statement without a WHERE clause.

(1 of 2)

Field	When Opening or Connecting to a Database	All Other Operations
Sixth	Set to W when the database server stores the FLOAT data type in DECIMAL form (done when the host system lacks support for FLOAT types).	Set to W following execution of a statement that does not use ANSI-standard SQL syntax (provided the **DBANSIWARN** environment variable is set).
Seventh	Set to W when the application is connected to a database server that is running in secondary mode. The database server is a secondary server in a data-replication pair (that is, the server is available only for read operations).	Set to W when a data fragment (a dbspace) has been skipped during query processing (when the DATASKIP feature is on).
Eighth	Set to W when client **DB_LOCALE** does not match the database locale. For more information, see the *Informix Guide to GLS Functionality*.	Reserved.

(2 of 2)

SQLERRM Character String

SQLERRM can store a character string of up to 70 bytes. The SQLERRM character string contains identifiers, such as a table names, that are placed in the error message. For some networked applications, it contains an error message that the networking software generates.

If an INSERT operation fails because a constraint is violated, the name of the constraint that failed is written to SQLERRM.

SQLSTATE Value

Certain Informix products, such as Informix ESQL/C, support the SQLSTATE value in compliance with X/Open and ANSI SQL standards. The GET DIAGNOSTICS statement reads the SQLSTATE value to diagnose errors after you run an SQL statement. The database server returns a result code in a five-character string that is stored in a variable called SQLSTATE. The SQLSTATE error code, or value, tells you the following information about the most recently executed SQL statement:

- If the statement was successful

- If the statement was successful but generated warnings
- If the statement was successful but generated no data
- If the statement failed

For more information on the GET DIAGNOSTICS statement, the SQLSTATE variable, and the meaning of the SQLSTATE return codes, see the GET DIAGNOSTICS statement in the *Informix Guide to SQL: Syntax*.

Tip: *If your Informix product supports GET DIAGNOSTICS and SQLSTATE, Informix recommends that you use them as the primary structure to detect, handle, and diagnose errors. Using SQLSTATE allows you to detect multiple errors, and it is ANSI compliant.*

Retrieving Single Rows

The set of rows that a SELECT statement returns is its *active set*. A *singleton* SELECT statement returns a single row. You can use embedded SELECT statements to retrieve single rows from the database into host variables. When a SELECT statement returns more than one row of data, however, a program must use a *cursor* to retrieve rows one at a time. Multiple-row select operations are discussed in "Retrieving Multiple Rows" on page 7-19.

To retrieve a single row of data, simply embed a SELECT statement in your program. The following example shows how you can write the embedded SELECT statement using Informix ESQL/C:

```
EXEC SQL SELECT avg (total_price)
    INTO :avg_price
    FROM items
    WHERE order_num in
        (SELECT order_num from orders
        WHERE order_date < date('6/1/98'));
```

The INTO clause is the only detail that distinguishes this statement from any example in Chapter 2 or Chapter 5. This clause specifies the host variables that are to receive the data that is produced.

When the program executes an embedded SELECT statement, the database server performs the query. The example statement selects an aggregate value so that it produces exactly one row of data. The row has only a single column, and its value is deposited in the host variable named **avg_price**. Subsequent lines of the program can use that variable.

You can use statements of this kind to retrieve single rows of data into host variables. The single row can have as many columns as desired. If a query produces more than one row of data, the database server cannot return any data. It returns an error code instead.

You should list as many host variables in the INTO clause as there are items in the select list. If, by accident, these lists are of different lengths, the database server returns as many values as it can and sets the warning flag in the fourth field of SQLWARN.

Data Type Conversion

The following ESQL/C example retrieves the average of a DECIMAL column, which is itself a DECIMAL value. However, the host variable into which the average of the DECIMAL column is placed is *not* required to have that data type.

```
EXEC SQL SELECT avg (total_price) into :avg_price
    FROM items;
```

The declaration of the receiving variable **avg_price** in the previous example of ESQL/C code is not shown. The declaration could be any one of the following definitions:

```
int avg_price;
double avg_price;
char avg_price[16];
dec_t avg_price; /* typedef of decimal number structure */
```

The data type of each host variable that is used in a statement is noted and passed to the database server with the statement. The database server does its best to convert column data into the form that the receiving variables use. Almost any conversion is allowed, although some conversions cause a precision loss. The results of the preceding example differ, depending on the data type of the receiving host variable, as the following table shows.

Data Type	Result
FLOAT	The database server converts the decimal result to FLOAT, possibly truncating some fractional digits.
	If the magnitude of a decimal exceeds the maximum magnitude of the FLOAT format, an error is returned.
INTEGER	The database server converts the result to INTEGER, truncating fractional digits if necessary.
	If the integer part of the converted number does not fit the receiving variable, an error occurs.
CHARACTER	The database server converts the decimal value to a CHARACTER string.
	If the string is too long for the receiving variable, it is truncated. The second field of SQLWARN is set to W and the value in the SQLSTATE variable is 01004.

Working with Null Data

What if the program retrieves a null value? Null values can be stored in the database, but the data types that programming languages support do not recognize a null state. A program must have some way to recognize a null item to avoid processing it as data.

Indicator variables meet this need in SQL APIs. An indicator variable is an additional variable that is associated with a host variable that might receive a null item. When the database server puts data in the main variable, it also puts a special value in the indicator variable to show whether the data is null. In the following Informix ESQL/C example, a single row is selected, and a single value is retrieved into the host variable **op_date**:

```
EXEC SQL SELECT paid_date
        INTO :op_date:op_d_ind
        FROM orders
        WHERE order_num = $the_order;
if (op_d_ind < 0) /* data was null */
    rstrdate ('01/01/1900', :op_date);
```

Because the value might be null, an indicator variable named **op_d_ind** is associated with the host variable. (It must be declared as a short integer elsewhere in the program.)

Following execution of the SELECT statement, the program tests the indicator variable for a negative value. A negative number (usually -1) means that the value retrieved into the main variable is null. If the variable is null, this program uses an ESQL/C library function to assign a default value to the host variable. (The function **rstrdate** is part of the Informix ESQL/C product.)

The syntax that you use to associate an indicator variable with a host variable differs with the language you are using, but the principle is the same in all languages.

Dealing with Errors

Although the database server handles conversion between data types automatically, several things still can go wrong with a SELECT statement. In SQL programming, as in any kind of programming, you must anticipate errors and provide for them at every point.

End of Data

One common event is that no rows satisfy a query. This event is signalled by an SQLSTATE code of 02000 and by a code of 100 in SQLCODE after a SELECT statement. This code indicates an error or a normal event, depending entirely on your application. If you are sure a row or rows should satisfy the query (for example, if you are reading a row using a key value that you just read from a row of another table), then the end-of-data code represents a serious failure in the logic of the program. On the other hand, if you select a row based on a key that a user supplies or some other source supplies that is less reliable than a program, a lack of data can be a normal event.

End of Data with Databases That Are Not ANSI Compliant

If your database is not ANSI compliant, the end-of-data return code, 100, is set in SQLCODE following SELECT statements only. In addition, the SQLSTATE value is set to 02000. (Other statements, such as INSERT, UPDATE, and DELETE, set the third element of SQLERRD to show how many rows they affected; Chapter 8 covers this topic.)

Serious Errors

Errors that set SQLCODE to a negative value or SQLSTATE to a value that begins with anything other than 00, 01, or 02 are usually serious. Programs that you have developed and that are in production should rarely report these errors. Nevertheless, it is difficult to anticipate every problematic situation, so your program must be able to deal with these errors.

For example, a query can return error -206, which means that a table specified in the query is not in the database. This condition occurs if someone dropped the table after the program was written, or if the program opened the wrong database through some error of logic or mistake in input.

Interpreting End of Data with Aggregate Functions

A SELECT statement that uses an aggregate function such as SUM, MIN, or AVG always succeeds in returning at least one row of data, even when no rows satisfy the WHERE clause. An aggregate value based on an empty set of rows is null, but it exists nonetheless.

However, an aggregate value is also null if it is based on one or more rows that all contain null values. If you must be able to detect the difference between an aggregate value that is based on no rows and one that is based on some rows that are all null, you must include a COUNT function in the statement and an indicator variable on the aggregate value. You can then work out the following cases.

Count Value	Indicator	Case
0	-1	Zero rows selected
>0	-1	Some rows selected; all were null
>0	0	Some non-null rows selected

Using Default Values

You can handle these inevitable errors in many ways. In some applications, more lines of code are used to handle errors than to execute functionality. In the examples in this section, however, one of the simplest solutions, the default value, should work, as the following example shows:

```
avg_price = 0; /* set default for errors */
EXEC SQL SELECT avg (total_price)
        INTO :avg_price:null_flag
        FROM items;
if (null_flag < 0) /* probably no rows */
    avg_price = 0; /* set default for 0 rows */
```

The previous example deals with the following considerations:

- If the query selects some non-null rows, the correct value is returned and used. This result is the expected and most frequent one.

- If the query selects no rows, or in the much less likely event that it selects only rows that have null values in the **total_price** column (a column that should never be null), the indicator variable is set, and the default value is assigned.

- If any serious error occurs, the host variable is left unchanged; it contains the default value initially set. At this point in the program, the programmer sees no need to trap such errors and report them.

Retrieving Multiple Rows

When any chance exists that a query could return more than one row, the program must execute the query differently. Multirow queries are handled in two stages. First, the program starts the query. (No data is returned immediately.) Then the program requests the rows of data one at a time.

These operations are performed using a special data object called a *cursor*. A cursor is a data structure that represents the current state of a query. The following list shows the general sequence of program operations:

1. The program *declares* the cursor and its associated SELECT statement, which merely allocates storage to hold the cursor.

2. The program *opens* the cursor, which starts the execution of the associated SELECT statement and detects any errors in it.

3. The program *fetches* a row of data into host variables and processes it.

4. The program *closes* the cursor after the last row is fetched.

5. When the cursor is no longer needed, the program *frees* the cursor to deallocate the resources it uses.

These operations are performed with SQL statements named DECLARE, OPEN, FETCH, CLOSE, and FREE.

Declaring a Cursor

You use the DECLARE statement to declare a cursor. This statement gives the cursor a name, specifies its use, and associates it with a statement. The following example is written in Informix ESQL/C:

```
EXEC SQL DECLARE the_item CURSOR FOR
    SELECT order_num, item_num, stock_num
        INTO o_num, i_num, s_num
        FROM items
    FOR READ ONLY;
```

The declaration gives the cursor a name (**the_item** in this case) and associates it with a SELECT statement. (Chapter 8 discusses how a cursor can also be associated with an INSERT statement.)

The SELECT statement in this example contains an INTO clause. The INTO clause specifies which variables receive data. You can also use the FETCH statement to specify which variables receive data, as "Locating the INTO Clause" on page 7-22 discusses.

The DECLARE statement is not an active statement; it merely establishes the features of the cursor and allocates storage for it. You can use the cursor declared in the preceding example to read through the **items** table once. Cursors can be declared to read backward and forward (see "Cursor Input Modes" on page 7-23). This cursor, because it lacks a FOR UPDATE clause and because it is designated FOR READ ONLY, is used only to read data, not to modify it. (Chapter 8 covers the use of cursors to modify data.)

Opening a Cursor

The program opens the cursor when it is ready to use it. The OPEN statement activates the cursor. It passes the associated SELECT statement to the database server, which begins the search for matching rows. The database server processes the query to the point of locating or constructing the first row of output. It does not actually return that row of data, but it does set a return code in SQLSTATE and in SQLCODE for SQL APIs. The following example shows the OPEN statement in ESQL/C:

```
EXEC SQL OPEN the_item;
```

Because the database server is seeing the query for the first time, it might detect a number of errors. After the program opens the cursor, it should test SQLSTATE or SQLCODE. If the SQLSTATE value is greater than 02000, or the SQLCODE contains a negative number, the cursor is not usable. An error might be present in the SELECT statement, or some other problem might prevent the database server from executing the statement.

If SQLSTATE is equal to 00000, or SQLCODE contains a zero, the SELECT statement is syntactically valid, and the cursor is ready to use. At this point, however, the program does not know if the cursor can produce any rows.

Fetching Rows

The program uses the FETCH statement to retrieve each row of output. This statement names a cursor and can also name the host variables that receive the data. The following example shows the completed Informix ESQL/C code:

```
EXEC SQL DECLARE the_item CURSOR FOR
    SELECT order_num, item_num, stock_num
        INTO :o_num, :i_num, :s_num
        FROM items;
EXEC SQL OPEN the_item;
while(SQLCODE == 0)
{
    EXEC SQL FETCH the_item;
    if(SQLCODE == 0)
        printf("%d, %d, %d", o_num, i_num, s_num);
}
```

Detecting End of Data

In the previous example, the WHILE condition prevents execution of the loop in case the OPEN statement returns an error. The same condition terminates the loop when SQLCODE is set to 100 to signal the end of data. However, the loop contains a test of SQLCODE. This test is necessary because, if the SELECT statement is valid yet finds no matching rows, the OPEN statement returns a zero, but the first fetch returns 100 (end of data) and no data. The following example shows another way to write the same loop:

```
EXEC SQL DECLARE the_item CURSOR FOR
    SELECT order_num, item_num, stock_num
    INTO :o_num, :i_num, :s_num
    FROM items;
EXEC SQL OPEN the_item;
if(SQLCODE == 0)
    EXEC SQL FETCH the_item;            /* fetch 1st row */
while(SQLCODE == 0)
{
    printf("%d, %d, %d", o_num, i_num, s_num);
    EXEC SQL FETCH the_item;
}
```

In this version, the case of no returned rows is handled early, so no second test of SQLCODE exists within the loop. These versions have no measurable difference in performance because the time cost of a test of SQLCODE is a tiny fraction of the cost of a fetch.

Locating the INTO Clause

The INTO clause names the host variables that are to receive the data that the database server returns. The INTO clause must appear in either the SELECT or the FETCH statement. However it cannot appear in both statements. The following example specifies host variables in the FETCH statement:

```
EXEC SQL DECLARE the_item CURSOR FOR
    SELECT order_num, item_num, stock_num
        FROM items;
EXEC SQL OPEN the_item;
while(SQLCODE == 0)
{
    EXEC SQL FETCH the_item INTO :o_num, :i_num, :s_num;
    if(SQLCODE == 0)
        printf("%d, %d, %d", o_num, i_num, s_num);
}
```

This form lets you fetch different rows into different locations. For example, you could use this form to fetch successive rows into successive elements of an array.

Cursor Input Modes

For purposes of input, a cursor operates in one of two modes, *sequential* or *scrolling*. A sequential cursor can fetch only the next row in sequence, so a sequential cursor can read through a table only once each time the cursor is opened. A scroll cursor can fetch the next row or any of the output rows, so a scroll cursor can read the same rows multiple times. The following example shows a sequential cursor declared in Informix ESQL/C:

```
EXEC SQL DECLARE pcurs cursor for
    SELECT customer_num, lname, city
        FROM customer;
```

After the cursor is opened, it can be used only with a sequential fetch that retrieves the next row of data, as the following example shows:

```
EXEC SQL FETCH p_curs into:cnum, :clname, :ccity;
```

Each sequential fetch returns a new row.

A scroll cursor is declared with the keywords SCROLL CURSOR, as the following example from Informix ESQL/C shows:

```
EXEC SQL DECLARE s_curs SCROLL CURSOR FOR
    SELECT order_num, order_date FROM orders
        WHERE customer_num > 104
```

Use the scroll cursor with a variety of fetch options. For example, the ABSOLUTE option specifies the absolute row position of the row to fetch.

```
EXEC SQL FETCH ABSOLUTE :numrow s_curs
    INTO :nordr, :nodat
```

This statement fetches the row whose position is given in the host variable **numrow**. You can also fetch the current row again, or you can fetch the first row and then scan through all the rows again. However, these features have a price, as the next section describes. For additional options that apply to scroll cursors, see the FETCH statement in the *Informix Guide to SQL: Syntax*.

Active Set of a Cursor

Once a cursor is opened, it stands for some selection of rows. The set of all rows that the query produces is called the *active set* of the cursor. It is easy to think of the active set as a well-defined collection of rows and to think of the cursor as pointing to one row of the collection. This situation is true as long as no other programs are modifying the same data concurrently.

Creating the Active Set

When a cursor is opened, the database server does whatever is necessary to locate the first row of selected data. Depending on how the query is phrased, this action can be easy, or it can require a great deal of work and time. Consider the following declaration of a cursor:

```
EXEC SQL DECLARE easy CURSOR FOR
    SELECT fname, lname FROM customer
        WHERE state = 'NJ'
```

Because this cursor queries only a single table in a simple way, the database server quickly determines whether any rows satisfy the query and identifies the first one. The first row is the only row the cursor finds at this time. The rest of the rows in the active set remain unknown. As a contrast, consider the following declaration of a cursor:

```
EXEC SQL DECLARE hard SCROLL CURSOR FOR
    SELECT C.customer_num, O.order_num, sum (items.total_price)
        FROM customer C, orders O, items I
        WHERE C.customer_num = O.customer_num
            AND O.order_num = I.order_num
            AND O.paid_date is null
        GROUP BY C.customer_num, O.order_num
```

The active set of this cursor is generated by joining three tables and grouping the output rows. The optimizer might be able to use indexes to produce the rows in the correct order, but generally the use of ORDER BY or GROUP BY clauses requires the database server to generate all the rows, copy them to a temporary table, and sort the table, before it can determine which row to present first.

In cases where the active set is entirely generated and saved in a temporary table, the database server can take quite some time to open the cursor. Afterwards, the database server could tell the program exactly how many rows the active set contains. However, this information is not made available. One reason is that you can never be sure which method the optimizer uses. If the optimizer can avoid sorts and temporary tables, it does so; but small changes in the query, in the sizes of the tables, or in the available indexes can change the methods of the optimizer.

Active Set for a Sequential Cursor

The database server attempts to use as few resources as possible to maintain the active set of a cursor. If it can do so, the database server never retains more than the single row that is fetched next. It can do this for most sequential cursors. On each fetch, it returns the contents of the current row and locates the next one.

Active Set for a Scroll Cursor

All the rows in the active set for a scroll cursor must be retained until the cursor closes because the database server cannot be sure which row the program will ask for next.

Most frequently, the database server implements the active set of a scroll cursor as a temporary table. The database server might not fill this table immediately, however (unless it created a temporary table to process the query). Usually it creates the temporary table when the cursor is opened. Then, the first time a row is fetched, the database server copies it into the temporary table and returns it to the program. When a row is fetched for a second time, it can be taken from the temporary table. This scheme uses the fewest resources in the event that the program abandons the query before it fetches all the rows. Rows that are never fetched are not created or saved.

Active Set and Concurrency

When only one program is using a database, the members of the active set cannot change. This situation describes most personal computers, and it is the easiest situation to think about. But some programs must be designed for use in a multiprogramming system, where two, three, or dozens of different programs can work on the same tables simultaneously.

When other programs can update the tables while your cursor is open, the idea of the active set becomes less useful. Your program can see only one row of data at a time, but all other rows in the table can be changing.

In the case of a simple query, when the database server holds only one row of the active set, any other row can change. The instant after your program fetches a row, another program can delete the same row or update it so that if it is examined again, it is no longer part of the active set.

When the active set, or part of it, is saved in a temporary table, *stale data* can present a problem. That is, the rows in the actual tables, from which the active-set rows are derived, can change. If they do, some of the active-set rows no longer reflect the current table contents.

These ideas seem unsettling at first, but as long as your program only reads the data, stale data does not exist, or rather, all data is equally stale. The active set is a snapshot of the data as it is at one moment in time. A row is different the next day; it does not matter if it is also different in the next millisecond. To put it another way, no practical difference exists between changes that occur while the program is running and changes that are saved and applied the instant that the program terminates.

The only time that stale data can cause a problem is when the program intends to use the input data to modify the same database; for example, when a banking application must read an account balance, change it, and write it back. Chapter 8 discusses programs that modify data.

Using a Cursor: A Parts Explosion

When you use a cursor, supplemented by program logic, you can solve problems that plain SQL cannot solve. One of these problems is the parts-explosion problem, sometimes called bill-of-materials processing. At the heart of this problem is a recursive relationship among objects; one object contains other objects, which contain yet others.

The problem is usually stated in terms of a manufacturing inventory. A company makes a variety of parts, for example. Some parts are discrete, but some are assemblages of other parts.

These relationships are documented in a single table, which might be called **contains**. The column **contains.parent** holds the part numbers of parts that are assemblages. The column **contains.child** has the part number of a part that is a component of the parent. If part number 123400 is an assembly of nine parts, nine rows exist with 123400 in the first column and other part numbers in the second. Figure 7-5 shows one of the rows that describe part number 123400.

Figure 7-5
*Parts-Explosion
Problem*

CONTAINS

PARENT	CHILD	
FK NN	FK NN	
123400	432100	
432100	765899	

Here is the parts-explosion problem: given a part number, produce a list of all parts that are components of that part. The following example is a sketch of one solution, as implemented in Informix ESQL/C:

```
int part_list[200];

boom(top_part)
int top_part;
{
    long this_part, child_part;
    int next_to_do = 0, next_free = 1;
    part_list[next_to_do] = top_part;

    EXEC SQL DECLARE part_scan CURSOR FOR
        SELECT child INTO child_part FROM contains
            WHERE parent = this_part;
    while(next_to_do < next_free)
    {
        this_part = part_list[next_to_do];
        EXEC SQL OPEN part_scan;
        while(SQLCODE == 0)
        {
            EXEC SQL FETCH part_scan;
            if(SQLCODE == 0)
            {
                part_list[next_free] = child_part;
                next_free += 1;
            }
        }
```

```
                    }
               EXEC SQL CLOSE part_scan;
               next_to_do += 1;
          }
     return (next_free - 1);
}
```

Technically speaking, each row of the **contains** table is the head node of a directed acyclic graph, or *tree*. The function performs a breadth-first search of the tree whose root is the part number passed as its parameter. The function uses a cursor named **part_scan** to return all the rows with a particular value in the **parent** column. The innermost `while` loop opens the **part_scan** cursor, fetches each row in the selection set, and closes the cursor when the part number of each component has been retrieved.

This function addresses the heart of the parts-explosion problem, but the function is not a complete solution. For example, it does not allow for components that appear at more than one level in the tree. Furthermore, a practical **contains** table would also have a column **count**, giving the count of **child** parts used in each **parent**. A program that returns a total count of each component part is much more complicated.

The iterative approach described previously is not the only way to approach the parts-explosion problem. If the number of generations has a fixed limit, you can solve the problem with a single SELECT statement using nested, outer self-joins.

If up to four generations of parts can be contained within one top-level part, the following SELECT statement returns all of them:

```
SELECT a.parent, a.child, b.child, c.child, d.child
   FROM contains a
        OUTER (contains b,
            OUTER (contains c, outer contains d))
   WHERE a.parent = top_part_number
        AND a.child = b.parent
        AND b.child = c.parent
        AND c.child = d.parent
```

This SELECT statement returns one row for each line of descent rooted in the part given as **top_part_number**. Null values are returned for levels that do not exist. (Use indicator variables to detect them.) To extend this solution to more levels, select additional nested outer joins of the **contains** table. You can also revise this solution to return counts of the number of parts at each level.

Dynamic SQL

Although static SQL is useful, it requires that you know the exact content of every SQL statement at the time you write the program. For example, you must state exactly which columns are tested in any WHERE clause and exactly which columns are named in any select list.

No problem exists when you write a program to perform a well-defined task. But the database tasks of some programs cannot be perfectly defined in advance. In particular, a program that must respond to an interactive user might need to compose SQL statements in response to what the user enters.

Dynamic SQL allows a program to form an SQL statement during execution, so that user input determines the contents of the statement. This action is performed in the following steps:

1. The program assembles the text of an SQL statement as a character string, which is stored in a program variable.

2. It executes a PREPARE statement, which asks the database server to examine the statement text and prepare it for execution.

3. It uses the EXECUTE statement to execute the prepared statement.

In this way, a program can construct and then use any SQL statement, based on user input of any kind. For example, it can read a file of SQL statements and prepare and execute each one.

DB-Access, a utility that you can use to explore SQL interactively, is an Informix ESQL/C program that constructs, prepares, and executes SQL statements dynamically. For example, DB-Access lets you use simple, interactive menus to specify the columns of a table. When you are finished, DB-Access builds the necessary CREATE TABLE or ALTER TABLE statement dynamically and prepares and executes it.

Preparing a Statement

In form, a dynamic SQL statement is like any other SQL statement that is written into a program, except that it cannot contain the names of any host variables.

A dynamic SQL statement has two restrictions. First, if it is a SELECT statement, it cannot include the INTO clause. The INTO clause names host variables into which column data is placed, and host variables are not allowed in a dynamic statement. Second, wherever the name of a host variable normally appears in an expression, a question mark (?) is written as a placeholder.

You can prepare a statement in this form for execution with the PREPARE statement. The following example is written in Informix ESQL/C:

```
EXEC SQL prepare query_2 from
        'SELECT * from orders
            WHERE customer_num = ? and order_date > ?';
```

The two question marks in this example indicate that when the statement is executed, the values of host variables are used at those two points.

You can prepare almost any SQL statement dynamically. The only statements that you cannot prepare are the ones directly concerned with dynamic SQL and cursor management, such as the PREPARE and OPEN statements. After you prepare an UPDATE or DELETE statement, it is a good idea to test the fifth field of SQLWARN to see if you used a WHERE clause (see "SQLWARN Array" on page 7-11).

The result of preparing a statement is a data structure that represents the statement. This data structure is not the same as the string of characters that produced it. In the PREPARE statement, you give a name to the data structure; it is **query_2** in the preceding example. This name is used to execute the prepared SQL statement.

The PREPARE statement does not limit the character string to one statement. It can contain multiple SQL statements, separated by semicolons. The following example shows a fairly complex transaction in Informix ESQL/C:

```
strcpy(big_query, "UPDATE account SET balance = balance + ?
WHERE customer_id = ?; \ UPDATE teller SET balance =
balance + ? WHERE teller_id = ?;");
EXEC SQL PREPARE big1 FROM :big_query;
```

When this list of statements is executed, host variables must provide values for six place-holding question marks. Although it is more complicated to set up a multistatement list, performance is often better because fewer exchanges take place between the program and the database server.

Executing Prepared SQL

After you prepare a statement, you can execute it multiple times. Statements other than SELECT statements, and SELECT statements that return only a single row, are executed with the EXECUTE statement.

The following Informix ESQL/C code prepares and executes a multistatement update of a bank account:

```
EXEC SQL BEGIN DECLARE SECTION;
char bigquery[270] = "begin work;";
EXEC SQL END DECLARE SECTION;
stcat ("update account set balance = balance + ? where ", bigquery);
stcat ("acct_number = ?;', bigquery);
stcat ("update teller set balance = balance + ? where ", bigquery);
stcat ("teller_number = ?;', bigquery);
stcat ("update branch set balance = balance + ? where ", bigquery);
stcat ("branch_number = ?;', bigquery);
stcat ("insert into history values(timestamp, values);", bigquery);

EXEC SQL prepare bigq from :bigquery;

EXEC SQL execute bigq using :delta, :acct_number, :delta,
    :teller_number, :delta, :branch_number;

EXEC SQL commit work;
```

The USING clause of the EXECUTE statement supplies a list of host variables whose values are to take the place of the question marks in the prepared statement. If a SELECT (or EXECUTE FUNCTION) returns only one row, you can use the INTO clause of EXECUTE to specify the host variables that receive the values.

Dynamic Host Variables

SQL APIs, which support dynamically allocated data objects, take dynamic statements one step further. They let you dynamically allocate the host variables that receive column data.

Dynamic allocation of variables makes it possible to take an arbitrary SELECT statement from program input, determine how many values it produces and their data types, and allocate the host variables of the appropriate types to hold them.

The key to this ability is the DESCRIBE statement. It takes the name of a prepared SQL statement and returns information about the statement and its contents. It sets SQLCODE to specify the type of statement; that is, the verb with which it begins. If the prepared statement is a SELECT statement, the DESCRIBE statement also returns information about the selected output data. If the prepared statement is an INSERT statement, the DESCRIBE statement returns information about the input parameters. The data structure to which a DESCRIBE statement returns information is a predefined data structure that is allocated for this purpose and is known as a system-descriptor area. If you are using Informix ESQL/C, you can use a system-descriptor area or, as an alternative, an **sqlda** structure.

The data structure that a DESCRIBE statement returns or references for a SELECT statement includes an array of structures. Each structure describes the data that is returned for one item in the select list. The program can examine the array and discover that a row of data includes a decimal value, a character value of a certain length, and an integer.

With this information, the program can allocate memory to hold the retrieved values and put the necessary pointers in the data structure for the database server to use.

Freeing Prepared Statements

A prepared SQL statement occupies space in memory. With some database servers, it can consume space that the database server owns as well as space that belongs to the program. This space is released when the program terminates, but in general, you should free this space when you finish with it.

You can use the FREE statement to release this space. The FREE statement takes either the name of a statement or the name of a cursor that was declared for a statement name, and releases the space allocated to the prepared statement. If more than one cursor is defined on the statement, freeing the statement does not free the cursor.

Quick Execution

For simple statements that do not require a cursor or host variables, you can combine the actions of the PREPARE, EXECUTE, and FREE statements into a single operation. The following example shows how the EXECUTE IMMEDIATE statement takes a character string, prepares it, executes it, and frees the storage in one operation:

```
EXEC SQL execute immediate 'drop index my_temp_index';
```

This capability makes it easy to write simple SQL operations. However, because no USING clause is allowed, the EXECUTE IMMEDIATE statement cannot be used for SELECT statements.

Embedding Data-Definition Statements

Data-definition statements, the SQL statements that create databases and modify the definitions of tables, are not usually put into programs. The reason is that they are rarely performed. A database is created once, but it is queried and updated many times.

The creation of a database and its tables is generally done interactively, using DB-Access or the Relational Object Manager. These tools can also be run from a file of statements, so that the creation of a database can be done with one operating-system command. The data-definition statements are documented in the *Informix Guide to SQL: Syntax* and the *Informix Guide to Database Design and Implementation*.

Embedding Grant and Revoke Privileges

One task related to data definition is performed repeatedly: granting and revoking privileges. Because privileges must be granted and revoked frequently, and possibly by users who are not skilled in SQL, it can be useful to package the GRANT and REVOKE statements in programs to give them a simpler, more convenient user interface.

The GRANT and REVOKE statements are especially good candidates for dynamic SQL. Each statement takes the following parameters:

- A list of one or more privileges
- A table name
- The name of a user

You probably need to supply at least some of these values based on program input (from the user, command-line parameters, or a file) but none can be supplied in the form of a host variable. The syntax of these statements does not allow host variables at any point.

The only alternative is to assemble the parts of a statement into a character string and to prepare and execute the assembled statement. Program input can be incorporated into the prepared statement as characters.

The following Informix ESQL/C function assembles a GRANT statement from parameters, and then prepares and executes it:

```
char priv_to_grant[100];
char table_name[20];
char user_id[20];

table_grant(priv_to_grant, table_name, user_id)
char *priv_to_grant;
char *table_name;
char *user_id;
{
    EXEC SQL BEGIN DECLARE SECTION;
    char grant_stmt[200];
    EXEC SQL END DECLARE SECTION;

    sprintf(grant_stmt, " GRANT %s ON %s TO %s",
        priv_to_grant, table_name, user_id);
    PREPARE the_grant FROM :grant_stmt;
    if(SQLCODE == 0)
        EXEC SQL EXECUTE the_grant;
    else
        printf("Sorry, got error # %d attempting %s",
            SQLCODE, grant_stmt);

    EXEC SQL FREE the_grant;
}
```

The opening statement of the function that the following example shows specifies its name and its three parameters. The three parameters specify the privileges to grant, the name of the table on which to grant privileges, and the ID of the user to receive them.

```
table_grant(priv_to_grant, table_name, user_id)
char *priv_to_grant;
char *table_name;
char *user_id;
```

The function uses the statements in the following example to define a local variable, **grant_stmt,** which is used to assemble and hold the GRANT statement:

```
EXEC SQL BEGIN DECLARE SECTION;
    char grant_stmt[200];
EXEC SQL END DECLARE SECTION;
```

As the following example illustrates, the GRANT statement is created by concatenating the constant parts of the statement and the function parameters:

```
sprintf(grant_stmt, " GRANT %s ON %s TO %s",priv_to_grant, table_name, user_id);
```

This statement concatenates the following six character strings:

- 'GRANT'
- The parameter that specifies the privileges to be granted
- 'ON'
- The parameter that specifies the table name
- 'TO'
- The parameter that specifies the user

The result is a complete GRANT statement composed partly of program input. The PREPARE statement passes the assembled statement text to the database server for parsing.

If the database server returns an error code in SQLCODE following the PREPARE statement, the function displays an error message. If the database server approves the form of the statement, it sets a zero return code. This action does not guarantee that the statement is executed properly; it means only that the statement has correct syntax. It might refer to a nonexistent table or contain many other kinds of errors that can be detected only during execution. The following portion of the example checks that **the_grant** was prepared successfully before executing it:

```
if(SQLCODE == 0)
    EXEC SQL EXECUTE the_grant;
else
    printf("Sorry, got error # %d attempting %s", SQLCODE, grant_stmt);
```

If the preparation is successful, SQLCODE = = 0, the next step executes the prepared statement.

Summary

SQL statements can be written into programs as if they were normal statements of the programming language. Program variables can be used in WHERE clauses, and data from the database can be fetched into them. A preprocessor translates the SQL code into procedure calls and data structures.

Statements that do not return data, or queries that return only one row of data, are written like ordinary imperative statements of the language. Queries that can return more than one row are associated with a cursor that represents the current row of data. Through the cursor, the program can fetch each row of data as it is needed.

Static SQL statements are written into the text of the program. However, the program can form new SQL statements dynamically, as it runs, and execute them also. In the most advanced cases, the program can obtain information about the number and types of columns that a query returns and dynamically allocate the memory space to hold them.

Modifying Data Through SQL Programs

In This Chapter 8-3

Using DELETE 8-3
    Direct Deletions 8-4
        Errors During Direct Deletions 8-4
        Using Transaction Logging 8-5
        Coordinated Deletions 8-6
    Deleting with a Cursor 8-7

Using INSERT 8-9
    Using an Insert Cursor 8-9
        Declaring an Insert Cursor 8-9
        Inserting with a Cursor. 8-10
        Status Codes After PUT and FLUSH 8-11
    Rows of Constants. 8-12
    An Insert Example. 8-12

Using UPDATE 8-15
    Using an Update Cursor 8-15
        The Purpose of the Keyword UPDATE 8-16
        Updating Specific Columns 8-16
        UPDATE Keyword Not Always Needed 8-16
    Cleaning Up a Table 8-17

Summary 8-18

In This Chapter

The previous chapter describes how to insert or embed SQL statements, especially the SELECT statement, into programs written in other languages. Embedded SQL enables a program to retrieve rows of data from a database.

This chapter discusses the issues that arise when a program needs to delete, insert, or update rows to modify the database. As in Chapter 7, this chapter prepares you for reading your Informix embedded language manual.

The general use of the INSERT, UPDATE, and DELETE statements is discussed in Chapter 6. This chapter examines their use from within a program. You can easily embed the statements in a program, but it can be difficult to handle errors and to deal with concurrent modifications from multiple programs.

Using DELETE

To delete rows from a table, a program executes a DELETE statement. The DELETE statement can specify rows in the usual way with a WHERE clause, or it can refer to a single row, the last one fetched through a specified cursor.

Whenever you delete rows, you must consider whether rows in other tables depend on the deleted rows. This problem of coordinated deletions is covered in Chapter 6. The problem is the same when deletions are made from within a program.

Direct Deletions

You can embed a DELETE statement in a program. The following example uses Informix ESQL/C:

```
EXEC SQL delete from items
    WHERE order_num = :onum;
```

You can also prepare and execute a statement of the same form dynamically. In either case, the statement works directly on the database to affect one or more rows.

The WHERE clause in the example uses the value of a host variable named **onum**. Following the operation, results are posted in SQLSTATE and in the **sqlca** structure, as usual. The third element of the SQLERRD array contains the count of rows deleted even if an error occurs. The value in SQLCODE shows the overall success of the operation. If the value is not negative, no errors occurred and the third element of SQLERRD is the count of all rows that satisfied the WHERE clause and were deleted.

Errors During Direct Deletions

When an error occurs, the statement ends prematurely. The values in SQLSTATE and in SQLCODE and the second element of SQLERRD explain its cause, and the count of rows reveals how many rows were deleted. For many errors, that count is zero because the errors prevented the database server from beginning the operation. For example, if the named table does not exist, or if a column tested in the WHERE clause is renamed, no deletions are attempted.

However, certain errors can be discovered after the operation begins and some rows are processed. The most common of these errors is a lock conflict. The database server must obtain an exclusive lock on a row before it can delete that row. Other programs might be using the rows from the table, preventing the database server from locking a row. Because the issue of locking affects all types of modifications, Chapter 9 discusses it.

Other, rarer types of errors can strike after deletions begin. For example, hardware errors that occur while the database is being updated.

Using Transaction Logging

The best way to prepare for any kind of error during a modification is to use transaction logging. In the event of an error, you can tell the database server to put the database back the way it was. The following example is based on the example in the section, "Direct Deletions" on page 8-4, which is extended to use transactions:

```
EXEC SQL begin work;/* start the transaction*/
EXEC SQL delete from items
     where order_num = :onum;
del_result = sqlca.sqlcode;/* save two error */
del_isamno = sqlca.sqlerrd[1];/* ...code numbers */
del_rowcnt = sqlca.sqlerrd[2];/* ...and count of rows */
if (del_result < 0)/* some problem, */
    EXEC SQL rollback work;/* ...put everything back */
else    /* everything worked OK, */
    EXEC SQL commit work;/* ...finish transaction */
```

A key point in this example is that the program saves the important return values in the **sqlca** structure before it ends the transaction. Both the ROLLBACK WORK and COMMIT WORK statements, like other SQL statements, set return codes in the **sqlca** structure. Executing a ROLLBACK WORK statement after an error wipes out the error code, unless it was saved, cannot be reported to the user.

The advantage of using transactions is that the database is left in a known, predictable state no matter what goes wrong. No question remains about how much of the modification is completed; either all of it or none of it is completed.

In a database with logging, if a user does not start an explicit transaction, the database server initiates an internal transaction prior to execution of the statement and terminates the transaction after execution completes or fails. If the statement execution succeeds, the internal transaction is committed. If the statement fails, the internal transaction is rolled back.

Coordinated Deletions

The usefulness of transaction logging is particularly clear when you must modify more than one table. For example, consider the problem of deleting an order from the demonstration database. In the simplest form of the problem, you must delete rows from two tables, **orders** and **items**, as the following example of Informix ESQL/C shows:

```
EXEC SQL BEGIN WORK;
EXEC SQL DELETE FROM items
    WHERE order_num = :o_num;
if (SQLCODE >= 0)
{
    EXEC SQL DELETE FROM orders
        WHERE order_num == :o_num;
{
    if (SQLCODE >= 0)
        EXEC SQL COMMIT WORK;
{
    else
{
        printf("Error %d on DELETE", SQLCODE);
        EXEC SQL ROLLBACK WORK;
}
```

The logic of this program is much the same whether or not transactions are used. If they are not used, the person who sees the error message has a much more difficult set of decisions to make. Depending on when the error occurred, one of the following situations applies:

- No deletions were performed; all rows with this order number remain in the database.

- Some, but not all, item rows were deleted; an order record with only some items remains.

- All item rows were deleted, but the order row remains.

- All rows were deleted.

In the second and third cases, the database is corrupted to some extent; it contains partial information that can cause some queries to produce wrong answers. You must take careful action to restore consistency to the information. When transactions are used, all these uncertainties are prevented.

Deleting with a Cursor

You can also write a DELETE statement with a cursor to delete the row that was last fetched. Deleting rows in this manner lets you program deletions based on conditions that cannot be tested in a WHERE clause, as the following example shows. The following example applies only to databases that are not ANSI compliant because of the way that the beginning and end of the transaction are set up.

Warning: *The design of the ESQL/C function in this example is unsafe. It depends on the current isolation level for correct operation. Isolation levels are discussed later in the chapter. For more information on isolation levels, see Chapter 9. Even when the function works as intended, its effects depend on the physical order of rows in the table, which is not generally a good idea.*

```
int delDupOrder()
{
    int ord_num;
    int dup_cnt, ret_code;

    EXEC SQL declare scan_ord cursor for
        select order_num, order_date
            into :ord_num, :ord_date
            from orders for update;
    EXEC SQL open scan_ord;
    if (sqlca.sqlcode != 0)
        return (sqlca.sqlcode);
    EXEC SQL begin work;
    for(;;)
    {
        EXEC SQL fetch next scan_ord;
        if (sqlca.sqlcode != 0) break;
        dup_cnt = 0; /* default in case of error */
        EXEC SQL select count(*) into dup_cnt from orders
            where order_num = :ord_num;
        if (dup_cnt > 1)
        {
            EXEC SQL delete from orders
                where current of scan_ord;
            if (sqlca.sqlcode != 0)
                break;
        }
    }
    ret_code = sqlca.sqlcode;
    if (ret_code == 100) /* merely end of data */
        EXEC SQL commit work;
    else    /* error on fetch or on delete */
        EXEC SQL rollback work;
    return (ret_code);
}
```

The purpose of the function is to delete rows that contain duplicate order numbers. In fact, in the demonstration database, the **orders.order_num** column has a unique index, so duplicate rows cannot occur in it. However, a similar function can be written for another database; this one uses familiar column names.

The function declares **scan_ord**, a cursor to scan all rows in the **orders** table. It is declared with the FOR UPDATE clause, which states that the cursor can modify data. If the cursor opens properly, the function begins a transaction and then loops over rows of the table. For each row, it uses an embedded SELECT statement to determine how many rows of the table have the order number of the current row. (This step fails without the correct isolation level, as Chapter 9 describes.)

In the demonstration database, with its unique index on this table, the count returned to **dup_cnt** is always one. However, if it is greater, the function deletes the current row of the table, reducing the count of duplicates by one.

Clean-up functions of this sort are sometimes needed, but they generally need more sophisticated design. This function deletes all duplicate rows except the last one that the database server returns. That order has nothing to do with the contents of the rows or their meanings. You can improve the function in the previous example by adding, perhaps, an ORDER BY clause to the cursor declaration. However, you cannot use ORDER BY and FOR UPDATE together. "An Insert Example" on page 8-12 presents a better approach.

Using INSERT

You can embed the INSERT statement in programs. Its form and use in a program are the same as Chapter 6 describes with the additional feature that you can use host variables in expressions, both in the VALUES and WHERE clauses. Moreover, a program has the additional ability to insert rows with a cursor.

Using an Insert Cursor

The DECLARE CURSOR statement has many variations. Most are used to create cursors for different kinds of scans over data, but one variation creates a special kind of cursor called an *insert cursor*. You use an insert cursor with the PUT and FLUSH statements to insert rows into a table in bulk efficiently.

Declaring an Insert Cursor

To create an insert cursor, declare a cursor to be for an INSERT statement instead of a SELECT statement. You cannot use such a cursor to fetch rows of data; you can use it only to insert them. The following code example shows the declaration of an insert cursor:

```
DEFINE the_company LIKE customer.company,
    the_fname LIKE customer.fname,
    the_lname LIKE customer.lname
DECLARE new_custs CURSOR FOR
    INSERT INTO customer (company, fname, lname)
        VALUES (the_company, the_fname, the_lname)
```

When you open an insert cursor, a buffer is created in memory to hold a block of rows. The buffer receives rows of data as the program produces them; then they are passed to the database server in a block when the buffer is full. The buffer reduces the amount of communication between the program and the database server, and it lets the database server insert the rows with less difficulty. As a result, the insertions go faster.

The buffer is always made large enough to hold at least two rows of inserted values. It is large enough to hold more than two rows when the rows are shorter than the minimum buffer size.

Inserting with a Cursor

The code in the previous example prepares an insert cursor for use. The continuation, as the following example shows, demonstrates how the cursor can be used. For simplicity, this example assumes that a function named **next_cust** returns either information about a new customer or null data to signal the end of input.

```
EXEC SQL BEGIN WORK;
EXEC SQL OPEN new_custs;
while(SQLCODE == 0)
{
    next_cust();
    if(the_company == NULL)
        break;
    EXEC SQL PUT new_custs;
}
if(SQLCODE == 0) /* if no problem with PUT */
{
    EXEC SQL FLUSH new_custs;/* write any rows left */
    if(SQLCODE == 0)/* if no problem with FLUSH */
        EXEC SQL COMMIT WORK;/* commit changes */
}
else
    EXEC SQL ROLLBACK WORK;/* else undo changes */
```

The code in this example calls **next_cust** repeatedly. When it returns non-null data, the PUT statement sends the returned data to the row buffer. When the buffer fills, the rows it contains are automatically sent to the database server. The loop normally ends when **next_cust** has no more data to return. Then the FLUSH statement writes any rows that remain in the buffer, after which the transaction terminates.

Re-examine the INSERT statement on page 8-9. The statement by itself, not part of a cursor definition, inserts a single row into the **customer** table. In fact, the whole apparatus of the insert cursor can be dropped from the example code, and the INSERT statement can be written into the code where the PUT statement now stands. The difference is that an insert cursor causes a program to run somewhat faster.

Status Codes After PUT and FLUSH

When a program executes a PUT statement, the program should test whether the row is placed in the buffer successfully. If the new row fits in the buffer, the only action of PUT is to copy the row to the buffer. No errors can occur in this case. However, if the row does not fit, the entire buffer load is passed to the database server for insertion, and an error can occur.

The values returned into the SQL Communications Area (SQLCA) give the program the information it needs to sort out each case. SQLCODE and SQLSTATE are set after every PUT statement to zero if no error occurs and to a negative error code if an error occurs.

The third element of SQLERRD is set to the number of rows actually inserted into the table. It is set to zero if the new row is merely moved to the buffer; to the count of rows that are in the buffer if the buffer load is inserted without error; or to the count of rows inserted before an error occurs, if one does occur.

Read the code once again to see how SQLCODE is used (see the previous example). First, if the OPEN statement yields an error, the loop is not executed because the WHILE condition fails, the FLUSH operation is not performed, and the transaction rolls back. Second, if the PUT statement returns an error, the loop ends because of the WHILE condition, the FLUSH operation is not performed, and the transaction rolls back. This condition can occur only if the loop generates enough rows to fill the buffer at least once; otherwise, the PUT statement cannot generate an error.

The program might end the loop with rows still in the buffer, possibly without inserting any rows. At this point, the SQL status is zero, and the FLUSH operation occurs. If the FLUSH operation produces an error code, the transaction rolls back. Only when all inserts are successfully performed is the transaction committed.

Rows of Constants

The insert cursor mechanism supports one special case where high performance is easy to obtain. In this case, all the values listed in the INSERT statement are constants: no expressions and no host variables are listed, just literal numbers and strings of characters. No matter how many times such an INSERT operation occurs, the rows it produces are identical. When the rows are identical, copying, buffering, and transmitting each identical row is pointless.

Instead, for this kind of INSERT operation, the PUT statement does nothing except to increment a counter. When a FLUSH operation is finally performed, a single copy of the row, and the count of inserts, is passed to the database server. The database server creates and inserts that many rows in one operation.

You do not usually insert a quantity of identical rows. You can insert identical rows when you first establish a database to populate a large table with null data.

An Insert Example

"Deleting with a Cursor" on page 8-7 contains an example of the DELETE statement whose purpose is to look for and delete duplicate rows of a table. A better way to perform this task is to select the desired rows instead of deleting the undesired ones. The code in the following Informix ESQL/C example shows one way to do this task:

```
EXEC SQL BEGIN DECLARE SECTION;
    long last_ord = 1;
    struct {
        long int o_num;
        date     o_date;
        long     c_num;
        char     o_shipinst[40];
        char     o_backlog;
        char     o_po[10];
        date     o_shipdate;
        decimal  o_shipwt;
        decimal  o_shipchg;
        date     o_paiddate;
    } ord_row;
EXEC SQL END DECLARE SECTION;

EXEC SQL BEGIN WORK;
```

```
EXEC SQL INSERT INTO new_orders
    SELECT * FROM orders main
        WHERE 1 = (SELECT COUNT(*) FROM orders minor
            WHERE main.order_num = minor.order_num);
EXEC SQL COMMIT WORK;

EXEC SQL DECLARE dup_row CURSOR FOR
    SELECT * FROM orders main INTO :ord_row
        WHERE 1 < (SELECT COUNT(*) FROM orders minor
            WHERE main.order_num = minor.order_num)
        ORDER BY order_date;
EXEC SQL DECLARE ins_row CURSOR FOR
    INSERT INTO new_orders VALUES (:ord_row);

EXEC SQL BEGIN WORK;
EXEC SQL OPEN ins_row;
EXEC SQL OPEN dup_row;
while(SQLCODE == 0)
{
    EXEC SQL FETCH dup_row;
    if(SQLCODE == 0)
    {
        if(ord_row.o_num != last_ord)
            EXEC SQL PUT ins_row;
        last_ord = ord_row.o_num
        continue;
    }
    break;
}
if(SQLCODE != 0 && SQLCODE != 100)
    EXEC SQL ROLLBACK WORK;
else
    EXEC SQL COMMIT WORK;
EXEC SQL CLOSE ins_row;
EXEC SQL CLOSE dup_row;
```

This example begins with an ordinary INSERT statement, which finds all the nonduplicated rows of the table and inserts them into another table, presumably created before the program started. That action leaves only the duplicate rows. (In the demonstration database, the **orders** table has a unique index and cannot have duplicate rows. Assume that this example deals with some other database.)

The code in the previous example then declares two cursors. The first, called **dup_row**, returns the duplicate rows in the table. Because **dup_row** is for input only, it can use the ORDER BY clause to impose some order on the duplicates other than the physical record order used in the example on page 8-7. In this example, the duplicate rows are ordered by their dates (the oldest one remains), but you can use any other order based on the data.

The second cursor, **ins_row**, is an insert cursor. This cursor takes advantage of the ability to use a C structure, **ord_row**, to supply values for all columns in the row.

The remainder of the code examines the rows that are returned through **dup_row**. It inserts the first one from each group of duplicates into the new table and disregards the rest.

For the sake of brevity, the preceding example uses the simplest kind of error handling. If an error occurs before all rows have been processed, the sample code rolls back the active transaction.

How Many Rows Were Affected?

When your program uses a cursor to select rows, it can test SQLCODE for 100 (or SQLSTATE for 02000), the end-of-data return code. This code is set to indicate that no rows, or no more rows, satisfy the query conditions. For databases that are not ANSI compliant, the end-of-data return code is set in SQLCODE or SQLSTATE only following SELECT statements; it is not used following DELETE, INSERT, or UPDATE statements. For ANSI-compliant databases, SQLCODE is also set to 100 for updates, deletes, and inserts that affect zero rows.

A query that finds no data is not a success. However, an UPDATE or DELETE statement that happens to update or delete no rows is still considered a success. It updated or deleted the set of rows that its WHERE clause said it should; however, the set was empty.

In the same way, the INSERT statement does not set the end-of-data return code even when the source of the inserted rows is a SELECT statement, and the SELECT statement selected no rows. The INSERT statement is a success because it inserted as many rows as it was asked to (that is, zero).

To find out how many rows are inserted, updated, or deleted, a program can test the third element of SQLERRD. The count of rows is there, regardless of the value (zero or negative) in SQLCODE.

Using UPDATE

You can embed the UPDATE statement in a program in any of the forms that Chapter 6 describes with the additional feature that you can name host variables in expressions, both in the SET and WHERE clauses. Moreover, a program can update the row that a cursor addresses.

Using an Update Cursor

An *update cursor* permits you to delete or update the current row; that is, the most recently fetched row. The following example in Informix ESQL/C shows the declaration of an update cursor:

```
EXEC SQL
     DECLARE names CURSOR FOR
          SELECT fname, lname, company
          FROM customer
     FOR UPDATE;
```

The program that uses this cursor can fetch rows in the usual way.

```
EXEC SQL
     FETCH names INTO :FNAME, :LNAME, :COMPANY;
```

If the program then decides that the row needs to be changed, it can do so.

```
if (strcmp(COMPANY, "SONY") ==0)
     {
     EXEC SQL
          UPDATE customer
               SET fname = 'Midori', lname = 'Tokugawa'
               WHERE CURRENT OF names;
     }
```

The words CURRENT OF names take the place of the usual test expressions in the WHERE clause. In other respects, the UPDATE statement is the same as usual, even including the specification of the table name, which is implicit in the cursor name but still required.

The Purpose of the Keyword UPDATE

The purpose of the keyword UPDATE in a cursor is to let the database server know that the program can update (or delete) any row that it fetches. The database server places a more demanding lock on rows that are fetched through an update cursor and a less demanding lock when it fetches a row for a cursor that is not declared with that keyword. This action results in better performance for ordinary cursors and a higher level of concurrent use in a multiprocessing system. (Chapter 9 discusses levels of locks and concurrent use.)

Updating Specific Columns

The following example has updated specific columns of the preceding example of an update cursor:

```
EXEC SQL
    DECLARE names CURSOR FOR
        SELECT fname, lname, company, phone
            INTO  :FNAME,:LNAME,:COMPANY,:PHONE FROM customer
    FOR UPDATE OF fname, lname
END-EXEC.
```

Only the **fname** and **lname** columns can be updated through this cursor. A statement such as the following one is rejected as an error:

```
EXEC SQL
    UPDATE customer
        SET company = 'Siemens'
        WHERE CURRENT OF names
END-EXEC.
```

If the program attempts such an update, an error code is returned and no update occurs. An attempt to delete with WHERE CURRENT OF is also rejected because deletion affects all columns.

UPDATE Keyword Not Always Needed

The ANSI standard for SQL does not provide for the FOR UPDATE clause in a cursor definition. When a program uses an ANSI-compliant database, it can update or delete with any cursor.

Cleaning Up a Table

A final, hypothetical example of how to use an update cursor presents a problem that should never arise with an established database but could arise in the initial design phases of an application.

In the example, a large table named **target** is created and populated. A character column, **datcol**, inadvertently acquires some null values. These rows should be deleted. Furthermore, a new column, **serials**, is added to the table with the ALTER TABLE statement. This column is to have unique integer values installed. The following example shows the Informix ESQL/C code you use to accomplish these tasks:

```
EXEC SQL BEGIN DECLARE SECTION;
char dcol[80];
short dcolint;
int sequence;
EXEC SQL END DECLARE SECTION;

EXEC SQL DECLARE target_row CURSOR FOR
    SELECT datcol
        INTO :dcol:dcolint
        FROM target
    FOR UPDATE OF serials;
EXEC SQL BEGIN WORK;
EXEC SQL OPEN target_row;
if (sqlca.sqlcode == 0) EXEC SQL FETCH NEXT target_row;
for(sequence = 1; sqlca.sqlcode == 0; ++sequence)
{
    if (dcolint < 0) /* null datcol */
        EXEC SQL DELETE WHERE CURRENT OF target_row;
    else
        EXEC SQL UPDATE target SET serials = :sequence
            WHERE CURRENT OF target_row;
}
if (sqlca.sqlcode >= 0)
    EXEC SQL COMMIT WORK;
else EXEC SQL ROLLBACK WORK;
```

Summary

A program can execute the INSERT, DELETE, and UPDATE statements, as Chapter 6 describes. A program can also scan through a table with a cursor, updating or deleting selected rows. It can also use a cursor to insert rows, with the benefit that the rows are buffered and sent to the database server in blocks.

In all these activities, you must make sure that the program detects errors and returns the database to a known state when an error occurs. The most important tool for doing this is transaction logging. Without transaction logging, it is more difficult to write programs that can recover from errors.

Programming for a Multiuser Environment

In This Chapter 9-3

Concurrency and Performance 9-3

Locking and Integrity 9-4

Locking and Performance 9-4

Concurrency Issues 9-5

How Locks Work 9-6
   Kinds of Locks 9-7
   Lock Scope 9-7
      Database Locks 9-8
      Table Locks 9-8
      Row and Key Locks 9-10
      Page Locks 9-11
      Coarse Index Locks 9-11
      Smart-Large-Object Locks 9-12
   Duration of a Lock 9-13
   Locks While Modifying 9-13

Locking with the SELECT Statement 9-14
   Setting the Isolation Level 9-14
      Comparing SET TRANSACTION with SET ISOLATION . . . 9-14
      ANSI Read Uncommitted and Informix Dirty
         Read Isolation 9-16
      ANSI Read Committed and Informix Committed
         Read Isolation 9-16
      Informix Cursor Stability Isolation 9-17
      ANSI Serializable, ANSI Repeatable Read, and
         Informix Repeatable Read Isolation 9-19
   Update Cursors 9-20

Retaining Update Locks 9-21

Locks Placed with INSERT, UPDATE, and DELETE. 9-22

Understanding the Behavior of the Lock Types 9-22

Controlling Data Modification with Access Modes 9-24

Setting the Lock Mode 9-24
    Waiting for Locks 9-25
    Not Waiting for Locks 9-25
    Waiting a Limited Time 9-26
    Handling a Deadlock 9-26
    Handling External Deadlock 9-26

Simple Concurrency 9-27

Hold Cursors 9-27

Using the SQL Statement Cache 9-29

Summary 9-30

In This Chapter

This chapter describes several programming issues you need to be aware of when you work in a multiuser environment.

If your database is contained in a single-user workstation and is not connected on a network to other computers, your programs can modify data freely. In all other cases, you must allow for the possibility that, while your program is modifying data, another program is reading or modifying the same data. This situation describes *concurrency*: two or more independent uses of the same data at the same time. This chapter addresses concurrency, locking, and isolation levels.

This chapter also describes the statement cache feature, which can reduce per-session memory allocation and speed up query processing. The statement cache stores statements that can then be shared among different user sessions that use identical SQL statements.

Concurrency and Performance

Concurrency is crucial to good performance in a multiprogramming system. When access to the data is *serialized* so that only one program at a time can use it, processing slows dramatically.

Locking and Integrity

Unless controls are placed on the use of data, concurrency can lead to a variety of negative effects. Programs can read obsolete data, or modifications can be lost even though they were apparently completed.

To prevent errors of this kind, the database server imposes a system of *locks*. A lock is a claim, or reservation, that a program can place on a piece of data. The database server guarantees that, as long as the data is locked, no other program can modify it. When another program requests the data, the database server either makes the program wait or turns it back with an error.

Locking and Performance

Because a lock serializes access to one piece of data, it reduces concurrency; any other programs that want access to that data must wait. The database server can place a lock on a single row, a disk page, a whole table, or an entire database. (A disk page might hold multiple rows and a row might require multiple disk pages.) The more locks it places and the larger the objects it locks, the more concurrency is reduced. The fewer the locks and the smaller the locked objects, the greater concurrency and performance can be.

The following sections discuss how you can achieve the following goals with your program:

- Place all the locks necessary to ensure data integrity
- Lock the fewest, smallest pieces of data possible consistent with the preceding goal

Concurrency Issues

To understand the hazards of concurrency, you must think in terms of multiple programs, each executing at its own speed. Suppose that your program is fetching rows through the following cursor:

```
EXEC SQL DECLARE sto_curse CURSOR FOR
    SELECT * FROM stock
        WHERE manu_code = 'ANZ';
```

The transfer of each row from the database server to the program takes time. During and between transfers, other programs can perform other database operations. At about the same time that your program fetches the rows produced by that query, another user's program might execute the following update:

```
EXEC SQL UPDATE stock
    SET unit_price = 1.15 * unit_price
        WHERE manu_code = 'ANZ';
```

In other words, both programs are reading through the same table, one fetching certain rows and the other changing the same rows. The following possibilities are concerned with what happens next:

1. The other program finishes its update before your program fetches its first row.

   Your program shows you only updated rows.

2. Your program fetches every row before the other program has a chance to update it.

   Your program shows you only original rows.

3. After your program fetches some original rows, the other program catches up and goes on to update some rows that your program has yet to read; then it executes the COMMIT WORK statement.

   Your program might return a mixture of original rows and updated rows.

4. Same as number 3, except that after updating the table, the other program issues a ROLLBACK WORK statement.

   Your program can show you a mixture of original rows and updated rows that no longer exist in the database.

The first two possibilities are harmless. In possibility number 1, the update is complete before your query begins. It makes no difference whether the update finished a microsecond ago or a week ago.

In possibility number 2, your query is, in effect, complete before the update begins. The other program might have been working just one row behind yours, or it might not start until tomorrow night; it does not matter.

The last two possibilities, however, can be important to the design of some applications. In possibility number 3, the query returns a mix of updated and original data. That result can be detrimental in some applications. In others, such as one that is taking an average of all prices, it might not matter at all.

In possibility number 4, it can be disastrous if a program returns some rows of data that, because their transaction was cancelled, can no longer be found in the table.

Another concern arises when your program uses a cursor to update or delete the last-fetched row. Erroneous results occur with the following sequence of events:

- Your program fetches the row.
- Another program updates or deletes the row.
- Your program updates or deletes WHERE CURRENT OF *cursor_name*.

To control concurrent events such as these, use the locking and *isolation level* features of the database server.

How Locks Work

Informix database servers support a complex, flexible set of locking features that this section describes. For a summary of locking features, see your *Getting Started* manual.

Kinds of Locks

The following table shows the types of locks that Informix database servers support for different situations.

Lock Type	Use
Shared	A shared lock reserves its object for reading only. It prevents the object from changing while the lock remains. More than one program can place a shared lock on the same object. More than one object can read the record while it is locked in shared mode.
Exclusive	An exclusive lock reserves its object for the use of a single program. This lock is used when the program intends to change the object.
	You cannot place an exclusive lock where any other kind of lock exists. After you place an exclusive lock, you cannot place another lock on the same object.
Promotable/Update	A promotable (or update) lock establishes the intent to update. You can only place it where no other promotable or exclusive lock exists. You can place promotable locks on records that already have shared locks. When the program is about to change the locked object, you can promote the promotable lock to an exclusive lock, but only if no other locks, including shared locks, are on the record at the time the lock would change from promotable to exclusive. If a shared lock was on the record when the promotable lock was set, you must drop the shared lock before the promotable lock can be promoted to an exclusive lock.

Lock Scope

You can apply locks to entire databases, entire tables, disk pages, single rows, or index-key values. The size of the object that is being locked is referred to as the *scope* of the lock (also called the *lock granularity*). In general, the larger the scope of a lock, the more concurrency is reduced, but the simpler programming becomes.

Database Locks

You can lock an entire database. The act of opening a database places a shared lock on the name of the database. A database is opened with the CONNECT, DATABASE, or CREATE DATABASE statements. As long as a program has a database open, the shared lock on the name prevents any other program from dropping the database or putting an exclusive lock on it.

The following statement shows how you might lock an entire database exclusively:

```
DATABASE database_one EXCLUSIVE
```

This statement succeeds if no other program has opened that database. After the lock is placed, no other program can open the database, even for reading, because its attempt to place a shared lock on the database name fails.

A database lock is released only when the database closes. That action can be performed explicitly with the DISCONNECT or CLOSE DATABASE statements or implicitly by executing another DATABASE statement.

Because locking a database reduces concurrency in that database to zero, it makes programming simple; concurrent effects cannot happen. However, you should lock a database only when no other programs need access. Database locking is often used before applying massive changes to data during off-peak hours.

Table Locks

You can lock entire tables. In some cases, the database server performs this action automatically. You can also use the LOCK TABLE statement to lock an entire table explicitly.

The LOCK TABLE statement or the database server can place the following types of table locks:

- Shared lock

  No users can write to the table. In shared mode, the database server places one shared lock on the table, which informs other users that no updates can be performed. In addition, the database server adds locks for every row updated, deleted, or inserted.

- Exclusive lock

  No other users can read from or write to the table. In exclusive mode, the database server places only one exclusive lock on the table, no matter how many rows it updates. An exclusive table lock prevents any concurrent use of the table and, therefore, can have a serious effect on performance if many other programs are contending for the use of the table. However, when you need to update most of the rows in a table, place an exclusive lock on the table.

Locking a Table with the LOCK TABLE Statement

A transaction tells the database server to use table-level locking for a table with the LOCK TABLE statement. The following example shows how to place an exclusive lock on a table:

```
LOCK TABLE tab1 IN EXCLUSIVE MODE
```

The following example shows how to place a shared lock on a table:

```
LOCK TABLE tab2 IN SHARE MODE
```

Tip: *You can set the isolation level for your database server to achieve the same degree of protection as the shared table lock while providing greater concurrency.*

When the Database Server Automatically Locks a Table

The database server always locks an entire table while it performs operations for any of the following statements:

- ALTER FRAGMENT
- ALTER INDEX ♦
- ALTER TABLE
- CREATE INDEX
- DROP INDEX
- RENAME COLUMN
- RENAME TABLE

Completion of the statement (or end of the transaction) releases the lock. An entire table can also be locked automatically during certain queries.

IDS

EDS

Placing a Table Lock with the LOCK MODE Clause

Enterprise Decision Server allows you to lock a table with either the LOCK TABLE statement or the TABLE lock mode of a LOCK MODE clause in a CREATE TABLE statement. All transactions that access a table whose lock mode is set to TABLE acquire a table lock for that table, if the isolation level for the transaction requires the transaction to acquire any locks at all. The following statement shows how to use the TABLE lock mode when you create a table:

```
CREATE TABLE tab1
(
    col1 ...
) LOCK MODE TABLE
```

You can use the ALTER TABLE statement to switch a table from one lock mode to any other lock mode (TABLE, PAGE, or ROW).

Whether you specify the TABLE lock mode for the LOCK MODE clause of a CREATE TABLE or ALTER TABLE statement, or use a LOCK TABLE statement to acquire a table lock, the effect is the same.

The TABLE lock mode is particularly useful in a data-warehousing environment where query efficiency increases because, instead of acquiring (or trying to acquire, depending on the isolation level) page- or row-level locks, the transaction acquires table locks. Table-level locks can significantly reduce the number of lock requests. The disadvantage of table locks is that they radically reduce update concurrency, but in a data warehousing environment this reduction is generally not a problem. ♦

Row and Key Locks

You can lock one row of a table. A program can lock one row or a selection of rows while other programs continue to work on other rows of the same table.

Row and key locking are not the default behaviors. You must specify row-level locking when you create the table. The following example creates a table with row-level locking:

```
CREATE TABLE tab1
(
col1...
) LOCK MODE ROW;
```

If you specify a LOCK MODE clause when you create a table, you can later change the lock mode with the ALTER TABLE statement. The following statement changes the lock mode on the reservations table to page-level locking:

```
ALTER TABLE tab1 LOCK MODE PAGE
```

In certain cases, the database server has to lock a row that does not exist. To do this, the database server places a lock on an index-key value. Key locks are used identically to row locks. When the table uses row locking, key locks are implemented as locks on imaginary rows. When the table uses page locking, a key lock is placed on the index page that contains the key or that would contain the key if it existed.

When you insert, update, or delete a key (performed automatically when you insert, update, or delete a row), the database server creates a lock on the key in the index.

Row and key locks generally provide the best performance overall when you update a relatively small number of rows because they increase concurrency. However, the database server incurs some overhead in obtaining a lock.

Page Locks

The database server stores data in units called *disk pages*. A disk page contains one or more rows. In some cases, it is better to lock a disk page than to lock individual rows on it. For example, with operations that require changing a large number of rows, you might choose page-level locking because row-level locking (one lock per row) might not be cost effective.

If you do not specify a LOCK MODE clause when you create a table, the default behavior for the database server is page-level locking. With page locking, the database server locks the entire page that contains the row. If you update several rows that are stored on the same page, the database server uses only one lock for the page.

Coarse Index Locks

When you change the lock mode of an index from normal to coarse lock mode, index-level locks are acquired on the index instead of item-level or page-level locks, which are the normal locks. This mode reduces the number of lock calls on an index.

Use the coarse lock mode when you know the index is not going to change, that is, when read-only operations are performed on the index.

Use the normal lock mode to have the database server place item-level or page-level locks on the index as necessary. Use this mode when the index gets updated frequently.

When the database server executes the command to change the lock mode to coarse, it acquires an exclusive lock on the table for the duration of the command. Any transactions that are currently using a lock of finer granularity must complete before the database server switches to the coarse lock mode.

IDS

Smart-Large-Object Locks

Locks on a CLOB or BLOB column are separate from the lock on the row. Smart large objects are locked only when they are accessed. When you lock a table that contains a CLOB or BLOB column, no smart large objects are locked. If accessed for writing, the smart large object is locked in update mode, and the lock is promoted to exclusive when the actual write occurs. If accessed for reading, the smart large object is locked in shared mode. The database server recognizes the transaction isolation mode, so if Repeatable Read isolation level is set, the database server does not release smart-large-object read locks before end of transaction.

When the database server retrieves a row and updates a smart large object that the row points to, only the smart large object is exclusively locked during the time it is being updated.

Byte-Range Locks

You can lock a range of bytes for a smart large object. Byte-range locks allow a transaction to selectively lock only those bytes that are accessed so that writers and readers simultaneously can access different byte ranges in the same smart large object.

For information about how to use byte-range locks, see your *Performance Guide*.

Byte-range locks support deadlock detection. For information about deadlock detection, see "Handling a Deadlock" on page 9-26.

Duration of a Lock

The program controls the duration of a database lock. A database lock is released when the database closes.

Depending on whether the database uses transactions, table lock durations vary. If the database does not use transactions (that is, if no transaction log exists and you do not use a COMMIT WORK statement), a table lock remains until it is removed by the execution of the UNLOCK TABLE statement.

The duration of table, row, and index locks depends on what SQL statements you use and on whether transactions are in use.

When you use transactions, the end of a transaction releases all table, row, page, and index locks. When a transaction ends, *all locks are released*.

Locks While Modifying

When the database server fetches a row through an update cursor, it places a promotable lock on the fetched row. If this action succeeds, the database server knows that no other program can alter that row. Because a promotable lock is not exclusive, other programs can continue to read the row. A promotable lock can improve performance because the program that fetched the row can take some time before it issues the UPDATE or DELETE statement, or it can simply fetch the next row. When it is time to modify a row, the database server obtains an exclusive lock on the row. If it already has a promotable lock, it changes that lock to exclusive status.

The duration of an exclusive row lock depends on whether transactions are in use. If they are not in use, the lock is released as soon as the modified row is written to disk. When transactions are in use, all such locks are held until the end of the transaction. This action prevents other programs from using rows that might be rolled back to their original state.

When transactions are in use, a key lock is used whenever a row is deleted. Using a key lock prevents the following error from occurring:

- Program A deletes a row.
- Program B inserts a row that has the same key.

■ Program A rolls back its transaction, forcing the database server to restore its deleted row.

What is to be done with the row inserted by Program B?

By locking the index, the database server prevents a second program from inserting a row until the first program commits its transaction.

The locks placed while the database server reads various rows are controlled by the current isolation level, which is discussed in the next section.

Locking with the SELECT Statement

The type and duration of locks that the database server places depend on the isolation set in the application and if the SELECT statement is within an update cursor. This section describes the different isolation levels and update cursors.

Setting the Isolation Level

The *isolation level* is the degree to which your program is isolated from the concurrent actions of other programs. The database server offers a choice of isolation levels that reflect a different set of rules for how a program uses locks when it reads data. The type and duration of locks that the database server places depend on the isolation level set in the application and on whether or not the SELECT statement is within an update cursor.

To set the isolation level, use either the SET ISOLATION or SET TRANSACTION statement. The SET TRANSACTION statement also lets you set access modes. For more information about access modes, see "Controlling Data Modification with Access Modes" on page 9-24.

Comparing SET TRANSACTION with SET ISOLATION

The SET TRANSACTION statement complies with ANSI SQL-92. This statement is similar to the Informix SET ISOLATION statement; however, the SET ISOLATION statement is not ANSI compliant and does not provide access modes.

The following table shows the relationships between the isolation levels that you set with the SET TRANSACTION and SET ISOLATION statements.

SET TRANSACTION	→	Correlates to	→	SET ISOLATION
Read Uncommitted				Dirty Read
Read Committed				Committed Read
Not Supported				Cursor Stability
(ANSI) Repeatable Read				(Informix) Repeatable Read
Serializable				(Informix) Repeatable Read

The major difference between the SET TRANSACTION and SET ISOLATION statements is the behavior of the isolation levels within transactions. The SET TRANSACTION statement can be issued only once for a transaction. Any cursors opened during that transaction are guaranteed to have that isolation level (or access mode if you are defining an access mode). With the SET ISOLATION statement, after a transaction is started, you can change the isolation level more than once within the transaction. The following examples illustrate the difference between how you can use the SET ISOLATION and SET TRANSACTION statements:

SET ISOLATION

```
EXEC SQL BEGIN WORK;
EXEC SQL SET ISOLATION TO DIRTY READ;
EXEC SQL SELECT ... ;
EXEC SQL SET ISOLATION TO REPEATABLE READ;
EXEC SQL INSERT ... ;
EXEC SQL COMMIT WORK;
   -- Executes without error
```

SET TRANSACTION

```
EXEC SQL BEGIN WORK;
EXEC SQL SET TRANSACTION ISOLATION LEVEL TO SERIALIZABLE;
EXEC SQL SELECT ... ;
EXEC SQL SET TRANSACTION ISOLATION LEVEL TO READ COMMITTED;
Error 876: Cannot issue SET TRANSACTION more than once in an
active transaction.
```

ANSI Read Uncommitted and Informix Dirty Read Isolation

The simplest isolation level, ANSI Read Uncommitted and Informix Dirty Read, amounts to virtually no isolation. When a program fetches a row, it places no locks, and it respects none; it simply copies rows from the database without regard for what other programs are doing.

A program always receives complete rows of data; even under ANSI Read Uncommitted or Informix Dirty Read isolation, a program never sees a row in which some columns are updated and some are not. However, a program that uses ANSI Read Uncommitted or Informix Dirty Read isolation sometimes reads updated rows before the updating program ends its transaction. If the updating program later rolls back its transaction, the reading program processed data that never really existed (possibility number 4 in the list of concurrency issues on page 9-5).

ANSI Read Uncommitted or Informix Dirty Read is the most efficient isolation level. The reading program never waits and never makes another program wait. It is the preferred level in any of the following cases:

- All tables are static; that is, concurrent programs only read and never modify data.
- The table is held in an exclusive lock.
- Only one program is using the table.

ANSI Read Committed and Informix Committed Read Isolation

When a program requests the ANSI Read Committed or Informix Committed Read isolation level, the database server guarantees that it never returns a row that is not committed to the database. This action prevents reading data that is not committed and that is subsequently rolled back.

ANSI Read Committed or Informix Committed Read is implemented simply. Before it fetches a row, the database server tests to determine whether an updating process placed a lock on the row; if not, it returns the row. Because rows that are updated but do not have committed locks on them, this test ensures that the program does not read uncommitted data.

ANSI Read Committed or Informix Committed Read does not actually place a lock on the fetched row, so this isolation level is almost as efficient as ANSI Read Uncommitted or Informix Dirty Read. This isolation level is appropriate to use when each row of data is processed as an independent unit, without reference to other rows in the same or other tables.

Informix Cursor Stability Isolation

The next level, Cursor Stability, is available only with the Informix SQL statement SET ISOLATION.

IDS

When Cursor Stability is in effect, Dynamic Server places a lock on the latest row fetched. It places a shared lock for an ordinary cursor or a promotable lock for an update cursor. Only one row is locked at a time; that is, each time a row is fetched, the lock on the previous row is released (unless that row is updated, in which case the lock holds until the end of the transaction). ♦

EDS

When Cursor Stability is in effect, Enterprise Decision Server places a lock on one or more rows. It places a shared lock for an ordinary cursor or a promotable lock for an update cursor. Use the ISOLATION_LOCKS configuration parameter to specify the maximum number of rows to be locked at any given time on any given scan. The database server includes the user's current row in the set of rows currently locked. As the next row is read from the cursor, the previous row might or might not be released. The user does not have control over which rows are locked or when those rows are released. The database server guarantees only that a maximum of n rows are locked at any given time for any given cursor and that the current row is in the set of rows currently locked. (The default value is one row.) For more information about the ISOLATION_LOCKS parameter, see your *Performance Guide* and *Administrator's Guide*. ♦

Because Cursor Stability locks only one row (Dynamic Server) or a specified number of rows (Enterprise Decision Server) at a time, it restricts concurrency less than a table lock or database lock.

Cursor Stability ensures that a row does not change while the program examines it. Such row stability is important when the program updates some other table based on the data it reads from the row. Because of Cursor Stability, the program is assured that the update is based on current information. It prevents the use of *stale data*.

The following example illustrates effective use of Cursor Stability isolation. In terms of the demonstration database, Program A wants to insert a new stock item for manufacturer Hero (HRO). Concurrently, Program B wants to delete manufacturer HRO and all stock associated with it. The following sequence of events can occur:

1. Program A, operating under Cursor Stability, fetches the HRO row from the **manufact** table to learn the manufacturer code: This action places a shared lock on the row.

2. Program B issues a DELETE statement for that row. Because of the lock, the database server makes the program wait.

3. Program A inserts a new row in the **stock** table using the manufacturer code it obtained from the **manufact** table.

4. Program A closes its cursor on the **manufact** table or reads a different row of it, releasing its lock.

5. Program B, released from its wait, completes the deletion of the row and goes on to delete the rows of **stock** that use manufacturer code HRO, including the row that Program A just inserted.

If Program A used a lesser level of isolation, the following sequence could occur:

1. Program A reads the HRO row of the **manufact** table to learn the manufacturer code. No lock is placed.

2. Program B issues a DELETE statement for that row. It succeeds.

3. Program B deletes all rows of **stock** that use manufacturer code HRO.

4. Program B ends.

5. Program A, not aware that its copy of the HRO row is now invalid, inserts a new row of **stock** using the manufacturer code HRO.

6. Program A ends.

At the end, a row occurs in **stock** that has no matching manufacturer code in **manufact**. Furthermore, Program B apparently has a bug; it did not delete the rows that it was supposed to delete. Use of the Cursor Stability isolation level prevents these effects.

The preceding scenario could be rearranged to fail even with Cursor Stability. All that is required is for Program B to operate on tables in the reverse sequence to Program A. If Program B deletes from **stock** before it removes the row of **manufact**, no degree of isolation can prevent an error. Whenever this kind of error is possible, all programs that are involved must use the same sequence of access.

ANSI Serializable, ANSI Repeatable Read, and Informix Repeatable Read Isolation

The definitions for ANSI Serializable, ANSI Repeatable Read, and Informix Repeatable Read isolation levels are all the same.

The Repeatable Read isolation level asks the database server to put a lock on every row the program examines and fetches. The locks that are placed are shareable for an ordinary cursor and promotable for an update cursor. The locks are placed individually as each row is examined. They are not released until the cursor closes or a transaction ends.

Repeatable Read allows a program that uses a scroll cursor to read selected rows more than once and to be sure that they are not modified or deleted between readings. (Chapter 7 describes scroll cursors.) No lower isolation level guarantees that rows still exist and are unchanged the second time they are read.

Repeatable Read isolation places the largest number of locks and holds them the longest. Therefore, it is the level that reduces concurrency the most. If your program uses this level of isolation, think carefully about how many locks it places, how long they are held, and what the effect can be on other programs.

In addition to the effect on concurrency, the large number of locks can be a problem. The database server records the number of locks by each program in a lock table. If the maximum number of locks is exceeded, the lock table fills up, and the database server cannot place a lock. An error code is returned. The person who administers an Informix database server system can monitor the lock table and tell you when it is heavily used.

The isolation level in an ANSI-compliant database is set to Serializable by default. The isolation level of Serializable is required to ensure that operations behave according to the ANSI standard for SQL.

Update Cursors

An update cursor is a special kind of cursor that applications can use when the row might potentially be updated. To use an update cursor, execute SELECT FOR UPDATE in your application. Update cursors use *promotable locks*; that is, the database server places an update lock (meaning other users can still view the row) when the application fetches the row, but the lock is changed to an exclusive lock when the application updates the row using an update cursor and UPDATE...WHERE CURRENT OF.

The advantage of using an update cursor is that you can view the row with the confidence that other users cannot change it or view it with an update cursor while you are viewing it and before you update it.

 Tip: *In an ANSI-compliant database, update cursors are unnecessary because any select cursor behaves the same as an update cursor.*

The pseudocode in Figure 9-1 shows when the database server places and releases locks with a cursor.

Figure 9-1
Locks Placed for
Update Cursors

```
declare update cursor
begin work
open the cursor
fetch the row          ◄──────────── Add an update lock for this row.
do stuff
update the row (use WHERE CURRENT OF) ◄── Promote lock to
commit work    ◄── Release lock.              exclusive.
```

Retaining Update Locks

If a user has the isolation level set lower than repeatable read, the database server releases update locks placed on rows as soon as the next row is fetched from a cursor. With this feature, you can use the RETAIN UPDATE LOCKS clause to retain an update lock until the end of a transaction when you set any of the following isolation levels:

- Dirty Read
- Committed Read
- Cursor Stability

This feature lets you avoid the overhead of Repeatable Read isolation level or work arounds such as dummy updates on a row. When the RETAIN UPDATE LOCKS feature is turned on and an update lock is implicitly placed on a row during a FETCH of a SELECT...FOR UPDATE statement, the update lock is not released until the end of the transaction. With the RETAIN UPDATE LOCKS feature, only update locks are held until end of transaction whereas Repeatable Read isolation level holds both update locks and shared locks until end of transaction.

The following example shows how to use the RETAIN UPDATE LOCKS clause when you set the isolation level to Committed Read:

```
SET ISOLATION TO COMMITTED READ RETAIN UPDATE LOCKS
```

To turn off the RETAIN UPDATE LOCKS feature, set the isolation level without the RETAIN UPDATE LOCKS clause. When you turn off the feature, update locks are not released directly. However, from this point on, a subsequent fetch releases the update lock of the immediately preceding fetch but not of earlier fetch operations. A close cursor releases the update lock on the current row.

For more information about how to use the RETAIN UPDATE LOCKS feature when you specify an isolation level, see the *Informix Guide to SQL: Syntax*.

Locks Placed with INSERT, UPDATE, and DELETE

When you execute an INSERT, UPDATE, or DELETE statement, the database server uses exclusive locks. An exclusive lock means that no other users can view the row unless they are using the Dirty Read isolation level. In addition, no other users can update or delete the item until the database server removes the lock.

When the database server removes the exclusive lock depends on the type of logging set for the database. If the database has logging, the database server removes all exclusive locks when the transaction completes (commits or rolls back). If the database does not have logging, the database server removes all exclusive locks immediately after the INSERT, UPDATE, or DELETE statement completes.

Understanding the Behavior of the Lock Types

Informix database servers store locks in an internal lock table. When the database server reads a row, it checks if the row or its associated page, table, or database is listed in the lock table. If it is in the lock table, the database server must also check the lock type. The lock table can contain the following types of locks.

Lock Name	Description	Statement Usually Placing the Lock
S	Shared lock	SELECT
X	Exclusive lock	INSERT, UPDATE, DELETE
U	Update lock	SELECT in an update cursor
B	Byte lock	Any statement that updates VARCHAR columns

In addition, the lock table might store *intent locks*. An intent lock can be an intent shared (IS), intent exclusive (IX), or intent shared exclusive (SIX). An intent lock is the lock the database server (lock manager) places on a higher granularity object when a lower granularity object needs to be locked. For example, when a user locks a row or page in Shared lock mode, the database server places an IS (Intent shared) lock on the table to provide an instant check that no other user holds an X lock on the table. In this case, intent locks are placed on the table only and not on the row or page. Intent locks can be placed at the level of a row, page, or table only.

The user does not have direct control over intent locks; the lock manager internally manages all intent locks.

The following table shows what locks a user (or the database server) can place if another user (or the database server) holds a certain type of lock. For example, if one user holds an exclusive lock on an item, another user requesting any kind of lock (exclusive, update or shared) receives an error. In addition, the database server is unable to place any intent locks on an item if a user holds an exclusive lock on the item.

	Hold X Lock	Hold U Lock	Hold S Lock	Hold IS Lock	Hold SIX Lock	Hold IX Lock
Request X lock	No	No	No	No	No	No
Request U lock	No	No	Yes	Yes	No	No
Request S lock	No	Yes	Yes	Yes	No	No
Request IS lock	No	Yes	Yes	Yes	Yes	Yes
Request SIX lock	No	No	No	Yes	No	No
Request IX lock	No	No	No	Yes	No	Yes

For information about how locking affects performance, see your *Performance Guide*.

Controlling Data Modification with Access Modes

Informix database servers support access modes. Access modes affect read and write concurrency for rows within transactions and are set with the SET TRANSACTION statement. You can use access modes to control data modification among shared files.

Transactions are read-write by default. If you specify that a transaction is read-only, that transaction cannot perform the following tasks:

- Insert, delete, or update table rows
- Create, alter, or drop any database object such as a schema, table, temporary table, index, or stored routine
- Grant or revoke privileges
- Update statistics
- Rename columns or tables

Read-only access mode prohibits updates.

You can execute stored routines in a read-only transaction as long as the routine does not try to perform any restricted statements.

For information about how to use the SET TRANSACTION statement to specify an access mode, see the *Informix Guide to SQL: Syntax*.

Setting the Lock Mode

The lock mode determines what happens when your program encounters locked data. One of the following situations occurs when a program attempts to fetch or modify a locked row:

- The database server immediately returns an error code in SQLCODE or SQLSTATE to the program.
- The database server suspends the program until the program that placed the lock removes the lock.
- The database server suspends the program for a time and then, if the lock is not removed, the database server sends an error-return code to the program.

You choose among these results with the SET LOCK MODE statement.

Waiting for Locks

When a user encounters a lock, the default behavior of a database server is to return an error to the application. If you prefer to wait indefinitely for a lock (this choice is best for many applications), you can execute the following SQL statement:

```
SET LOCK MODE TO WAIT
```

When this lock mode is set, your program usually ignores the existence of other concurrent programs. When your program needs to access a row that another program has locked, it waits until the lock is removed, then proceeds. In most cases, the delays are imperceptible.

You can also wait for a specific number of seconds, as in the following example:

```
SET LOCK MODE TO WAIT 20
```

Not Waiting for Locks

The disadvantage of waiting for locks is that the wait might become long (although properly designed applications should hold their locks briefly). When the possibility of a long delay is not acceptable, a program can execute the following statement:

```
SET LOCK MODE TO NOT WAIT
```

When the program requests a locked row, it immediately receives an error code (for example, error -107 `Record is locked`), and the current SQL statement terminates. The program must roll back its current transaction and try again.

The initial setting is *not waiting* when a program starts up. If you are using SQL interactively and see an error related to locking, set the lock mode to wait. If you are writing a program, consider making that one of the first embedded SQL statements that the program executes.

Waiting a Limited Time

You can ask the database server to set an upper limit on a wait with the following statement:

```
SET LOCK MODE TO WAIT 17
```

This statement places an upper limit of 17 seconds on the length of any wait. If a lock is not removed in that time, the error code is returned.

Handling a Deadlock

A *deadlock* is a situation in which a pair of programs blocks the progress of each other. Each program has a lock on some object that the other program wants to access. A deadlock arises only when all programs concerned set their lock modes to wait for locks.

An Informix database server detects deadlocks immediately when they involve only data at a single network server. It prevents the deadlock from occurring by returning an error code (error -143 ISAM error: deadlock detected) to the second program to request a lock. The error code is the one the program receives if it sets its lock mode to not wait for locks. If your program receives an error code related to locks even after it sets lock mode to wait, you know the cause is an impending deadlock.

Handling External Deadlock

A deadlock can also occur between programs on different database servers. In this case, the database server cannot instantly detect the deadlock. (Perfect deadlock detection requires excessive communications traffic among all database servers in a network.) Instead, each database server sets an upper limit on the amount of time that a program can wait to obtain a lock on data at a different database server. If the time expires, the database server assumes that a deadlock was the cause and returns a lock-related error code.

In other words, when external databases are involved, every program runs with a maximum lock-waiting time. The DBA can set or modify the maximum for the database server.

Simple Concurrency

If you are not sure which choice to make concerning locking and concurrency, and if your application is straightforward, have your program execute the following statements when it starts up (immediately after the first DATABASE statement):

```
SET LOCK MODE TO WAIT
SET ISOLATION TO REPEATABLE READ
```

Ignore the return codes from both statements. Proceed as if no other programs exist. If no performance problems arise, you do not need to read this section again.

Hold Cursors

IDS

When transaction logging is used, Dynamic Server guarantees that anything done within a transaction can be rolled back at the end of it. To handle transactions reliably, the database server normally applies the following rules:

- When a transaction ends, all cursors are closed.
- When a transaction ends, all locks are released. ♦

EDS

Enterprise Decision Server might not release locks at the end of a transaction. To demonstrate how to acquire a table lock, suppose the database server acquires a lock on all coservers that store a part of the table. If a transaction first acquires a SHARED mode table lock and tries to upgrade to EXCLUSIVE mode table lock, locks might not be released at the end of the transaction. This can happen if the transaction performs a SELECT and then performs an INSERT on a table with lock mode TABLE. In this case, the upgrade might succeed on some coservers and fail on other coservers. No attempt is made to roll back the successful upgrades, which means that the transaction might end with EXCLUSIVE locks on the table for some coservers. ♦

The rules that are used to handle transactions reliably are normal with most database systems that support transactions, and they do not cause any trouble for most applications. However, circumstances exist in which using standard transactions with cursors is not possible. For example, the following code works fine without transactions. However, when transactions are added, closing the cursor conflicts with using two cursors simultaneously.

```
EXEC SQL DECLARE master CURSOR FOR . . .
EXEC SQL DECLARE detail CURSOR FOR . . . FOR UPDATE
EXEC SQL OPEN master;
while(SQLCODE == 0)
{
    EXEC SQL FETCH master INTO . . .
    if(SQLCODE == 0)
    {
        EXEC SQL BEGIN WORK;
        EXEC SQL OPEN detail USING . . .
        EXEC SQL FETCH detail . . .
        EXEC SQL UPDATE . . . WHERE CURRENT OF detail
        EXEC SQL COMMIT WORK;
    }
}
EXEC SQL CLOSE master;
```

In this design, one cursor is used to scan a table. Selected records are used as the basis for updating a different table. The problem is that when each update is treated as a separate transaction (as the pseudocode in the previous example shows), the COMMIT WORK statement following the UPDATE closes all cursors, including the master cursor.

The simplest alternative is to move the COMMIT WORK and BEGIN WORK statements to be the last and first statements, respectively, so that the entire scan over the master table is one large transaction. Treating the scan of the master table as one large transaction is sometimes possible, but it can become impractical if many rows need to be updated. The number of locks can be too large, and they are held for the duration of the program.

A solution that Informix database servers support is to add the keywords WITH HOLD to the declaration of the master cursor. Such a cursor is referred to as a *hold cursor* and is not closed at the end of a transaction. The database server still closes all other cursors, and it still releases all locks, but the hold cursor remains open until it is explicitly closed.

Before you attempt to use a hold cursor, you must be sure that you understand the locking mechanism described here, and you must also understand the programs that are running concurrently. Whenever COMMIT WORK is executed, all locks are released, including any locks placed on rows fetched through the hold cursor.

The removal of locks has little importance if the cursor is used as intended, for a single forward scan over a table. However, you can specify WITH HOLD for any cursor, including update cursors and scroll cursors. Before you do this, you must understand the implications of the fact that all locks (including locks on entire tables) are released at the end of a transaction.

Using the SQL Statement Cache

The SQL statement cache is a feature that lets you store in a buffer identical SQL statements that are executed repeatedly so the statements can be reused among different user sessions without the need for per-session memory allocation. Statement caching can dramatically improve performance for applications that contain a large number of prepared statements. However, performance improvements are less dramatic when statement caching is used to cache statements that are prepared once and executed many times.

Use SQL to turn on or turn off statement caching for an individual database session when statement caching is enabled for the database server. The following statement shows how to use SQL to turn on caching for the current database session:

```
SET STATEMENT_CACHE ON
```

The following statement shows how to use SQL to turn off caching for the current database session:

```
SET STATEMENT_CACHE OFF
```

If you attempt to turn on or turn off statement caching when caching is disabled, the database server returns an error.

For information about syntax for the SET STATEMENT CACHE statement, see the *Informix Guide to SQL: Syntax*. For information about the **STMT_CACHE** and **STMT_CACHE_SIZE** configuration parameters, see the *Administrator's Reference* and your *Performance Guide*. For information about the **STMT_CACHE** environment variable, see the *Informix Guide to SQL: Reference*.

Summary

Whenever multiple programs have access to a database concurrently (and when at least one of them can modify data), all programs must allow for the possibility that another program can change the data even as they read it. The database server provides a mechanism of locks and isolation levels that usually allow programs to run as if they were alone with the data.

The SET STATEMENT CACHE statement allows you to store in a buffer identical SQL statements that are used repeatedly. When statement caching is turned on, the database server stores the identical statements so they can be reused among different user sessions without the need for per-session memory allocation.

Creating and Using SPL Routines

In This Chapter 10-5

Introduction to SPL Routines 10-6
   What You Can Do with SPL Routines 10-6
   SPL Routine Behavior for Enterprise Decision Server 10-7

Writing SPL Routines 10-8
   Using the CREATE PROCEDURE or CREATE
      FUNCTION Statement 10-8
      Beginning and Ending the Routine 10-8
      Specifying a Routine Name 10-9
      Adding a Specific Name 10-10
      Adding a Parameter List 10-11
      Adding a Return Clause 10-13
      Specifying Whether or Not the SPL Function is Variant . . . 10-14
      Adding a Modifier 10-14
      Specifying a Document Clause 10-16
      Specifying a Listing File 10-16
      Adding Comments 10-17
   Example of a Complete Routine 10-18
   Creating an SPL Routine in a Program 10-18
   Dropping an SPL Routine 10-19

Defining and Using Variables 10-20
   Declaring Local Variables 10-21
      Scope of Local Variables 10-22
      Declaring Built-In Type Variables 10-22
      Declaring Variables for Smart Large Objects 10-23
      Declaring Variables for Simple Large Objects 10-23
      Declaring Collection Variables 10-23
      Declaring Row-Type Variables 10-24
      Declaring Opaque- and Distinct-Type Variables 10-25

Declaring Variables for Column Data with the LIKE Clause . . 10-26
Declaring PROCEDURE Type Variables 10-26
Using Subscripts with Variables 10-27
Variable and Keyword Ambiguity 10-27
Declaring Global Variables 10-29
Assigning Values to Variables 10-30
The LET Statement 10-31
Other Ways to Assign Values to Variables 10-33

Expressions in SPL Routines 10-33

Writing the Statement Block 10-34
Implicit and Explicit Statement Blocks 10-34
Using Cursors 10-35
Using the FOREACH Loop to Define Cursors 10-35
Using an IF - ELIF - ELSE Structure 10-38
Adding WHILE and FOR Loops 10-40
Exiting a Loop 10-42

Returning Values from an SPL Function 10-43
Returning a Single Value 10-44
Returning Multiple Values 10-44

Handling Row-Type Data 10-46
Precedence of Dot Notation 10-46
Updating a Row-Type Expression 10-47

Handling Collections 10-48
Collection Examples 10-48
The First Steps 10-49
Declaring a Collection Variable 10-50
Declaring an Element Variable 10-50
Selecting a Collection into a Collection Variable 10-50
Inserting Elements into a Collection Variable 10-51
Inserting into a SET or MULTISET 10-51
Inserting into a LIST 10-52
Checking the Cardinality of a LIST Collection 10-53
Syntax of the VALUES Clause 10-54

Selecting Elements from a Collection 10-54
   The Collection Query 10-55
   Adding the Collection Query to the SPL Routine 10-56
Deleting a Collection Element 10-57
   Updating the Collection in the Database 10-59
   Deleting the Entire Collection 10-60
Updating a Collection Element 10-61
   Updating a Collection with a Variable 10-62
Updating the Entire Collection 10-63
   Updating a Collection of Row Types 10-63
   Updating a Nested Collection 10-64
Inserting into a Collection 10-66
   Inserting into a Nested Collection 10-67

Executing Routines 10-71
   Using the EXECUTE Statements 10-71
   Using the CALL Statement 10-73
   Executing Routines in Expressions 10-74
   Executing an External Function with the RETURN Statement . . .10-75
   Executing Cursor Functions from an SPL Routine 10-75
   Dynamic Routine-Name Specification 10-76

Privileges on Routines 10-78
   Privileges for Registering a Routine 10-79
   Privileges for Executing a Routine 10-79
      Granting and Revoking the Execute Privilege 10-80
      Execute Privileges with COMMUTATOR and
         NEGATOR Functions 10-80
   Privileges on Objects Associated with a Routine 10-81
   DBA Privileges for Executing a Routine 10-82

Finding Errors in an SPL Routine 10-84
   Looking at Compile-Time Warnings 10-85
   Generating the Text of the Routine 10-85

Debugging an SPL Routine 10-86

Exception Handling. 10-88
   Trapping an Error and Recovering 10-89
   Scope of Control of an ON EXCEPTION Statement 10-90
   User-Generated Exceptions. 10-91
      Simulating SQL Errors 10-91
      Using RAISE EXCEPTION to Exit Nested Code 10-92

Checking the Number of Rows Processed in an SPL Routine 10-93

Summary 10-93

In This Chapter

This chapter describes how to create and use SPL routines. An SPL routine is a user-defined routine written in Informix Stored Procedure Language (SPL). Informix SPL is an extension to SQL that provides flow control, such as looping and branching. Anyone who has the Resource privilege on a database can create an SPL routine.

Routines written in SQL are parsed, optimized as far as possible, and then stored in the system catalog tables in executable format. An SPL routine might be a good choice for SQL-intensive tasks. SPL routines can execute routines written in C or other external languages, and external routines can execute SPL routines.

You can use SPL routines to perform any task that you can perform in SQL and to expand what you can accomplish with SQL alone. Because SPL is a language native to the database, and because SPL routines are parsed and optimized when they are created rather than at runtime, SPL routines can improve performance for some tasks. SPL routines can also reduce traffic between a client application and the database server and reduce program complexity.

The syntax for each SPL statement is described in the *Informix Guide to SQL: Syntax*. Examples accompany the syntax for each statement.

Introduction to SPL Routines

SPL *routine* is a generic term that includes SPL *procedures* and SPL *functions*. An SPL *procedure* is a routine written in SPL and SQL that does not return a value. An SPL *function* is a routine written in SPL and SQL that returns a single value, a value with a complex data type, or multiple values. Generally, a routine written in SPL that returns a value is an SPL function.

You use SQL and SPL statements to write an SPL routine. SPL statements can be used only inside the CREATE PROCEDURE, CREATE PROCEDURE FROM, CREATE FUNCTION, and CREATE FUNCTION FROM statements. All these statements are available with SQL APIs such as Informix ESQL/C. The CREATE PROCEDURE and CREATE FUNCTION statements are available with DB-Access and the Relational Object Manager.

What You Can Do with SPL Routines

You can accomplish a wide range of objectives with SPL routines, including improving database performance, simplifying writing applications, and limiting or monitoring access to data.

Because an SPL routine is stored in an executable format, you can use it to execute frequently repeated tasks to improve performance. When you execute an SPL routine rather than straight SQL code, you can bypass repeated parsing, validity checking, and query optimization.

You can use an SPL routine in a data-manipulation SQL statement to supply values to that statement. For example, you can use a routine to perform the following actions:

- Supply values to be inserted into a table
- Supply a value that makes up part of a condition clause in a SELECT, DELETE, or UPDATE statement

These actions are two possible uses of a routine in a data-manipulation statement, but others exist. In fact, any expression in a data-manipulation SQL statement can consist of a routine call.

You can also issue SQL statements in an SPL routine to hide those SQL statements from a database user. Rather than having all users learn how to use SQL, one experienced SQL user can write an SPL routine to encapsulate an SQL activity and let others know that the routine is stored in the database so that they can execute it.

You can write an SPL routine to be run with the DBA privilege by a user who does not have the DBA privilege. This feature allows you to limit and control access to data in the database. Alternatively, an SPL routine can monitor the users who access certain tables or data. For more information about how to use SPL routines to control access to data, see the *Informix Guide to Database Design and Implementation*.

SPL Routine Behavior for Enterprise Decision Server

EDS

Enterprise Decision Server supports SPL procedures but not SPL functions.

With Enterprise Decision Server, the following SPL procedure features behave differently than they do in Dynamic Server:

- SYSPROCPLAN system catalog table

  All Informix database servers modify the SYSPROCPLAN system catalog table whenever an SPL procedure is created. For Dynamic Server, the SYSPROCPLAN system catalog table is also modified during execution of an SPL procedure, if the SPL procedure generates any new query-execution plans during execution. However, Enterprise Decision Server does not modify the SYSPROCPLAN table when execution of an SPL procedure results in new query-execution plans. For example, if plans are deleted from the SYSPROCPLAN system catalog table, and the procedure is executed from any coserver, the plans are not restored in SYSPROCPLAN. However, an UPDATE STATISTICS FOR PROCEDURE statement that is executed from any coserver updates the plans in SYSPROCPLAN.

- SPL Procedure calls

  An SPL procedure call can be made only to SPL procedures that are in the current database and the current database server.

Writing SPL Routines

An SPL routine consists of a beginning statement, a statement block, and an ending statement. Within the statement block, you can use SQL or SPL statements.

The maximum size of an SPL routine is 64 kilobytes. The maximum size includes any SPL global variables in the database and the routine itself.

Using the CREATE PROCEDURE or CREATE FUNCTION Statement

You must first decide if the routine that you are creating returns values or not. If the routine does not return a value, use the CREATE PROCEDURE statement to create an SPL procedure. If the routine returns a value, use the CREATE FUNCTION statement to create an SPL function.

To create an SPL routine, use one CREATE PROCEDURE or CREATE FUNCTION statement to write the body of the routine and register it.

Beginning and Ending the Routine

To create an SPL routine that does not return values, start with the CREATE PROCEDURE statement and end with the END PROCEDURE keyword. Figure 10-1 shows how to begin and end an SPL procedure.

Figure 10-1

```
CREATE PROCEDURE new_price( per_cent REAL )
  .
  .
  .
END PROCEDURE;
```

The name that you assign to the SPL procedure can be up to 18 characters long. For more information about naming conventions, see the Identifier segment in the *Informix Guide to SQL: Syntax*.

To create an SPL function that returns one or more values, start with the CREATE FUNCTION statement and end with the END FUNCTION keyword. Figure 10-2 shows how to begin and end an SPL function.

Figure 10-2

```
CREATE FUNCTION discount_price( per_cent REAL)
    RETURNING MONEY;
    .
    .
    .
END FUNCTION;
```

The entire text of an SPL routine, including spaces and tabs, must not exceed 64 kilobytes. In SPL routines, the END PROCEDURE or END FUNCTION keywords are required.

Important: *For compatibility with earlier Informix products, you can use CREATE PROCEDURE with a RETURNING clause to create a user-defined routine that returns a value. However, Informix recommends that you use CREATE PROCEDURE for SPL routines that do not return values (SPL procedures) and CREATE FUNCTION for SPL routines that return one or more values (SPL functions).*

Specifying a Routine Name

You specify a name for the UDR immediately following the CREATE PROCEDURE or CREATE FUNCTION statement and before the parameter list, as Figure 10-3 shows.

Figure 10-3

```
CREATE PROCEDURE add_price (arg INT )...
```

IDS

Dynamic Server allows you to create more than one SPL routine with the same name but with different parameters. This feature is known as *routine overloading*. For example, you might create each of the following SPL routines in your database:

```
CREATE PROCEDURE multiply (a INT, b basetype1)...
CREATE PROCEDURE multiply (a INT, b basetype2)...
CREATE PROCEDURE multiply (a REAL, b basetype3)...
```

If you call a UDR with the name **multiply()**, the database server evaluates the name of the UDR and its arguments to determine which UDR to execute. ♦

Routine resolution is the process in which the database server searches for a routine signature that it can use, given the name of the UDR and a list of arguments. Every UDR has a *signature* that uniquely identifies the UDR based on the following information:

- The type of UDR (procedure or function)
- The UDR name
- The number of parameters
- The data types of the parameters
- The order of the parameters

The UDR signature is used in a CREATE, DROP, or EXECUTE statement if you enter the full parameter list of the UDR. For example, each statement in Figure 10-4 uses a UDR signature.

Figure 10-4

```
CREATE FUNCTION multiply(a INT, b INT);
DROP PROCEDURE end_of_list(n SET, row_id INT);
EXECUTE FUNCTION compare_point(m point, n point);
```

IDS

Adding a Specific Name

Because Dynamic Server supports routine overloading, an SPL routine might not be uniquely identified by its name alone. However, a UDR can be uniquely identified by a *specific name*. A *specific name* is a unique identifier that you define in the CREATE PROCEDURE or CREATE FUNCTION statement, in addition to the UDR name. A specific name is defined with the SPECIFIC keyword and is unique in the database. Two UDRs in the same database cannot have the same specific name, even if they have different owners.

A specific name can be up to 18 characters long. Figure 10-5 shows how to define the specific name **calc** in a CREATE FUNCTION statement that creates the **calculate()** function.

Figure 10-5

```
CREATE FUNCTION calculate(a INT, b INT, c INT)
    RETURNING INT
    SPECIFIC calc1;
.
.
.
END FUNCTION;
```

Because the owner **bsmith** has given the SPL function the specific name **calc1**, no other user can define a UDR—SPL or external—with the specific name **calc1**. Now you can refer to the UDR as **bsmith.calculate** or with the SPECIFIC keyword **calc1** in any statement that requires the SPECIFIC keyword.

Adding a Parameter List

When you create an SPL UDR, you can define a parameter list so that the UDR accepts one or more arguments when it is invoked. The parameter list is optional.

A parameter to an SPL routine must have a name and can be defined with a default value. The following table lists the categories of data types that a parameter can specify for the different Informix database servers.

Dynamic Server	Enterprise Decision Server
Built-in data types	Built-in data types
Opaque data types	
Distinct data types	
Row types	
Collection types	
Smart large objects (CLOB and BLOB)	

For all Informix database servers, a parameter cannot specify any of the following data types:

- SERIAL
- SERIAL8
- TEXT
- BYTE

Figure 10-6 shows examples of different parameter lists.

Figure 10-6

```
CREATE PROCEDURE raise_price(per_cent INT)

CREATE FUNCTION  raise_price(per_cent INT DEFAULT 5)

CREATE PROCEDURE update_emp(n employee_t)
CREATE FUNCTION  update_nums( list1 LIST (ROW a varchar(10),
                                          b varchar(10),
                                          c int) NOT NULL )
```

When you define a parameter, you accomplish two tasks at once:

- You request that the user supply a value when the routine is executed.

- You implicitly define a variable (with the same name as the parameter name) that you can use as a local variable in the body of the routine.

If you define a parameter with a default value, the user can execute the SPL routine with or without the corresponding argument. If the user executes the SPL routine without the argument, the database server assigns the parameter the default value as an argument.

When you invoke an SPL routine, you can give an argument a null value. SPL routines handle null values by default. However, you cannot give an argument a null value if the argument is a collection element.

Using Simple Large Objects as Parameters

Although you cannot define a parameter with a simple large object (a large object that contains TEXT or BYTE data types), you can use the REFERENCES keyword to define a parameter that points to a simple large object, as Figure 10-7 shows.

Figure 10-7

```
CREATE PROCEDURE proc1(lo_text REFERENCES TEXT)

CREATE FUNCTION proc2(lo_byte REFERENCES BYTE DEFAULT NULL)
```

The REFERENCES keyword means that the SPL routine is passed a descriptor that contains a pointer to the simple large object, not the object itself.

Undefined Arguments

When you invoke an SPL routine, you can specify all, some, or none of the defined arguments. If you do not specify an argument, and if its corresponding parameter does not have a default value, the argument, which is used as a variable within the SPL routine, is given a status of *undefined*.

Undefined is a special status used for SPL variables that have no value. The SPL routine executes without error, as long as you do not attempt to use the variable that has the status *undefined* in the body of the routine.

The *undefined* status is not the same as a null value. Null means the value is not available or not applicable.

Adding a Return Clause

If you use CREATE FUNCTION to create an SPL routine, you must specify a return clause that returns one or more values.

Tip: *If you use the CREATE PROCEDURE statement to create an SPL routine, you have the option of specifying a return clause. However, Informix recommends that you always use the CREATE FUNCTION statement to create a routine that returns values.*

To specify a return clause, use the RETURNING or RETURNS keyword with a list of data types the UDR will return. The data types can be any SQL data types except SERIAL, SERIAL8, TEXT, or BYTE.

The return clause in Figure 10-8 specifies that the SPL routine will return an INT value and a REAL value.

Figure 10-8

```
CREATE FUNCTION find_group(id INT)
    RETURNING INT, REAL;
    .
    .
    .
END FUNCTION;
```

After you specify a return clause, you must also specify a RETURN statement in the body of the UDR that explicitly returns the values to the calling UDR. For more information on writing the RETURN statement, see "Returning Values from an SPL Function" on page 10-43.

To specify that the function should return a simple large object (a TEXT or BYTE value), you must use the REFERENCES clause, as in Figure 10-9, because an SPL routine returns only a pointer to the object, not the object itself.

Figure 10-9

```
CREATE FUNCTION find_obj(id INT)
    RETURNING REFERENCES BYTE;
```

Specifying Whether or Not the SPL Function is Variant

When you create an SPL function, the function is variant by default. A function is variant if it returns different results when it is invoked with the same arguments or if it modifies a database or variable state. For example, a function that returns the current date or time is a variant function.

By default, SPL functions are variant. If you specify WITH NOT VARIANT when you create a function, the function cannot contain any SQL statements. You can create a functional index on a nonvariant function.

IDS

Adding a Modifier

When you write SPL functions, you can use the WITH clause to add a modifier to the CREATE FUNCTION statement. In the WITH clause, you can specify the COMMUTATOR or NEGATOR functions. The other modifiers are for external routines.

Important: *You can use the COMMUTATOR or NEGATOR modifiers with SPL functions only. You cannot use any modifiers with SPL procedures.*

The COMMUTATOR Modifier

The COMMUTATOR modifier allows you to specify an SPL function that is the *commutator function* of the SPL function you are creating. A commutator function accepts the same arguments as the SPL function you are creating, but in opposite order, and returns the same value. The commutator function might be more cost effective for the SQL optimizer to execute.

For example, the functions **lessthan(a,b)**, which returns TRUE if **a** is less than **b**, and **greaterthan(b,a)**, which returns TRUE if **b** is greater than or equal to **a**, are commutator functions. Figure 10-10 uses the WITH clause to define a commutator function.

WIN NT

Figure 10-14 shows how to log the compile-time warnings in *tmp**listfile* when you work in Windows NT.

Figure 10-14

```
CREATE FUNCTION raise_prices(per_cent INT)
    .
    .
    .
END FUNCTION
    WITH LISTING IN 'C:\tmp\listfile'
    ◆
```

Always remember to place single or double quotation marks around the filename or pathname.

Adding Comments

You can add a comment to any line of an SPL routine, even a blank line.

To add a comment, place a double dash (--) before the comment or enclose the comment in braces ({ }). The double dash complies with the ANSI standard. The braces are an Informix extension to the ANSI standard.

To add a multiple-line comment, you can either

- place a double dash before each line of the comment.
- enclose the entire comment within braces.

All the examples in Figure 10-15 are valid comments.

Figure 10-15

```
SELECT * FROM customer -- Selects all columns and rows

SELECT * FROM customer
    -- Selects all columns and rows
    -- from the customer table

SELECT * FROM customer
    { Selects all columns and rows
      from the customer table }
```

Warning: *Braces ({ }) can be used to delimit both comments and the list of elements in a collection. To ensure that the parser correctly recognizes the end of a comment or list of elements in a collection, Informix recommends that you use the double dash for comments in an SPL routine that handles collection types.*

Example of a Complete Routine

The following CREATE FUNCTION statement creates a routine that reads a customer address:

```
CREATE FUNCTION read_address (lastname CHAR(15)) -- one
argument
    RETURNING CHAR(15), CHAR(15), CHAR(20), CHAR(15),CHAR(2)
        CHAR(5); -- 6 items

    DEFINE p_lname,p_fname, p_city CHAR(15); --define each
        routine variable
    DEFINE p_add CHAR(20);
    DEFINE p_state CHAR(2);
    DEFINE p_zip CHAR(5);

    SELECT fname, address1, city, state, zipcode
        INTO p_fname, p_add, p_city, p_state, p_zip
        FROM customer
        WHERE lname = lastname;

    RETURN p_fname, lastname, p_add, p_city, p_state, p_zip;
        --6 items
END FUNCTION;

DOCUMENT 'This routine takes the last name of a customer
    as', --brief description
    'its only argument. It returns the full name and address
    of the customer.'

WITH LISTING IN 'pathname' -- modify this pathname according
-- to the conventions that your operating system requires

-- compile-time warnings go here
; -- end of the routine read_address
```

Creating an SPL Routine in a Program

To use an SQL API to create an SPL routine, put the text of the CREATE PROCEDURE or CREATE FUNCTION statement in a file. Use the CREATE PROCEDURE FROM or CREATE FUNCTION FROM statement and refer to that file to compile the routine. For example, to create a routine to read a customer name, you can use a statement such as the one in the previous example and store it in a file. If the file is named **read_add_source**, the following statement compiles the **read_address** routine:

```
CREATE PROCEDURE FROM 'read_add_source';
```

The following example shows how the previous SQL statement looks in an ESQL/C program:

```
/* This program creates whatever routine is in *
 * the file 'read_add_source'.
 */
#include <stdio.h>
EXEC SQL include sqlca;
EXEC SQL include sqlda;
EXEC SQL include datetime;
/* Program to create a routine from the pwd */

main()
{
EXEC SQL database play;
EXEC SQL create procedure from 'read_add_source';
}
```

Dropping an SPL Routine

After you create an SPL routine, you cannot change the body of the routine. Instead, you need to drop the routine and re-create it. Before you drop the routine, however, make sure that you have a copy of its text somewhere outside the database.

In general, use DROP PROCEDURE with an SPL procedure name and DROP FUNCTION with an SPL function name, as Figure 10-16 shows.

Figure 10-16

```
DROP PROCEDURE raise_prices;
DROP FUNCTION read_address;
```

Tip: *You can also use DROP PROCEDURE with a function name to drop an SPL function. However, Informix recommends that you use DROP PROCEDURE only with procedure names and DROP FUNCTION only with function names.*

However, if the database has other routines of the same name (overloaded routines), you cannot drop the SPL routine by its routine name alone. To drop a routine that has been overloaded, you must specify either its signature or its specific name. Figure 10-17 shows two ways that you might drop a routine that is overloaded.

Figure 10-17

```
DROP FUNCTION calculate( a INT, b INT, c INT);
    -- this is a signature

DROP SPECIFIC FUNCTION calc1;
    -- this is a specific name
```

If you do not know the type of a routine (function or procedure), you can use the DROP ROUTINE statement to drop it. DROP ROUTINE works with either functions or procedures. DROP ROUTINE also has a SPECIFIC keyword, as Figure 10-18 shows.

Figure 10-18

```
DROP ROUTINE calculate;
DROP SPECIFIC ROUTINE calc1;
```

Before you drop an SPL routine stored on a remote database server, be aware of the following restriction. You can drop an SPL routine with a fully qualified routine name in the form *database@dbservername:owner.routinename* only if the routine name alone, without its arguments, is enough to identify the routine. Because user-defined data types on one database might not exist on another database, you cannot use qualified names with arguments that are user-defined data types.

Defining and Using Variables

Any variable that you use in an SPL routine, other than a variable that is implicitly defined in the parameter list of the routine, must be defined in the body of the routine.

The value of a variable is held in memory; the variable is not a database object. Therefore, rolling back a transaction does not restore the values of SPL variables.

To define a variable in an SPL routine, use the DEFINE statement. DEFINE is not an executable statement. DEFINE must appear after the CREATE PROCEDURE statement and before any other statements. The examples in Figure 10-19 are all legal variable definitions.

Figure 10-19

```
DEFINE a INT;
DEFINE person person_t;
DEFINE GLOBAL gl_out INT DEFAULT 13;
```

For more information on DEFINE, see the description in the *Informix Guide to SQL: Syntax.*

An SPL variable has a name and a data type. The variable name must be a valid identifier, as described in the Identifier segment in the *Informix Guide to SQL: Syntax.*

Declaring Local Variables

You can define a variable to be either *local* or *global* in scope. This section describes local variables. In an SPL routine, *local variables:*

- are valid only for the duration of the SPL routine.

- are reset to their initial values or to a value the user passes to the routine, each time the routine is executed.

- cannot have default values.

You can define a local variable on any of the following data types:

- Built-in data types (except SERIAL, SERIAL8, TEXT, or BYTE)

- Any extended data type (row type, opaque, distinct, or collection type) that is defined in the database prior to execution of the SPL routine

The scope of a local variable is the statement block in which it is declared. You can use the same variable name outside the statement block with a different definition.

For more information on defining global variables, see "Declaring Global Variables" on page 10-29.

Scope of Local Variables

A local variable is valid within the statement block in which it is defined and within any nested statement blocks, unless you redefine the variable within the statement block.

In the beginning of the SPL procedure in Figure 10-20, the integer variables **x**, **y**, and **z** are defined and initialized.

Figure 10-20

```
CREATE PROCEDURE scope()
    DEFINE x,y,z INT;
    LET x = 5;
    LET y = 10;
    LET z = x + y; --z is 15
    BEGIN
        DEFINE x, q INT;
        DEFINE z CHAR(5);
        LET x = 100;
        LET q = x + y;    -- q = 110
        LET z = 'silly'; -- z receives a character value
    END
    LET y = x; -- y is now 5
    LET x = z; -- z is now 15, not 'silly'
END PROCEDURE;
```

The BEGIN and END statements mark a nested statement block in which the integer variables **x** and **q** are defined as well as the CHAR variable **z**. Within the nested block, the redefined variable **x** masks the original variable **x**. After the END statement, which marks the end of the nested block, the original value of **x** is accessible again.

Declaring Built-In Type Variables

Built-in type variables hold data retrieved from built-in data types. You can define an SPL variable with any built-in type, except SERIAL and SERIAL8 as Figure 10-21 shows.

Figure 10-21

```
DEFINE x INT;
DEFINE y INT8;
DEFINE name CHAR(15);
DEFINE today DATETIME YEAR TO DAY;
```

Declaring Variables for Smart Large Objects

A variable for a BLOB or CLOB object (or a data type that contains a smart large object) does not contain the object itself but rather a pointer to the object. Figure 10-22 shows how to define a variable for BLOB and CLOB objects.

Figure 10-22

```
DEFINE a_blob BLOB;
DEFINE b_clob CLOB;
```

Declaring Variables for Simple Large Objects

A variable for a simple large object (a TEXT or BYTE object) does not contain the object itself but rather a pointer to the object. When you define a variable on the TEXT or BYTE data type, you must use the keyword REFERENCES before the data type, as Figure 10-23 shows.

Figure 10-23

```
DEFINE t REFERENCES TEXT;
DEFINE b REFERENCES BYTE;
```

Declaring Collection Variables

In order to hold a collection fetched from the database, a variable must be of type SET, MULTISET, or LIST.

Important: *A collection variable must be defined as a local variable. You cannot define a collection variable as a global variable.*

A variable of SET, MULTISET, or LIST type is a *collection variable* that holds a collection of the type named in the DEFINE statement. Figure 10-24 shows how to define typed collection variables.

Figure 10-24

```
DEFINE a SET ( INT NOT NULL );

DEFINE b MULTISET ( ROW (  b1 INT,
                           b2 CHAR(50),
                         ) NOT NULL );

DEFINE c LIST ( SET (DECIMAL NOT NULL) NOT NULL);
```

You must always define the elements of a collection variable as NOT NULL. In this example, the variable **a** is defined to hold a SET of non-null integers; the variable **b** holds a MULTISET of non-null row types; and the variable **c** holds a LIST of non-null sets of non-null decimal values.

In a variable definition, you can nest complex types in any combination or depth to match the data types stored in your database.

You cannot assign a collection variable of one type to a collection variable of another type. For example, if you define a collection variable as a SET, you cannot assign another collection variable of MULTISET or LIST type to it.

IDS

Declaring Row-Type Variables

Row-type variables hold data from named or unnamed row types. You can define a *named row variable* or an *unnamed row variable*. Suppose you define the named row types that Figure 10-25 shows.

Figure 10-25
Some Example Row Types

```
CREATE ROW TYPE zip_t
(
    z_code      CHAR(5),
    z_suffix    CHAR(4)
);

CREATE ROW TYPE address_t
(
    street      VARCHAR(20),
    city        VARCHAR(20),
    state       CHAR(2),
    zip         zip_t
);

CREATE ROW TYPE employee_t
(
    name        VARCHAR(30),
    address     address_t,
    salary      INTEGER
);

CREATE TABLE employee OF TYPE employee_t;
```

If you define a variable with the name of a named row type, the variable can only hold data of that row type. In Figure 10-26, the **person** variable can only hold data of **employee_t** type.

Figure 10-26

```
DEFINE person employee_t;
```

To define a variable that holds data stored in an unnamed row type, use the ROW keyword followed by the fields of the row type, as Figure 10-27 shows.

Figure 10-27

```
DEFINE manager ROW ( nameVARCHAR(30),
                     department VARCHAR(30),
                     salaryINTEGER );
```

Because unnamed row types are type-checked for structural equivalence only, a variable defined with an unnamed row type can hold data from any unnamed row type that has the same number of fields and the same type definitions. Therefore, the variable **manager** can hold data from any of the row types in Figure 10-28.

Figure 10-28

```
ROW ( name       VARCHAR(30),
      department VARCHAR(30),
      salary     INTEGER );

ROW ( french     VARCHAR(30),
      spanish    VARCHAR(30),
      number     INTEGER );

ROW ( title      VARCHAR(30),
      musician   VARCHAR(30),
      price      INTEGER );
```

Important: *Before you can use a row type variable, you must initialize the row variable with a LET statement or SELECT...INTO statement.*

IDS

Declaring Opaque- and Distinct-Type Variables

Opaque-type variables hold data retrieved from opaque data types. *Distinct-type variables* hold data retrieved from distinct data types. If you define a variable with an opaque data type or a distinct data type, the variable can only hold data of that type.

If you define an opaque data type named **point** and a distinct data type named **centerpoint**, you can define SPL variables to hold data from the two types, as Figure 10-29 shows.

Figure 10-29

```
DEFINE a point;
DEFINE b centerpoint;
```

The variable **a** can only hold data of type **point**, and **b** can only hold data of type **centerpoint**.

Declaring Variables for Column Data with the LIKE Clause

If you use the LIKE clause, the database server defines a variable to have the same data type as a column in a table or view.

If the column contains a collection, row type, or nested complex type, the variable has the complex or nested complex type defined in the column.

In Figure 10-30, the variable **loc1** defines the data type for the **locations** column in the **image** table.

Figure 10-30

```
DEFINE loc1 LIKE image.locations;
```

Declaring PROCEDURE Type Variables

In an SPL routine, you can define a variable of type PROCEDURE and assign the variable the name of an existing SPL routine or external routine. Defining a variable of PROCEDURE type indicates that the variable is a call to a user-defined routine, not a built-in routine of the same name.

For example, the statement in Figure 10-31 defines **length** as an SPL procedure or SPL function, not as the built-in LENGTH function.

Figure 10-31

```
DEFINE length PROCEDURE;
LET x = length( a,b,c );
```

This definition disables the built-in LENGTH function within the scope of the statement block. You would use such a definition if you had already created an SPL or external routine with the name LENGTH.

Because Dynamic Server supports routine overloading, you can define more than one SPL routine or external routine with the same name. If you call any routine from an SPL routine, Dynamic Server determines which routine to use, based on the arguments specified and the routine determination rules. For information about routine overloading and routine determination, see *Extending Informix Dynamic Server 2000.* ♦

Tip: *If you create an SPL routine with the same name as an aggregate function (SUM, MAX, MIN, AVG, COUNT) or with the name **extend**, you must qualify the routine name with an owner name.*

Using Subscripts with Variables

You can use subscripts with variables of CHAR, VARCHAR, NCHAR, NVARCHAR, BYTE, or TEXT data type. The subscripts indicate the starting and ending character positions that you want to use within the variable.

Subscripts must always be constants. You cannot use variables as subscripts. Figure 10-32 illustrates how to use a subscript with a CHAR(15) variable.

Figure 10-32

```
DEFINE name CHAR(15);
LET name[4,7] = 'Ream';
SELECT fname[1,3] INTO name[1,3] FROM customer
    WHERE lname = 'Ream';
```

In this example, the customer's last name is placed between positions 4 and 7 of **name**. The first three characters of the customer's first name is retrieved into positions 1 through 3 of **name**. The part of the variable that is delimited by the two subscripts is referred to as a *substring*.

Variable and Keyword Ambiguity

If you define a variable as an SQL keyword, ambiguities can occur. The following rules for identifiers help you avoid ambiguities for SPL variables, SPL routine names, and built-in function names:

- Defined variables take the highest precedence.
- Routines defined with the PROCEDURE keyword in a DEFINE statement take precedence over SQL functions.
- SQL functions take precedence over SPL routines that exist but are *not* identified with the PROCEDURE keyword in a DEFINE statement.

In general, avoid using an ANSI-reserved word for the name of the variable. For example, you cannot define a variable with the name **count** or **max** because they are the names of aggregate functions. For a list of the reserved keywords that you should avoid using as variable names, see the Identifier segment in the *Informix Guide to SQL: Syntax*.

Variables and Column Names

If you use the same identifier for an SPL variable that you use for a column name, the database server assumes that each instance of the identifier is a variable. Qualify the column name with the table name, using dot notation, in order to use the identifier as a column name.

In the SELECT statement in Figure 10-33, **customer.lname** is a column name and **lname** is a variable name.

Figure 10-33

```
CREATE PROCEDURE table_test()

    DEFINE lname CHAR(15);
    LET lname = 'Miller';

    SELECT customer.lname INTO lname FROM customer
        WHERE customer_num = 502;
    .
    .
    .
END PROCEDURE;
```

Variables and SQL Functions

If you use the same identifier for an SPL variable as for an SQL function, the database server assumes that an instance of the identifier is a variable and disallows the use of the SQL function. You cannot use the SQL function within the block of code in which the variable is defined. The example in Figure 10-34 shows a block within an SPL procedure in which the variable called **user** is defined. This definition disallows the use of the USER function in the BEGIN ... END block.

Figure 10-34

```
CREATE PROCEDURE user_test()
    DEFINE name CHAR(10);
    DEFINE name2 CHAR(10);
    LET name = user; -- the SQL function

    BEGIN
        DEFINE user CHAR(15); -- disables user function
        LET user = 'Miller';
        LET name = user; -- assigns 'Miller' to variable name

    END
    .
    .
    .
    LET name2 = user; -- SQL function again
```

SPL Routine Names and SQL Functions

For information about ambiguities between SPL routine names and SQL function names, see the *Informix Guide to SQL: Syntax*.

Declaring Global Variables

A *global variable* has its value stored in memory and is available to other SPL routines, run by the same user session, on the same database. A global variable has the following characteristics:

- It requires a default value.

- It can be used in any SPL routine, although it must be defined in each routine in which it is used.

- It carries its value from one SPL routine to another until the session ends.

Important: *You cannot define a collection variable as a global variable.*

Figure 10-35 shows two SPL functions that share a global variable.

Figure 10-35

```
CREATE FUNCTION func1()
    RETURNING INT;
    DEFINE GLOBAL gvar INT DEFAULT 2;
    LET gvar = gvar + 1;
    RETURN gvar;
END FUNCTION;

CREATE FUNCTION func2()
    RETURNING INT;
    DEFINE GLOBAL gvar INT DEFAULT 5;
    LET gvar = gvar + 1;
    RETURN gvar;
END FUNCTION;
```

Although you must define a global variable with a default value, the variable is only set to the default the first time you use it. If you execute the two functions in Figure 10-36 in the order given, the value of **gvar** would be 4.

Figure 10-36

```
EXECUTE FUNCTION func1();
EXECUTE FUNCTION func2();
```

But if you execute the functions in the opposite order, as Figure 10-37 shows, the value of **gvar** would be 7.

Figure 10-37

```
EXECUTE FUNCTION func2();
EXECUTE FUNCTION func1();
```

For more information, see "Executing Routines" on page 10-71.

Assigning Values to Variables

Within an SPL routine, use the LET statement to assign values to the variables you have already defined.

If you do not assign a value to a variable, either by an argument passed to the routine or by a LET statement, the variable has an undefined value. An undefined value is different than a null value. If you attempt to use a variable with an undefined value within the SPL routine, you receive an error.

You can assign a value to a routine variable in any of the following ways:

- Use a LET statement.
- Use a SELECT...INTO statement.
- Use a CALL statement with a procedure that has a RETURNING clause.
- Use an EXECUTE PROCEDURE...INTO or EXECUTE FUNCTION...INTO statement.

The LET Statement

With a LET statement, you can use one or more variable names with an equal (=) sign and a valid expression or function name. Each example in Figure 10-38 is a valid LET statement.

Figure 10-38

```
LET a = 5;
LET b = 6; LET c = 10;
LET a,b = 10,c+d;
LET a,b = (SELECT cola,colb FROM tab1 WHERE cola=10);
LET d = func1(x,y);
```

IDS

Dynamic Server allows you to assign a value to an opaque-type variable, a row-type variable, or a field of a row type. You can also return the value of an external function or another SPL function to an SPL variable. ♦

Suppose you define the named row types **zip_t** and **address_t**, as Figure 10-25 on page 10-24 shows. Anytime you define a row-type variable, you must initialize the variable before you can use it. Figure 10-39 shows how you might define and initialize a row-type variable. You can use any row-type value to initialize the variable.

Figure 10-39

```
DEFINE a address_t;
LET a = ROW ('A Street', 'Nowhere', 'AA',
          ROW(NULL, NULL))::address_t
```

After you define and initialize the row-type variable, you can write the LET statements that Figure 10-40 shows.

Figure 10-40

```
  .
  .
LET a.zip.z_code = 32601;
LET a.zip.z_suffix = 4555;
    -- Assign values to the fields of address_t
```

Tip: *Use dot notation in the form **variable.field** or **variable.field.field** to access the fields of a row type, as "Handling Row-Type Data" on page 10-46 describes.*

Suppose you define an opaque-type **point** that contains two values that define a two-dimensional point, and the text representation of the values is **'(x,y)'**. You might also have a function **circum()** that calculates the circumference of a circle, given the point **'(x,y)'** and a radius **r**.

If you define an opaque-type **center** that defines a point as the center of a circle, and a function **circum()** that calculates the circumference of a circle, based on a point and the radius, you can write variable declarations for each. In Figure 10-41, **c** is an opaque type variable and **d** holds the value that the external function **circum()** returns.

Figure 10-41

```
DEFINE c point;
DEFINE r REAL;
DEFINE d REAL;

LET c = '(29.9,1.0)' ;
    -- Assign a value to an opaque type variable

LET d = circum( c, r );
    -- Assign a value returned from circum()
```

The *Informix Guide to SQL: Syntax* describes in detail the syntax of the LET statement.

Other Ways to Assign Values to Variables

You can use the SELECT statement to fetch a value from the database and assign it directly to a variable, as Figure 10-42 shows.

Figure 10-42

```
SELECT fname, lname INTO a, b FROM customer
    WHERE customer_num = 101
```

Use the CALL or EXECUTE PROCEDURE statements to assign values returned by an SPL function or an external function to one or more SPL variables. You might use either of the statements in Figure 10-43 to return the full name and address from the SPL function **read_address** into the specified SPL variables.

Figure 10-43

```
EXECUTE FUNCTION read_address('Smith')
    INTO p_fname, p_lname, p_add, p_city, p_state, p_zip;

CALL read_address('Smith')
    RETURNING p_fname, p_lname, p_add, p_city, p_state, p_zip;
```

Expressions in SPL Routines

You can use any SQL expression in an SPL routine except for an aggregate expression. The *Informix Guide to SQL: Syntax* provides the complete syntax and descriptions for SQL expressions.

The following examples contain SQL expressions:

```
var1
var1 + var2 + 5
read_address('Miller')
read_address(lastname = 'Miller')
get_duedate(acct_num) + 10 UNITS DAY
fname[1,5] || '' || lname
'(415)' || get_phonenum(cust_name)
```

Writing the Statement Block

Every SPL routine has at least one statement block, which is a group of SQL and SPL statements between the CREATE statement and the END statement. You can use any SPL statement or any allowed SQL statement within a statement block. For a list of SQL statements that are not allowed within an SPL statement block, see the description of the Statement Block segment in the *Informix Guide to SQL: Syntax*.

Implicit and Explicit Statement Blocks

In an SPL routine, the *implicit statement block* extends from the end of the CREATE statement to the beginning of the END statement. You can also define an *explicit statement block*, which starts with a BEGIN statement and ends with an END statement, as Figure 10-44 shows.

Figure 10-44

```
BEGIN
    DEFINE distance INT;
    LET distance = 2;
END
```

The explicit statement block allows you to define variables or processing that are valid only within the statement block. For example, you can define or redefine variables, or handle exceptions differently, for just the scope of the explicit statement block.

The SPL function in Figure 10-45 has an explicit statement block that redefines a variable defined in the implicit block.

Figure 10-45

```
CREATE FUNCTION block_demo()
    RETURNING INT;

    DEFINE distance INT;
    LET distance = 37;
    BEGIN
        DEFINE distance INT;
        LET distance = 2;
    END
    RETURN distance;

END FUNCTION;
```

In this example, the implicit statement block defines the variable **distance** and gives it a value of 37. The explicit statement block defines a different variable named **distance** and gives it a value of 2. However, the RETURN statement returns the value stored in the first **distance** variable, or 37.

Using Cursors

A FOREACH loop defines a *cursor,* a specific identifier that points to one item in a group, whether a group of rows or the elements in a collection.

The FOREACH loop declares and opens a cursor, fetches rows from the database, works on each item in the group, and then closes the cursor. You must declare a cursor if a SELECT, EXECUTE PROCEDURE, or EXECUTE FUNCTION statement might return more than one row. After you declare the cursor, you place the SELECT, EXECUTE PROCEDURE, or EXECUTE FUNCTION statement within it.

An SPL routine that returns a group of rows is called a *cursor routine* because you must use a cursor to access the data it returns. An SPL routine that returns no value, a single value, or any other value that does not require a cursor is called a *noncursor routine.* The FOREACH loop declares and opens a cursor, fetches rows or a collection from the database, works on each item in the group, and then closes the cursor. You must declare a cursor if a SELECT, EXECUTE PROCEDURE, or EXECUTE FUNCTION statement might return more than one row or a collection. After you declare the cursor, you place the SELECT, EXECUTE PROCEDURE, or EXECUTE FUNCTION statement within it.

In a FOREACH loop, you can use an EXECUTE FUNCTION or SELECT...INTO statement to execute an external function that is an iterator function.

Using the FOREACH Loop to Define Cursors

A FOREACH loop begins with the FOREACH keyword and ends with END FOREACH. Between FOREACH and END FOREACH, you can declare a cursor or use EXECUTE PROCEDURE or EXECUTE FUNCTION. The two examples in Figure 10-46 show the structure of FOREACH loops.

Figure 10-46

```
FOREACH cursor FOR
    SELECT column FROM table INTO variable;
.
.
.
END FOREACH

FOREACH
    EXECUTE FUNCTION name() INTO variable;
END FOREACH
```

The semicolon is placed after each statement within the FOREACH loop and after END FOREACH.

Figure 10-47 creates a routine that uses a FOREACH loop to operate on the **employee** table.

Figure 10-47

```
CREATE_PROCEDURE increase_by_pct( pct INTEGER )

    DEFINE s INTEGER;

    FOREACH sal_cursor FOR

        SELECT salary INTO s FROM employee
            WHERE salary > 35000

        LET s = s + s * ( pct/100 );

        UPDATE employee SET salary = s
            WHERE CURRENT OF sal_cursor;

    END FOREACH

END PROCEDURE;
```

The routine in Figure 10-47 performs the following tasks within the FOREACH loop:

- Declares a cursor
- Selects one **salary** value at a time from **employee**
- Increases the salary by a percentage
- Updates employee with the new salary
- Fetches the next salary value

The SELECT statement is placed within a cursor because it returns all the salaries in the table greater than 35000.

The WHERE CURRENT OF clause in the UPDATE statement updates only the row on which the cursor is currently positioned. The clause also automatically sets an *update cursor* on the current row. An update cursor places an update lock on the row so that no other user can update the row until your update occurs.

An SPL routine will set an update cursor automatically if an UPDATE or DELETE statement within the FOREACH loop uses the WHERE CURRENT OF clause. If you use WHERE CURRENT OF, you must explicitly name the cursor in the FOREACH statement.

If you are using an update cursor, you can add a BEGIN WORK statement before the FOREACH statement and a COMMIT WORK statement after END FOREACH, as Figure 10-48 shows.

Figure 10-48

```
BEGIN WORK;

    FOREACH sal_cursor FOR
        SELECT salary INTO s FROM employee
            WHERE salary > 35000;
        LET s = s + s * ( pct/100 );
        UPDATE employee SET salary = s
            WHERE CURRENT OF sal_cursor
    END FOREACH
COMMIT WORK;
```

For each iteration of the FOREACH loop, the COMMIT WORK statement commits the work done since the BEGIN WORK statement and releases the lock on the updated row.

Using an IF - ELIF - ELSE Structure

The SPL routine in Figure 10-49 uses an IF - ELIF - ELSE structure to compare the two arguments that the routine accepts.

Figure 10-49

```
CREATE FUNCTION str_compare( str1 CHAR(20), str2 CHAR(20))
    RETURNING INTEGER;

    DEFINE result INTEGER;

    IF str1 > str2 THEN
        result = 1;
    ELIF str2 > str1 THEN
        result = -1;
    ELSE
        result = 0;
    END IF
    RETURN result;
END FUNCTION;
```

Suppose you define a table named **manager** with the columns that Figure 10-50 shows.

Figure 10-50

```
CREATE TABLE manager
(
    mgr_name         VARCHAR(30),
    department       VARCHAR(12),
    dept_no          SMALLINT,
    direct_reports   SET( VARCHAR(30) NOT NULL ),
    projects         LIST( ROW ( pro_name VARCHAR(15),
                     pro_members SET( VARCHAR(20) NOT NULL ) )
                     NOT NULL),
    salary           INTEGER,
);
```

The SPL routine in Figure 10-51 uses an IF - ELIF - ELSE structure to check the number of elements in the SET in the **direct_reports** column and call various external routines based on the results.

Figure 10-51

```
CREATE FUNCTION check_set( d SMALLINT )
    RETURNING VARCHAR(30), VARCHAR(12), INTEGER;

    DEFINE name VARCHAR(30);
    DEFINE dept VARCHAR(12);
    DEFINE num INTEGER;

    SELECT mgr_name, department, CARDINALITY(direct_reports)
        FROM manager INTO name, dept, num
        WHERE dept_no = d;
    IF num > 20 THEN
        EXECUTE FUNCTION add_mgr(dept);
    ELIF num = 0 THEN
        EXECUTE FUNCTION del_mgr(dept);
    ELSE
        RETURN name, dept, num;
    END IF;

END FUNCTION;
```

The CARDINALITY() function counts the number of elements that a collection contains. For more information, see "Cardinality Function" on page 4-19.

An IF - ELIF - ELSE structure in an SPL routine has up to the following four parts:

■ An IF... THEN condition

If the condition following the IF statement is TRUE, the routine executes the statements in the IF block. If the condition is false, the routine evaluates the ELIF condition.

The expression in an IF statement can be any valid condition, as the Condition segment of the *Informix Guide to SQL: Syntax* describes. For the complete syntax and a detailed discussion of the IF statement, see the *Informix Guide to SQL: Syntax*.

■ One or more ELIF conditions (optional)

The routine evaluates the ELIF condition only if the IF condition is false. If the ELIF condition is true, the routine executes the statements in the ELIF block. If the ELIF condition is false, the routine either evaluates the next ELIF block or executes the ELSE statement.

- An ELSE condition (optional)

  The routine executes the statements in the ELSE block if the IF condition and all of the ELIF conditions are false.

- An END IF statement

  The END IF statement ends the statement block.

Adding WHILE and FOR Loops

Both the WHILE and FOR statements create execution loops in SPL routines. A WHILE loop starts with a WHILE *condition*, executes a block of statements as long as the condition is true, and ends with END WHILE.

Figure 10-52 shows a valid WHILE condition. The routine executes the WHILE loop as long as the condition specified in the WHILE statement is true.

Figure 10-52

```
CREATE PROCEDURE test_rows( num INT )

    DEFINE i INTEGER;
    LET i = 1;

    WHILE i < num
        INSERT INTO table1 (numbers) VALUES (i);
        LET i = i + 1;
    END WHILE;

END PROCEDURE;
```

The SPL routine in Figure 10-52 accepts an integer as an argument and then inserts an integer value into the **numbers** column of **table1** each time it executes the WHILE loop. The values inserted start at 1 and increase to num - 1.

Be careful that you do not create an endless loop, as Figure 10-53 shows.

Figure 10-53

```
CREATE PROCEDURE endless_loop()

    DEFINE i INTEGER;
    LET i = 1;
    WHILE ( 1 = 1 ) -- don't do this!
        LET i = i + 1;
        INSERT INTO table1 VALUES (i);
    END WHILE;

END PROCEDURE;
```

A FOR loop extends from a FOR statement to an END FOR statement and executes for a specified number of iterations, which are defined in the FOR statement. Figure 10-54 shows several ways to define the iterations in the FOR loop.

Figure 10-54

```
FOR i = 1 TO 10
    .
    .
END FOR;


FOR i = 1 TO 10 STEP 2
    .
    .
END FOR;


FOR i IN (2,4,8,14,22,32)
    .
    .
END FOR;


FOR i IN (1 TO 20 STEP 5, 20 to 1 STEP -5, 1,2,3,4,5)
    .
    .
END FOR:
```

In the first example, the SPL procedure executes the FOR loop as long as **i** is between 1 and 10, inclusive. In the second example, **i** steps from 1 to 3, 5, 7, and so on, but never exceeds 10. The third example checks whether **i** is within a defined set of values. In the fourth example, the SPL procedure executes the loop when **i** is 1, 6, 11, 16, 20, 15, 10, 5, 1, 2, 3, 4, or 5—in other words, 11 times, because the list has two duplicate values, 1 and 5.

Tip: *The main difference between a WHILE loop and a FOR loop is that a FOR loop is guaranteed to finish, but a WHILE loop is not. The FOR statement specifies the exact number of times the loop executes, unless a statement causes the routine to exit the loop. With WHILE, it is possible to create an endless loop.*

Exiting a Loop

In a FOR, FOREACH, or WHILE loop, you can use a CONTINUE or EXIT statement to control the execution of the loop.

CONTINUE causes the routine to skip the statements in the rest of the loop and move to the next iteration of the FOR statement. EXIT ends the loop and causes the routine to continue executing with the first statement following END FOR. Remember that EXIT must be followed by the keyword of the loop the routine is executing—for example, EXIT FOR or EXIT FOREACH.

Figure 10-55 shows examples of CONTINUE and EXIT within a FOR loop.

Figure 10-55

```
FOR i = 1 TO 10
    IF i = 5 THEN
        CONTINUE FOR;

    .
    .
    .

    ELIF i = 8 THEN
        EXIT FOR;
    END IF;

END FOR;
```

Tip: *You can use CONTINUE and EXIT to improve the performance of SPL routines so that loops do not execute unnecessarily.*

Returning Values from an SPL Function

SPL functions can return one or more values. To have your SPL function return values, you need to include the following two parts:

1. Write a RETURNING clause in the CREATE PROCEDURE or CREATE FUNCTION statement that specifies the number of values to be returned and their data types.

2. In the body of the function, enter a RETURN statement that explicitly returns the values.

Tip: *You can define a routine with the CREATE PROCEDURE statement that returns values, but in that case, the routine is actually a function. Informix recommends that you use the CREATE FUNCTION statement when the routine returns values.*

After you define a return clause (with a RETURNING statement), the SPL function can return values that match those specified in number and data type, or no values at all. If you specify a return clause, and the SPL routine returns no actual values, it is still considered a function. In that case, the routine returns a null value for each value defined in the return clause.

An SPL function can return variables, expressions, or the result of another function call. If the SPL function returns a variable, the function must first assign the variable a value by one of the following methods:

- A LET statement
- A default value
- A SELECT statement
- Another function that passes a value into the variable

Each value an SPL function returns can be up to 32 kilobytes long.

Important: *The return value for an SPL function must be a specific data type. You cannot specify a generic row or generic collection data type as a return type.*

Returning a Single Value

Figure 10-56 shows how an SPL function can return a single value.

Figure 10-56

```
CREATE FUNCTION increase_by_pct(amt DECIMAL, pct DECIMAL)
    RETURNING DECIMAL;

    DEFINE result DECIMAL;

    LET result = amt + amt * (pct/100);

    RETURN result;

END FUNCTION;
```

The **increase_by_pct** function receives two arguments of DECIMAL value, an amount to be increased and a percentage by which to increase it. The return clause specifies that the function will return one DECIMAL value. The RETURN statement returns the DECIMAL value stored in **result**.

Returning Multiple Values

An SPL function can return more than one value from a single row of a table. Figure 10-57 shows an SPL function that returns two column values from a single row of a table.

Figure 10-57

```
CREATE FUNCTION birth_date( num INTEGER )
    RETURNING VARCHAR(30), DATE;

    DEFINE n VARCHAR(30);
    DEFINE b DATE;

    SELECT name, bdate INTO n, b FROM emp_tab
        WHERE emp_no = num;

    RETURN n, b;

END FUNCTION;
```

The function in Figure 10-57 returns to the calling routine, two values (a name and birthdate) from one row of the **emp_tab** table. In this case, the calling routine must be prepared to handle the VARCHAR and DATE values returned.

Figure 10-58 shows an SPL function that returns more than one value from more than one row.

Figure 10-58

```
CREATE FUNCTION birth_date_2( num INTEGER )
    RETURNING VARCHAR(30), DATE;

    DEFINE n VARCHAR(30);
    DEFINE b DATE;

    FOREACH cursor1 FOR
        SELECT name, bdate INTO n, b FROM emp_tab
            WHERE emp_no > num;
        RETURN n, b WITH RESUME;
    END FOREACH

END FUNCTION;
```

In Figure 10-58, the SELECT statement fetches two values from the set of rows whose employee number is higher than the number the user enters. The set of rows that satisfy the condition could contain one row, many rows, or zero rows. Because the SELECT statement can return many rows, it is placed within a cursor.

Tip: *When a statement within an SPL routine returns no rows, the corresponding SPL variables are assigned null values.*

The RETURN statement uses the WITH RESUME keywords. When RETURN WITH RESUME is executed, control is returned to the calling routine. But the next time the SPL function is called (by a FETCH or the next iteration of a cursor in the calling routine), all the variables in the SPL function keep their same values, and execution continues at the statement immediately following the RETURN WITH RESUME statement.

If your SPL routine returns multiple values, the calling routine must be able to handle the multiple values through a cursor or loop, as follows:

- If the calling routine is an SPL routine, it needs a FOREACH loop.
- If the calling routine is an ESQL/C program, it needs a cursor declared with the DECLARE statement.
- If the calling routine is an external routine, it needs a cursor or loop appropriate to the language in which the routine is written.

IDS

Handling Row-Type Data

In an SPL routine, you can use named row types and unnamed row types as parameter definitions, arguments, variable definitions, and return values. For information about how to declare a row variable in SPL, see "Declaring Row-Type Variables" on page 10-24.

Figure 10-59 defines a row type **salary_t** and an **emp_info** table, which are the examples that this section uses.

Figure 10-59
The salary_t Row Type and emp_info Table

```
CREATE ROW TYPE salary_t(base MONEY(9,2), bonus MONEY(9,2))

CREATE TABLE emp_info (emp_name VARCHAR(30), salary salary_t);
```

The **emp_info** table has columns for the employee name and salary information.

Precedence of Dot Notation

With Dynamic Server, a value that uses dot notation (as in **proj.name**) in an SQL statement in an SPL routine has one of three meanings, in the following order:

1. **variable.field**
2. **column.field**
3. **table.column**

In other words, the expression proj.name is first evaluated as **variable.field**. If the routine does not find a variable **proj**, it evaluates the expression as **column.field**. If the routine does not find a column **proj**, it evaluates the expression as **table.column**.

Updating a Row-Type Expression

From within an SPL routine, you can use a row variable to update a row-type expression. Figure 10-60 shows an SPL procedure **emp_raise** that is used to update the **emp_info** table when an employee's base salary increases by a certain percentage.

Figure 10-60

```
CREATE PROCEDURE emp_raise( name VARCHAR(30),
                  pct DECIMAL(3,2) )

   DEFINE row_var salary_t;

   SELECT salary INTO row_var FROM emp_info
      WHERE emp_name = name;

   LET row_var.base = row_var.base * pct;

   UPDATE emp_info SET salary = row_var
      WHERE emp_name = name;
END PROCEDURE;
```

The SELECT statement selects a row from the **salary** column of **emp_info table** into the row variable **row_var**.

The **emp_raise** procedure uses SPL dot notation to directly access the **base** field of the variable **row_var**. In this case, the dot notation means *variable.field*. The **emp_raise** procedure recalculates the value of **row_var.base** as (row_var.base * pct). The procedure then updates the **salary** column of the **emp_info** table with the new **row_var** value.

Important: *A row-type variable must be initialized as a row before its fields can be set or referenced. You can initialize a row-type variable with a SELECT...INTO statement or LET statement.*

Handling Collections

A *collection* is a group of elements of the same data type, such as a SET, MULTISET, or LIST.

A table might contain a collection stored as the contents of a column or as a field of a row type within a column. A collection can be either simple or nested. A *simple collection* is a SET, MULTISET, or LIST of built-in, opaque, or distinct data types. A *nested collection* is a collection that contains other collections.

Collection Examples

The following sections of the chapter rely on several different examples to show how you can manipulate collections in SPL programs.

The basics of handling collections in SPL programs are illustrated with the **numbers** table, as Figure 10-61 shows.

Figure 10-61
The numbers Table

```
CREATE TABLE numbers
(
    id           INTEGER PRIMARY KEY,
    primes       SET( INTEGER NOT NULL ),
    evens        LIST( INTEGER NOT NULL ),
    twin_primes  LIST( SET( INTEGER NOT NULL ) NOT NULL )
);
```

The **primes** and **evens** columns hold simple collections. The **twin_primes** column holds a nested collection, a LIST of SETs. (Twin prime numbers are pairs of consecutive prime numbers whose difference is 2, such as 5 and 7, or 11 and 13. The **twin_primes** column is designed to allow you to enter such pairs.

Some examples in this chapter use the **polygons** table in Figure 10-62 to illustrate how to manipulate collections. The **polygons** table contains a collection to represent two-dimensional graphical data. For example, suppose that you define an opaque data type named **point** that has two double-precision values that represent the **x** and **y** coordinates of a two-dimensional point whose coordinates might be represented as '1.0, 3.0'. Using the **point** data type, you can create a table that contains a set of points that define a polygon, as Figure 10-62 shows.

Figure 10-62
The polygons Table

```
CREATE OPAQUE TYPE point ( INTERNALLENGTH = 8);

CREATE TABLE polygons
(
    id              INTEGER PRIMARY KEY,
    definition   SET( point NOT NULL )
);
```

The **definition** column in the **polygons** table contains a simple collection, a SET of **point** values.

The First Steps

Before you can access and handle an individual element of a simple or nested collection, you must follow a basic set of steps:

- Declare a collection variable to hold the collection.
- Declare an element variable to hold an individual element of the collection.
- Select the collection from the database into the collection variable.

After you take these initial steps, you can insert elements into the collection or select and handle elements that are already in the collection.

Each of these steps is explained in the following sections, using the **numbers** table as an example.

Tip: *You can handle collections in any SPL routine.*

Declaring a Collection Variable

Before you can retrieve a collection from the database into an SPL routine, you must declare a collection variable. Figure 10-63 shows how to declare a collection variable to retrieve the **primes** column from the **numbers** table.

Figure 10-63

```
DEFINE p_coll SET( INTEGER NOT NULL );
```

The DEFINE statement declares a collection variable **p_coll**, whose type matches the data type of the collection stored in the **primes** column.

Declaring an Element Variable

After you declare a collection variable, you declare an element variable to hold individual elements of the collection. The data type of the element variable must match the data type of the collection elements.

For example, to hold an element of the SET in the **primes** column, use an element variable declaration such as the one that Figure 10-64 shows.

Figure 10-64

```
DEFINE p INTEGER;
```

To declare a variable that holds an element of the **twin_primes** column, which holds a nested collection, use a variable declaration such as the one that Figure 10-65 shows.

Figure 10-65

```
DEFINE s SET( INTEGER NOT NULL );
```

The variable **s** holds a SET of integers. Each SET is an element of the LIST stored in **twin_primes**.

Selecting a Collection into a Collection Variable

After you declare a collection variable, you can fetch a collection into it. To fetch a collection into a collection variable, enter a SELECT... INTO statement that selects the collection column from the database into the collection variable you have named.

For example, to select the collection stored in one row of the **primes** column of **numbers**, add a SELECT statement, such as the one that Figure 10-66 shows, to your SPL routine.

Figure 10-66

```
SELECT primes INTO p_coll FROM numbers
    WHERE id = 220;
```

The WHERE clause in the SELECT statement specifies that you want to select the collection stored in just one row of **numbers**. The statement places the collection into the collection variable **p_coll**, which Figure 10-63 on page 10-50 declares.

The variable **p_coll** now holds a collection from the **primes** column, which could contain the value SET {5,7,31,19,13}.

Inserting Elements into a Collection Variable

After you retrieve a collection into a collection variable, you can insert a value into the collection variable. The syntax of the INSERT statement varies slightly, depending on the type of the collection to which you want to add values.

Inserting into a SET or MULTISET

To insert into a SET or MULTISET stored in a collection variable, use an INSERT statement with the TABLE keyword followed by the collection variable, as Figure 10-67 shows.

Figure 10-67

```
INSERT INTO TABLE(p_coll) VALUES(3);
```

The TABLE keyword makes the collection variable a collection-derived table. Collection-derived tables are described in the section "Handling Collections in SELECT Statements" on page 5-30. The collection that Figure 10-67 derives is a virtual table of one column, with each element of the collection representing a row of the table. Before the insert, consider **p_coll** as a virtual table that contains the rows (elements) that Figure 10-68 shows.

Figure 10-68

```
5
7
31
19
13
```

After the insert, **p_coll** might look like the virtual table that Figure 10-69 shows.

Figure 10-69

```
5
7
31
19
13
3
```

Because the collection is a SET, the new value is added to the collection, but the position of the new element is undefined. The same principle is true for a MULTISET.

Tip: *You can only insert one value at a time into a simple collection.*

Inserting into a LIST

If the collection is a LIST, you can add the new element at a specific point in the LIST or at the end of the LIST. As with a SET or MULTISET, you must first define a collection variable and select a collection from the database into the collection variable.

Figure 10-70 shows the statements you need to define a collection variable and select a LIST from the **numbers** table into the collection variable.

Figure 10-70

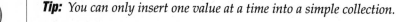

```
.
.
DEFINE e_coll LIST(INTEGER NOT NULL);

SELECT evens INTO e_coll FROM numbers
    WHERE id = 99;
.
.
```

At this point, the value of **e_coll** might be LIST {2,4,6,8,10}. Because **e_coll** holds a LIST, each element has a numbered position in the list. To add an element at a specific point in a LIST, add an AT *position* clause to the INSERT statement, as Figure 10-71 shows.

Figure 10-71

```
INSERT AT 3 INTO TABLE(e_coll) VALUES(12);
```

Now the LIST in **e_coll** has the elements {2,4,12,6,8,10}, in that order.

The value you enter for the *position* in the AT clause can be a number or a variable, but it must have an INTEGER or SMALLINT data type. You cannot use a letter, floating-point number, decimal value, or expression.

Checking the Cardinality of a LIST Collection

At times you might want to add an element at the end of a LIST. In this case, you can use the CARDINALITY() function to find the number of elements in a LIST and then enter a position that is greater than the value CARDINALITY() returns.

IDS

Dynamic Server allows you to use the CARDINALITY() function with a collection that is stored in a column but not with a collection that is stored in a collection variable. In an SPL routine, you can check the cardinality of a collection in a column with a SELECT statement and return the value to a variable. ♦

Suppose that in the **numbers** table, the **evens** column of the row whose **id** column is 99 still contains the collection LIST {2,4,6,8,10}. This time, you want to add the element 12 at the end of the LIST. You can do so with the SPL procedure **end_of_list**, as Figure 10-72 on page 10-54 shows.

Figure 10-72

```
CREATE PROCEDURE end_of_list()

    DEFINE n SMALLINT;
    DEFINE list_var LIST(INTEGER NOT NULL);

    SELECT CARDINALITY(evens) FROM numbers INTO n
        WHERE id = 100;

    LET n = n + 1;

    SELECT evens INTO list_var FROM numbers
        WHERE id = 100;

    INSERT AT n INTO TABLE(list_var) VALUES(12);

END PROCEDURE;
```

In **end_of_list**, the variable **n** holds the value that CARDINALITY() returns, that is, the count of the items in the LIST. The LET statement increments **n**, so that the INSERT statement can insert a value at the last position of the LIST. The SELECT statement selects the collection from one row of the table into the collection variable **list_var**. The INSERT statement inserts the element 12 at the end of the list.

Syntax of the VALUES Clause

The syntax of the VALUES clause is different when you insert into an SPL collection variable than when you insert into a collection column. The syntax rules for inserting literals into collection variables are as follows:

- Use parentheses after the VALUES keyword to enclose the complete list of values.

- If you are inserting into a simple collection, you do not need to use a type constructor or brackets.

- If you are inserting into a nested collection, you need to specify a literal collection.

Selecting Elements from a Collection

Suppose you want your SPL routine to select elements from the collection stored in the collection variable, one at time, so that you can handle the elements.

To move through the elements of a collection, you first need to declare a cursor using a FOREACH statement, just as you would declare a cursor to move through a set of rows. Figure 10-73 shows the FOREACH and END FOREACH statements, but with no statements between them yet.

Figure 10-73

```
FOREACH cursor1 FOR
.
.
.
END FOREACH
```

The FOREACH statement is described in "Using Cursors" on page 10-35 and the *Informix Guide to SQL: Syntax*.

The next section, "The Collection Query," describes the statements that are omitted between the FOREACH and END FOREACH statements.

The examples in the following sections are based on the **polygons** table of Figure 10-62 on page 10-49.

The Collection Query

After you declare the cursor between the FOREACH and END FOREACH statements, you enter a special, restricted form of the SELECT statement known as a *collection query*.

A collection query is a SELECT statement that uses the FROM TABLE keywords followed by the name of a collection variable. Figure 10-74 shows this structure, which is known as a *collection-derived table*.

Figure 10-74

```
.
.
.
FOREACH cursor1 FOR
    SELECT * INTO pnt FROM TABLE(vertexes)
    .
    .
    .
END FOREACH
```

The SELECT statement in Figure 10-74 uses the collection variable **vertexes** as a collection-derived table. You can think of a collection-derived table as a table of one column, with each element of the collection being a row of the table. For example, you can visualize the SET of four points stored in **vertexes** as a *table* with four rows, such as the one that Figure 10-75 shows.

Figure 10-75

```
'(3.0,1.0)'
'(8.0,1.0)'
'(3.0,4.0)'
'(8.0,4.0)'
```

After the first iteration of the FOREACH statement in Figure 10-75, the collection query selects the first element in **vertexes** and stores it in **pnt**, so that **pnt** contains the value '(3.0,1.0)'.

Tip: *Because the collection variable **vertexes** contains a SET, not a LIST, the elements in **vertexes** have no defined order. In a real database, the value* '(3.0,1.0)' *might not be the first element in the SET.*

Adding the Collection Query to the SPL Routine

Now you can add the cursor defined with FOREACH and the collection query to the SPL routine, as Figure 10-76 shows.

Figure 10-76

```
CREATE PROCEDURE shapes()

    DEFINE vertexes SET( point NOT NULL );
    DEFINE pnt point;

    SELECT definition INTO vertexes FROM polygons
        WHERE id = 207;

    FOREACH cursor1 FOR
        SELECT * INTO pnt FROM TABLE(vertexes);
    .
    .
    END FOREACH
    .
    .
END PROCEDURE;
```

The statements that Figure 10-76 shows form the framework of an SPL routine that handles the elements of a collection variable. To decompose a collection into its elements, use a *collection-derived table*. After the collection is decomposed into its elements, the routine can access elements individually as table rows of the collection-derived table. Now that you have selected one element in **pnt**, you can update or delete that element, as "Updating a Collection Element" on page 10-61 and "Deleting a Collection Element" on page 10-57 describe.

For the complete syntax of the collection query, see the SELECT statement in the *Informix Guide to SQL: Syntax*. For the syntax of a collection-derived table, see the Collection-Derived Table segment in the *Informix Guide to SQL: Syntax*.

Tip: *If you are selecting from a collection that contains no elements or zero elements, you can use a collection query without declaring a cursor. However, if the collection contains more than one element, and you do not use a cursor, you will receive an error message.*

Deleting a Collection Element

After you select an individual element from a collection variable into an element variable, you can delete the element from the collection. For example, after you select a point from the collection variable **vertexes** with a collection query, you can remove the point from the collection.

The steps involved in deleting a collection element include:

1. Declare a collection variable and an element variable.

2. Select the collection from the database into the collection variable.

3. Declare a cursor so that you can select elements one at a time from the collection variable.

4. Write a loop or branch that locates the element that you want to delete.

5. Delete the element from the collection using a DELETE... WHERE CURRENT OF statement that uses the collection variable as a collection-derived table.

Figure 10-77 shows a routine that deletes one of the four points in **vertexes**, so that the polygon becomes a triangle instead of a rectangle.

Figure 10-77

```
CREATE PROCEDURE shapes()

    DEFINE vertexes SET( point NOT NULL );
    DEFINE pnt point;

    SELECT definition INTO vertexes FROM polygons
        WHERE id = 207;

    FOREACH cursor1 FOR
        SELECT * INTO pnt FROM TABLE(vertexes)
        IF pnt = '(3,4)' THEN
                -- calls the equals function that
                -- compares two values of point type
            DELETE FROM TABLE(vertexes)
                WHERE CURRENT OF cursor1;
            EXIT FOREACH;
        ELSE
            CONTINUE FOREACH;
        END IF;
    END FOREACH
    .
    .
    .
END PROCEDURE;
```

In Figure 10-77, the FOREACH statement declares a cursor. The SELECT statement is a collection-derived query that selects one element at a time from the collection variable **vertexes** into the element variable **pnt**.

The IF... THEN... ELSE structure tests the value currently in **pnt** to see if it is the point '(3,4)'. Note that the expression pnt = '(3,4)' calls the instance of the **equal()** function defined on the **point** data type. If the current value in **pnt** is '(3,4)', the DELETE statement deletes it, and the EXIT FOREACH statement exits the cursor.

 Tip: *Deleting an element from a collection stored in a collection variable does not delete it from the collection stored in the database. After you delete the element from a collection variable, you must update the collection stored in the database with the new collection. For an example that shows how to update a collection column, see "Updating the Collection in the Database" on page 10-59.*

The syntax for the DELETE statement is described in the *Informix Guide to SQL: Syntax.*

Updating the Collection in the Database

After you change the contents of a collection variable in an SPL routine (by deleting, updating, or inserting an element), you must update the database with the new collection.

To update a collection in the database, add an UPDATE statement that sets the collection column in the table to the contents of the updated collection variable. For example, the UPDATE statement in Figure 10-78 shows how to update the **polygons** table to set the **definition** column to the new collection stored in the collection variable **vertexes**.

Figure 10-78

```
CREATE PROCEDURE shapes()

    DEFINE vertexes SET(point NOT NULL);
    DEFINE pnt point;

    SELECT definition INTO vertexes FROM polygons
        WHERE id = 207;

    FOREACH cursor1 FOR
        SELECT * INTO pnt FROM TABLE(vertexes)
        IF pnt = '(3,4)' THEN
                -- calls the equals function that
                -- compares two values of point type
            DELETE FROM TABLE(vertexes)
                WHERE CURRENT OF cursor1;
            EXIT FOREACH;
        ELSE
            CONTINUE FOREACH;
        END IF;
    END FOREACH

    UPDATE polygons SET definition = vertexes
        WHERE id = 207;

END PROCEDURE;
```

Now the **shapes()** routine is complete. After you run **shapes()**, the collection stored in the row whose ID column is 207 is updated so that it contains three values instead of four.

You can use the **shapes()** routine as a framework for writing other SPL routines that manipulate collections.

The elements of the collection now stored in the **definition** column of row 207 of the **polygons** table are listed as follows:

```
'(3,1)'
'(8,1)'
'(8,4)'
```

Deleting the Entire Collection

If you want to delete all the elements of a collection, you can use a single SQL statement. You do not need to declare a cursor. To delete an entire collection, you must perform the following tasks:

- Define a collection variable.
- Select the collection from the database into a collection variable.
- Enter a DELETE statement that uses the collection variable as a collection-derived table.
- Update the collection from the database.

Figure 10-79 shows the statements that you might use in an SPL routine to delete an entire collection.

Figure 10-79

```
DEFINE vertexes SET( INTEGER NOT NULL );

SELECT definition INTO vertexes FROM polygons
    WHERE id = 207;

DELETE FROM TABLE(vertexes);

UPDATE polygons SET definition = vertexes
    WHERE id = 207;
```

This form of the DELETE statement deletes the entire collection in the collection variable **vertexes**. You cannot use a WHERE clause in a DELETE statement that uses a collection-derived table.

After the UPDATE statement, the **polygons** table contains an empty collection where the **id** column is equal to 207.

The syntax for the DELETE statement is described in the *Informix Guide to SQL: Syntax*.

Updating a Collection Element

You can update a collection element by accessing the collection within a cursor just as you select or delete an individual element.

If you want to update the collection SET{100, 200, 300, 500} to change the value 500 to 400, retrieve the SET from the database into a collection variable and then declare a cursor to move through the elements in the SET, as Figure 10-80 shows.

Figure 10-80

```
DEFINE s SET(INTEGER NOT NULL);
DEFINE n INTEGER;

SELECT numbers INTO s FROM orders
    WHERE order_num = 10;

FOREACH cursor1 FOR
    SELECT * INTO n FROM TABLE(s)
    IF ( n == 500 ) THEN
        UPDATE TABLE(s)(x)
            SET x = 400 WHERE CURRENT OF cursor1;
        EXIT FOREACH;
    ELSE
        CONTINUE FOREACH;
    END IF;
END FOREACH
```

The UPDATE statement uses the collection variable **s** as a collection-derived table. To specify a collection-derived table, use the TABLE keyword. The value (x) that follows (s) in the UPDATE statement is a *derived column*, a column name you supply because the SET clause requires it, even though the collection-derived table does not have columns.

You can think of the collection-derived table as having one row and looking something like the following example:

```
100     200     300     500
```

In this example, x is a fictitious column name for the "column" that contains the value 500. You only specify a derived column if you are updating a collection of built-in, opaque, distinct, or collection type elements. If you are updating a collection of row types, use a field name instead of a derived column, as "Updating a Collection of Row Types" on page 10-63 describes.

Updating a Collection with a Variable

You can also update a collection with the value stored in a variable instead of a literal value.

The SPL procedure in Figure 10-81 uses statements that are similar to the ones that Figure 10-80 shows, except that this procedure updates the SET in the **direct_reports** column of the **manager** table with a variable, rather than with a literal value. Figure 10-51 on page 10-39 defines the **manager** table.

Figure 10-81

```
CREATE PROCEDURE new_report(mgr VARCHAR(30),
    old VARCHAR(30), new VARCHAR(30) )

    DEFINE s SET (VARCHAR(30) NOT NULL);
    DEFINE n VARCHAR(30);

    SELECT direct_reports INTO s FROM manager
        WHERE mgr_name = mgr;

    FOREACH cursor1 FOR
        SELECT * INTO n FROM TABLE(s)
        IF ( n == old ) THEN
            UPDATE TABLE(s)(x)
                SET x = new WHERE CURRENT OF cursor1;
            EXIT FOREACH;
        ELSE
            CONTINUE FOREACH;
        END IF;
    END FOREACH

    UPDATE manager SET mgr_name = s
        WHERE mgr_name = mgr;

END PROCEDURE;
```

The UPDATE statement nested in the FOREACH loop uses the collection-derived table **s** and the derived column **x**. If the current value of **n** is the same as **old**, the UPDATE statement changes it to the value of **new**. The second UPDATE statement stores the new collection in the **manager** table.

Updating the Entire Collection

If you want to update all the elements of a collection to the same value, or if the collection contains only one element, you do not need to use a cursor. The statements in Figure 10-82 show how you can retrieve the collection into a collection variable and then update it with one statement.

Figure 10-82

```
   .
   .

   DEFINE s SET (INTEGER NOT NULL);

   SELECT numbers INTO s FROM orders
       WHERE order_num = 10;

   UPDATE TABLE(s)(x) SET x = 0;

   UPDATE orders SET numbers = s
       WHERE order_num = 10;  .

   .
   .
```

The first UPDATE statement in this example uses a derived column named **x** with the collection-derived table **s** and gives all the elements in the collection the value 0. The second UPDATE statement stores the new collection in the database.

Updating a Collection of Row Types

To update a collection of row types, you can use the name of the field you want to update in the UPDATE statement, instead of a derived column name.

The **manager** table in Figure 10-51 on page 10-39 has a column named **projects** that contains a LIST of row types with the definition that Figure 10-83 shows.

Figure 10-83

```
projects    LIST( ROW( pro_name VARCHAR(15),
            pro_members SET(VARCHAR(20) NOT NULL) ) NOT NULL)
```

To access the individual row types in the LIST, declare a cursor and select the LIST into a collection variable. After you retrieve an individual row type, you can update the **pro_name** or **pro_members** fields by supplying a field name and the new data, as Figure 10-84 shows.

Figure 10-84

```
CREATE PROCEDURE update_pro( mgr VARCHAR(30),
    pro VARCHAR(15) )

    DEFINE p LIST(ROW(a VARCHAR(15), b SET(VARCHAR(20)
            NOT NULL) ) NOT NULL);
    DEFINE r ROW(p_name VARCHAR(15), p_member SET(VARCHAR(20)
NOT NULL) );
    LET r = ROW("project", "SET{'member'}");

SELECT projects INTO p FROM manager
        WHERE mgr_name = mgr;

    FOREACH cursor1 FOR
        SELECT * INTO r FROM TABLE(p)
        IF (r.p_name == 'Zephyr') THEN
            UPDATE TABLE(p) SET pro_name = pro
                WHERE CURRENT OF cursor1;
            EXIT FOREACH;
        END IF;
    END FOREACH

    UPDATE manager SET projects = p
        WHERE mgr_name = mgr;

END PROCEDURE;
```

Before you can use a row-type variable in an SPL program, you must initialize the row variable with a LET statement or a SELECT...INTO statement. The UPDATE statement nested in the FOREACH loop of Figure 10-84 sets the **pro_name** field of the row type to the value supplied in the variable **pro**.

Tip: *To update a value in a SET in the **pro_members** field of the row type, declare a cursor and use an UPDATE statement with a derived column, as "Updating a Collection Element" on page 10-61 explains.*

Updating a Nested Collection

If you want to update a collection of collections, you must declare a cursor to access the outer collection and then declare a nested cursor to access the inner collection.

For example, suppose that the **manager** table has an additional column, **scores**, which contains a LIST whose element type is a MULTISET of integers, as Figure 10-85 shows.

Figure 10-85

```
scores        LIST(MULTISET(INT NOT NULL) NOT NULL)
```

To update a value in the MULTISET, declare a cursor that moves through each value in the LIST and a nested cursor that moves through each value in the MULTISET, as Figure 10-86 shows.

Figure 10-86

```
CREATE FUNCTION check_scores ( mgr VARCHAR(30) )
    SPECIFIC NAME nested;
    RETURNING INT;

    DEFINE l LIST( MULTISET( INT NOT NULL ) NOT NULL );
    DEFINE m MULTISET( INT NOT NULL );
    DEFINE n INT;
    DEFINE c INT;

    SELECT scores INTO l FROM manager
        WHERE mgr_name = mgr;

    FOREACH list_cursor FOR
        SELECT * FROM TABLE(l) INTO m;

        FOREACH set_cursor FOR
            SELECT * FROM TABLE(m) INTO n;
            IF (n == 0) THEN
                DELETE FROM TABLE(m)
                    WHERE CURRENT OF set_cursor;
            ENDIF;
        END FOREACH;
        LET c = CARDINALITY(m);
        RETURN c WITH RESUME;
    END FOREACH

END FUNCTION
    WITH LISTING IN '/tmp/nested.out';
```

The SPL function in Figure 10-86 selects each MULTISET in the **scores** column into **l**, and then each value in the MULTISET into **m**. If a value in **m** is 0, the function deletes it from the MULTISET. After the values of 0 are deleted, the function counts the remaining elements in each MULTISET and returns an integer.

Tip: *Because this function returns a value for each MULTISET in the LIST, you must use a cursor to enclose the EXECUTE FUNCTION statement when you execute the function.*

Inserting into a Collection

You can insert a value into a collection without declaring a cursor. If the collection is a SET or MULTISET, the value is added to the collection but the position of the new element is undefined because the collection has no particular order. If the value is a LIST, you can add the new element at a specific point in the LIST or at the end of the LIST.

In the **manager** table, the **direct_reports** column contains collections of SET type, and the **projects** column contains a LIST. To add a name to the SET in the **direct_reports** column, use an INSERT statement with a collection-derived table, as Figure 10-87 shows.

Figure 10-87

```
CREATE PROCEDURE new_emp( emp VARCHAR(30), mgr VARCHAR(30) )

    DEFINE r SET(VARCHAR(30) NOT NULL);

    SELECT direct_reports INTO r FROM manager
        WHERE mgr_name = mgr;

    INSERT INTO TABLE (r) VALUES(emp);

    UPDATE manager SET direct_reports = r
        WHERE mgr_name = mgr;

END PROCEDURE;
```

This SPL procedure takes an employee name and a manager name as arguments. The procedure then selects the collection in the **direct_reports** column for the manager the user has entered, adds the employee name the user has entered, and updates the **manager** table with the new collection.

The INSERT statement in Figure 10-87 inserts the new employee name that the user supplies into the SET contained in the collection variable **r**. The UPDATE statement then stores the new collection in the **manager** table.

Notice the syntax of the VALUES clause. The syntax rules for inserting literal data and variables into collection variables are as follows:

- Use parentheses after the VALUES keyword to enclose the complete list of values.

- If the collection is SET, MULTISET, or LIST, use the type constructor followed by brackets to enclose the list of values to be inserted. In addition, the collection value must be enclosed in quotes.

```
VALUES( "SET{ 1,4,8,9 }" )
```

- If the collection contains a row type, use ROW followed by parentheses to enclose the list of values to be inserted:

```
VALUES( ROW( 'Waters', 'voyager_project' ) )
```

- If the collection is a nested collection, nest keywords, parentheses, and brackets according to how the data type is defined:

```
VALUES( "SET{ ROW('Waters', 'voyager_project'),
              ROW('Adams', 'horizon_project') }")
```

For more information on inserting values into collections, see Chapter 6.

Inserting into a Nested Collection

If you want to insert into a nested collection, the syntax of the VALUES clause changes. Suppose, for example, that you want to insert a value into the **twin_primes** column of the **numbers** table that Figure 10-61 on page 10-48 shows.

With the **twin_primes** column, you might want to insert a SET into the LIST or an element into the inner SET. The following sections describe each of these tasks.

Inserting a Collection into the Outer Collection

Inserting a SET into the LIST is similar to inserting a single value into a simple collection.

To insert a SET into the LIST, declare a collection variable to hold the LIST and select the entire collection into it. When you use the collection variable as a collection-derived table, each SET in the LIST becomes a *row* in the *table*. You can then insert another SET at the end of the LIST or at a specified point.

For example, the **twin_primes** column of one row of numbers might contain the following LIST, as Figure 10-88 shows.

Figure 10-88

```
LIST( SET{3,5}, SET{5,7}, SET{11,13} )
```

If you think of the LIST as a collection-derived table, it might look similar to the one that Figure 10-89 shows.

Figure 10-89

```
{3,5}
{5,7}
{11,13}
```

You might want to insert the value "SET{17,19}" as a second item in the LIST. The statements in Figure 10-90 show how to do this.

Figure 10-90

```
CREATE PROCEDURE add_set()

    DEFINE l_var LIST( SET( INTEGER NOT NULL ) NOT NULL );

    SELECT twin_primes INTO l_var FROM numbers
        WHERE id = 100;

    INSERT AT 2 INTO TABLE (l_var) VALUES( "SET{17,19}" );

    UPDATE numbers SET twin_primes = 1
        WHERE id = 100;

END PROCEDURE;
```

In the INSERT statement, the VALUES clause inserts the value SET {17,19} at the second position of the LIST. Now the LIST looks like the one that Figure 10-91 shows.

Figure 10-91

```
{3,5}
{17,19}
{5,7}
{11,13}
```

You can perform the same insert by passing a SET to an SPL routine as an argument, as Figure 10-92 shows.

Figure 10-92

```
CREATE PROCEDURE add_set( set_var SET(INTEGER NOT NULL),
    row_id INTEGER );

    DEFINE list_var LIST( SET(INTEGER NOT NULL) NOT NULL );
    DEFINE n SMALLINT;

    SELECT CARDINALITY(twin_primes) INTO n FROM numbers
        WHERE id = row_id;

    LET n = n + 1;

    SELECT twin_primes INTO list_var FROM numbers
        WHERE id = row_id;

    INSERT AT n INTO TABLE( list_var ) VALUES( set_var );

    UPDATE numbers SET twin_primes = list_var
        WHERE id = row_id;

END PROCEDURE;
```

In **add_set()**, the user supplies a SET to add to the LIST and an INTEGER value that is the **id** of the row in which the SET will be inserted.

Inserting a Value into the Inner Collection

In an SPL routine, you can also insert a value into the inner collection of a nested collection. In general, to access the inner collection of a nested collection and add a value to it, perform the following steps:

1. Declare a collection variable to hold the entire collection stored in one row of a table.

2. Declare an element variable to hold one element of the outer collection. The element variable is itself a collection variable.

3. Select the entire collection from one row of a table into the collection variable.

4. Declare a cursor so that you can move through the elements of the outer collection.

5. Select one element at a time into the element variable.

6. Use a branch or loop to locate the inner collection you want to update.

7. Insert the new value into the inner collection.

8. Close the cursor.

9. Update the database table with the new collection.

As an example, you can use this process on the **twin_primes** column of **numbers**. For example, suppose that **twin_primes** contains the values that Figure 10-93 shows, and you want to insert the value 18 into the last SET in the LIST.

Figure 10-93

```
LIST( SET( {3,5}, {5,7}, {11,13}, {17,19} ) )
```

Figure 10-94 shows the beginning of a procedure that inserts the value.

Figure 10-94

```
CREATE PROCEDURE add_int()

    DEFINE list_var LIST( SET( INTEGER NOT NULL ) NOT NULL );
    DEFINE set_var SET( INTEGER NOT NULL );

        SELECT twin_primes INTO list_var FROM numbers
            WHERE id = 100;
    .
    .
```

So far, the **add_int** procedure has performed steps 1, 2, and 3. The first DEFINE statement declares a collection variable that holds the entire collection stored in one row of numbers.

The second DEFINE statement declares an element variable that holds an element of the collection. In this case, the element variable is itself a collection variable because it holds a SET. The SELECT statement selects the entire collection from one row into the collection variable, **list_var**.

Figure 10-95 shows how to declare a cursor so that you can move through the elements of the outer collection.

Figure 10-95

```
    .
    .
    FOREACH list_cursor FOR
        SELECT * INTO set_var FROM TABLE( list_var);

        FOREACH element_cursor FOR
```

Executing Routines

You can execute an SPL routine or external routine in any of the following ways:

- Using a stand-alone EXECUTE PROCEDURE or EXECUTE FUNCTION statement that you execute from DB-Access
- Calling the routine explicitly from another SPL routine or an external routine
- Using the routine name with an expression in an SQL statement

An *external routine* is a routine written in C or some other external language.

Using the EXECUTE Statements

You can use EXECUTE PROCEDURE or EXECUTE FUNCTION to execute an SPL routine or external routine. In general, it is best to use EXECUTE PROCEDURE with procedures and EXECUTE FUNCTION with functions.

Tip: *For backward compatibility, the EXECUTE PROCEDURE statement allows you to use an SPL function name and an INTO clause to return values. However, Informix recommends that you use EXECUTE PROCEDURE only with procedures and EXECUTE FUNCTION only with functions.*

You can issue EXECUTE PROCEDURE and EXECUTE FUNCTION statements as stand-alone statements from DB-Access or the Relational Object Manager from within an SPL routine or external routine.

If the routine name is unique within the database, and if it does not require arguments, you can execute it by entering just its name and parentheses after EXECUTE PROCEDURE, as Figure 10-96 shows.

Figure 10-96

```
EXECUTE PROCEDURE update_orders();
```

The INTO clause is never present when you invoke a procedure with the EXECUTE statement because a procedure does not return a value.

If the routine expects arguments, you must enter the argument values within parentheses, as Figure 10-97 shows.

Figure 10-97

```
EXECUTE FUNCTION scale_rectangles(107, 1.9)
     INTO new;
```

The statement in Figure 10-97 executes a function. Because a function returns a value, EXECUTE FUNCTION uses an INTO clause that specifies a variable where the return value is stored. The INTO clause must always be present when you use an EXECUTE statement to execute a function.

If the database has more than one procedure or function of the same name, Dynamic Server locates the right function based on the data types of the arguments. For example, the statement in Figure 10-97 supplies INTEGER and REAL values as arguments, so if your database contains multiple routines named **scale_rectangles()**, the database server executes only the **scale_rectangles()** function that accepts INTEGER and REAL data types.

The parameter list of an SPL routine always has parameter names, as well as data types. When you execute the routine, the parameter names are optional. However, if you pass arguments by name (instead of just by value) to EXECUTE PROCEDURE or EXECUTE FUNCTION, as in Figure 10-98, Dynamic Server resolves the routine-by-routine name and arguments only, a process known as *partial routine resolution*.

Figure 10-98

```
EXECUTE FUNCTION scale_rectangles( rectid = 107,
     scale = 1.9 ) INTO new_rectangle;
```

◆

You can also execute an SPL routine stored on another database server by adding a *qualified routine name* to the statement, that is, a name in the form *database@dbserver:owner_name.routine_name,* as in Figure 10-99.

Figure 10-99

```
EXECUTE PROCEDURE informix@davinci:bsmith.update_orders();
```

When you execute a routine remotely, the *owner_name* in the qualified routine name is optional.

Using the CALL Statement

You can call an SPL routine or an external routine from an SPL routine using the CALL statement. CALL can execute both procedures and functions. If you use CALL to execute a function, add a RETURNING clause and the name of an SPL variable (or variables) that will receive the value (or values) the function returns.

Suppose, for example, that you want the **scale_rectangles** function to call an external function that calculates the area of the rectangle and then returns the area with the rectangle description, as in Figure 10-100.

Figure 10-100

```
CREATE FUNCTION scale_rectangles( rectid INTEGER,
        scale REAL )
    RETURNING rectangle_t, REAL;

    DEFINE rectv rectangle_t;
    DEFINE a REAL;
    SELECT rect INTO rectv
        FROM rectangles WHERE id = rectid;
    IF ( rectv IS NULL ) THEN
        LET rectv.start = (0.0,0.0);
        LET rectv.length = 1.0;
        LET rectv.width = 1.0;
        LET a = 1.0;
        RETURN rectv, a;
    ELSE
        LET rectv.length = scale * rectv.length;
        LET rectv.width = scale * rectv.width;
        CALL area(rectv.length, rectv.width) RETURNING a;
        RETURN rectv, a;
    END IF;

END FUNCTION;
```

The SPL function in Figure 10-100 uses a CALL statement that executes the external function **area()**. The value **area()** returns is stored in **a** and returned to the calling routine by the RETURN statement.

In this example, **area()** is an external function, but you can use CALL in the same manner with an SPL function.

Executing Routines in Expressions

Just as with built-in functions, you can execute SPL routines (and external routines from SPL routines) by using them in expressions in SQL and SPL statements. A routine used in an expression is usually a function because it returns a value to the rest of the statement.

For example, you might execute a function by a LET statement that assigns the return value to a variable. The statements in Figure 10-101 perform the same task. They execute an external function within an SPL routine and assign the return value to the variable **a**.

Figure 10-101

```
LET a = area( rectv.length, rectv.width );

CALL area( rectv.length, rectv.width ) RETURNING a;
        -- these statements are equivalent
```

You can also execute an SPL routine from an SQL statement, as Figure 10-102 shows. Suppose you write an SPL function, **increase_by_pct**, which increases a given price by a given percentage. After you write an SPL routine, it is available for use in any other SPL routine.

Figure 10-102

```
CREATE FUNCTION raise_price ( num INT )
    RETURNING DECIMAL;

    DEFINE p DECIMAL;

    SELECT increase_by_pct(price, 20) INTO p
        FROM inventory WHERE prod_num = num;

    RETURN p;

END FUNCTION;
```

The example in Figure 10-102 selects the **price** column of a specified row of **inventory** and uses the value as an argument to the SPL function **increase_by_pct**. The function then returns the new value of price, increased by 20 percent, in the variable **p**.

Executing an External Function with the RETURN Statement

You can use a RETURN statement to execute any external function from within an SPL routine. Figure 10-103 shows an external function that is used in the RETURN statement of an SPL program.

Figure 10-103

```
CREATE FUNCTION c_func() RETURNS int
LANGUAGE C;

CREATE FUNCTION spl_func() RETURNS INT;
    RETURN(c_func());
END FUNCTION;

EXECUTE FUNCTION spl_func();
```

When you execute the **spl_func()** function, the **c_func()** function is invoked, and the SPL function returns the value that the external function returns.

Executing Cursor Functions from an SPL Routine

A cursor function is a user-defined function that returns one or more rows of data and therefore requires a cursor to execute. A cursor function can be either of the following functions:

■   An SPL function with a RETURN statement that contains the WITH RESUME keywords

■   An external function that is defined as an iterator function

The behavior of a cursor function is the same whether the function is an SPL function or an external function. However, an SPL cursor function can return more than one value per iteration, whereas an external cursor function (iterator function) can return only one value per iteration.

To execute a cursor function from an SPL routine, you must include the function in a FOREACH loop of an SPL routine. The following examples show different ways to execute a cursor function in a FOREACH loop:

```
FOREACH SELECT cur_func1(col_name) INTO spl_var FROM tab1
    INSERT INTO tab2 VALUES (spl_var);
END FOREACH

FOREACH EXECUTE FUNCTION cur_func2() INTO spl_var
    INSERT INTO tab2 VALUES (spl_var);
END FOREACH
```

Dynamic Routine-Name Specification

Dynamic routine-name specification allows you to execute an SPL routine from another SPL routine by building the name of the called routine within the calling routine. Dynamic routine-name specification simplifies how you can write an SPL routine that calls another SPL routine whose name is not known until runtime. The database server lets you specify an SPL variable instead of the explicit name of an SPL routine in the EXECUTE PROCEDURE or EXECUTE FUNCTION statement.

In Figure 10-104 on page 10-77, the SPL procedure **company_proc** updates a large company sales table and then assigns an SPL variable named **salesperson_proc** to hold the dynamically created name of an SPL procedure that updates another, smaller table that contains the monthly sales of an individual salesperson.

Figure 10-104

```
CREATE PROCEDURE company_proc ( no_of_items INT,
    itm_quantity SMALLINT, sale_amount MONEY,
    customer VARCHAR(50), sales_person VARCHAR(30) )

DEFINE salesperson_proc VARCHAR(60);

-- Update the company table

INSERT INTO company_tbl VALUES (no_of_items, itm_quantity,
    sale_amount, customer, sales_person);

-- Generate the procedure name for the variable
-- salesperson_proc

LET salesperson_proc = sales_person || "." || "tbl" ||
    current_month || "_" || current_year || "_proc" ;

-- Execute the SPL procedure that the salesperson_proc
-- variable names

EXECUTE PROCEDURE salesperson_proc (no_of_items,
    itm_quantity, sale_amount, customer)

END PROCEDURE;
```

In Figure 10-104, the procedure **company _proc** accepts five arguments and inserts them into **company_tbl.** Then the LET statement uses various values and the concatenation operator | | to generate the name of another SPL procedure to execute. In the LET statement:

- **sales_person** is an argument passed to the **company_proc** procedure.
- **current_month** is the current month in the system date.
- **current_year** is the current year in the system date.

Therefore, if a salesperson named Bill makes a sale in July 1998, **company_proc** inserts a record in **company_tbl** and executes the SPL procedure **bill.tbl07_1998_proc,** which updates a smaller table that contains the monthly sales of an individual salesperson.

Rules for Dynamic Routine-Name Specification

You must define the SPL variable that holds the name of the dynamically executed SPL routine as CHAR, VARCHAR, NCHAR, or NVARCHAR type. You must also give the SPL variable a valid and non-null name.

The SPL routine that the dynamic routine-name specification identifies must exist before it can be executed. If you assign the SPL variable the name of a valid SPL routine, the EXECUTE PROCEDURE or EXECUTE FUNCTION statement executes the routine whose name is contained in the variable, even if a built-in function of the same name exists.

In an EXECUTE PROCEDURE or EXECUTE FUNCTION statement, you cannot use two SPL variables to create a variable name in the form *owner.routine_name*. However, you can use an SPL variable that contains a fully qualified routine name, for example, *bill.proc1*. Figure 10-105 shows both cases.

Figure 10-105

```
EXECUTE PROCEDURE owner_variable.proc_variable
    -- this is not allowed ;

LET proc1 = bill.proc1;
EXECUTE PROCEDURE proc1 -- this is allowed ;
```

Privileges on Routines

Privileges differentiate users who can create a routine from users who can execute a routine. Some privileges accrue as part of other privileges. For example, the DBA privilege includes permissions to create routines, execute routines, and grant these privileges to other users.

Privileges for Registering a Routine

To register a routine in the database, an authorized user wraps the SPL commands in a CREATE FUNCTION or CREATE PROCEDURE statement. The database server stores a registered SPL routine internally. The following users qualify to register a new routine in the database:

■ Any user with the DBA privilege can register a routine with or without the DBA keyword in the CREATE statement.

For an explanation of the DBA keyword, see "DBA Privileges for Executing a Routine" on page 10-82.

■ A user who does not have the DBA privilege needs the Resource privilege to register an SPL routine. The creator is the owner of the routine.

A user who does not have the DBA privilege cannot use the DBA keyword to register the routine.

A DBA must give other users the Resource privilege needed to create routines. The DBA can also revoke the Resource privilege, preventing the revokee from creating further routines.

A DBA and the routine owner can cancel the registration with the DROP FUNCTION or DROP PROCEDURE statement.

Privileges for Executing a Routine

The Execute privilege enables users to invoke a routine. The routine might be invoked by the EXECUTE or CALL statements, or by using a function in an expression. The following users have a default Execute privilege, which enables them to invoke a routine:

■ By default, any user with the DBA privilege can execute any routine in the database.

■ If the routine is registered with the qualified CREATE DBA FUNCTION or CREATE DBA PROCEDURE statements, only users with the DBA privilege have a default Execution privilege for that routine.

ANSI

- If the database is not ANSI compliant, user **public** (any user with Connect database privilege) automatically has the Execute privilege to a routine that is not registered with the DBA keyword.

- In an ANSI-compliant database, the procedure owner and any user with the DBA privilege can execute the routine without receiving additional privileges. ♦

Granting and Revoking the Execute Privilege

Routines have the following GRANT and REVOKE requirements:

- The DBA can grant or revoke the Execute privilege to any routine in the database.

- The creator of a routine can grant or revoke the Execute privilege on that particular routine. The creator forfeits the ability to grant or revoke by including the AS *grantor* clause with the GRANT EXECUTE ON statement.

- Another user can grant the Execute privilege if the owner applied the WITH GRANT keywords in the GRANT EXECUTE ON statement.

A DBA or the routine owner must explicitly grant the Execute privilege to non-DBA users for the following conditions:

- A routine in an ANSI-compliant database
- A database with the **NODEFDAC** environment variable set to yes
- A routine that was created with the DBA keyword

An owner can restrict the Execute privilege on a routine even though the database server grants that privilege to public by default. To do this, issue the REVOKE EXECUTION ON.... PUBLIC statement. The DBA and owner can still execute the routine and can grant the Execute privilege to specific users, if applicable.

IDS

Execute Privileges with COMMUTATOR and NEGATOR Functions

Important: *If you must explicitly grant the Execute privilege on an SPL function that you create with a COMMUTATOR or NEGATOR modifier, you must also explicitly grant the Execute privilege on the COMMUTATOR or NEGATOR modifier before the grantee can use either. You cannot specify COMMUTATOR or NEGATOR modifiers with SPL procedures.*

The following example demonstrates both limiting privileges for a function and its negator to one group of users. Suppose you create the following pair of negator functions:

```
CREATE FUNCTION greater(y PERCENT, z PERCENT)
RETURNS BOOLEAN
NEGATOR= less(y PERCENT, z PERCENT)
...
CREATE FUNCTION less(y PERCENT, z PERCENT)
RETURNS BOOLEAN
NEGATOR= greater(y PERCENT, z PERCENT)
...
```

By default, any user can execute both the function and negator. The following statements allow only **accounting** to execute these functions:

```
REVOKE EXECUTE ON greater FROM PUBLIC
REVOKE EXECUTE ON less FROM PUBLIC
GRANT ROLE accounting TO mary, jim, ted
GRANT EXECUTE ON greater TO accounting
GRANT EXECUTE ON less TO accounting
```

A user might receive the Execute privilege accompanied by the WITH GRANT option authority to grant the Execute privilege to other users. If a user loses the Execute privilege on a routine, the Execute privilege is also revoked from all users who were granted the Execute privilege by that user.

For more information, see the GRANT and REVOKE statements in the *Informix Guide to SQL: Syntax*.

Privileges on Objects Associated with a Routine

The database server checks the existence of any referenced objects and verifies that the user invoking the routine has the necessary privileges to access the referenced objects. For example, if a user executes a routine that updates data in a table, the user must have the Update privilege for the table or columns referenced in the routine.

Objects referenced by a routine include:

- Tables and columns
- User-defined data types
- Other routines executed by the routine

When the owner of a routine grants the Execute privilege, some privileges on objects automatically accompany the Execute privilege. A GRANT EXECUTE ON statement confers to the grantee any table-level privileges that the grantor received from a GRANT statement that contained the WITH GRANT keywords.

The owner of the routine, and not the user who runs the routine, owns the unqualified objects created in the course of executing the routine. For example, assume user **howie** registers an SPL routine that creates two tables, with the following SPL routine:

```
CREATE PROCEDURE promo()
    .
    .
    .
    CREATE TABLE newcatalog
    (
    catlog_num INTEGER
    cat_advert VARCHAR(255, 65)
    cat_picture BLOB
    ) ;
    CREATE TABLE dawn.mailers
    (
    cust_num INTEGER
    interested_in SET(catlog_num INTEGER)
    );
END PROCEDURE;
```

User **julia** runs the routine, which creates the table **newcatalog**. Because no owner name qualifies table name **newcatalog**, the routine owner (**howie)** owns **newcatalog**. By contrast, the qualified name **dawn.maillist** identifies **dawn** as the owner of **maillist**.

DBA Privileges for Executing a Routine

If a DBA creates a routine using the DBA keyword, the database server automatically grants the Execute privilege only to other users with the DBA privilege. A DBA can, however, explicitly grant the Execute privilege on a DBA routine to a user who does not have the DBA privilege.

When a user executes a routine that was registered with the DBA keyword, that user assumes the privileges of a DBA for the duration of the routine. If a user who does not have the DBA privilege runs a DBA routine, the database server implicitly grants a temporary DBA privilege to the invoker. Before exiting a DBA routine, the database server implicitly revokes the temporary DBA privilege.

Objects created in the course of running a DBA routine are owned by the user who executes the routine, unless a statement in the routine explicitly names someone else as the owner. For example, suppose that **tony** registers the **promo()** routine with the DBA keyword, as follows:

```
CREATE DBA PROCEDURE promo()
   .
   .
   .
   CREATE TABLE catalog
   .
   CREATE TABLE libby.mailers
   .
   .

END PROCEDURE;
```

Although **tony** owns the routine, if **marty** runs it, then **marty** owns the **catalog** table, but user **libby** owns **libby.mailers** because her name qualifies the table name, making her the table owner.

A called routine does not inherit the DBA privilege. If a DBA routine executes a routine that was created without the DBA keyword, the DBA privileges do not affect the called routine.

If a routine that is registered without the DBA keyword calls a DBA routine, the caller must have Execute privileges on the called DBA routine. Statements within the DBA routine execute as they would within any DBA routine.

The following example demonstrates what occurs when a DBA and non-DBA routine interact. Suppose procedure **dbspc_cleanup()** executes another procedure **clust_catalog()**. Suppose also that the procedure **clust_catalog()** creates an index and that the SPL source code for **clust_catalog()** includes the following statements:

```
CREATE CLUSTER INDEX c_clust_ix ON catalog (catalog_num);
```

The DBA procedure **dbspc_cleanup()** invokes the other routine with the following statement:

```
EXECUTE PROCEDURE clust_catalog(catalog)
```

Assume **tony** registered **dbspc_cleanup()** as a DBA procedure and **clust_catalog()** is registered without the DBA keyword, as the following statements show:

```
CREATE DBA PROCEDURE dbspc_cleanup(loc CHAR)
CREATE PROCEDURE clust_catalog(catalog CHAR)
GRANT EXECUTION ON dbspc_cleanup(CHAR) to marty;
```

Suppose user **marty** runs **dbspc_cleanup()**. Because index **c_clust_ix** is created by a non-DBA routine, **tony,** who owns both routines, also owns **c_clust_ix**. By contrast, **marty** would own index **c_clust_ix** if **clust_catalog()** is a DBA procedure, as the following registering and grant statements show:

```
CREATE PROCEDURE dbspc_cleanup(loc CHAR)
CREATE DBA PROCEDURE clust_catalog(catalog CHAR)
GRANT EXECUTION ON clust_catalog(CHAR) to marty;
```

Notice that **dbspc_cleanup()** need not be a DBA procedure to call a DBA procedure.

Finding Errors in an SPL Routine

When you use CREATE PROCEDURE or CREATE FUNCTION to write an SPL routine with DB-Access or the Relational Object Manager, the statement fails when you select **Run** from the menu, if a syntax error occurs in the body of the routine.

If you are creating the routine in DB-Access or the Relational Object Manager, when you choose the **Modify** option from the menu, the cursor moves to the line that contains the syntax error. You can select **Run** and **Modify** again to check subsequent lines.

Looking at Compile-Time Warnings

If the database server detects a potential problem, but the syntax of the SPL routine is correct, the database server generates a warning and places it in a listing file. You can examine this file to check for potential problems before you execute the routine.

The filename and pathname of the listing file are specified in the WITH LISTING IN clause of the CREATE PROCEDURE or CREATE FUNCTION statement. For information about how to specify the pathname of the listing file, see "Specifying a Document Clause" on page 10-16.

If you are working on a network, the listing file is created on the system where the database resides. If you provide an absolute pathname and filename for the file, the file is created at the location you specify.

UNIX

If you provide a relative pathname for the listing file, the file is created in your home directory on the computer where the database resides. (If you do not have a home directory, the file is created in the **root** directory.) ♦

WIN NT

If you provide a relative pathname for the listing file, the default directory is your current working directory if the database is on the local computer. Otherwise the default directory is **%INFORMIXDIR%\bin**. ♦

After you create the routine, you can view the file that is specified in the WITH LISTING IN clause to see the warnings that it contains.

Generating the Text of the Routine

After you create an SPL routine, it is stored in the **sysprocbody** system catalog table. The **sysprocbody** system catalog table contains the executable routine, as well as its text.

To retrieve the text of the routine, select the **data** column from the **sysprocbody** system catalog table. The **datakey** column for a text entry has the code **T**.

The SELECT statement in Figure 10-106 reads the text of the SPL routine **read_address**.

Figure 10-106

```
SELECT data FROM informix.sysprocbody
    WHERE datakey = 'T' -- find text lines
    AND procid =
        ( SELECT procid
        FROM informix.sysprocedures
        WHERE informix.sysprocedures.procname =
            'read_address' )
```

Debugging an SPL Routine

After you successfully create and run an SPL routine, you can encounter logic errors. If the routine has logic errors, use the TRACE statement to help find them. You can trace the values of the following items:

- Variables
- Arguments
- Return values
- SQL error codes
- ISAM error codes

To generate a listing of traced values, first use the SQL statement SET DEBUG FILE to name the file that is to contain the traced output. When you create the SPL routine, include a TRACE statement.

The following methods specify the form of TRACE output.

Statement	Action
TRACE ON	Traces all statements except SQL statements. Prints the contents of variables before they are used. Traces routine calls and returned values.
TRACE PROCEDURE	Traces only the routine calls and returned values.
TRACE *expression*	Prints a literal or an expression. If necessary, the value of the expression is calculated before it is sent to the file.

Figure 10-107 demonstrates how you can use the TRACE statement to monitor how an SPL function executes.

Figure 10-107

```
CREATE FUNCTION read_many  (lastname CHAR(15))
     RETURNING CHAR(15), CHAR(15), CHAR(20), CHAR(15),CHAR(2),
        CHAR(5);

     DEFINE p_lname,p_fname, p_city CHAR(15);
     DEFINE p_add CHAR(20);
     DEFINE p_state CHAR(2);
     DEFINE p_zip CHAR(5);
     DEFINE lcount, i INT;

     LET lcount = 1;

     TRACE ON; -- Every expression will be traced from here on
     TRACE 'Foreach starts';
        -- A trace statement with a literal

     FOREACH
     SELECT fname, lname, address1, city, state, zipcode
        INTO p_fname, p_lname, p_add, p_city, p_state, p_zip
        FROM customer
        WHERE lname = lastname
     RETURN p_fname, p_lname, p_add, p_city, p_state, p_zip
        WITH RESUME;
     LET lcount = lcount + 1;   -- count of returned addresses
     END FOREACH

     TRACE 'Loop starts'; -- Another literal
     FOR i IN (1 TO 5)
        BEGIN
           RETURN i , i+1, i*i, i/i, i-1,i with resume;
        END
     END FOR;

  END FUNCTION;
```

With the TRACE ON statement, each time you execute the traced routine, entries are added to the file you specified in the SET DEBUG FILE statement. To see the debug entries, view the output file with any text editor.

The following list contains some of the output that the function in Figure 10-107 generates. Next to each traced statement is an explanation of its contents.

Statement	Action
TRACE ON	Echoes TRACE ON statement.
TRACE Foreach starts	Traces expression, in this case, the literal string Foreach starts.
start select cursor	Provides notification that a cursor is opened to handle a FOREACH loop.
select cursor iteration	Provides notification of the start of each iteration of the select cursor.
expression: (+lcount, 1)	Evaluates the encountered expression, (lcount+1), to 2.
let lcount = 2	Echoes each LET statement with the value.

Exception Handling

You can use the ON EXCEPTION statement to trap any exception (or error) that the database server returns to your SPL routine or any exception that the routine raises. The RAISE EXCEPTION statement lets you generate an exception within the SPL routine.

In an SPL routine, you cannot use exception handling to handle the following conditions:

- Success (row returned)
- Success (no rows returned)

Trapping an Error and Recovering

The ON EXCEPTION statement provides a mechanism to trap any error.

To trap an error, enclose a group of statements in a statement block marked with BEGIN and END and add an ON EXCEPTION IN statement at the beginning of the statement block. If an error occurs in the block that follows the ON EXCEPTION statement, you can take recovery action.

Figure 10-108 shows an ON EXCEPTION statement within a statement block.

Figure 10-108

```
BEGIN
DEFINE c INT;
ON EXCEPTION IN
    (
    -206, -- table does not exist
    -217  -- column does not exist
    ) SET err_num

IF err_num = -206 THEN
        CREATE TABLE t (c INT);
        INSERT INTO t VALUES (10);
        -- continue after the insert statement
    ELSE
        ALTER TABLE t ADD(d INT);
        LET c = (SELECT d FROM t);
        -- continue after the select statement.
    END IF
END EXCEPTION WITH RESUME

INSERT INTO t VALUES (10);  -- will fail if t does not exist

LET c = (SELECT d FROM t);  -- will fail if d does not exist
END
```

When an error occurs, the SPL interpreter searches for the innermost ON EXCEPTION declaration that traps the error. The first action after trapping the error is to reset the error. When execution of the error action code is complete, and if the ON EXCEPTION declaration that was raised included the WITH RESUME keywords, execution resumes automatically with the statement *following* the statement that generated the error. If the ON EXCEPTION declaration did not include the WITH RESUME keywords, execution exits the current block entirely.

Scope of Control of an ON EXCEPTION Statement

An ON EXCEPTION statement is valid for the statement block that follows the ON EXCEPTION statement, all the statement blocks nested within the following statement block, and all the statement blocks that follow the ON EXCEPTION statement. It is *not* valid in the statement block that contains the ON EXCEPTION statement.

The pseudo code in Figure 10-109 shows where the exception is valid within the routine. That is, if error 201 occurs in any of the indicated blocks, the action labeled **a201** occurs.

Figure 10-109

```
CREATE PROCEDURE scope()
    DEFINE i INT;
    .
    .
    .
    BEGIN    -- begin statement block A
    .
    .
    .
        ON EXCEPTION IN (201)
        -- do action a201
        END EXCEPTION
        BEGIN -- statement block aa
            -- do action, a201 valid here
        END
        BEGIN -- statement block bb
            -- do action, a201 valid here
        END
        WHILE i < 10
            -- do something, a201 is valid here
        END WHILE

    END
    BEGIN    -- begin statement block B
        -- do something
        -- a201 is NOT valid here
    END
END PROCEDURE;
```

User-Generated Exceptions

You can generate your own error using the RAISE EXCEPTION statement, as
Figure 10-110 shows.

Figure 10-110

```
BEGIN
    ON EXCEPTION SET esql, eisam   -- trap all errors
        IF esql = -206 THEN        -- table not found
            -- recover somehow
        ELSE
            RAISE exception esql, eisam ; -- pass the error up
        END IF
    END EXCEPTION
        -- do something
END
```

In Figure 10-110, the ON EXCEPTION statement uses two variables, **esql** and
eisam, to hold the error numbers that the database server returns. The IF
clause executes if an error occurs and if the SQL error number is -206. If any
other SQL error is caught, it is passed out of this BEGIN...END block to the last
BEGIN...END block of the previous example.

Simulating SQL Errors

You can generate errors to simulate SQL errors, as Figure 10-111 shows. If the
user is **pault**, then the SPL routine acts as if that user has no update privileges,
even if the user really does have that privilege.

Figure 10-111

```
BEGIN
    IF user = 'pault' THEN
        RAISE EXCEPTION -273;   -- deny Paul update privilege
    END IF
END
```

Using RAISE EXCEPTION to Exit Nested Code

Figure 10-112 shows how you can use the RAISE EXCEPTION statement to break out of a deeply nested block.

Figure 10-112

```
BEGIN
    ON EXCEPTION IN (1)
    END EXCEPTION WITH RESUME -- do nothing significant (cont)

    BEGIN
        FOR i IN (1 TO 1000)
            FOREACH select ..INTO aa FROM t
                IF aa < 0 THEN
                    RAISE EXCEPTION 1 ;    -- emergency exit
                END IF
            END FOREACH
        END FOR
        RETURN 1;
    END

    --do something;            -- emergency exit to
                               -- this statement.
    TRACE 'Negative value returned';
    RETURN -10;
END
```

If the innermost condition is true (if **aa** is negative), then the exception is raised and execution jumps to the code following the END of the block. In this case, execution jumps to the TRACE statement.

Remember that a BEGIN...END block is a *single* statement. If an error occurs somewhere inside a block and the trap is outside the block, the rest of the block is skipped when execution resumes and execution begins at the next statement.

Unless you set a trap for this error somewhere in the block, the error condition is passed back to the block that contains the call and back to any blocks that contain the block. If no ON EXCEPTION statement exists that is set to handle the error, execution of the SPL routine stops, creating an error for the routine that is executing the SPL routine.

Checking the Number of Rows Processed in an SPL Routine

Within SPL routines, you can use the **DBINFO** function to find out the number of rows that have been processed in SELECT, INSERT, UPDATE, DELETE, EXECUTE PROCEDURE, and EXECUTE FUNCTION statements.

Figure 10-113 shows an SPL function that uses the **DBINFO** function with the 'sqlca.sqlerrd2' option to determine the number of rows that are deleted from a table.

Figure 10-113

```
CREATE FUNCTION del_rows ( pnumb INT )
RETURNING INT;

DEFINE nrows INT;

DELETE FROM sec_tab WHERE part_num = pnumb;
LET nrows = DBINFO('sqlca.sqlerrd2');

RETURN nrows;

END FUNCTION;
```

To ensure valid results, use this option after SELECT and EXECUTE PROCEDURE or EXECUTE FUNCTION statements have completed executing. In addition, if you use the 'sqlca.sqlerrd2' option within cursors, make sure that all rows are fetched before the cursors are closed to ensure valid results.

Summary

SPL routines provide many opportunities for streamlining your database process, including enhanced database performance, simplified applications, and limited or monitored access to data. You can also use SPL routines to handle extended data types, such as collection types, row types, opaque types, and distinct types. For syntax diagrams of SPL statements, see the *Informix Guide to SQL: Syntax*.

Creating and Using Triggers

In This Chapter 11-3

When to Use Triggers 11-3

How to Create a Trigger 11-4
   Assigning a Trigger Name 11-5
   Specifying the Trigger Event 11-5
   Defining the Triggered Actions 11-6
   A Complete CREATE TRIGGER Statement 11-7

Using Triggered Actions 11-7
   Using BEFORE and AFTER Triggered Actions 11-7
   Using FOR EACH ROW Triggered Actions 11-9
      Using the REFERENCING Clause 11-9
      Using the WHEN Condition 11-10
   Using SPL Routines as Triggered Actions 11-11
      Passing Data to an SPL Routine 11-11
      Using SPL 11-12
      Updating Nontriggering Columns with Data from an
        SPL Routine 11-12

Triggers in a Table Hierarchy 11-13

Using Select Triggers 11-13
   SELECT Statements that Execute Triggered Actions 11-13
      Stand-Alone SELECT Statements 11-14
      Collection Subqueries in the Select List of a
        SELECT Statement 11-14
      SELECT Statements Embedded in User-Defined Routines . . 11-14
      Views 11-15
   Restrictions on Execution of Select Triggers 11-15
   Select Triggers on Tables in a Table Hierarchy 11-16

Re-Entrant Triggers 11-16

Tracing Triggered Actions 11-17
    Example of TRACE Statements in an SPL Routine 11-17
    Example of TRACE Output. 11-18

Generating Error Messages 11-18
    Applying a Fixed Error Message 11-19
    Generating a Variable Error Message 11-20

Summary 11-22

In This Chapter

This chapter describes the purpose of each component of the CREATE TRIGGER statement, illustrates some uses for triggers, and describes the advantages of using an SPL routine as a triggered action.

An SQL trigger is a mechanism that resides in the database. It is available to any user who has permission to use it. An SQL trigger specifies that when a particular action, an insert, a select, a delete, or an update, occurs on a particular table, the database server should automatically perform one or more additional actions. The additional actions can be INSERT, DELETE, UPDATE, EXECUTE PROCEDURE or EXECUTE FUNCTION statements.

IDS

Dynamic Server also supports user-defined routines written in C language as triggered actions. ◆

When to Use Triggers

Because a trigger resides in the database and anyone who has the required privilege can use it, a trigger lets you write a set of SQL statements that multiple applications can use. It lets you avoid redundant code when multiple programs need to perform the same database operation.

You can use triggers to perform the following actions as well as others that are not found in this list:

- Create an audit trail of activity in the database. For example, you can track updates to the orders table by updating corroborating information to an audit table.

- Implement a business rule. For example, you can determine when an order exceeds a customer's credit limit and display a message to that effect.

■ Derive additional data that is not available within a table or within the database. For example, when an update occurs to the quantity column of the **items** table, you can calculate the corresponding adjustment to the **total_price** column.

■ Enforce referential integrity. When you delete a customer, for example, you can use a trigger to delete corresponding rows (that is, rows that have the same customer number) in the **orders** table.

How to Create a Trigger

You use the CREATE TRIGGER statement to create a trigger. The CREATE TRIGGER statement is a data-definition statement that associates SQL statements with a precipitating action on a table. When the precipitating action occurs, it triggers the associated SQL statements, which are stored in the database. Figure 11-1 illustrates the relationship of the precipitating action, or trigger event, to the triggered action.

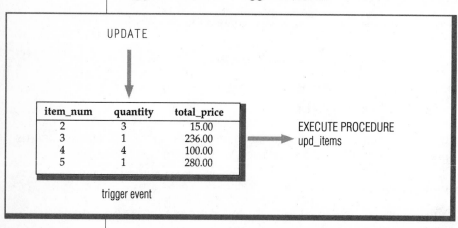

Figure 11-1
Trigger Event and
Triggered Action

The CREATE TRIGGER statement consists of clauses that perform the following actions:

■ Assign a trigger name.

■ Specify the trigger event, that is, the table and the type of action that initiate the trigger.

■ Define the SQL actions that are triggered.

An optional clause, called the REFERENCING clause, is discussed in "Using FOR EACH ROW Triggered Actions" on page 11-9.

To create a trigger, use DB-Access, the Relational Object Manager, or one of the SQL APIs. This section describes the CREATE TRIGGER statement as you enter it with the interactive Query-language option in DB-Access or the Relational Object Manager. In an SQL API, you precede the statement with the symbol or keywords that identify it as an embedded statement.

Assigning a Trigger Name

The trigger name identifies the trigger. It follows the words CREATE TRIGGER in the statement. It can be up to 18 characters in length, beginning with a letter and consisting of letters, the digits 0 to 9, and the underscore. In the following example, the portion of the CREATE TRIGGER statement that is shown assigns the name **upqty** to the trigger:

```
CREATE TRIGGER upqty    -- assign trigger name
```

Specifying the Trigger Event

The *trigger event* is the type of statement that activates the trigger. When a statement of this type is performed on the table, the database server executes the SQL statements that make up the triggered action. The trigger event can be an INSERT, SELECT, DELETE, or UPDATE statement. When you define an UPDATE or SELECT trigger event, you can name one or more columns in the table to activate the trigger. If you do not name any columns, then an update or SELECT of any column in the table activates the trigger. You can create only one INSERT and one DELETE trigger per table, but you can create multiple UPDATE or SELECT triggers as long as the triggering columns are mutually exclusive.

In the following excerpt of a CREATE TRIGGER statement, the trigger event is defined as an update of the **quantity** column in the **items** table:

```
CREATE TRIGGER upqty
UPDATE OF quantity ON items-- an UPDATE trigger event
```

This portion of the statement identifies the table on which you create the trigger. If the trigger event is an insert or delete, only the type of statement and the table name are required, as the following example shows:

```
CREATE TRIGGER ins_qty
INSERT ON items          -- an INSERT trigger event
```

Defining the Triggered Actions

The *triggered actions* are the SQL statements that are performed when the trigger event occurs. The triggered actions can consist of INSERT, DELETE, UPDATE, and EXECUTE PROCEDURE statements. In addition to specifying what actions are to be performed, however, you must also specify *when* they are to be performed in relation to the triggering statement. You have the following choices:

- Before the triggering statement executes
- After the triggering statement executes
- For each row that is affected by the triggering statement

A single trigger can define actions for each of these times.

To define a triggered action, specify when it occurs and then provide the SQL statement or statements to execute. You specify when the action is to occur with the keywords BEFORE, AFTER, or FOR EACH ROW. The triggered actions follow, enclosed in parentheses. The following triggered-action definition specifies that the SPL routine **upd_items_p1** is to be executed before the triggering statement:

```
BEFORE(EXECUTE PROCEDURE upd_items_p1)-- a BEFORE action
```

A Complete CREATE TRIGGER Statement

To define a complete CREATE TRIGGER statement, combine the trigger-name clause, the trigger-event clause, and the triggered-action clause. The following CREATE TRIGGER statement is the result of combining the components of the statement from the preceding examples. This trigger executes the SPL routine **upd_items_p1** whenever the **quantity** column of the **items** table is updated.

```
CREATE TRIGGER upqty
UPDATE OF quantity ON items
BEFORE(EXECUTE PROCEDURE upd_items_p1)
```

If a database object in the trigger definition, such as the SPL routine **upd_items_p1** in this example, does not exist when the database server processes the CREATE TRIGGER statement, it returns an error.

Using Triggered Actions

To use triggers effectively, you need to understand the relationship between the triggering statement and the resulting triggered actions. You define this relationship when you specify the time that the triggered action occurs; that is, BEFORE, AFTER, or FOR EACH ROW.

Using BEFORE and AFTER Triggered Actions

Triggered actions that occur before or after the trigger event execute only once. A BEFORE triggered action executes before the *triggering statement*, that is, before the occurrence of the trigger event. An AFTER triggered action executes after the action of the triggering statement is complete. BEFORE and AFTER triggered actions execute even if the triggering statement does not process any rows.

Among other uses, you can use BEFORE and AFTER triggered actions to determine the effect of the triggering statement. For example, before you update the **quantity** column in the **items** table, you could call the SPL routine **upd_items_p1** to calculate the total quantity on order for all items in the table, as the following example shows. The procedure stores the total in a global variable called **old_qty**.

```
CREATE PROCEDURE upd_items_p1()
    DEFINE GLOBAL old_qty INT DEFAULT 0;
    LET old_qty = (SELECT SUM(quantity) FROM items);
END PROCEDURE;
```

After the triggering update completes, you can calculate the total again to see how much it has changed. The following SPL routine, **upd_items_p2**, calculates the total of **quantity** again and stores the result in the local variable **new_qty**. Then it compares **new_qty** to the global variable **old_qty** to see if the total quantity for all orders has increased by more than 50 percent. If so, the procedure uses the RAISE EXCEPTION statement to simulate an SQL error.

```
CREATE PROCEDURE upd_items_p2()
    DEFINE GLOBAL old_qty INT DEFAULT 0;
    DEFINE new_qty INT;
    LET new_qty = (SELECT SUM(quantity) FROM items);
    IF new_qty > old_qty * 1.50 THEN
        RAISE EXCEPTION -746, 0, 'Not allowed - rule violation';
    END IF
END PROCEDURE;
```

The following trigger calls **upd_items_p1** and **upd_items_p2** to prevent an extraordinary update on the **quantity** column of the **items** table:

```
CREATE TRIGGER up_items
UPDATE OF quantity ON items
BEFORE(EXECUTE PROCEDURE upd_items_p1())
AFTER(EXECUTE PROCEDURE upd_items_p2());
```

If an update raises the total quantity on order for all items by more than 50 percent, the RAISE EXCEPTION statement in **upd_items_p2** terminates the trigger with an error. When a trigger fails in the database server and the database has logging, the database server rolls back the changes that both the triggering statement and the triggered actions make. For more information on what happens when a trigger fails, see the CREATE TRIGGER statement in the *Informix Guide to SQL: Syntax*.

Using FOR EACH ROW Triggered Actions

A FOR EACH ROW triggered action executes once for each row that the triggering statement affects. For example, if the triggering statement has the following syntax, a FOR EACH ROW triggered action executes once for each row in the **items** table in which the **manu_code** column has a value of 'KAR':

```
UPDATE items SET quantity = quantity * 2 WHERE manu_code = 'KAR'
```

If the triggering statement does not process any rows, a FOR EACH ROW triggered action does not execute.

If the triggering statement is a SELECT statement (the trigger is a select trigger), the triggered actions execute after all processing on the retrieved row is complete. However, the triggered actions might not execute immediately; a FOR EACH ROW action executes for every instance of a row that is returned to the user. For example, in a SELECT statement with an ORDER BY clause, all rows must be qualified against the WHERE clause before they are sorted and returned.

Using the REFERENCING Clause

When you create a FOR EACH ROW triggered action, you must usually indicate in the triggered action statements whether you are referring to the value of a column before or after the effect of the triggering statement. For example, imagine that you want to track updates to the **quantity** column of the **items** table. To do this, create the following table to record the activity:

```
CREATE TABLE log_record
    (item_num     SMALLINT,
     ord_num      INTEGER,
     username     CHARACTER(8),
     update_time  DATETIME YEAR TO MINUTE,
     old_qty      SMALLINT,
     new_qty      SMALLINT);
```

To supply values for the **old_qty** and **new_qty** columns in this table, you must be able to refer to the old and new values of **quantity** in the **items** table; that is, the values before and after the effect of the triggering statement. The REFERENCING clause enables you to do this.

The REFERENCING clause lets you create two prefixes that you can combine with a column name, one to reference the old value of the column and one to reference its new value. These prefixes are called *correlation names*. You can create one or both correlation names, depending on your requirements. You indicate which one you are creating with the keywords OLD and NEW. The following REFERENCING clause creates the correlation names **pre_upd** and **post_upd** to refer to the old and new values in a row:

```
REFERENCING OLD AS pre_upd NEW AS post_upd
```

The following triggered action creates a row in **log_record** when **quantity** is updated in a row of the **items** table. The INSERT statement refers to the old values of the **item_num** and **order_num** columns and to both the old and new values of the **quantity** column.

```
FOR EACH ROW(INSERT INTO log_record
    VALUES (pre_upd.item_num, pre_upd.order_num, USER, CURRENT,
            pre_upd.quantity, post_upd.quantity));
```

The correlation names defined in the REFERENCING clause apply to all rows that the triggering statement affects.

Important: *If you refer to a column name in the triggering table and do not use a correlation name, the database server makes no special effort to search for the column in the definition of the triggering table. You must always use a correlation name with a column name in SQL statements in a FOR EACH ROW triggered action, unless the statement is valid independent of the triggered action. For more information, see the CREATE TRIGGER statement in the "Informix Guide to SQL: Syntax."*

Using the WHEN Condition

As an option, you can precede a triggered action with a WHEN clause to make the action dependent on the outcome of a test. The WHEN clause consists of the keyword WHEN followed by the condition statement given in parentheses. In the CREATE TRIGGER statement, the WHEN clause follows the keywords BEFORE, AFTER, or FOR EACH ROW and precedes the triggered-action list.

When a WHEN condition is present, if it evaluates to *true*, the triggered actions execute in the order in which they appear. If the WHEN condition evaluates to *false* or *unknown*, the actions in the triggered-action list do not execute. If the trigger specifies FOR EACH ROW, the condition is evaluated for each row also.

In the following trigger example, the triggered action executes only if the condition in the WHEN clause is true; that is, if the post-update unit price is greater than two times the pre-update unit price:

```
CREATE TRIGGER up_price
UPDATE OF unit_price ON stock
REFERENCING OLD AS pre NEW AS post
FOR EACH ROW WHEN(post.unit_price > pre.unit_price * 2)
    (INSERT INTO warn_tab VALUES(pre.stock_num, pre.manu_code,
        pre.unit_price, post.unit_price, CURRENT))
```

For more information on the WHEN condition, see the CREATE TRIGGER statement in the *Informix Guide to SQL: Syntax*.

Using SPL Routines as Triggered Actions

Probably the most powerful feature of triggers is the ability to call an SPL routine as a triggered action. The EXECUTE PROCEDURE statement, which calls an SPL routine, lets you pass data from the triggering table to the SPL routine and also to update the triggering table with data returned by the SPL routine. SPL also lets you define variables, assign data to them, make comparisons, and use procedural statements to accomplish complex tasks within a triggered action.

Passing Data to an SPL Routine

You can pass data to an SPL routine in the argument list of the EXECUTE PROCEDURE statement. The EXECUTE PROCEDURE statement in the following trigger example passes values from the **quantity** and **total_price** columns of the **items** table to the SPL routine **calc_totpr**:

```
CREATE TRIGGER upd_totpr
UPDATE OF quantity ON items
REFERENCING OLD AS pre_upd NEW AS post_upd
FOR EACH ROW(EXECUTE PROCEDURE calc_totpr(pre_upd.quantity,
    post_upd.quantity, pre_upd.total_price) INTO total_price)
```

Passing data to an SPL routine lets you use it in the operations that the procedure performs.

Using SPL

The EXECUTE PROCEDURE statement in the preceding trigger calls the SPL routine that the following example shows. The procedure uses SPL to calculate the change that needs to be made to the **total_price** column when **quantity** is updated in the **items** table. The procedure receives both the old and new values of **quantity** and the old value of **total_price**. It divides the old total price by the old quantity to derive the unit price. It then multiplies the unit price by the new quantity to obtain the new total price.

```
CREATE PROCEDURE calc_totpr(old_qty SMALLINT, new_qty SMALLINT,
    total MONEY(8)) RETURNING MONEY(8);
    DEFINE u_price LIKE items.total_price;
    DEFINE n_total LIKE items.total_price;
    LET u_price = total / old_qty;
    LET n_total = new_qty * u_price;
    RETURN n_total;
END PROCEDURE;
```

In this example, SPL lets the trigger derive data that is not directly available from the triggering table.

Updating Nontriggering Columns with Data from an SPL Routine

Within a triggered action, the INTO clause of the EXECUTE PROCEDURE statement lets you update nontriggering columns in the triggering table. The EXECUTE PROCEDURE statement in the following example calls the **calc_totpr** SPL procedure that contains an INTO clause, which references the column **total_price**:

```
FOR EACH ROW(EXECUTE PROCEDURE calc_totpr(pre_upd.quantity,
    post_upd.quantity, pre_upd.total_price) INTO total_price);
```

The value that is updated into **total_price** is returned by the RETURN statement at the conclusion of the SPL procedure. The **total_price** column is updated for each row that the triggering statement affects.

IDS

Triggers in a Table Hierarchy

When you define a trigger on a supertable, any subtables in the table hierarchy also inherit the trigger. Consequently when you perform operations on tables in the hierarchy, triggers can execute for any table in the hierarchy that is a subtable of the table on which a trigger is defined.

You can create a trigger on a subtable to override any trigger that the subtable inherits from a supertable in the hierarchy.

To disable a trigger that a subtable inherits, create an empty trigger on the subtable to override the trigger from the supertable. Because triggers are not additive, this empty trigger executes for the subtable and any subtables under the subtable, which are not subject to further overrides.

IDS

Using Select Triggers

You can create a select trigger on a table or column(s) to perform certain types of application-specific auditing, such as tracking the number of hits on a table. You might create a select trigger to insert an audit record to an audit table each time a user queries a certain table. For example, a DBA might create a select trigger to provide a Web transaction history for Web DataBlade modules.

SELECT Statements that Execute Triggered Actions

When you create a select trigger, only certain types of select statements can execute the actions defined on that trigger. A select trigger executes for the following types of SELECT statements only:

- Stand-alone SELECT statements
- Collection subqueries in the select list of a SELECT statement
- SELECT statements embedded in user-defined routines
- Views

Stand-Alone SELECT Statements

Suppose you define the following select trigger on a table:

```
CREATE TRIGGER hits_trig SELECT OF col_a ON tab_a
REFERENCING OLD AS hit
FOR EACH ROW (INSERT INTO hits_log
VALUES (hit.col_a, CURRENT, USER));
```

A select trigger executes when the triggering column appears in the select list of a stand-alone SELECT statement. The following statement executes a triggered action on the **hits_trig** trigger for each instance of a row that the database server returns:

```
SELECT col_a FROM tab_a
```

Collection Subqueries in the Select List of a SELECT Statement

A select trigger executes when the triggering column appears in a collection subquery that occurs in the select list of another SELECT statement. The following statement executes a triggered action on the **hits_trig** trigger for each instance of a row that the collection subquery returns:

```
SELECT MULTISET(SELECT col_a FROM tab_a) FROM ...
```

SELECT Statements Embedded in User-Defined Routines

A select trigger that is defined on a SELECT statement embedded in a user defined routine (UDR) executes a triggered action in the following instances only:

- The UDR appears in the select list of a SELECT statement
- The UDR is invoked with an execute procedure statement

Suppose you create a routine **new_proc** that contains the statement `SELECT col_a FROM tab_a`. Each of the following statements executes a triggered action on the **hits_trig** trigger for each instance of a row that the embedded SELECT statement returns:

```
SELECT new_proc() FROM tab_b
```

```
EXECUTE PROCEDURE new_proc
```

Views

Select triggers execute a triggered action for views whose base tables contain a reference to a triggering column. However, you cannot define a select trigger on a view.

Suppose you create the following view:

```
CREATE VIEW view_tab AS
SELECT * FROM tab_a
```

The following statements execute a triggered action on the **hits_trig** trigger for each instance of a row that the view returns:

```
SELECT * FROM view_tab
```

```
SELECT col_a FROM tab_a
```

Restrictions on Execution of Select Triggers

The following types of statements do not trigger any actions on select triggers:

- The triggering column or columns are not in the select list (for example, a column that appears in the WHERE clause of a SELECT statement does not execute a select trigger).
- The SELECT statement contains an aggregate function
- The SELECT statement includes UNION or UNION ALL operations
- The SELECT statement includes a DISTINCT or UNIQUE keyword
- The UDR expression that contains the SELECT statement is not in the select list
- The SELECT select statement appears within an INSERT INTO statement
- The SELECT statement appears within a scroll cursor
- Cascading select triggers

    A cascading select trigger is a trigger whose actions includes an SPL routine that itself has a triggering select statement. However, the actions of a cascading select trigger do not execute and the database server does not return an error.

Select Triggers on Tables in a Table Hierarchy

When you define a select trigger on a supertable, any subtables in the table hierarchy also inherit the trigger. Consequently when you perform SELECT operations on tables in the hierarchy, select triggers execute for any table in the hierarchy that is a subtable of the table on which you define the select trigger.

For information about overriding and disabling inherited triggers, see "Triggers in a Table Hierarchy" on page 11-13.

Re-Entrant Triggers

A *re-entrant trigger* refers to a case in which the triggered action can reference the triggering table. In other words, both the triggering event and the triggered action can operate on the same table. For example, suppose the following UPDATE statement represents the triggering event:

```
UPDATE tab1 SET (col_a, col_b) = (col_a + 1, col_b + 1)
```

The following triggered action is legal because column **col_c** is not a column that the triggering event has updated:

```
UPDATE tab1 SET (col_c) = (col_c + 3)
```

In the preceding example, a triggered action on **col_a** or **col_b** would be illegal because a triggered action cannot be an UPDATE statement that references a column that was updated by the triggering event.

 Important: *Select triggers cannot be re-entrant triggers. If the triggering event is a SELECT statement, the triggered action cannot operate on the same table.*

For a list of the rules that describe those situations in which a trigger can and cannot be re-entrant, see the CREATE TRIGGER statement in the *Informix Guide to SQL: Syntax.*

Tracing Triggered Actions

If a triggered action does not behave as you expect, place it in an SPL routine and use the SPL TRACE statement to monitor its operation. Before you start the trace, you must direct the output to a file with the SET DEBUG FILE TO statement.

Example of TRACE Statements in an SPL Routine

The following example shows TRACE statements that you add to the SPL routine **items_pct.** The SET DEBUG FILE TO statement directs the trace output to the file that the pathname specifies. The TRACE ON statement begins tracing the statements and variables within the procedure.

```
CREATE PROCEDURE items_pct(mac CHAR(3))
DEFINE tp MONEY;
DEFINE mc_tot MONEY;
DEFINE pct DECIMAL;
SET DEBUG FILE TO 'pathname'; -- modify this pathname according to the
                   -- conventions that your operating system requires

TRACE 'begin trace';
TRACE ON;
LET tp = (SELECT SUM(total_price) FROM items);
LET mc_tot = (SELECT SUM(total_price) FROM items
    WHERE manu_code = mac);
LET pct = mc_tot / tp;
IF pct > .10 THEN
    RAISE EXCEPTION -745;
END IF
TRACE OFF;
END PROCEDURE;

CREATE TRIGGER items_ins
INSERT ON items
REFERENCING NEW AS post_ins
FOR EACH ROW(EXECUTE PROCEDURE items_pct (post_ins.manu_code));
```

Example of TRACE Output

The following example shows sample trace output from the **items_pct**
procedure as it appears in the file that was named in the SET DEBUG FILE TO
statement. The output reveals the values of procedure variables, procedure
arguments, return values, and error codes.

```
trace expression :begin trace
trace on
expression:
  (select (sum total_price)
    from items)
evaluates to $18280.77 ;
let  tp = $18280.77
expression:
  (select (sum total_price)
    from items
    where (= manu_code, mac))
evaluates to $3008.00 ;
let  mc_tot = $3008.00
expression:(/ mc_tot, tp)
evaluates to 0.16
let  pct = 0.16
expression:(> pct, 0.1)
evaluates to 1
expression:(- 745)
evaluates to -745
raise exception :-745, 0, ''
exception : looking for handler
SQL error = -745 ISAM error = 0  error string = = ''
exception : no appropriate handler
```

For more information about how to use the TRACE statement to diagnose
logic errors in SPL routines, see Chapter 10, "Creating and Using SPL
Routines."

Generating Error Messages

When a trigger fails because of an SQL statement, the database server returns
the SQL error number that applies to the specific cause of the failure.

When the triggered action is an SPL routine, you can generate error messages
for other error conditions with one of two reserved error numbers. The first
one is error number -745, which has a generalized and fixed error message.
The second one is error number -746, which allows you to supply the
message text, up to a maximum of 71 characters.

Applying a Fixed Error Message

You can apply error number -745 to any trigger failure that is not an SQL error. The following fixed message is for this error:

```
-745 Trigger execution has failed.
```

You can apply this message with the RAISE EXCEPTION statement in SPL. The following example generates error -745 if **new_qty** is greater than **old_qty** multiplied by 1.50:

```
CREATE PROCEDURE upd_items_p2()
    DEFINE GLOBAL old_qty INT DEFAULT 0;
    DEFINE new_qty INT;
    LET new_qty = (SELECT SUM(quantity) FROM items);
    IF new_qty > old_qty * 1.50 THEN
        RAISE EXCEPTION -745;
    END IF
END PROCEDURE
```

If you are using DB-Access, the text of the message for error -745 displays on the bottom of the screen, as Figure 11-2 shows.

Figure 11-2
Error Message -745 with Fixed Message

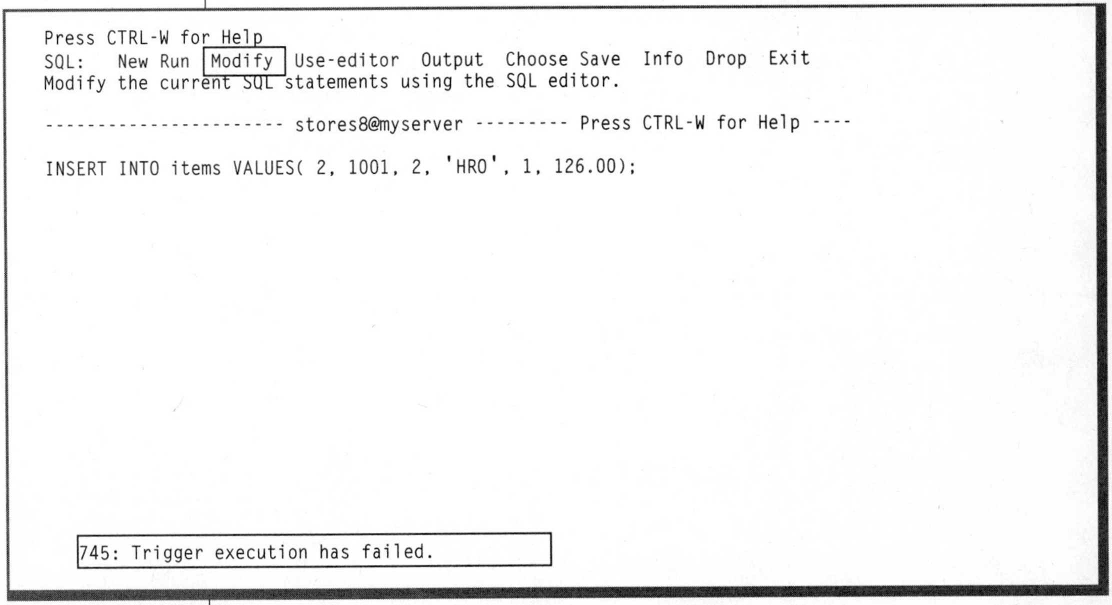

```
Press CTRL-W for Help
SQL:   New Run  Modify  Use-editor  Output  Choose Save  Info  Drop  Exit
Modify the current SQL statements using the SQL editor.

---------------------- stores8@myserver --------- Press CTRL-W for Help ----

INSERT INTO items VALUES( 2, 1001, 2, 'HRO', 1, 126.00);
```

```
745: Trigger execution has failed.
```

If you trigger the erring procedure through an SQL statement in your SQL API, the database server sets the SQL error status variable to -745 and returns it to your program. To display the text of the message, follow the procedure that your Informix application development tool provides for retrieving the text of an SQL error message.

Generating a Variable Error Message

Error number -746 allows you to provide the text of the error message. Like the preceding example, the following one also generates an error if **new_qty** is greater than **old_qty** multiplied by 1.50. However, in this case the error number is -746, and the message text Too many items for Mfr. is supplied as the third argument in the RAISE EXCEPTION statement. For more information on the syntax and use of this statement, see the RAISE EXCEPTION statement in Chapter 10, "Creating and Using SPL Routines."

```
CREATE PROCEDURE upd_items_p2()
    DEFINE GLOBAL old_qty INT DEFAULT 0;
    DEFINE new_qty INT;
    LET new_qty = (SELECT SUM(quantity) FROM items);
    IF new_qty > old_qty * 1.50 THEN
        RAISE EXCEPTION -746, 0, 'Too many items for Mfr.';
    END IF
END PROCEDURE;
```

If you use DB-Access to submit the triggering statement, and if **new_qty** is greater than **old_qty**, you will get the result that Figure 11-3 shows.

Figure 11-3
Error Number -746 with User-Specified Message Text

```
Press CTRL-W for Help
SQL:   New  Run  Modify  Use-editor  Output  Choose  Save  Info  Drop  Exit
Modify the current SQL statements using the SQL editor.

-------------------- store7@myserver --------- Press CTRL-W for Help -----

INSERT INTO items VALUES( 2, 1001, 2, 'HRO', 1, 126.00);
```

```
746: Too many items for Mfr.
```

If you invoke the trigger through an SQL statement in an SQL API, the
database server sets **sqlcode** to -746 and returns the message text in the
sqlerrm field of the SQL communications area (SQLCA). For more information
about how to use the SQLCA, see your SQL API manual.

Summary

To introduce triggers, this chapter discussed the following topics:

- The purpose of each component of the CREATE TRIGGER statement
- How to create BEFORE and AFTER triggered actions and how to use them to determine the impact of the triggering statement
- How to create a FOR EACH ROW triggered action and how to use the REFERENCING clause to refer to the values of columns both before and after the action of the triggering statement
- The advantages of using SPL routines as triggered actions
- How to trace triggered actions if they behave unexpectedly
- How to generate two types of error messages within a triggered action

Index

A

Access modes, description of 9-24
Accessing tables 2-69
Active set
  definition of 2-25, 7-14
  of a cursor 7-24
Aggregate function
  and GROUP BY clause 5-5
  AVG 4-6
  COUNT 4-5
  description of 4-4, 4-15
  in ESQL 7-15
  in expressions 4-4
  in SPL routine 10-33
  in subquery 5-24
  MAX 4-7
  MIN 4-7
  null value signalled 7-12
  RANGE 4-7
  standard deviation 4-8
  STDEV 4-8
  SUM 4-7
  VARIANCE 4-9
Alias
  for table name 2-64
  to assign column names in
      temporary table 5-12
  using
      as a query shortcut 2-64
      with a supertable 3-17
  with self-join 5-11
ALL keyword, beginning a
    subquery 5-22

ALTER INDEX statement, locking
    table 9-8
AND logical operator 2-33
ANSI 1-15
ANSI compliance
  icon Intro-11
  level Intro-16
ANSI-compliant database
  FOR UPDATE not required
      in 8-16
  signalled in SQLWARN 7-11
ANY keyword, beginning a
    subquery 5-24
Application
  design of order-entry 6-52
  handling errors 7-17
  isolation level 9-14
  update cursor 9-20
Archiving
  database server methods 6-56
  description of 6-56
  transaction log 6-56
Arithmetic operator, in
    expression 2-44
Ascending order in SELECT 2-13
Asterisk notation, in a SELECT
    statement 3-10
Asterisk, wildcard character in
    SELECT 2-11
AVG function, as aggregate
    function 4-6

B

BEGIN WORK statement 6-55
BETWEEN keyword
  testing for equality in WHERE
    clause 2-26
  using to specify a range of
    rows 2-29
Boldface type Intro-9
Boolean expression, and logical
  operator 2-33
Built-in type variable 10-22
BYTE data type
  restrictions
    with GROUP BY 5-6
    with relational expression 2-26
  using LENGTH function on 4-30

C

CARDINALITY function 4-19
Cartesian product
  basis of any join 2-58
  description of 2-56
Cascading deletes
  definition of 6-39
  locking associated with 6-39
  logging 6-40
  restriction 6-41
Case conversion
  with INITCAP function 4-23
  with LOWER function 4-22
  with UPPER function 4-22
CASE expression
  description of 2-49
  using 2-50
CHAR data type
  converting to a DATE value 4-15
  converting to a DATETIME
    value 4-17
  in relational expressions 2-26
  subscripting 2-40
  substrings of 2-22
  truncation signalled 7-12
Character string
  converting to a DATE value 4-15
  converting to a DATETIME
    value 4-17

Check constraint, definition of 6-37
Class libraries, shared 1-13
CLOSE DATABASE statement,
  effect on database locks 9-8
Code set, ISO 8859-1 Intro-4
Code, sample, conventions
  for Intro-12
Collation order and GLS 2-23
Collection data type
  accessing 3-4, 3-11
  counting elements in 4-19
  description of 3-11
  element, searching for with
    IN 3-13
  simple 3-11
  updating 6-29
  using the CARDINALITY
    function 4-19
Collection subquery
  description of 5-30
  omitting ITEM keyword in 5-31
  using ITEM keyword in 5-32
Collection types, in an SPL
  routine 10-17
Collection values, inserting into
  columns 6-18
Collection variable
  defining, restrictions on 10-23
  nested 3-11, 3-12
  selecting 3-12
Collection-derived table
  accessing elements in a
    collection 5-33
  description of 5-30, 10-57
  restrictions on 5-34
  using in SPL 10-61
Column
  definition of 2-5
  description of 1-11
  in relational model 1-11
  label on 5-39
  row-type, definition of 3-6
Column number, using 2-21
Comment icons Intro-10
COMMIT WORK statement
  closing cursors 9-27
  releasing locks 9-13, 9-27
  setting SQLCODE 8-5

Committed Read, isolation level
  (Informix) 9-16
commutator function
  definition 10-14
Comparison condition, description
  of 2-26
Compliance
  icons Intro-11
  with industry standards Intro-16
Compound query 5-35
Concurrency
  access modes 9-24
  ANSI Read Committed
    isolation 9-16
  ANSI Read Uncommitted
    isolation 9-16
  ANSI Repeatable Read
    isolation 9-19
  ANSI Serializable isolation 9-19
  database lock 9-8
  deadlock 9-26
  description of 6-57, 9-3
  effect on performance 9-3
  Informix Cursor Stability
    isolation 9-17
  Informix Dirty Read
    isolation 9-16
  Informix Read Committed
    isolation 9-16
  Informix Repeatable Read
    isolation 9-19
  isolation level 9-14
  kinds of locks 9-7
  lock duration 9-13
  lock scope 9-7
  table lock 9-8
Configuration parameter,
  ISOLATION_LOCKS 9-17
Constraint, entity integrity 6-36
Contact information Intro-16
Conventions,
  documentation Intro-8
Conversion function, description
  of 4-15
Coordinated deletes 8-6
Correlated subquery
  definition of 5-21
  restriction with cascading
    deletes 6-41

COUNT function
  and GROUP BY 5-6
  as aggregate function 4-5
  count rows to delete 6-7
  use in a subquery 6-10
  with DISTINCT 4-6
CREATE DATABASE statement
  setting shared lock 9-8
  SQLWARN after 7-11
CREATE FUNCTION FROM
  statement, in embedded
  languages 10-18
CREATE FUNCTION statement
  inside CREATE FUNCTION
    FROM statement 10-18
  using 10-8
  WITH LISTING IN clause 10-85
CREATE INDEX statement, locking
  table 9-8
CREATE PROCEDURE FROM
  statement, in embedded
  languages 10-18
CREATE PROCEDURE statement
  inside CREATE PROCEDURE
    FROM 10-18
  using 10-8
  WITH LISTING IN clause 10-85
CURRENT function, comparing
  column values 4-10
Cursor
  active set of 7-24
  closing 9-27
  declaring 7-20
  definition of 7-19
  for insert 8-9
  for update 8-15, 9-13
  hold 9-27
  opening 7-21, 7-24
  retrieving values with
    FETCH 7-21
  scroll 7-23
  sequence of program
    operations 7-19
  sequential 7-23, 7-25
  WITH HOLD 9-27
Cursor Stability isolation level
  (Informix) 9-17
Cyclic query 6-41

D

Data definition statements 7-33
Data integrity 6-51 to 6-55
Data loading 6-57
Data model, description of 1-3
Data replication 6-58
Data type
  automatic conversions 7-15
  collection, accessing 3-4, 3-11
  conversion 6-13
  differences in how query results
    are displayed 2-10
  hashable, description of 5-4
Database
  ANSI-compliant 1-17
  concurrent use 1-8
  definition of 1-10
  GLS 1-17
  management of 1-9
  object-relational, description
    of 1-13
  relational, description of 1-10
  server 1-8
  table names 2-69
Database lock 9-8
Database object
  constraints as a 6-41
  index as a 6-41
  object modes 6-41
  trigger as a 6-41
  violation detection 6-41
Database object mode
  examples 6-43
Database server
  archiving 6-56
  identifying host computer
    name 4-33
  identifying version number 4-33
  locking tables 9-8
  signalled in SQLWARN 7-11
  statement caching 9-29
DATABASE statement
  exclusive mode 9-8
  locking 9-8
  SQLWARN after 7-11
Database-level privilege 6-32

database@dbservername
  owner.routinename 10-20
DataBlade modules 1-13
DATE data type
  converting to a character
    string 4-16
  functions returning 4-10
  in ORDER BY sequence 2-13
  in relational expressions 2-26
  international date formats 1-17
DATE function, as conversion
  function 4-15
DATETIME data type
  converting to a character
    string 4-16
  displaying format 4-14
  functions returning 4-10
  in ORDER BY sequence 2-13
  in relational expressions 2-26
DAY function, as time
  function 4-11
DB-Access utility Intro-5
DB-Access, creating database
  with 7-33
DBDATE environment
  variable 6-13
DBINFO function, in SELECT
  statement 4-32
DBSERVERNAME function, in
  SELECT statement 2-55, 4-31,
  4-41
dbspace, name returned by
  DBINFO function 4-32
Deadlock detection 9-26
DECIMAL data type, signalled in
  SQLWARN 7-11
DECLARE statement
  description of 7-20
  FOR INSERT clause 8-9
  FOR UPDATE 8-15
  SCROLL keyword 7-23
  WITH HOLD clause 9-28
DECODE function 4-33
Default locale Intro-4
Default value, in column 6-37
Delete join 6-10

DELETE statement
  all rows of table 6-6
  coordinated deletes 8-6
  count of rows 8-4
  description of 6-6
  embedded 7-6, 8-3 to 8-8
  number of rows 7-10
  preparing 7-30
  transactions with 8-5
  using subquery 6-10
  WHERE clause restricted 6-10
  with cursor 8-7
Demonstration databases Intro-5
Dependencies, software Intro-4
Descending order in SELECT 2-13
Diagnostics table
  example of privileges 6-50
  examples of starting 6-47
Difference set operation 5-43
Dirty Read isolation level
  (Informix) 9-16
Display label
  in ORDER BY clause 2-51
  with SELECT 2-47
DISTINCT keyword
  relation to GROUP BY 5-5
  using in SELECT 2-17
  using with COUNT function 4-6
Distinct-type variable 10-25
Distributed deadlock 9-26
DOCUMENT clause, use in SPL
  routine 10-16
Documentation notes Intro-15
Documentation, types of
  documentation notes Intro-15
  error message files Intro-14
  machine notes Intro-15
  on-line help Intro-14
  on-line manuals Intro-13
  printed manuals Intro-13
  related reading Intro-16
  release notes Intro-15
Domain of column 6-37
Dominant table 5-15
Dot notation 3-8
DROP INDEX statement, locking
  table 9-8
Duplicate values, finding 2-52, 4-38
Dynamic 1-13

Dynamic routine-name
  specification
  for SPL function 10-76
  for SPL routine 10-76
  rules for 10-78
Dynamic SQL
  description of 7-5, 7-29
  freeing prepared statements 7-32

E

Embedded SQL
  definition of 7-4
  languages available 7-4
End of data
  signal in SQLCODE 7-9, 7-17
  signal only for SELECT 8-14
  when opening cursor 7-21
Entity, definition of 6-36
Environment variables Intro-9
en_us.8859-1 locale Intro-4
Equals (=) relational operator 2-27,
  2-58
Equi-join 2-58
Error checking
  simulating errors 10-91
  SPL routine 10-88 to 10-92
Error message files Intro-14, 7-13
Error messages
  for trigger failure 11-18
  generating in a trigger 11-18
  retrieving trigger text in a
    program 11-20, 11-21
Errors
  after DELETE 8-4
  codes for 7-10
  dealing with 7-17
  detected on opening cursor 7-21
  during updates 6-51
  inserting with a cursor 8-11
  ISAM error code 7-10
ESCAPE 2-40
ESCAPE keyword, using in
  WHERE clause 2-40
ESQL
  cursor use 7-19 to 7-28
  DELETE statement in 8-3
  delimiting host variables 7-7

dynamic embedding 7-5, 7-29
error handling 7-17
fetching rows from cursor 7-21
host variable 7-6, 7-8
indicator variable 7-16
INSERT in 8-9
overview 7-3 to 7-37, 8-3 to 8-18
preprocessor 7-4
scroll cursor 7-23
selecting single rows 2-25, 7-14
SQL Communications Area
  (SQLCA) 7-8
SQLCODE 7-9
SQLERRD fields 7-10
static embedding 7-5
UPDATE in 8-15
Exclusive lock 9-7
EXECUTE IMMEDIATE statement,
  description of 7-33
Execute privilege
  DBA keyword, effect of 10-82
  objects referenced by a
    routine 10-82
EXISTS keyword, in a WHERE
  clause 5-22
Expression
  CASE 2-49
  date-oriented 4-10
  description of 2-44
  display label for 2-47
  in SPL routine 10-33
EXTEND function
  using in expression 4-14
  with DATE, DATETIME and
    INTERVAL 4-10
Extensibility, description of 1-13
External tables 6-57

F

Feature icons Intro-10
Features of this product,
  new Intro-5
FETCH statement
  ABSOLUTE keyword 7-23
  description of 7-21
  sequential 7-23
  with sequential cursor 7-25

Field projection 3-8
Field, definition of 3-6
File, compared to database 1-3
Find Error utility Intro-14
finderr utility Intro-14
FIRST clause
  description of 2-41
  in a union query 2-44
  using 2-42
  with ORDER BY clause 2-43
FLUSH statement
  count of rows inserted 8-11
  writing rows to buffer 8-10
FOR UPDATE keywords
  conflicts with ORDER BY 8-8
  not needed in ANSI-compliant
    database 8-16
  specific columns 8-16
Foreign key 6-38
Fragmented table, using primary
  keys 2-52, 4-38
FREE statement, freeing prepared
  statements 7-32
FROM keyword, alias names 2-64
Function
  aggregate 4-4
  applying to expressions 4-10
  conversion 4-15
  DATE 4-15
  date-oriented 4-10
  DBINFO 4-32
  DECODE 4-33
  in SELECT statements 4-3
  INITCAP 4-23
  LOWER 4-22
  LPAD 4-27
  name confusion in SPL
    routine 10-28
  NVL 4-35
  REPLACE 4-24
  RPAD 4-28
  smart large object 4-20
  string manipulation 4-21
  SUBSTR 4-26
  SUBSTRING 4-25
  time 4-10
  TO_CHAR 4-16
  TO_DATE 4-17
  UPPER 4-22

G

Global Language Support
  (GLS) Intro-4
  and MATCHES keyword 2-39
  and ORDER BY keywords 2-23,
    2-39
  database, description of 1-17
  default locale 2-23
  sort order 2-23
Global variable
  declaring 10-29
  description of 10-29
GLS. See Global Language Support.
GRANT statement, in embedded
  SQL 7-33 to 7-36
Greater than or equal to (>=)
  relational operator 2-29
Greater than (>) relational
  operator 2-28
GROUP BY keywords
  column number with 5-7
  description of 5-4

H

Hashable data, description of 5-4
HAVING keyword 5-8
HEX function, using in
  expression 4-32
Hold cursor, definition of 9-27
Host variable
  delimiter for 7-7
  description of 7-6
  fetching data into 7-21
  in DELETE statement 8-4
  in INSERT statement 8-9
  in UPDATE statement 8-15
  in WHERE clause 7-15
  INTO keyword sets 7-14
  null indicator 7-16
  restrictions in prepared
    statement 7-29
  truncation signalled 7-12
Hostname of computer, returned by
  DBINFO function 4-33

I

Icons
  compliance Intro-11
  feature Intro-10
  Important Intro-10
  platform Intro-10
  product Intro-10
  Tip Intro-10
  Warning Intro-10
Important paragraphs, icon
  for Intro-10
IN keyword
  using in WHERE clause 2-26
IN relational operator 5-22
Index, table locks 9-9
Indicator variable, definition
  of 7-16
Industry standards, compliance
  with Intro-16
INFORMIXDIR/bin
  directory Intro-5
INITCAP function, as string
  manipulation function 4-23
Insert cursor
  definition of 8-9
  using 8-12
INSERT statement
  and end of data 8-14
  constant data with 8-12
  count of rows inserted 8-11
  duplicate values in 6-12
  embedded 8-9 to 8-14
  inserting
    collections 6-18
    into supertables 6-17
    multiple rows 6-21
    rows 6-11
    single rows 6-11
  null values in 6-12
  number of rows 7-10
  SELECT statement in 6-21
  smart large objects in 6-20
  VALUES clause 6-11
Inserting rows of constant
  data 8-12
Interrupted modifications 6-51
Intersection set operation 5-41

INTERVAL data type, in relational
expressions 2-26
INTO keyword
choice of location 7-22
in FETCH statement 7-22
mismatch signalled in
SQLWARN 7-12
restrictions in INSERT 6-22
restrictions in prepared
statement 7-29
retrieving multiple rows 7-20
retrieving single rows 7-14
INTO TEMP keywords, description
of 2-67
IS NOT NULL keywords 2-32
IS NULL keywords 2-32
ISAM error code 7-10
ISO 8859-1 code set Intro-4, 2-23
Isolation level
ANSI Read Committed 9-16
ANSI Read Uncommitted 9-16
ANSI Repeatable Read 9-19
ANSI Serializable 9-19
description of 9-14
Informix Committed Read 9-16
Informix Cursor Stability 9-17
Informix Dirty Read 9-16
Informix Repeatable Read 9-19
setting 9-14
ISOLATION_LOCKS configuration
parameter, specifying number
of rows to lock 9-17

J

Join
associative 2-62
composite 2-56
condition 2-56
creating 2-58
definition of 2-8, 2-56
delete join 6-10
dominant table 5-15
equi-join 2-58
in an UPDATE statement 6-32
multiple-table join 2-63
natural 2-61
nested simple 5-17
outer, definition of 5-15

outer, types of 5-15
self-join 5-11
simple 2-56
subservient table 5-15

K

Keywords
in a subquery 5-22
in a WHERE clause 2-26

L

Label 2-47, 5-39
Last SERIAL value, returned by
DBINFO function 4-32
LENGTH function 4-4
on TEXT or BYTE strings 4-30
on VARCHAR 4-30
use in expression 4-29
Less than or equal to (<=) relational
operator 2-29
Less than (<) relational
operator 2-28
LET statement 10-31
LIKE keyword
description of 2-35
using in WHERE clause 2-26
Local variable, description of 10-21
Locale Intro-4, 1-17
default Intro-4
en_us.8859-1 Intro-4
Lock mode, TABLE 9-10
LOCK TABLE statement, locking a
table explicitly 9-8
Locking
and concurrency 6-57
and integrity 9-4
behavior of different lock
types 9-22
deadlock 9-26
description of 9-6
granularity 9-7
lock duration 9-13
lock mode 9-24
not wait 9-25
setting 9-24
wait 9-25

locks released at end of
transaction 9-27
scope of lock 9-7
specifying number of rows to
lock 9-17
types of locks
coarse index lock 9-11, Index-1
database lock 9-8
exclusive lock 9-7
page lock 9-10, 9-11
promotable lock 9-7, 9-13
row and key locks 9-10
shared lock 9-7
smart-large-object locks 9-12
table lock 9-8
with
DELETE 8-4
update cursor 9-13
Locks, retaining update 9-21
Logical log
and backups 6-56
description of 6-53
Logical operator
AND 2-33
NOT 2-33
OR 2-33
Logslice, description of 6-53
Loop, exiting with RAISE
exception 10-92
LOWER function, as string
manipulation function 4-22
LPAD function, as string
manipulation function 4-27

M

Machine notes Intro-15
MATCHES keyword
using GLS 2-39
using in WHERE clause 2-26
MATCHES relational operator
how locale affects 2-39
in WHERE clause 2-35
MAX function, as aggregate
function 4-7
MDY function, as time
function 4-10
Message file for error
messages Intro-14

MIN function, as aggregate
    function 4-7
MODE ANSI keywords, specifying
    transactions 6-55
MONEY data type
    in INSERT statement 6-12
    international money formats 1-17
MONTH function, as time
    function 4-10
Multiple-table join 2-63
MULTISET keyword
    creating a collection
        subquery 5-30
    in a collection subquery
        expression 5-31
Multithreaded application,
    definition of 7-5

N

Naming convention, tables 2-69
Natural join 2-61
NCHAR data type, querying
    on 2-10
Nested ordering, in SELECT 2-14
New features of this
    product Intro-5
NODEFDAC environment variable,
    effect on privileges granted to
    public 10-80
Nonlogging tables 6-54
Not equal (!=) relational
    operator 2-28
NOT logical operator 2-33
Null value
    detecting in ESQL 7-16
    in INSERT statement 6-12
    testing for 2-32
    with logical operator 2-33
NVARCHAR data type, querying
    on 2-10
NVL function 4-35

O

Object mode, description of 6-41
Object-relational database,
    description of 1-13
ON EXCEPTION statement
    scope of control 10-90
    trapping errors 10-88
    user-generated errors 10-91
On-line help Intro-14
On-line manuals Intro-13
onload utility 6-56
onunload utility 6-56
Opaque-type variable 10-25
OPEN statement 7-21
Opening a cursor 7-24
OR logical operator 2-33
OR relational operator 2-30
ORDER BY keywords
    and GLS 2-23
    ascending order 2-13
    DESC keyword 2-14, 2-22
    display label with 2-51
    multiple columns 2-14
    relation to GROUP BY 5-6
    restrictions in INSERT 6-22
    restrictions with FOR
        UPDATE 8-8
    select columns by number 2-21
    sorting rows 2-12
Outer join 5-15
Output from TRACE
    statement 11-18

P

Page lock 9-10
Parts explosion 7-26
Performance
    depends on concurrency 9-3
    increasing with stored
        routines 10-6
Platform icons Intro-10
PREPARE statement
    description of 7-30
    error return in SQLERRD 7-10
    multiple SQL statements 7-30

Primary key
    definition of 6-36
    in fragmented table 2-52, 4-38
Primary key constraint, definition
    of 6-39
Printed manuals Intro-13
Privilege
    database-level 6-32
    displaying 6-34
    needed to modify data 6-32
    overview 1-8
Procedure-type variables 10-26
Product icons Intro-10
Program group
    Documentation notes Intro-15
    Release notes Intro-15
Projection, definition of 2-7
Project, description of 1-12
Promotable lock 9-7, 9-13
PUT statement
    constant data with 8-12
    count of rows inserted 8-11
    sends returned data to buffer 8-10

Q

Qualifier, existential 5-27
Query
    audit 5-29
    compound 5-35
    cyclic 6-41
    self-referencing 6-41
    stated in terms of data model 1-6

R

RAISE EXCEPTION
    statement 10-88
RANGE function, as aggregate
    function 4-7
Re 11-16
Read Committed isolation level
    (ANSI) 9-16
Read Uncommitted isolation level
    (ANSI) 9-16
Recursive relationship, example
    of 7-26

Re-entrant trigger, description
    of 11-16
REFERENCING clause 11-9
Referential constraint, definition
    of 6-39
Referential integrity, definition
    of 6-37
Related reading Intro-16
Relational database, description
    of 1-10
Relational model
    join 2-8
    projection 2-6
    selection 2-6
Relational Object Manager 1-16
Relational operation 2-5
Relational operator
    BETWEEN 2-29
    EXISTS 5-22
    IN 5-22
    in a WHERE clause 2-26 to 2-28
    LIKE 2-35
    NULL 2-32
    OR 2-30
Release notes Intro-15
Repeatable Read isolation level
    (Informix and ANSI) 9-19
REPLACE function, as string
    manipulation function 4-24
Replication
    of data 6-58
    transparency 6-58
Return types, in SPL function 10-13
REVOKE statement, in embedded
    SQL 7-33 to 7-36
rofferr utility Intro-14
ROLLBACK WORK statement
    closes cursors 9-27
    releases locks 9-13, 9-27
    setting SQLCODE 8-5
Row
    checking rows processed in SPL
        routines 10-93
    definition of 1-11, 2-5
    deleting 6-6
    finding number of rows
        processed 4-32

finding rows that a user
    modified 2-54, 4-39
in relational model 1-11
inserting 6-11
specifying number of rows
    returned with FIRST
    clause 2-41
Row lock 9-10
Row type
    dot notation with 3-8
    field projection 3-8
    field projections in SELECT 3-9
    field, definition of 3-6
    selecting columns from 3-6
    selecting data from 3-4
    updating 6-27
    using asterisk notation with
        SELECT 3-10
Rowid
    using in self-join 5-14
    using to find modified rows 2-54,
        4-39
    using to locate internal row
        numbers 2-52, 4-38
Row-type column, definition of 3-6
Row-type variables,
    delcaring 10-24
RPAD function, as string
    manipulation function 4-28

S

sales_demo database Intro-5
Sample-code conventions Intro-12
Scroll cursor
    active set 7-25
    definition of 7-23
SCROLL keyword, using in
    DECLARE 7-23
searching for collection
    element 2-26
Select cursor
    opening 7-21
    using 7-20

Select list
    display label 2-47
    expressions in 2-44
    functions in 4-3 to 4-32
    labels in 5-39
    selecting all columns 2-11
    selecting specific columns 2-17
    specifying a substring in 2-22
SELECT statement
    accessing collections 3-4, 3-11
    active set 2-25, 7-14
    advanced 5-4 to 5-45
    aggregate functions in 4-4, 4-15
    alias names 2-64
    and end-of-data return code 8-14
    compound query 5-35
    cursor for 7-19, 7-20
    date-oriented functions in 4-10
    display label 2-47
    DISTINCT keyword 2-17
    embedded 7-14 to 7-17
    FIRST clause 2-41
    for joined tables 2-68
    for single tables 2-10 to 4-32
    functions 4-3 to 4-32
    GROUP BY clause 5-5
    HAVING clause 5-8
    INTO clause with ESQL 7-14
    INTO TEMP clause 2-67
    join 2-58 to 2-64
    multiple-table 2-56
    natural join 2-61
    ORDER BY clause 2-12
    outer join 5-15 to 5-19
    rowid 2-55, 4-41
    SELECT clause 2-11 to 2-23
    select list 2-7
    selecting a row type 3-4
    selecting a substring 2-22
    selecting expressions 2-44
    selection list 2-11
    self-join 5-11
    simple 2-3 to 2-68
    single-table 2-10
    singleton 2-25, 7-14
    smart-large-objects functions
        in 4-20
    subquery 5-20 to 5-29

UNION operator 5-35
using
  for join 2-8
  for projection 2-7
  for selection 2-6
Select trigger, description of 11-13
Selection, description of 2-6
Select, description of 1-12
Self-join
  assigning column names with
    INTO TEMP 5-12
  description of 5-11
Self-referencing query 5-11, 6-41
Semantic integrity 6-37
Sequential cursor, definition
  of 7-23
SERIAL data type
  finding last SERIAL value
    inserted 4-32
  generated number in
    SQLERRD 7-10
  inserting a starting value 6-12
Serializable isolation level (ANSI),
  description of 9-19
Session ID, returned by DBINFO
  function 4-33
SET clause 6-26
Set difference 5-43
Set intersection 5-41
SET ISOLATION statement
  compared with SET
    TRANSACTION
    statement 9-14
  description of 9-14
SET keyword, use in UPDATE 6-24
SET LOCK MODE statement,
  description of 9-24
Set operation 5-34
  difference 5-43
  intersection 5-41
  union 5-35
SET TRANSACTION statement,
  compared with SET
    ISOLATION statement 9-15
Shared class libraries 1-13
Singleton SELECT statement 2-25,
  7-14

SITENAME function, in SELECT
  statement 2-55, 4-31, 4-41
Smart large object
  declaring variables for 10-23
  functions for copying 4-20
  importing and exporting 4-20,
    6-20
  using SQL functions
    in a SELECT statement 4-20
    in an INSERT statement 6-20
    in an UPDATE statement 6-31
Software dependencies Intro-4
SOME keyword, beginning a
  subquery 5-22
Sorting
  as affected by a locale 2-23
  effects of GLS 2-23
  nested 2-14
  with ORDER BY 2-13
SPL
  program variable 7-6
  relation to SQL 10-5, 10-6
  tracing triggered actions 11-17
SPL function
  definition of 10-6
  dynamic routine-name
    specification 10-76
  variant vs. not variant 10-14
SPL routine
  adding comments to 10-16
  as triggered action 11-11
  compiler warning 10-85
  debugging 10-86
  definition of 10-6
  dynamic routine-name
    specification 10-76
  example of 10-18
  exceptions 10-88 to 10-92
  finding in system catalog 10-85
  FOR loop 10-40
  IF..ELIF..ELSE structure 10-38
  in an embedded language 10-18
  in SELECT statements 4-36
  introduction to 10-6
  listing compiler messages 10-85
  loop 10-35, 10-40

name confusion with SQL
  functions 10-29
return types 10-13
SQL expressions in 10-33
syntax error 10-84
uses 10-6
variables, scope of 10-22
WHILE loop 10-40
writing 10-8
SQL
  Application Programming
    Interfaces 7-4
  compliance of statements with
    ANSI standard 1-15
  cursor 7-19
  description of 1-14
  error handling 7-17
  history 1-15
  Informix SQL and ANSI SQL 1-15
  interactive use 1-16
  standardization 1-15
SQL code Intro-12
SQL Communications Area
  (SQLCA)
  altered by end of transaction 8-5
  description of 7-8
  inserting rows 8-11
SQL statement cache 9-29
SQLCODE field
  after opening cursor 7-21
  and FLUSH operation 8-11
  description of 7-9
  end of data on SELECT only 8-14
  end of data signalled 7-17
  set by DELETE statement 8-4
  set by PUT statement 8-11
SQLERRD array
  count of deleted rows 8-4
  count of inserted rows 8-11
  count of rows 8-14
  description of 7-10
  syntax of naming 7-8
SQLERRM Character String 7-13
SQLSTATE variable
  in non-ANSI-compliant
    databases 7-17
  using with a cursor 7-21

SQLWARN array
  description of 7-11
  syntax of naming 7-8
  with PREPARE 7-30
Standard deviation, aggregate
      function 4-8
Statement cache, SQL 9-29
Static SQL 7-5
STDEV function, as aggregate
      function 4-8
Stored procedure language.
  See SPL.
Stored routine, general
      programming 1-16
stores_demo database Intro-5
Subquery
  correlated 5-21, 6-41
  in DELETE statement 6-10
  in SELECT statement 5-20 to 5-29
  in UPDATE statement
    with SET clause 6-25
    with WHERE clause 6-24
Subscripting
  in a WHERE clause 2-40
  SPL variables 10-27
Subservient table 5-15
SUBSTR function, as string
      manipulation function 4-26
Substring 2-22, 10-27
SUBSTRING function, as string
      manipulation function 4-25
SUM function, as aggregate
      function 4-7
superstores Intro-5
superstores_demo database Intro-5
Supertable
  in a table hierarchy 3-15
  inserting into 6-17
  selecting from 3-16
  using an alias 3-17
System catalog
  privileges in 6-34
  querying 6-34
  sysprocbody 10-85
  systabauth 6-34
System descriptor area 7-32
System requirements
  database Intro-4
  software Intro-4

T

Table
  accessing 2-69
  description of 1-10
  in relational model 1-10
  loading data
    with external tables 6-57
    with onload utility 6-56
  lock 9-8
  logging 6-54
  names 2-69
  nonlogging 6-54
  not in the current database 2-34
Table hierarchy, triggers in 11-13
TABLE lock mode 9-10
Temporary table
  and active set of cursor 7-24
  assigning column names 5-12
  example 6-23
TEXT data type
  restrictions
    with GROUP BY 5-6
    with relational expression 2-26
  using LENGTH function on 4-30
Time function
  description of 4-10
  use in SELECT 4-4
Tip icons Intro-10
TODAY function, in constant
      expression 4-31, 6-13
TO_CHAR function, as conversion
      function 4-16
TO_DATE function, as conversion
      function 4-17
TRACE statement
  debugging an SPL routine 10-86
  output from 11-18
Transaction
  cursors closed at end 9-27
  description of 6-51
  example with DELETE 8-5
  locks held to end of 9-13
  locks released at end of 9-13, 9-27
  transaction log 6-53
  use signalled in SQLWARN 7-11
Transaction logging
  contents of log 6-56
  description of 6-53

Trigger
  creating 11-4
  definition of 11-3
  in a table hierarchy 11-13
  name assigning 11-5
  re-entrant, description of 11-16
  select
    defining on a table
      hierarchy 11-16
    description of 11-13
    restrictions on execution 11-15
  when to use 11-3
Trigger event
  definition of 11-5
  example of 11-5
Triggered action
  BEFORE and AFTER 11-7
  FOR EACH ROW 11-9
  generating an error
      message 11-18
  in relation to triggering
      statement 11-6
  statements 11-3
  tracing 11-17
  using 11-7
  using SPL routines 11-11
  WHEN condition 11-10
Truncation, signalled in
      SQLWARN 7-12
Typed table
  definition of 3-5
  inserting rows 6-14
  selecting from 3-5

U

UNION operator
  description of 5-35
  display labels with 5-39
Union set operation 5-35
UNIQUE keyword, in SELECT
      statement 2-17
UNIX operating system
  default locale for Intro-4
untyped 10-23
Update cursor 9-20
Update cursor, definition of 8-15
Update locks, retaining 9-21

UPDATE statement
  and end of data 8-14
  description of 6-23
  embedded 8-15 to 8-17
  multiple assignment 6-26
  number of rows 7-10
  preparing 7-30
  restrictions on subqueries 6-26
  smart large objects in 6-31
  using a join to update a
    column 6-32
UPPER function, as string
  manipulation function 4-22
USER function, in expression 2-54,
  4-30, 4-39
Users, types of Intro-3
Utility program
  onload 6-56
  onunload 6-56

V

VALUES clause, in INSERT
  statement 6-11
VARCHAR data type, using
  LENGTH function on 4-30
Variable
  defining and using in SPL
    routine 10-20
  scope in SPL routine 10-22
  with same name as a
    keyword 10-27
VARIANCE function, as aggregate
  function 4-9
variant SPL function 10-14
Version number, returned by
  DBINFO function 4-33
Violations table
  example of privileges 6-49
  examples 6-43
  examples of starting 6-47

W

Warning icons Intro-10
Warning, with SPL routine at
  compile time 10-85
WEEKDAY function, as time
  function 4-10, 4-13
WHERE clause
  Boolean expression in 2-33
  comparison condition 2-26
  date-oriented functions in 4-13
  host variables in 7-15
  in DELETE 6-6 to 6-10
  relational operators 2-26
  selecting rows 2-25
  subqueries in 5-22
  subscripting 2-40
  testing a subscript 2-40
  wildcard comparisons 2-35
  with NOT keyword 2-30
  with OR keyword 2-30
WHERE CURRENT OF clause
  in DELETE statement 8-7
  in UPDATE statement 8-15
WHERE keyword
  null data tests 2-32
  range of values 2-29
Wildcard character, asterisk 2-11
Wildcard comparison in WHERE
  clause 2-35 to 2-40
Windows NT
  default locale for Intro-4
WITH HOLD keywords, declaring
  a hold cursor 9-28
WITH LISTING IN clause, use in
  SPL routine 10-16

X

X/Open compliance level Intro-16

Y

YEAR function, as time
  function 4-10

Symbols

!=, not equal, relational
  operator 2-28
<, less than, relational
  operator 2-28
<=, less than or equal to, relational
  operator 2-29
=, equals, relational operator 2-27,
  2-58
>, greater than, relational
  operator 2-28
>=, greater than or equal to,
  relational operator 2-29
?, question mark
  as placeholder in PREPARE 7-30

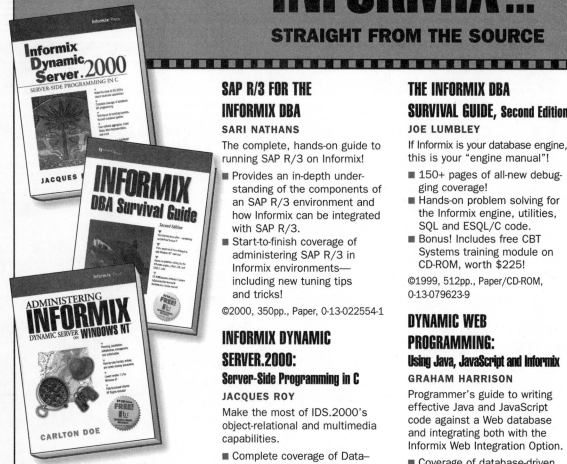